PRAISE FOR THE NINTH EDITION

"For most teachers of Scripture and pastors the problem is not finding good resources for biblical study—with limited funds for books, the issue is determining the best resources. Thanks to Glynn's thorough research, this problem will be solved for many."

—DANIEL I. BLOCK
Professor of Old Testament
Wheaton College and Graduate School

"It's great to have a consensus commentary and reference survey that combines the judgments of many other surveys. I highly recommend it."

—GEORGE W. KNIGHT III
Adjunct Professor of New Testament
Greenville Presbyterian Theological Seminary

"In this excellent survey, Glynn has provided novice and expert alike with a very full listing of commentaries. He has solicited input from many qualified experts and on that basis has developed this extremely useful tool. All of us stand in his debt for having pulled together a listing of what surely represents the best of contemporary as well as classical scholarship."

—EUGENE H. MERRILL
Distinguished Professor of Old Testament Studies
Dallas Theological Seminary

"Preachers need books. Preachers need good books. Preachers need workable leads about which books to buy. Glynn has served the church well by producing this marvelous bibliographic reference. For students, preachers, and teachers, there is much here that can be found no place else in a similar form. This survey answers the question, Where will I get the best book for my bucks?"

—HADDON W. ROBINSON
Harold John Ockenga
Distinguished Professor of Preaching
Gordon-Conwell Theological Seminary

"Glynn's work is not just another listing of books, but a useful method by which the busy pastor can maintain currency on interpretative issues and methodology, and theological students can begin to acquire a 'center of gravity' in sorting out all of the books and series available in different categories. His listings represent the most significant titles (both current and forthcoming) in biblical and theological scholarship. The author has a watchful eye on the publishing landscape, alerting his readers to the new features in an ever-changing terrain."

—DENNIS M. SWANSON
Seminary Librarian
The Master's Seminary

"My students approach me constantly with questions about library building and commentary recommendations. I am delighted to be able to direct them to Glynn's *Commentary and Reference Survey*. His assessment of student needs and quality of reference works are consistently on-target. If you want to do Bible study, this is the help you need."

—JOHN H. WALTON
Professor of Old Testament and Hebrew
Wheaton College and Graduate School

Commentary & Reference Survey

TENTH EDITION
FULLY REVISED AND UPDATED

COMMENTARY & REFERENCE SURVEY

A COMPREHENSIVE GUIDE TO BIBLICAL AND THEOLOGICAL RESOURCES

JOHN GLYNN

FOREWORD BY DARRELL L. BOCK

Kregel
Academic & Professional

*Commentary and Reference Survey: A Comprehensive Guide
to Biblical and Theological Resources*

© 1994, 2003, 2007 by John Glynn
Tenth Edition

Published by Kregel Publications, a division of Kregel, Inc.,
P.O. Box 2607, Grand Rapids, MI 49501.

ISBN 978-0-8254-2737-4

Printed in the United States of America

07 08 09 10 11 / 5 4 3 2 1

To my parents,
Jack and Ann Glynn,
for imparting to me a love of reading
and a moral compass.

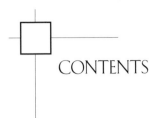

CONTENTS

FOREWORD

This survey is a genuine service to the student of the Bible. Often, I am asked what books are best for the serious study of Scripture, and many times I am forced to make the question more precise because of the varied elements that go into serious engagement of the Bible's message and background. Now I have a place to which I can send students that gives them both a clear array of choices and good guidance.

John Glynn started work on this survey as a labor of love years ago as a seminary student. He has run it by dozens of professors, and has written publishers to stay current on what is coming next. The book has gone through multiple editions and updates. It is as thorough a presentation of works on biblical studies as one could hope to find, a ready reference into the seeming maze of serious Bible study. But that maze, once understood, can be a source of rich reflection.

In Glynn's survey, he classifies works by theme and theological orientation. One can consider the various types of commentaries on any book or the themes that the book raises by consulting the "Special Studies" sections.

Like a map taking one on a great tour of a wonderful city, this survey orients the student about where to find the rich and varied discussion that is a part of biblical study. So pick up the map and begin the tour. In this book you have a faithful and helpful guide.

—Darrell L. Bock

ACKNOWLEDGMENTS

I would like to thank two fellow students at Dallas Theological Seminary—John Day and Barry Gin—who provided invaluable data-entry help for the first three self-published editions of my survey back in the day when I was computer illiterate. Also, I am indebted to Dr. Robert Chisholm for my third-semester class on Hebrew exegesis. There, most students learned that glad-handing papers wouldn't suffice. Dr. Chisholm taught me the meaning of true exegesis and that standard references are not always right.

Finally, Parableman (aka Jeremy Pierce) was extremely helpful in keeping me in the loop concerning forthcoming commentaries at http://parablemania.ektopos.com/archives/2006/05/forthcombook .html.

INTRODUCTION

In the late springtime of 1992, while I was fishing through the "missionary" basket where departing Moody Bible Institute students left behind items they didn't care to take home for summer, I discovered a copy of Douglas Moo's edited *Annotated Bibliography of the Bible and the Church*.[1] Having just begun to build a personal reference library in preparation for attending Dallas Theological Seminary, I was immediately interested, especially because it contained sections on the best available commentaries at that time.

When I arrived at Dallas Theological Seminary, I found that the school bookstore had surveys that had been compiled by the Old Testament and the New Testament departments. Comparing Moo's book and the surveys, I began to get a better idea of which commentaries I should purchase—and purchase I did. Over the next several years, I continued to acquire other surveys and sources, periodically refining my list and adding additional categories to cover other examples of extrabiblical literature.

Now, after fifteen years of analyzing and reviewing books, I can safely say that I have received an additional theological education. However, one maxim I have continued to observe is that I should maintain only a library that will continue to be useful, even if only a few pages of a certain book clarifies an answer that I am seeking.

What are the salient features of this survey? About 40 percent of the total books mentioned in this survey are commentaries, which

---

1. Douglas Moo, *Annotated Bibliography of the Bible and the Church*, 2d ed. (Alumni Publications, 1986).

comprise the largest single category. Given the high cost of most commentaries, it is imperative that readers derive from each volume as much value as possible. Therefore, commentaries mentioned herein are noted in each biblical book in two categories: Technical and Semitechnical for the student trained in the original languages, and Exposition for the informed layman or pastor who has more general biblical training. Technical, or exegetical, commentaries concentrate principally on the interpretation of the original languages *in the main text,* whereas semitechnical commentaries generally relegate grammatical, textual, and historical problems to footnotes. Because the main text of semitechnical works are primarily expositional, they can also be used by the informed layman.

Commentaries that are geared toward application are subsumed under the Exposition rubric. These include titles from Zondervan's NIV Application Commentary (NIVAC), InterVarsity's Bible Speaks Today (BST) and IVP New Testament Commentary (IVPNTC), the Interpretation series from Westminster John Knox (IBC), and The Preacher's Commentary (TPC; previously titled the Communicator's Commentary) published by Thomas Nelson.

Furthermore, given the wide range of theological perspectives in most categories, each entry is further delineated by the following codes:

- E   =   Evangelical
- E/Cr   =   Evangelical/Critical
- C/M   =   Conservative/Moderate
- L/Cr   =   Liberal/Critical
- All   =   Edited volumes with essays across a theological spectrum

What this means is that commentaries on a specific biblical book may run the gamut from evangelicals who affirm "the idea that Scripture in the original manuscripts does not affirm anything that is contrary to fact"[2] to Liberal/Critical scholars who believe that the Bible

---

2. Wayne Grudem, *Bible Doctrine* (Zondervan, 1999), 487.

contains clear errors and may or may not affirm what it says about itself and God. Between these two perspectives exist varying degrees of inerrancy where the Bible could be in error concerning some minor historical facts (Evangelical/Critical), or that it only affirms what is normative in faith and practice rather than in historical or scientific detail (Conservative/Moderate).[3] The titles are listed alphabetically, and boldfaced entries represent titles that I highly recommend and consider the "best of the best." The full names of series mentioned can be found under "Abbreviations."

Apparently, one reviewer of my last edition did not think I was skeptical enough, while another thought I was too skeptical. To the first charge, the orientation of the boldfaced recommendations in the survey proper broke down as follows:

- 163   Evangelical
- 83   Evangelical/Critical
- 55   Conservative/Moderate
- 68   Liberal/Critical

---

3. The gospel of Matthew is an example of how these criteria can be applied. For example, although no explicit references to Matthew as the author of the gospel exist, Craig Keener accepts on the basis of the earliest patristic materials that the author is indeed Matthew. His approach is evangelical. Donald Hagner, WBC, 2 vols. (Word/Nelson, 1993–95), on the other hand, fudges around on some historical issues, suggesting a single feeding rather than two in 14:13–21 (5,000) and 15:29–39 (4,000), though Jesus himself refers to two (16:9–10). Likewise, Hagner gets antsy over the resurrection of the dead, suggesting this miracle makes little historical sense (Matt. 27:51–52). Thus, even though Hagner's commentary is essentially evangelical, the occasional nods to critical scholarship call into question the absolute veracity of the text and is, thus, Evangelical/Critical. As for W. D. Davies and Dale Allison's massive work, *A Critical and Exegetical Commentary on the Gospel According to St. Matthew*, ICC, 3 vols. (T & T Clark, 1988–97), they essentially conclude that we can accept on face value what Matthew affirms about faith and God, but the historical events must be evaluated independently. This earns them the Conservative/Moderate moniker. Finally, Ulrich Luz's first two volumes of a projected three-volume project in the Hermeneia series (Fortress, 2001–) is so thoroughly form and redaction-critical that virtually any assertion by any so-called author is to be regarded with a thorough-going skepticism. In this approach, Luz even goes so far as to suggest that Matthew was written in the mid-second century. Thus, he is classified as Liberal/Critical.

In "The Ultimate Commentary Collection" in the back of this book, the disparity is even greater:

- 75   Evangelical
- 35   Evangelical/Critical
- 15   Conservative/Moderate
- 22   Liberal/Critical

In this edition, the emergence of key evangelical treatments in the past few years has tipped the scale even more. That said, here follows a paradigm of the previously mentioned criteria.

Matthew
Technical, Semitechnical

L/Cr	1. Boring, Eugene. NIB, vol. 8 (Abingdon, 1995).
E	**2. Carson, D. A. EBC, vol. 9, rev. ed. (Zondervan, 2006).**
C/M	**3. Davies, W. D., and Dale Allison. ICC, 3 vols. (T & T Clark, 1988–97).**
E/Cr	4. Gundry, Robert. *Matthew*, 2d ed. (Eerdmans, 1994).
E/Cr	**5. Hagner, Donald. WBC, 2 vols. (Word, 1993–94).**
E	6. Keener, Craig (Eerdmans, 1999).
L/Cr	7. Luz, Ulrich. Hermeneia, 3 vols. (Fortress, 1998–).
C/M	**8. Nolland, John. NIGTC (Eerdmans, 2005).**

Exposition (Partial list)

E	**1. Blomberg, Craig. NAC (Broadman & Holman, 1993).**
C/M	2. Davies, W. D., and Dale Allison. *Matthew: A Shorter Commentary* (T & T Clark, 2005).
E/Cr	**3. France, Richard. TOTC (Eerdmans, 1988).**
E	4. Green, Michael. BST (IVP, 2001).
E	**5. Keener, Craig. IVPNTC (IVP, 1997).**

A Special Studies section, which includes particularly useful monographs, augments each book list of commentaries. Asterisked footnotes throughout the survey generally indicate forthcoming titles to appear and provide a capsule summary of the present and future possibilities of what might actually constitute an ideal library. Numbered footnotes, however, offer more detail on a particular book or subject.

The rest of the survey covers resources for other biblical and theological disciplines, including Biblical Hebrew, New Testament Greek, Systematic Theology, and Church History. Here, too, outstanding entries are listed in bold. In addition, a list of computer resources and Internet sites are offered.

Finally, I have included a few special features to elucidate further specific recommendations. "On Commentary Series" provides the big picture of the individual titles alluded to in each biblical book. Please read "Building a 'Must-Have' Personal Reference Library." When approaching the daunting task of assembling a library (which might cost the equivalent of a good secondhand car), it is advisable to develop a consumer strategy. This might not be a consumer report, but it might help steer you clear of unnecessary frills.

Also for your benefit, "The Ultimate Commentary Collection" charts the best exegetical and expositional commentaries for each book. Here, I have done my best to list the primary exegetical choice first, followed by the best expositional commentary.

For sake of brevity, all subtitles are omitted unless they are absolutely necessary to explain a book's contents. Since this volume is primarily a buyer's guide, I have omitted the name of the city of the publisher. Often, I will simply add a short note for explanation.

Appraisal

First, although I have not read all of the approximately 2,500 books listed in this survey, I rely principally on the consensus of other published bibliographies and surveys. Second, each quarter I photocopy reviews from twenty-five theological journals (British journals also inform me of books of which I might be otherwise unaware).[4] Third, I receive review copies from more than a dozen publishers.

---

4. Periodicals worth considering are the *Ashland Theological Journal, Bibliotheca Sacra, Bulletin for Biblical Research, Catholic Biblical Quarterly, Churchman, Denver Journal* (online at denver-journal.densem.edu), *Expository Times, Interpretation, Journal of Biblical Literature, Journal of the Evangelical Theological Society, Religious Studies Review, Review and Expositor, The Southern Baptist Journal of Theology, Themelios, Trinity Journal,* and the *Westminster Theological Journal.*

When I receive a new book, I first check the endorsements. An author's reputation has already raised the level of anticipation attending the release of a new book. The reputation of the author's endorsers adds further weight to how well professors, pastors, and other interested professionals might receive it. Generally, subsequent reviews of new books appearing in journals follow the suit of endorsements (if the reviewer is of the same persuasion as the endorser and the author). Next, I'll turn to the table of contents and select sample sections to peruse. From these, I am able to discern the general thrust of the authors' approach and how they have handled a particular interpretative issue. Bibliographies and indices are also of great interest to me. I often refer to the author index to note which commentators the author cites most often. If the richness of citation matches an informed and current bibliography, things are looking good.

Finally, I scan each book's bibliography religiously to spot titles that are being mentioned continually by different authors. Thus, this survey attempts to represent the best books available in each category.

A Word on Exegetical Forecasting

Though recommending forthcoming commentaries may seem a bit presumptuous, my rationale is as follows. Of the more than seventy new evangelical titles slated to appear in the next few years (delays, however, are inevitable), more than half are from scholars who have already written one or more studies. For instance, D. A. Carson has written two semitechnical commentaries (Matthew and John) as well as several other books. He is scheduled to write two technical commentaries (Hebrews and 1–3 John) and two semitechnical works (Galatians and Revelation), which will ultimately place him in the exalted company of F. F. Bruce, C. K. Barrett, and I. Howard Marshall as a premier commentator on the New Testament. Peter O'Brien finds himself in such company with his recent, outstanding semitechnical effort on Ephesians, technical commentaries on Philippians and Colossians/Philemon, and a forthcoming commentary on Hebrews (PNTC). I think it fair to say that we can expect more of the same from these men (although, admittedly, this is not always the case). But bear in mind that it is possible for a commentary to be reassigned or delayed significantly.

In many instances, you will discover that a particular book, such as Genesis or Romans, is already well served. A small percentage (5–10 percent) of the books in this survey may also be currently out of print, but some publishers such as Good Books and Wipf & Stock specialize in reprinting discontinued titles. Occasionally, the original publisher will reprint one of their backlisted titles. I think it important to mention these inasmuch as they can often be obtained secondhand (see Internet Web Sites: Used Books) or can be found in theological libraries for purposes of study.

You might want to consult the used booksellers if you would like to sell some of your library to finance newer acquisitions. The best of new commentaries, of course, will still take into account the old masters, but they will especially focus on commentators of the last twenty-five years.

These are the methods by which I keep this survey current, in both reassessing aging titles and assessing the new titles that have emerged. The purpose of my survey is to evaluate the length and breadth of current scholarship; it is not intended as a history of interpretation.

In an effort to keep this survey as current and useful as possible, please send any suggestions or criticisms to me at the following address or telephone number.

JOHN GLYNN
81 Perry Avenue
Stoughton, MA 02072
781-341-4515

ABBREVIATIONS

Bible Versions

AMPLIFIED	*Amplified Bible*
ESV	*English Standard Version*
HCSB	*Holman Christian Standard Bible* (Broadman & Holman)
KJV	King James Version
MSG	*The Message* (NavPress)
NASB	New American Standard Bible (various publishers)
NCV	New Century Version
NIV	*New International Version* (Zondervan)
NKJV	New King James Version
NLT	*New Living Translation* (Tyndale)
NRSV	*New Revised Standard Version* (various publishers)
RSV	Revised Standard Version
TNIV	*Today's New International Version* (Zondervan)

General Abbreviations

AB	Anchor Bible (Doubleday)
ABRL	Anchor Bible Reference Library
ABS	American Bible Society
ACCS	Ancient Christian Commentary on the Scripture (IVP)
AGNT	Friberg, Timothy and Barbara. *Analytical Greek New Testament*. Baker, 1981.
ANE	Ancient Near East
ANTC	Abingdon New Testament Commentary

AOTC	Abingdon Old Testament Commentary
Apollos	Apollos Old Testament Commentary Series (IVP)
ATJ	*Ashland Theological Journal*
BAS	Biblical Archaeology Society
BBC	Blackwell Bible Commentary
BCBC	Believers Church Bible Commentary (Herald)
BCOTWP	Baker Commentary on the Old Testament: Wisdom and Psalms
BDAG	Bauer, Walter, Frederick Danker, William Arndt, and F. Wilbur Gingrich. *A Greek-English Lexicon of the New Testament and Other Early Christian Literature.* 3d ed. University of Chicago Press, 2000.
BDB	Brown, F., S. R. Driver, and C. A. Briggs. *A Hebrew and English Lexicon of the Old Testament.* Oxford, 1907.
BECNT	Baker Exegetical Commentary on the New Testament
BHL	*Biblia Hebraica Leningradensia*
BHS	*Biblia Hebraica Stuttgartensia*
BibSac	*Bibliotheca Sacra* (Dallas Theological Seminary)
BNTC	Black's New Testament Commentaries (formerly Harper's New Testament Commentaries [HNTC]) (Black/Harper/Hendrickson/Continuum)
BSC	Bible Study Commentary (Zondervan)
BST	The Bible Speaks Today (IVP)
BTCB	Brazos Theological Commentary on the Bible (Baker)
CAH	Cambridge Ancient History
CBC	Cornerstone Biblical Commentary (Tyndale)
CCNT	Crossroad Companions to the New Testament
DBC	Doubleday Bible Commentary
DJG	*Dictionary of Jesus and the Gospels* (IVP)
DLNTD	*Dictionary of the Latter New Testament and Its Developments* (IVP)
DNTB	*Dictionary of New Testament Background* (IVP)
DPL	*Dictionary of Paul and His Letters* (IVP)
DSB	Daily Study Bible (Westminster John Knox)

DSS	Dead Sea Scrolls
EBC	Expositor's Bible Commentary (Zondervan)
ECC	Eerdmans Critical Commentary
EDB	*Eerdmans Dictionary of the Bible*
EDNT	*Exegetical Dictionary of the New Testament* (Eerdmans)
EGGNT	Exegetical Guides to the Greek New Testament (Eerdmans)
Emmaus	*Emmaus Theological Journal*
EPSC	Evangelical Press Study Commentary
Epworth	Epworth Commentary Series
EvBC	Everyman's Bible Commentary (Moody)
ExpTim	*Expository Times*
FOTL	The Forms of the Old Testament Literature (Eerdmans)
GAP	Guides to the Apocrypha and Pseudepigrapha (Sheffield)
GBS	German Bible Society
G/K	Goodrick/Kohlenberger
GNT	Greek New Testament
GTJ	*Grace Theological Journal*
HALOT	Koehler, L., and W. Baumgartner. *A Hebrew-Aramaic Lexicon of the Old Testament.* 3d ed. Brill, 1994–2002.
HCOT	Historical Commentary on the Old Testament (Peeters)
HCSB	*Holman Christian Standard Bible* (Broadman & Holman)
Hermeneia	Hermeneia: A Critical and Historical Commentary (Fortress)
HOTE	Handbooks for Old Testament Exegesis (Kregel)
IBC	Interpretation: A Bible Commentary for Teaching and Preaching (Westminster John Knox)
IBR	Institute for Biblical Research (Baker)
IBT	Interpreting Biblical Texts (Abingdon)
ICC	International Critical Commentary (T & T Clark)

IES	Israel Exploration Society
ISBE	*International Standard Bible Encyclopedia.* Edited by G. W. Bromiley. 4 vols. Eerdmans, 1979–1988.
ITC	International Theological Commentary (Eerdmans/ Handsel)
IVP	InterVarsity Press
IVPNTC	IVP New Testament Commentary
JBI	*Journal of Biblical Interpretation*
JBMW	*Journal of Biblical Manhood and Womanhood*
JEDP	Documentary hypothesis sources
JETS	*Journal of the Evangelical Theological Society*
JPS	Jewish Publication Society
JPSTC	Jewish Publication Society Torah Commentary
JPT	*Journal of Pentecostal Theology*
JSNT	*Journal for the Study of the New Testament*
JSOT	*Journal for the Study of the Old Testament*
JTS	*Journal of Theological Studies*
KECOT	Kregel Expository Commentary on the Old Testament
LEC	Library of Early Christianity (Westminster John Knox)
LEH	Lust, Johan, Erik Eynikel, and Katrin Hauspie, eds. *A Greek-English Lexicon of the Septuagint.* GBS, 2003.
LXX	Septuagint; Greek translation of the Old Testament
Mentor	Mentor Old Testament Commentary (Christian Focus)
MT	Masoretic Text
NA^{26}	*Nestle-Aland Novum Testamentum Graece.* 26th ed. GBS, 1979.
NA^{27}	*Nestle-Aland Novum Testamentum Graece.* 27th ed. GBS, 1993.
NAC	New American Commentary (Broadman & Holman)
NACSBT	New American Commentary Studies in Bible and Theology
NBC	*New Bible Commentary* (IVP)

NBD	*New Bible Dictionary* (IVP)
NCamBC	New Cambridge Bible Commentary (Cambridge University Press)
NCBC	New Century Bible Commentary (Eerdmans/ Sheffield)
NIB	The New Interpreter's Bible (Abingdon)
NIBCNT	New International Bible Commentary on the New Testament (Hendrickson)
NIBCOT	New International Bible Commentary on the Old Testament (Hendrickson)
NICNT	New International Commentary on the New Testament (Eerdmans)
NICOT	New International Commentary on the Old Testament (Eerdmans)
NIDNTT	*New International Dictionary of New Testament Theology* (Zondervan)
NIDOTTE	*New International Dictionary of Old Testament Theology and Exegesis* (Zondervan)
NIGTC	New International Greek Testament Commentary (Eerdmans)
NIVAC	The NIV Application Commentary (Zondervan)
NIVTDNTW	*NIV Theological Dictionary of New Testament Words* (Zondervan)
NT	New Testament
NTC	New Testament in Context Commentaries (Trinity)
NTG	New Testament Guides (Cornell/Sheffield Academic Press)
NTL	New Testament Library (Westminster John Knox)
NTT	New Testament Theology (Cambridge University Press)
OT	Old Testament
OTG	Old Testament Guides (Cornell/Sheffield Academic Press)
OTL	Old Testament Library (Westminster John Knox)
PCA	Presbyterian Church in America
PNTC	The Pillar New Testament Commentary (Eerdmans)

Q	Siglum for the Synoptic sayings-source
REC	Reformed Expository Commentary (Presbyterian & Reformed)
RevExp	*Review and Expositor*
SBJT	*Southern Baptist Journal of Theology*
SBL	Society of Biblical Literature
SHBC	Smyth and Helwys Bible Commentary
SIL	Summer Institute of Linguistics
SJOT	*Scandinavian Journal of the Old Testament*
TDNT	*Theological Dictionary of the New Testament* (Eerdmans)
THNTC	The Two Horizons New Testament Commentary
TJ	*Trinity Journal*
TLNT	*Theological Lexicon of the New Testament* (Hendrickson)
TLOT	*Theological Lexicon of the Old Testament* (Hendrickson)
TMSTJ	*The Master's Seminary Theological Journal*
TNTC	Tyndale New Testament Commentaries (Eerdmans)
TOTC	Tyndale Old Testament Commentaries (IVP)
TPC	The Preacher's Commentary (Thomas Nelson)
TWOT	*Theological Wordbook of the Old Testament*
UBS	United Bible Societies
UBS[4]	Aland, B., et al., eds. *The Greek New Testament.* 4th ed. UBS, 1993.
VT	*Vetus Testamentum*
WBC	Word Biblical Commentary (Word/Thomas Nelson)
WBComp	Westminster Bible Companion
WEC	Wycliffe Exegetical Commentary (Moody)
WTJ	*Westminster Theological Journal*
ZEC	Zondervan Exegetical Commentary
ZIBBC	*Zondervan Illustrated Bible Backgrounds Commentary*

1

BUILDING A "MUST-HAVE" PERSONAL REFERENCE LIBRARY

How do you build a basic working reference library? Which books do you absolutely require when you find yourself in the perplexing position in which you can find no satisfactory solution to an apparent exegetical conundrum?

While perusing the libraries of various pastors, I have observed that ministers often either do not possess the essential tools necessary for quality inductive Bible study or simply could make better choices. Many such mini-libraries are cluttered with titles destined to gather dust or disseminate inferior information. Paradoxically, I have also witnessed fully equipped libraries accumulated by those who never end up in full-time ministry.

Thus, in attempting to determine a list of titles for an ideal "must-have" personal reference library, one must discern between the "must-have" volumes and the "dare-not" titles for the benefit of the occasional pathological bibliophile (such as myself) who lies in perpetual danger of sacrificing his final semester's tuition (if a pending Bible college or seminary graduate) in the pursuit of the "ideal" reference set. With this concern in view, I have tried to construct a recommendation geared for the layman, the student, and the pastor of a church, each of whom lacks a nearby Bible college or seminary library on which to fall back. First, every Christian should purchase a core group of resources for the benefit of his or her own study.

For Laymen

To learn how to conduct an inductive Bible study, I would recommend that the informed layman begin by reading Duvall and Hays.[1] For more advanced students, a more excellent guide is Klein, Blomberg, and Hubbard.[2] Then, having learned how to conduct an inductive Bible study, both layman and student must acquire the minimum number of basic tools. The start-up cost of the following titles is approximately $450 retail.

Bibles[3]

1. Barker, Kenneth, ed. *Zondervan NIV Study Bible, 10th Anniversary Edition* (Zondervan, 2002). Thought for thought.[4]
2. Blum, Ed, ed. *The Holman Christian Standard Bible* (Broadman & Holman, 2004).[5]
3. *New Living Translation* (Tyndale, 1996). Provides general nuance; dynamic equivalence (thought for thought).
4. Packer, J. I., ed. *English Standard Version* (Crossway, 2001). The ESV, an outstanding translation, is like a cross between NASB and the RSV.

References

1. Brisco, Thomas. *Holman Bible Atlas* (Broadman & Holman, 1999).

---

1. Scott Duvall and Daniel Hays, *Grasping God's Word,* 2d ed. (Zondervan, 2005); and idem, *Grasping God's Word Workbook,* 2d ed. (Zondervan, 2005).
2. William Klein, Craig Blomberg, and Robert Hubbard, *Introduction to Biblical Interpretation,* 2d ed. (Thomas Nelson, 2004).
3. Other possibilities for strong consideration are John Kohlenberger, ed., *The Essential Evangelical Parallel Bible* (Oxford University Press, 2004); and idem, *The Evangelical Parallel New Testament* (Oxford University Press, 2004). The first parallels the NKJV, ESV, NLT, and MSG. To these the second adds the NIV, HCSB, TNIV, and NCV.
4. Many prefer the NIV because so many commentary series are based on it (i.e., IVPNTC, NAC, NICNT [partial], NIVAC, PNTC, TOTC, etc.).
5. *The Holman Christian Standard Bible* (*HCSB*) by Broadman & Holman Publishers strives for the middle ground between the NASB and NIV. Also, there is a companion *HCSB Pocket Bible Concordance* (Broadman & Holman, 2005).

2. Elwell, Walter, ed. *Baker Encyclopedia of the Bible,* 4 vols. (Baker, 1992).[6]
3. Erickson, Millard. *Christian Theology,* 2d ed. (Baker, 1998); **or** Grudem, Wayne. *Systematic Theology* (Zondervan, 1994).
4. Marshall, I. Howard, et al., eds. *New Bible Dictionary,* 3d ed. (IVP, 1996).
5. Wenham, Gordon, et al., eds. *New Bible Commentary: Twenty-First Century Edition* (IVP, 1994).

For Bible College and Seminary Students

Assuming that the previously mentioned titles have been secured, the next order of business for the prospective ministry student is to begin assembling language resources that will facilitate study while he or she is in school. For first-year Greek students, whether in Bible college or seminary, at least a basic grammar, a workbook, and a copy of the Greek New Testament will be required texts.[7] Once you have ascertained which school you will be attending, you might want to "get a leg up" by calling the school bookstore to determine if a standard text is used in all beginning Greek courses.

Many professors will also require the purchase of the *BDAG* lexicon (see the following list), if not a Greek-English concordance and an exhaustive concordance to the Greek New Testament (which lists every occurrence of a Greek word). In any case, all of these tools will continue to be of value in future ministry and can be obtained for around $250.

The titles that I suggest for a basic Greek reference set are as follows:

1. Bauer, Walter, Frederick Danker, William Arndt, and F. Wilbur Gingrich. *A Greek-English Lexicon of the New Testament,* 3d ed. (University of Chicago, 2000).

---

6. Advanced students should purchase *ISBE* instead.
7. Either E. Nestle, and Kurt Aland, eds., *Novum Testamentum Graece,* 27th ed. (GBS, 1993), which gives the most comprehensive listings of variant readings, or Barbara Aland et al., eds., *The Greek New Testament,* 4th ed. (UBS, 1994), which is the same text with a shorter evaluation of variants. Both editions are now available with Newman's *Concise Greek-English Dictionary.*

2. Guthrie, George, and Scott Duvall. *Biblical Greek Exegesis* (Zondervan, 1998). Intermediate, advanced; selected readings, grammatical and semantic diagramming, how-to-do exegeticals; companion to Daniel Wallace's *Greek Grammar Beyond the Basics* (Zondervan, 1996).
3. Kohlenberger, John, Edward Goodrick, and James Swanson. *The Exhaustive Concordance to the Greek New Testament* (Zondervan, 1995). UBS[4] text.
4. Kohlenberger, John, Edward Goodrick, and James Swanson. *The Greek-English Concordance to the New Testament* (Zondervan, 1997). NIV text; G/K numbering system.
5. Mounce, William. *Basics of Biblical Greek,* 2d ed. (Zondervan, 2003). Includes interactive study aid CD.
———. *Basics of Biblical Greek: Workbook,* 2d ed. (Zondervan, 2003).

Then you will need to acquire a basic set of language helps to fertilize your growing knowledge of the New Testament in its original tongue. Elementary helps include an analytical lexicon to the GNT, which indicates every form of a Greek word found in the New Testament and provides its lexical root and basic definition.[8]

An interlinear Greek-English New Testament also proves to be of inestimable help in a pinch, especially when double-checking your own translation and comparing the various ways Greek words have been translated in English versions.[9] A sister-companion to an interlinear translation is Timothy and Barbara Friberg, *Analytical Greek New Testament,* which parses the GNT word by word and has placated many of the frantic nights when paradigm memorization failed me.[10]

---

8. Either William Mounce, *The Analytical Lexicon to the GNT* (Zondervan, 1992), which features the G/K numbering system, or the Friberg, Friberg, and Miller, *Analytical Lexicon of the GNT* (Baker, 1999), which is based on the NA[27] and UBS[4] texts.
9. Options include J. D. Douglas, ed., *The New Interlinear Greek-English New Testament* (Tyndale, 1990), which is based on the NA[26], the UBS[4] corrected, and the NRSV texts.
10. Timothy and Barbara Friberg, *Analytical Greek New Testament* (Baker, 1981).

Nevertheless, learning New Testament Greek is nothing of which to be afraid (which, for that matter, is also true of Hebrew). By exercising diligence, one can master both of the sacred languages, eventually rendering some helps anachronistic.

Two other Greek helps will produce dividends later in one's pastorate, yet they will be most beneficial during second and third year Greek while the student is preparing the daunting exegetical paper. These resources are an intermediate Greek grammar, to explain the interrelationship of Greek words in phrases and sentences (syntax),[11] and the word-study reference edited by Colin Brown, *The New International Dictionary of New Testament Theology.*[12]

A student can borrow reference titles from other students or photocopy relevant passages in the school library. However, the same tools that *assist* in learning while one is in training are the same tools that enable the minister to *persist* in learning when the graduate moves on.

Some of the tools you can sell secondhand (e.g., first-year grammars, *AGNT,* and analytical lexicons) before departing school. Thus, the "must-have" cost of a library for a Bible college or seminary graduate (with Greek training) is to date approximately $1,300.

The same basic components will ensure future proficiency for Hebrew study: a *BHS* Hebrew Bible,[13] a basic grammar and workbook, a lexicon, a Hebrew-English concordance, and an exhaustive concordance. Depending on the specific requirements of your school's language department, I recommend the following:

1. Even-Shoshan, Abraham. *A New Concordance of the Old Testament,* 2d ed. (Baker, 1989).

---

11. Daniel Wallace, *Greek Grammar Beyond the Basics* (Zondervan, 1996). For pastors, a helpful supplement to Wallace with some variegation of syntactical categories is Richard Young, *Intermediate New Testament Greek* (Broadman & Holman, 1994).

12. Colin Brown, ed., *The New International Dictionary of New Testament Theology,* 4 vols. (Zondervan, 1975–1978).

13. K. Elliger and W. Rudolph, eds., *Biblia Hebraica Stuttgartensia,* 5th ed. (GBS, 1997). The *Biblia Hebraica Quinta* is currently in the process of publication and ultimately will be superior to *BHS.*

2. Koehler, L., W. Baumgartner, and John Stamm, eds. *The Hebrew and Aramaic Lexicon of the Old Testament: Study Edition*, 2 vols. (Brill, 2001).[14]

3. Kohlenberger, John, and James Swanson, eds. *The Hebrew-English Concordance to the Old Testament* (Zondervan, 1999).

4. Pratico, Gary, and Brad Van Pelt. *Basics of Biblical Hebrew*, 2d ed. (Zondervan, 2007).[15]

———. *Basics of Biblical Hebrew: Workbook*, 2d ed. (Zondervan, 2007).

For Hebrew, the suggested counterparts are as follows:

1. Kohlenberger, John, ed. *The NIV Hebrew-English Interlinear Old Testament* (Zondervan, 1987).

2. Owens, John. *Analytical Key to the Old Testament,* 4 vols. (Baker, 1989–92).

3. VanGemeren, Willem, ed. *The New International Dictionary of Old Testament Theology and Exegesis,* 5 vols. (Zondervan, 1997). G/K numbering system.

4. Waltke, Bruce, and Michael O'Connor. *An Introduction to Biblical Hebrew Syntax* (Eisenbrauns, 1990).

Worth mentioning are features contained in both Owens and the *NIDOTTE*. Owens actually does double duty as a Hebrew-English Old Testament (RSV) and a parsing guide. Passage by passage, it parses

---

14. The most important feature of this lexicon is that it is alphabetized according to how each word appears in *BHS* rather than by root. It is also eminently more current than *BDB* relative to etymology and ANE parallels. If not for its exorbitant cost ($180 retail), it would be vastly preferable to *BDB*. Nevertheless, obtain it.

15. Other options include Allen Ross, *Introducing Biblical Hebrew* (Baker, 2000); Russell Fuller and Kyoungwon Choi, *Invitation to Biblical Hebrew* (Kregel, 2006); and Duane Garrett, *A Modern Grammar for Classical Hebrew* (Broadman & Holman, 2002). For second-year Hebrew and rusty pastors, *From Exegesis to Exposition* (Baker, 1999) by Robert Chisholm is useful for exegetical papers and sermon preparation.

every Hebrew word in the Old Testament, identifies the page number where it appears in *BDB*, supplies the root for verb forms, and lists the frequency of occurrences of each word. This feature makes it a valuable tool for exegetical papers. The *NIDOTTE* does much the same as its New Testament counterpart (providing the ancient Near Eastern, OT, LXX, Qumran, Rabbinic, and NT background to each Hebrew word). But it does one better by including a volume on topical entries (such as biblical concepts, places, persons, and events) and an index of semantic fields. Its contributors are evangelical.

The cost to date for the Hebrew-Greek graduate, which includes the basic reference set ($450), Greek grammars and language helps ($650), and the Hebrew grammars and language helps ($900), is $2,000.

For Pastors

Students in seminary and Bible college should plan to acquire a working set of commentaries while they are still in school. By scanning for book sales on bulletin boards, trolling the used-book room at the school bookstore, and taking advantage of the occasional publisher discounts, significant savings can be realized.

But why, you might ask, should I burden myself with so many books that I will rarely read from cover to cover? First, commentaries equip the pastor with a ready answer to any biblical question. One never knows when an inquiry concerning Obadiah or Jude could come your way. Otherwise, you could end up ruining the day for lack of references.[16]

Second, commentaries can furnish comprehensive coverage against shaky sermons, if, in a weak moment, the pastor's usual caution gives way to a homiletic flight of fancy. Commentaries suggest not only a range of possible solutions to problem passages but also a wealth of theological, literary, and cultural background material to ensure that the general tenor of a pulpit message remains sound.

---

16. I am not suggesting that a pastor replace an already existing working library. First, as a general rule, libraries need to become fully equipped (expanded). Then, older commentaries and references can be updated as needed. Computer options enable the user both to update language and reference helps and to save enormous time in sermon preparation.

The kind of commentaries one buys must be reflective of the training that one has received. For the seminary-trained professional, a mix-and-match, hodge-podge approach to commentary collecting is still the best route to follow because many complete testament or Bible series are uneven in quality and might cover a wider theological spectrum than that with which you are comfortable.

A pastor should have two technical (or one technical and one semi-technical) commentaries on each book of the Bible and an expositional commentary to provide a general overview of each book (with an eye toward application) if the budget allows. The pastor can assume that approximately two-thirds of his "must-have" library will consist of commentaries and commentary sets. Thus, the cost for a library of 100–120 commentaries alone can be expected to approach $3,200.

I recommend both the technical Word Biblical Commentary series (WBC) and the semitechnical New International Commentary series on both testaments published by Eerdmans (NICOT, NICNT). It would be better to substitute deficient titles in either series with available titles from Eerdmans' New International Greek Testament Commentary (NIGTC), the Eerdmans Critical Commentary (ECC), Broadman & Holman's whole-Bible New American Commentary (NAC), the newly emerging Apollos Old Testament Commentary, and the Baker Exegetical Commentary on the New Testament (BECNT) series.

For Bible college or M.A. students with two to three years of Greek background, the best combination is WBC (Word/Thomas Nelson) and NIGTC (Eerdmans) series in the New Testament. For those with less Greek background, NICNT (Eerdmans), Pillar New Testament Commentary (Eerdmans), and BECNT (Baker) are to be preferred. In the Old Testament, a combination of the NICOT (Eerdmans), the NAC (Broadman & Holman), Hendrickson's The New International Biblical Commentary on the Old Testament (NIBCOT), the Apollos Old Testament Commentary (IVP), and another IVP series, the Tyndale Old Testament Commentary (TOTC), would be your best choices. Depending on the number of paperbacks purchased (TOTC and NIBCOT), the overall commentary costs for Greek-only ministers comes to approximately $2,500–$3,000.

Finally, for the pastor or layman without training in the original languages, several very worthwhile preaching, application, and expositional commentary series are available.[17] Of these, the best combination for the New Testament is The NIV Application Commentary (NIVAC) by Zondervan, the Pillar series (PNTC) by Eerdmans, the Cornerstone Biblical Commentary (CBC) by Tyndale, and a collection of four other series.[18] The Old Testament is best covered by the NIVAC, the TOTC (IVP), and The Bible Speaks Today series (BST), also by IVP. The estimated price for a solid expositional library is approximately $1,300.

Now that I have gone to the wire (and the limits of your expense account) in championing the fat commentary bookcase, I am compelled by the ghosts of Hebrew and Greek professors to extend a caveat. Commentaries are not intended to take the place of your own intensive Bible study (and use of language helps and references where applicable) as illustrated in hermeneutics texts. They are meant to be an *aid* to study, such as gaining a perspective on background, or analyzing phrases with cultural, historical, or theological nuance, or as a last line of defense in double-checking the integrity of your own conclusions.

Owning and soaking in your own message is vital to your own growth and that of your congregation. The last thing you need is a videotaped sermon rented from a commentary (at the expense of the Holy Spirit). Having said all that, and having spent this much money, following are fourteen more titles that you should obtain.

1. Alexander, Desmond, et al., eds. *New Dictionary of Biblical Theology* (IVP, 2000). Three parts: introductory articles, individual book theologies, 215 (A–Z) topics.

---

17. Expositional as opposed to technical, exegetically based commentaries often succeed better at providing the general theological and applicational thrust of a given passage or biblical book. Therefore, they can be equally valuable to the seminary-trained pastor. Indeed, some series such as the NIVAC (Zondervan), Interpretation (Westminster John Knox), the IVP New Testament Commentary (IVPNTC), and The Preacher's Commentary by Thomas Nelson are designed specifically for preachers. Also, the New Interpreter's Bible commentary series (Abingdon) follows each block of commentary with a very helpful "Reflections" section.

18. The Tyndale New Testament Commentary (TNTC) from Eerdmans, Black's New Testament Commentary (BNTC) from Hendrickson Publishers, the NAC (Broadman & Holman), and the IVPNTC series (IVP).

2. Arnold, Bill, and Hugh Williamson, eds. *Dictionary of the Old Testament: Historical Books* (IVP, 2005).

3. Baker, David, and Desmond Alexander, eds. *Dictionary of the Old Testament: The Pentateuch* (IVP, 2002).

4. Carson, D. A., and Douglas Moo. *An Introduction to the New Testament*, rev. ed. (Zondervan, 2006).

5. Davids, Peter, and Ralph Martin, eds. *Dictionary of the Later New Testament and Its Developments* (IVP, 1997).

6. Dillard, Raymond, and Tremper Longman. *Introduction to the Old Testament*, 2d. ed. (Zondervan, 2006).[19]

7. Elwell, Walter, ed. *Baker Theological Dictionary of the Bible* (Baker, 1994, 2001). Formerly *Evangelical Dictionary of Biblical Theology,* **or** Elwell, Walter, ed. *Evangelical Dictionary of Theology,* 2d ed. (Baker, 2001).

8. Evans, Craig, and Stanley Porter, eds. *Dictionary of New Testament Backgrounds* (IVP, 2000). Highly academic (i.e., Qumran documents, apocryphal writings, etc.).

9. Green, Joel, Scot McKnight, and I. Howard Marshall, eds. *Dictionary of Jesus and the Gospels* (IVP, 1992).

10. Hawthorne, Gerald, Ralph Martin, and Daniel Reid, eds. *Dictionary of Paul and His Letters* (IVP, 1993).[20]

11. Keener, Craig. *The IVP Bible Background Commentary: New Testament* (IVP, 1993).[21]

12. Porter, Stanley, and Lee McDonald. *Early Christianity and Its Sacred Literature* (Hendrickson, 2000).

13. Provan, Iain, V. Philips Long, and Tremper Longman. *A Biblical History of Israel* (Westminster John Knox, 2003).

---

19. For courses requiring more survey than introductory material, choose Andrew Hill and John Walton, *A Survey of the Old Testament,* 2d ed. (Zondervan, 2000); or Colin Smith, *Unfolding the Bible Story,* 4 vols. (Moody, 2002), whose two Old Testament volumes are ideal for two-semester surveys.

20. For a condensation of the four NT volumes, see Daniel Reid, ed., *The IVP Dictionary of the New Testament* (IVP, 2004).

21. For a comprehensive, single-volume treatment of the cultural, political, and religious environment during New Testament times, another alternative is Everett Ferguson, *Backgrounds of Early Christianity,* 2d ed. (Eerdmans, 1993).

14. Walton, John, Victor Matthews, and Mark Chavalas. *The IVP Bible Background Commentary: Old Testament* (IVP, 2000).

The "must-have" cost of a personal biblical reference library is as follows:

Seminary-trained student (about 165 volumes):	$5,700[22]
Bible college with Greek (about 145 volumes):	$4,400
Computer programs (15–25 print resources):	$2,900
Layman (about 120 volumes):	$2,300

---

22. Retail cost. Taking advantage of discounts, used books, and selling of the language helps that are designed specifically for seminary use should reduce each number by 40 percent. Consider this a wise investment. A library that is approximately the same cost as a semester of school will help you retain three to four years of learning. Second, the average time a pastor spends on preparing a weekly message or two (over a period of thirty to forty years) amply justifies the initial down payment. In my mind, that's the best way to stretch your ministry dollar.

2

ON COMMENTARY SERIES

For specific recommendations on whole sets, I recommend both the Word Biblical Commentary (WBC) and Eerdmans' New International Greek Testament Commentary (NIGTC), which are technical. Also, excellent choices are the semitechnical New International Commentary on both testaments, also published by Eerdmans (NICOT, NICNT); Baker Exegetical Commentary on the New Testament (BECNT); and the nascent Apollos Old Testament Commentary (IVP),[1] which is formatted like the WBC with a theological emphasis in the explanation section following each pericope. It is also advisable to consult commentaries from series that generally run moderate-liberal in their persuasion.

The WBC series, formerly published by Word and now carried by Thomas Nelson, has a fairly equal combination of evangelical and moderate (with some liberal) commentators. A commentary with an evangelical bias would typically subscribe to the belief that all Scripture is absolutely inerrant, that is, the Bible is written with full historical and scientific accuracy on all matters that it affirms and thus is completely truthful. A moderate view would affirm that the inerrancy of Scripture is restricted to its theological content rather than its historical or scientific statements. A moderate, for instance, could hold that the actual author of 2 Peter is someone other than the

---

1. Specifically intended for pastors, Apollos follows the format of the WBC series with special emphasis on theological reflection and applicational possibilities in the corresponding "Explanations" section. As such, it is more scholarly than the applicational series mentioned below, with some commentaries indicating an evangelical/critical slant (i.e., Gordon McConville on Deuteronomy).

apostle himself but that its theological truths are still consistent with the rest of Scripture. A liberal view, however, would generally assert that Scripture's claim to divine origin is dubious (i.e., the JEDP documentary hypothesis of Pentateuchal redaction).

In recent years, evangelicals have been forced to play catch-up in writing commentaries that supply the advanced philology, text-critical notes, theological implications, socioliterary background, and extrabiblical parallels that have characterized liberal scholarship for decades. Particularly noteworthy liberal commentary series are Hermeneia (Fortress), and the Old Testament Library (OTL)[2] and the New Testament Library (NTL), both from Westminster John Knox.

Series of mixed theological persuasion (including liberal, evangelical, and moderate commentators) that deserve mention are the Eerdmans Critical Commentary (ECC), the revising ICC series (T & T Clark), and the Anchor Bible (Doubleday).

Other options include the new wave of commentaries that exclusively address cultural and literary backgrounds. Rather than following the verse-by-verse format of the traditional grammatical-historical commentaries, these generally exposit blocks of text. This format includes the New Testament in Context (NTC) by Trinity Press International and the socio-rhetorical commentaries published by Eerdmans.

Some of the series that I include are semitechnical as well as expositional, namely, Broadman & Holman's whole-Bible New American Commentary (NAC)[3] and the Pillar New Testament Commentary (PNTC) series, which are designed specifically for the serious student and the general reader alike. As such, these commentaries usually are better than more technical treatments for grasping the overall flow of

---

2. The Old Testament Library was inaugurated by Westminster, but since merging with John Knox, the name of the publisher is Westminster John Knox. Also, titles in the Interpretation series were originally published by John Knox, but are now also available through Westminster John Knox. I have tried to make these distinctions throughout the book, including the WBC volumes.

3. Particularly outstanding in the NAC series and able to be used as a semitechnical commentary include David Garland on 2 Corinthians, Richard Taylor and Ray Clendenen on Haggai/Malachi, Duane Garrett on Hosea and Amos, Robert Bergen on 1–2 Samuel, Daniel Block on Judges and Ruth, David Howard on Joshua, Dennis Cole on Numbers, Doug Stuart on Exodus, and Mark Rooker on Leviticus.

the passage. In some cases, I have included them under Technical, Semitechnical references.

For expositional recommendations in addition to those mentioned earlier, I would also recommend the NIV Application Commentary (NIVAC),[4] the Tyndale Old Testament Commentary (TOTC), The Bible Speaks Today (BST), the Black's New Testament Commentary (BNTC), and an emerging series to watch from Hendrickson Publishers, the New International Biblical Commentary on the Old Testament (NIBCOT).

The following overview presents a list of series arranged according to my recommendations:

Evangelical and Technical, Semitechnical[5]

1. New International Greek Testament Commentary (NIGTC)
2. New International Commentary (NICOT, NICNT)
3. Baker Exegetical Commentary (BECNT)
4. Pillar New Testament Commentaries (PNTC)
5. Apollos Old Testament Commentary (Apollos)

Mixed, Technical, Semitechnical[6]

1. Word Biblical Commentaries (WBC)
2. International Critical Commentary (ICC)
3. The Anchor Bible (AB)
4. Eerdmans Critical Commentary (ECC)
5. Black's New Testament Commentaries (BNTC), formerly Harper's New Testament Commentaries (HNTC)

---

4. The NIVAC series is the best homiletic set current. It breaks the interpretation into three categories: original meaning, bridging contexts, and contemporary significance, thus following the accepted pattern for preparing sermons.
5. Note that the AB, Hermeneia, IBC, NIB, NICNT, NICOT, NIGTC, NIVAC, NTL, OTL, PNTC, and TNTC are all printed on acid-free paper, promising years of durability and clarity.
6. The commentaries of Milgrom, Christensen, Klein, McCarter, Cogan, Hobbs, Japhet, Williamson, Fox, Clines, Seow, Murphy, Andersen, Freedman, Barrett, Cranfield, Thrall, Best, Johnson, Achtemeier, Smalley, Boxall, and Schnackenburg are among those of the moderate-to-liberal persuasion (primarily in the Hermeneia, OTL, AB, ICC, and WBC series) that are considered as desirable selections for conservatives.

6. Sacra Pagina
7. Abingdon New Testament Commentaries (ANTC), Abingdon Old Testament Commentaries (AOTC)
8. New Century Bible Commentary (NCBC)
9. New Testament in Context Commentaries (NTC)[7]

Liberal, Technical

1. Hermeneia, Continental Commentaries
2. Old Testament Library (OTL), New Testament Library (NTL)

Exposition

1. New American Commentary (NAC)
2. Tyndale Old Testament Commentary (TOTC)
3. New International Biblical Commentary: OT and NT (NIBCOT, NIBCNT)
4. Cornerstone Biblical Commentary (CBC)
5. New Interpreter's Bible (NIB)[8]
6. Tyndale New Testament Commentary (TNTC)
7. Expositors Bible Commentary (EBC)
8. Believer's Church Bible Commentary (BCBC)
9. Daily Study Bible (DSB)

Preaching and Application

1. The NIV Application Commentary (NIVAC)
2. The Bible Speaks Today (BST)
3. IVP New Testament Commentary (IVPNTC)
4. Interpretation (IBC)
5. The Preacher's Commentary (TPC)

---

7. The NTC abbreviation is used for this series rather than the New Testament Commentary by William Hendriksen and Simon Kistemaker (Baker) because of more recommended titles.

8. Especially Walter Kaiser on Leviticus, Choon-Leong Seow on Kings, Leslie Allen on Chronicles, Ralph Klein on Ezra/Nehemiah, Clinton McCann on Psalms, Raymond Van Leeuwen on Proverbs, Christopher Seitz on Isaiah 40–66, Kathryn Pfisterer Darr on Ezekiel, Alan Culpepper on Luke, Gail O'Day on John, Robert Wall on Acts, Tom Wright on Romans, and Richard Hays on Galatians.

3

OLD TESTAMENT INTRODUCTION, SURVEY, AND THEOLOGY

Old Testament Introduction

1. Archer, Gleason. *A Survey of Old Testament Introduction,* rev. ed. (Moody, 1994).
2. Dillard, Raymond, and Tremper Longman. *Introduction to the Old Testament,* rev. ed. (Zondervan, 2006). Historical, theological, and literary background.
3. Dumbrell, William. *The Faith of Israel,* 2d ed. (Baker, 2002). Especially theology.
4. Harrison, R. K. *Introduction to the Old Testament* (Hendrickson, 2004).
5. Kaltner, John, and Steven McKenzie. *The Old Testament* (Abingdon, 2006).
6. LaSor, William, David Hubbard, and Frederic Bush. *Old Testament Survey,* 2d ed. (Eerdmans, 1996).
7. Matthews, Victor, and James Moyer. *The Old Testament: Text and Context,* 2d ed. (Hendrickson, 2005).

Old Testament Survey[*]

1. **Arnold, Bill, and Bryan Beyer. *Encountering the Old Testament* (Baker, 1999).** Includes multimedia, interactive CD-ROM, companion reader (*see under* Old Testament Background: Ancient Near East Parallels).

---

[*] Forthcoming: David Howard, *Invitation to the Old Testament* (Kregel). Probably the best combo is Sailhamer (Pentateuch), Hamilton (Historical), Estes (Wisdom), Wilson (Psalms), and Chisholm (Prophets).

2. Dyer, Charles, and Eugene Merrill. *Nelson's Old Testament Survey* (Thomas Nelson, 2003)
3. **Hill, Andrew, and John Walton.** *A Survey of the Old Testament,* **2d ed. (Zondervan, 2000).**
4. Walton, John, and Andrew Hill. *Old Testament Today* (Zondervan, 2004). Introductory, college-level.

Introduction to the Pentateuch*

1. **Alexander, Desmond.** *From Paradise to the Promised Land,* **2d ed. (Baker, 2002).**
2. Hamilton, Victor. *Handbook on the Pentateuch,* 2d ed. (Baker, 2005).
3. **Sailhamer, John.** *The Pentateuch as Narrative* **(Zondervan, 1992).**
4. Schnittjer, Gary. *The Torah Story* (Zondervan, 2006).
5. **Wenham, Gordon.** *Exploring the Old Testament: A Guide to the Pentateuch* **(IVP, 2003).**
6. *See* Critical Introductions.

Introduction to the Historic Books

1. Campbell, Antony. *Joshua to Chronicles* (Westminster John Knox, 2004).
2. Chisholm, Robert. *Interpreting the Historical Books* (Kregel, 2006).
3. **Hamilton, Victor.** *Handbook on the Historical Books* **(Baker, 2001).**
4. **Howard, David.** *An Introduction to the Old Testament Historical Books* **(Moody, 1993).**
5. Nelson, Richard. IBT (Abingdon, 1998). 2 Samuel 24 as test case.
6. **Satterthwaite, Philip, and Gordon McConville.** *Exploring the Old Testament,* **Volume Two (IVP, 2005).**

---

* Forthcoming: Peter Vogt, *Interpreting the Pentateuch* (Kregel).

Introduction to the Wisdom Literature*

1. Berry, Donald. *An Introduction to Wisdom and Poetry of the Old Testament* (Broadman & Holman, 1995).
2. Bullock, Hassell. *An Introduction to the Old Testament Poetic Books,* rev. ed. (Moody, 1988).
3. **Clifford, Richard. IBT (Abingdon, 1998).** Outstanding critical introduction.
4. Crenshaw, James. *Old Testament Wisdom,* rev. ed. (Westminster John Knox, 1998).
5. **Estes, Daniel. *Handbook on the Wisdom Books and Psalms* (Baker, 2005).**
6. Lucas, Ernest. *Exploring the Old Testament,* vol. 3 (IVP, 2004).
7. **Murphy, Roland. *The Tree of Life,* 3d ed. (Eerdmans, 2002).**

Introduction to the Psalms†

1. **Bullock, Hassell. *Encountering the Book of Psalms* (Baker, 2001).**
2. Crenshaw, James. *The Psalms, An Introduction* (Eerdmans, 2001).
3. **McCann, Clinton. *A Theological Introduction to the Book of Psalms* (Abingdon, 1993).**
4. Westermann, Claus. *The Living Psalms* (Eerdmans, 1989).
5. **Wilson, Gerald. *The Psalms*. IBT (Abingdon, 2005).**

Introduction to Prophetic Literature‡

1. Bullock, Hassell. *An Introduction to the Old Testament Prophetic Books* (Moody, 1986).
2. **Chisholm, Robert. *Handbook on the Prophets* (Baker, 2002).**
3. Hutton, Rodney. *Fortress Introduction to the Prophets* (Fortress, 2004).
4. **McConville, Gordon. *Exploring the Old Testament,* vol. 4 (IVP, 2003).**

---

* Forthcoming: Richard Schultz, *Interpreting the Wisdom Literature* (Kregel).
† Forthcoming: Mark Futato, *Interpreting the Psalms* (Kregel).
‡ Forthcoming: Michael Grisanti, *Interpreting the Prophets* (Kregel).

5. **Petersen, David.** *The Prophetic Literature* **(Westminster John Knox, 2002).** Includes Elijah, Elisha, etc.
6. Rofé, Alexander. *Introduction to Prophetic Literature* (Sheffield Academic Press, 1997).
7. Sweeney, Marvin. *The Prophetic Literature.* IBT (Abingdon, 2006).
8. VanGemeren, Willem. *Interpreting the Prophetic Word* (Zondervan, 1990).

Critical Introductions

1. Anderson, Bernhard. *Understanding the Old Testament,* 4th ed., abridged and updated (Prentice-Hall, 2000).
2. Birch, Bruce, et al. *A Theological Introduction to the Old Testament,* 2d ed. (Abingdon, 2005).
3. Blenkinsopp, Joseph. *The Pentateuch,* ABRL (Doubleday, 1992). Especially interpretation, 1800 to present.
4. Brueggemann, Walter. *An Introduction to the Old Testament* (Westminster John Knox, 2003).
5. Childs, Brevard. *Introduction to the Old Testament as Scripture* (Fortress, 1979). Moderate.
6. Collins, John. *Introduction to the Hebrew Bible* (Fortress, 2004). Book and CD.
7. Crenshaw, James. *Old Testament Story and Faith* (Hendrickson, 1992).
8. Drane, John. *Introducing the Old Testament,* rev. ed. (Fortress, 2001).
9. Eissfeldt, Otto. *The Old Testament* (Harper, 1965). Classic JEDP, dated.
10. Flanders, Henry, Robert Crapps, and David Smith. *People of the Covenant,* 3d ed. (Oxford University Press, 1988).
11. Fretheim, Terence. *The Pentateuch,* IBT (Abingdon, 1996).
12. Rendtorff, Rolf. *The Old Testament: An Introduction* (Fortress, 1986).
13. Schmidt, Werner. *Old Testament Introduction,* 2d ed. (Westminster John Knox, 2000).

14. Vriezen, T. C., and Adam van der Woude. *Ancient Israel and Early Jewish Literature* (Brill, 2005).
15. Whybray, Norman. *Introduction to the Pentateuch* (Eerdmans, 1995). As single author fiction.

Principal Old Testament Theologies

1. **Barr, James. *The Concept of Biblical Theology* (Fortress, 1999).**
2. Brueggemann, Walter. *Theology of the Old Testament* (Fortress, 1997). Studies metaphor and imagery of the courtroom.
3. Clements, Ronald. *Wisdom in Theology* (Eerdmans, 1992). Exilic developments.
4. Gerstenberger, Erhard. *Theologies of the Old Testament* (Fortress, 2002).
5. **Goldingay, John. *Old Testament Theology*, 3 vols. (IVP, 2003, 2006–).**
6. **House, Paul. *Old Testament Theology* (IVP, 1998).**
7. **Kaiser, Walter. *Toward an Old Testament Theology* (Zondervan, 1978).**
8. Knierim, Rolf. *The Task of Old Testament Theology* (Eerdmans, 1995).
9. Martens, Elmer. *God's Design*, 3d ed. (D & F Scott Publishing, 1998).
10. Merrill, Eugene. *Everlasting Dominion* (B & H Publishing Group, 2006).
11. Ollenburger, Ben, et al., eds. *The Flowering of Old Testament Theology* (Eisenbrauns, 1992).
12. Perdue, Leo. *Wisdom and Creation* (Abingdon, 1994). Wisdom theology.
13. Preuss, Horst. *Old Testament Theology*, OTL, 2 vols. (Westminster John Knox, 1995–96). Liberal focus on Yahweh.
14. Rendtorff, Rolf. *The Old Testament: An Introduction* (Fortress, 1986).
15. Robertson, O. Palmer. *The Christ of the Covenants* (Presbyterian & Reformed, 1981).

————. *The Christ of the Prophets* (Presbyterian & Reformed, 2004).

16. Sailhamer, John. *Introduction to Old Testament Theology* (Zondervan, 1995).
17. Smith, Ralph. *Old Testament Theology* (Broadman & Holman, 1994). Useful historical overview.
18. Von Rad, Gerhard. *Old Testament Theology,* 2 vols. (Westminster John Knox, 2001). Liberal, salvation-history approach.
19. **Waltke, Bruce, with Charles Yu.** *An Old Testament Theology: A Canonical and Thematic Approach* **(Zondervan, 2007).**

Supplemental Theologies

1. Barmash, Pamela. *Homicide in the Biblical World* (Cambridge University Press, 2005).
2. Bartholomew, Craig, et al., eds. *Out of Egypt* (Zondervan, 2004).
3. Brown, Michael. *Israel's Divine Healer* (Zondervan, 1995).
4. **Carroll, R., M. Daniel, and Richard Hess, eds.** *Israel's Messiah in the Bible and the Dead Sea Scrolls* **(Baker, 2003).**
5. **Cowles, C. S., et al.** *Show Them No Mercy* **(Zondervan, 2003).** Genocide.
6. Gowan, Donald. *Theology of the Prophetic Books* (Westminster John Knox, 1998).
7. Greenspahn, Frederick. *When Brothers Dwell Together* (Oxford University Press, 1994). Refutes primogeniture (right of firstborn).
8. Hasel, Gerhard. *Old Testament Theology: Basic Issues in the Current Debate*, 4th ed. (Eerdmans, 1991).
9. Hildebrandt, Wilf. *An Old Testament Theology of the Spirit of God* (Hendrickson, 1995).
10. Johnston, Philip, and Peter Walker, eds. *The Land of Promise* (IVP, 2000).
11. McEntire, Mark. *The Blood of Abel* (Mercer, 1999). OT violence.
12. Niehaus, Jeffrey. *God at Sinai* (Zondervan, 1996).

13. Ollenburger, Ben. *Old Testament Theology*, 2d ed. (Eisenbrauns, 2004).
14. Penchansky, David, and Paul Redditt, eds. *Shall Not the Judge of the Earth Do What Is Right?* (Eisenbrauns, 2000).
15. **Satterthwaite, Philip, Richard Hess, and Gordon Wenham, eds. *The Lord's Anointed: Interpretations of Old Testament Messianic Texts* (Baker, 1996).**
16. Seitz, Christopher. *Word Without End* (Baylor University Press, 2005).
17. Wisdom, Jeffrey. *Blessings for the Nations and the Curse of the Law* (Mohr, 2001).
18. Wood, John. *Perspectives on War in the Bible* (Mercer University Press, 1998).

Biblical Theologies of Both Testaments

1. Beale, Gregory. *The Temple and the Church's Mission* (IVP, 2004).
2. Childs, Brevard. *Biblical Theology of the Old and New Testaments* (Fortress, 1992).
3. Das, Andrew, and Frank Matera, eds. *The Forgotten God* (Westminster John Knox, 2002). Paul Achtemeier tribute.
4. Goldsworthy, Graeme. *According to Plan* (IVP, 2002). Introductory.
5. Hafemann, Scott, ed. *Biblical Theology* (IVP, 2002).
6. Kraftchick, Steven, et al., eds. *Biblical Theology* (Abingdon, 1995).
7. Scobie, Charles. *An Approach to Biblical Theology* (Eerdmans, 2002).
8. Sun, H., et al., eds. *Problems in Biblical Theology* (Eerdmans, 1997).
9. Zuck, Roy, and Darrell Bock, eds. *Biblical Theology of the New Testament* (Moody, 1994).
10. Zuck, Roy, Eugene Merrill, and Darrell Bock, eds. *Biblical Theology of the Old Testament* (Moody, 1992).

4

OLD TESTAMENT COMMENTARIES

Genesis[*]
Technical, Semitechnical[1]

C/M 1. Cassuto, Umberto. *A Commentary on Book of Genesis,* 2 vols. (Magnes, 1961, 1964). Covers 1:1–13:5. Alternative to Documentary Hypothesis.

L/Cr 2. Fretheim, Terence. NIB, vol. 1 (Abingdon, 1994). Appreciation for literary facets; particularly plots, structure, and sequence.

E **3. Hamilton, Victor. NICOT, 2 vols. (Eerdmans, 1990, 1995).** Especially comparative Semitics.

C/M 4. Sarna, Nahum. JPSTC (JPS, 1989). Incorporates rabbinic exegesis.

L/Cr 5. Von Rad, Gerhard. OTL, rev. ed. (Westminster, 1973). Theological interpretation.

E/Cr **6. Wenham, Gordon. WBC, 2 vols. (Word, 1987, 1994).** Especially form, structure, setting.

L/Cr **7. Westermann, Claus. Continental, 3 vols. (Fortress, 1984–86).** Tradition-critical.

---

[*] Forthcoming: Richard Clifford, Hermeneia (Fortress); David Baker, Apollos (IVP); Erhard Blum, HCOT (Peeters); Kathleen O'Connor, SHBC (Smyth & Helwys); Ronald Hendel, AB, 2 vols. (Doubleday); Bill Arnold, NCBC (Cambridge University Press); and Theodore Hiebert, AOTC (Abingdon).

[1] Given the breadth of Genesis, the choice of Wenham, Hamilton, and Mathews most comprehensively covers the terrain. Waltke is also of assistance. David Baker's forthcoming commentary should be obtained.

Exposition

E/Cr 1. Atkinson, David. *The Message of Genesis 1–11,* BST (IVP, 1990).

E/Cr 2. Baldwin, Joyce. *The Message of Genesis 12–50,* BST (IVP, 1986).

L/Cr 3. Brueggemann, Walter. IBC (John Knox, 1982). Especially theology.

E 4. Collins, C. John. *Genesis 1–4* (Presbyterian & Reformed, 2005).

E 5. Currid, John. EPSC, 2 vols. (Evangelical Press, 2003, 2004).

E 6. Eveson, Philip. *The Book of Origins* (Evangelical Press, 2001).

E/Cr 7. Hartley, John. NIBCOT (Hendrickson, 2001). Editing from Moses to time of Solomon.

E/Cr 8. Kidner, Derek. TOTC (IVP, 1967). Day-age creation view.

E 9. Mathews, Kenneth. NAC, 2 vols. (Broadman & Holman, 1996, 2005).

E 10. Ross, Allen. *Creation and Blessing* (Baker, 1988). Thorough expositional study guide.

E 11. Sailhamer, John. EBC, vol. 2 (Zondervan, 1990).

E 12. Waltke, Bruce, with Cathi Fredericks. *Genesis* (Zondervan, 2001). Especially theology, somewhat semitechnical.

E 13. Walton, John. NIVAC (Zondervan, 2001).

Special Studies

E/Cr 1. Alexander, Desmond. *Abraham in the Negev* (Paternoster, 1997). Genesis 20–22.

E 2. Arnold, Bill. *Encountering the Book of Genesis* (Baker, 1998). College-level introduction.

L/Cr 3. Bailey, Lloyd. *Noah: The Person and the Story in History and Tradition* (University of South Carolina, 1989).

L/Cr 4. Brodie, Thomas. *Genesis as Dialogue* (Oxford University Press, 2001).

L/Cr   5. Carr, David. *Reading the Fractures of Genesis* (Westminster John Knox, 1996).

L/Cr   6. Clifford, Richard. *Creation Accounts in the Ancient Near East and in the Bible* (Catholic Biblical Association, 1994).

L/Cr   7. Hendel, Ronald. *The Text of Genesis 1–11* (Oxford University Press, 1998). LXX instructive to original reading.

E   8. **Hess, Richard, and David Tsumura, eds.** *I Studied Inscriptions from Before the Flood* **(Eisenbrauns, 1994).**

E/Cr   9. **Hess, Richard, Philip Satterthwaite, and Gordon Wenham, eds.** *He Swore an Oath* **(Baker, 1994).** Themes from Genesis 12–50.

E   10. **Longman, Tremper.** *How to Read Genesis* **(IVP, 2005).**

E   11. Sheridan, Mark. *Genesis 12–50.* ACCS (IVP, 2002). Patristic commentary.

L/Cr   12. Thompson, Thomas. *The Historicity of the Patriarchal Narratives* (Trinity Press International, 2002).

L/Cr   13. Westermann, Claus. *Genesis: An Introduction* (Fortress, 1992). Three commentary introductions combined.

C/M   14. **Williamson, Paul.** *Abraham, Israel and the Nations* **(Sheffield Academic Press, 2000).** Genesis 15 and 17 as separate covenants.

Exodus[*]
Technical, Semitechnical

L/Cr   1. Brueggemann, Walter. NIB, vol. 1 (Abingdon, 1994).

L/Cr   2. Cassuto, Umberto. *A Commentary on the Book of Exodus* (Magnes, 1967).

---

[*] Forthcoming: Brent Strawn, NICOT (Eerdmans); Desmond Alexander, Apollos (IVP); James Bruckner, NIBCOT (Hendrickson); Dennis Olson, AOTC (Abingdon); G. I. Davies, ICC (T & T Clark); William Johnstone, SHBC (Smyth & Helwys); and Sean McBride, Hermeneia (Fortress). Obtain Stuart and Strawn (forthcoming). Enns is a should have.

L/Cr   3. **Childs, Brevard. OTL (Westminster, 1974).** Canonical
            approach with history of interpretation for each passage.
L/Cr   4. Durham, John. WBC (Word, 1987). Source-critical,
            dubious about historicity.
L/Cr   5. **Houtman, Cornelis. HCOT, 3 vols. (Peeters, 1993–
            2000).** Exodus written sixth century B.C.; historical-critical.
            Especially the "Book of the Covenant" (20:22–23:19) in
            vol. 3.
L/Cr   6. Propp, Brian. AB, 2 vols. (Doubleday, 1999, 2006).
            Argues for JEDP; excellent on textual criticism (with
            DSS readings), social background. Narrative study the
            principal focus of which is folktale analysis. Impractical
            for pastors.
C/M   7. Sarna, Nahum. JPSTC (JPS, 1991). Incorporates rabbinic
            exegesis.

Exposition

E   1. Cole, Alan. TOTC (IVP, 1973).
E   2. Currid, John. EPSC, 2 vols. (Evangelical Press, 2000–
            02).
E   3. **Enns, Peter. NIVAC (Zondervan, 2000).**
C/M   4. **Fretheim, Terence. IBC (Westminster John Knox,
            1991).** Creation theology.
E   5. Kaiser, Walter. EBC, vol. 2 (Zondervan, 1989).
E   6. Mackay, John. *Exodus,* Mentor (Christian Focus,
            2001).
C/M   7. Meyers, Carol. NCamBC (Cambridge University, 2005).
E   8. Motyer, J. A. BST (IVP, 2005).
E   9. Ryken, Philip. *Exodus* (Crossway, 2005).
E   10. **Stuart, Douglas. NAC (Broadman & Holman,
            2006).**[2]

---

2. What most impressed me about this commentary was the easy proficiency with
   which Dr. Stuart exegetes how a particular Hebrew word or phrase should be
   taken in context, weaves in the ancient Near Eastern background, and dem-
   onstrates the way the theology not only relates to Exodus and the rest of the
   Pentateuch but to the entire biblical corpus. Those familiar with Dr. Stuart's

Special Studies

L/Cr 1. Coats, George. *Exodus 1–18*, FOTL (Eerdmans, 1999).

E 2. Enns, Peter. *Exodus Retold* (Harvard University Press, 1995).

C/M 3. Galpaz-Feller, Pnina. *The Exodus from Egypt: Reality or Illusion (Exodus 1–15)* (Schocken, 2002).

C/M 4. Gowan, Donald. *Theology in Exodus* (Westminster John Knox, 1994). Especially Exodus 3–4, intertestamental, rabbinic development.

C/M 5. **Jackson, Bernard. *The Semiotics of Biblical Law* (Sheffield Academic Press, 2000).**

L/Cr 6. Loewenstamm, Samuel. *The Evolution of the Exodus Tradition* (Magnes, 1992). Distributed by Eisenbrauns.

E 7. **Sprinkle, Joe. *The Book of the Covenant* (JSOT Press, 1994).** Exodus 20:22–23:33.

All 8. Vervenne, Marc, ed. *Studies in the Book of Exodus* (Peeters, 1996).

Leviticus*
Technical, Semitechnical

L/Cr 1. Budd, Philip. NCBC (Eerdmans, 1996). Exilic, postexilic.

L/Cr 2. Gerstenberger, Erhard. OTL (Westminster, 1996). Leviticus as postexilic; from 1986–87 German edition.

E/Cr 3. **Hartley, John. WBC (Word, 1992).** Includes history of interpretation.

L/Cr 4. Levine, Baruch. JPSTC (JPS, 1989). Documentary hypothesis view; recent linguistic, archaeological data.

C/M 5. **Milgrom, Jacob. AB, 3 vols. (Doubleday, 1991, 2000, 2001).** Especially ancient interpretation.

---

prior work will not be surprised by the depth of scholarship undergirding his insights here. For a conservative commentary that is sufficiently meaty but still easy on the eyes, one could do no better.

* Forthcoming: Nobuyoshi Kiuchi, Apollos; Richard Hess, EBC; David Baker, CBC; and James Watts, HCOT.

| E/Cr | 6. | **Wenham, Gordon. NICOT (Eerdmans, 1979).** Includes rhetorical analysis, NT parallels. Influenced by anthropologist Mary Douglas. |

Exposition[3]

C/M	1.	Balentine, Samuel. IBC (Westminster, 2003).
C/M	2.	Bellinger, William. NICOT (Hendrickson, 2001).
E	3.	Currid, John. EPSC (Evangelical Press, 2005).
E	4.	**Gane, Roy. NIVAC (Zondervan, 2004).** Jacob Milgrom pupil.
E	5.	Harris, R. Laird. EBC, vol. 2 (Zondervan, 1990). Detailed philology and biblical theology.
E	6.	Harrison, R. K. TOTC (IVP, 1980).
E	7.	Kaiser, Walter. NIB, vol. 1 (Abingdon, 1994).
E	8.	Kleinig, John. Concordia Commentary (Concordia, 2003).
C/M	9.	Knight, George A. DSB (Westminster, 1981).
C/M	10.	**Milgrom, Jacob. Continental (Fortress, 2004).**
E	11.	Noordtzij, A. BSC (Zondervan, 1982).
E	12.	**Rooker, Mark. NAC (Broadman & Holman, 2000).**
E	13.	**Ross, Allen.** *Holiness to the Lord: A Guide to the Exposition of the Book of Leviticus* **(Baker, 2002).**
E	14.	Tidball, Derek. BST (IVP, 2005).

Special Studies

C/M	1.	Balentine, Samuel. *The Torah's Vision of Worship* (Fortress, 1999).
C/M	2.	Douglas, Mary. *Leviticus as Literature* (Oxford University Press, 2000).
L/Cr	3.	Gammie, John. *Holiness in Israel* (Fortress, 1989).
E	4.	Gane, Roy. *Cult and Character* (Eisenbrauns, 2005).

---

3. Although Allen Ross was emphatic that *Holiness to the Lord* be called a guide rather than a commentary, it qualifies as a very worthy supplement. Milgrom has come out with an excellent distillation of his magisterial magnum opus for the Anchor series. His student Roy Gane has done likewise for NIVAC. And then there is Rooker, Kleinig, and Currid (most lay-friendly) to consider.

L/Cr   5.   Gorman, Frank. ITC (Eerdmans, 1997).

L/Cr   6.   Grabbe, Lester. OTG (Sheffield Academic, 1993).

C/M   7.   Houston, Walter. *Purity and Monotheism: Clean and Unclean Animals in Biblical Law* (Sheffield Academic, 1993).

C/M   8.   Jenson, R. P. *Graded Holiness* (Sheffield Academic, 1992).

C/M   **9.**   **Klawans, Jonathan. *Impurity and Sin in Ancient Judaism* (Oxford University Press, 2000).**

C/M   ———. *Purity, Sacrifice, and the Temple* (Oxford University Press, 2005).

C/M   10.   Knohl, Israel. *The Sanctuary of Silence* (Fortress, 1995). Holiness code.

All   11.   Rendtorff, Rolf, and Robert Kugler, eds. *The Book of Leviticus* (Brill, 2003).

Numbers[*]
Technical, Semitechnical

E   **1.**   **Ashley, Timothy. NICOT (Eerdmans, 1993).** Especially philology and theology.

L/Cr   2.   Budd, Philip. WBC (Word, 1984). Form/redaction-critical, history of interpretation.

L/Cr   3.   Davies, Eryl. NCBC (Eerdmans, 1995). Redaction-critical.

L/Cr   4.   Levine, Baruch. AB, 2 vols. (Doubleday 1993, 2000). Documentary view, comparative study of priestly terms, especially volume 2.

C/M   **5.**   **Milgrom, Jacob. JPSTC (JPS, 1990).** Especially usage of priestly terms believes substantially historical.

---

[*]   Forthcoming: Moshe Weinfeld, Hermeneia (Fortress); Frank Gosling, HCOT (Peeters); David Baker, BCBC (Herald); Ronald Allen (EBC); and John Sailhamer, WBC (Thomas Nelson). Sailhamer has been assigned the replacement volume for Budd in the WBC series. Certainly, this commentary should be much anticipated because Sailhamer has already demonstrated proficiency in his commentary on Genesis and his exposition of the Pentateuch (both above).

Exposition

E 1. Allen, Ronald. EBC, vol. 2 (Zondervan, 1990).
E 2. Brown, Raymond. BST (IVP, 2002).[4]
E 3. **Cole, R. Dennis. NAC (Broadman & Holman, 2000).** Focuses on literary structure and theology. Excellent defense of Mosaic core.
L/Cr 4. Dozeman, Thomas. NIB, vol. 2 (Abingdon, 1998).
E 5. Gane, Roy. NIVAC (Zondervan, 2004). With Leviticus.
E 6. Harrison, R. K. *Numbers* (Baker, 1993).
L/Cr 7. **Olson, Dennis. IBC (Westminster John Knox, 1996).** Post-exilic.
E 8. Philip, James. TPC (Word, 1987).
E/Cr 9. **Wenham, Gordon. TOTC (IVP, 1981).** Especially structure, anthropology, and priestly ritual.

Special Studies

C/M 1. **Douglas, Mary. *In the Wilderness* (Oxford, 2001).**
L/Cr 2. Knierim, Rolf, and George Coats. FOTL (Eerdmans, 2005).
L/Cr 3. Kok, Johnson. *The Sin of Moses and the Staff of God* (Van Gorcum, 1997).
E 4. Lee, Won. *Punishment and Forgiveness in Israel's Migratory Campaign* (Eerdmans, 2003). Numbers 10–36. Literary/theological structure.
E 5. Moore, Michael. *The Balaam Tradition* (Scholars, 1990).
L/Cr 6. Nelson, Richard. *Raising Up a Faithful Priest* (Westminster John Knox, 1993).
L/Cr 7. Sakenfeld, Katharine. *Journeying with God,* ITC (Eerdmans, 1995).
E/Cr 8. **Wenham, Gordon. OTG (Sheffield Academic Press, 1997).** Outstanding introduction.

---

4. The conservative Raymond Brown (also author of BST entries on Deuteronomy, Nehemiah, and Hebrews) is to be distinguished from the now-deceased Catholic scholar Raymond E. Brown.

E/Cr   9. Widener, Michael. *Moses, God, and the Dynamics of Intercessory Prayer* (Mohr, 2004). Exodus 32–34; Numbers 13–14.

Deuteronomy*
Technical, Semitechnical

C/M   1. Christensen, Duane. *Deuteronomy 1–21:9,* WBC, rev. ed. (Thomas Nelson, 2001). Deuteronomy as a poem in five concentric units.

———. *Deuteronomy 21:10–34:12,* WBC (Thomas Nelson, 2002).

L/Cr   2. Clements, Ronald. NIB, vol. 2 (Abingdon, 1998).

E   **3. Craigie, Peter. NICOT (Eerdmans, 1976).** Ugaritic, ANE background.

L/Cr   4. Mayes, A. D. H. NCBC (Eerdmans, 1979). Theological, literary developments.

E/Cr   **5. McConville, J. Gordon. Apollos (IVP, 2002).** Pre-monarchic.

L/Cr   6. Nelson, Richard. OTL (Westminster, 2002).

L/Cr   **7. Tigay, Jeffrey. JPSTC (JPS, 1995).** Source-critical.

L/Cr   8. Weinfeld, Moshe. AB, 2 vols. (Doubleday, 1991, 2002).[5]

Exposition

E   **1. Block, Daniel. NIVAC (Zondervan).**

E   2. Brown, Raymond. BST (IVP, 1993).

L/Cr   3. Brueggeman, Walter. AOTC (Abingdon, 2001). Fall of northern kingdom provenance.

---

* Forthcoming: Norbert Lohfink and G. Braulik, Hermeneia (Fortress); Bill Arnold, NICOT (Eerdmans); Mark Biddle, SHBC (Smyth & Helwys); Eugene Merrill, CBC (Tyndale); Jack Lundbom, ECC (Eerdmans); and Cornelis Houtman, HCOT (Peeters). Use McConville with Block and Arnold, but consult Lundbom and Houtman if possible.

5. Especially textual criticism. Weinfeld's analysis, which advocates multiple redactions interspersed with reconstructions of cultic history, obscures its value for referencing early Jewish and medieval interpretation.

E   4. Merrill, Eugene. NAC (Broadman & Holman, 1994).
     Somewhat semitechnical.
C/M 5. **Miller, Patrick. IBC (John Knox, 1990).** NT, contem-
     porary, theological application.
L/Cr 6. Payne, David. DSB (Westminster, 1985).
E   7. Ridderbos, Herman. BSC (Zondervan, 1984).
E/Cr 8. Thompson, John. TOTC (IVP, 1974). Later 11th–10th
     century redactor, ANE background.
E   9. **Wright, Christopher. NIBCOT (Hendrickson, 1996).**
     Ethical implications.

Special Studies

E   1. Barker, Paul. *The Triumph of Grace in Deuteronomy*
     (Paternoster, 2004).
C/M 2. Christensen, Duane, ed. *A Song of Power and the Power
     of Song* (Eisenbrauns, 1993).
C/M 3. Knight, George A. *The Song of Moses* (Eerdmans, 1995).
     Deuteronomy 32.
L/Cr 4. Lohfink, Norbert. *Theology of the Pentateuch* (Fortress,
     1994).
E/Cr 5. McConville, J. Gordon. *Grace in the End* (Zondervan,
     1993). Theology.
E/Cr 6. McConville, J. Gordon, and J. Gary Millar. *Time and
     Place in Deuteronomy* (Sheffield Academic Press,
     1994).
E/Cr 7. Millar, Gary. *Now Choose Life* (Eerdmans, 1999). The-
     ology and ethics.
L/Cr 8. Olson, Dennis. *Deuteronomy and the Death of Moses*
     (Fortress, 1994).
L/Cr 9. Pitkänen, Pekka. *Central Sanctuary and the Centraliza-
     tion of Worship in Ancient Israel* (Gorgias, 2003).
L/Cr 10. Rofé, Alexander. *Deuteronomy: Issues and Interpreta-
     tion* (T & T Clark, 2001).

Joshua*
Technical, Semitechnical

L/Cr 1. Boling, Robert, and G. E. Wright. AB (Doubleday, 1982). Dated interpretation of archaeology.

E/Cr 2. **Butler, Trent. WBC (Word, 1983).** Literary-critical.

L/Cr 3. Nelson, Richard. OTL (Westminster John Knox, 1997). Especially Old Greek, Deuteronomistic history.

E 4. **Woudstra, Marten. NICOT (Eerdmans, 1981).**

Exposition[6]

L/Cr 1. Auld, Graeme. DSB (Westminster John Knox, 1984). With Judges, Ruth.

L/Cr 2. Creach, Jerome. IBC (Westminster John Knox, 2003).

E 3. Davis, Dale. *Joshua: No Falling Words* (Christian Focus, 2003).

E 4. **Hess, Richard. TOTC (IVP, 1996).** Especially archaeology.

E 5. **Howard, David. NAC (Broadman & Holman, 1998).** Especially theology and philology.

Special Studies

L/Cr 1. Auld, Graeme. *Joshua Retold* (T & T Clark, 1998). Especially LXX-MT divergence, Deuteronomic redaction.

---

* Forthcoming: Graeme Auld (T & T Clark); Kyle McCarter, Hermeneia (Fortress); Hartmut Rösel, HCOT (Peeters); Steven McKenzie, SHBC (Smyth & Helwys); Gordon Matties, BCBC (Herald); Pekka Pitkanen, Apollos (IVP); and Robert Hubbard, NIVAC (Zondervan). When Woudstra is supplemented with Howard, Hess, or Hubbard (to come), you'll have all of the bases covered, albeit in a more expositional fashion than usual. For more technical details, use Butler's commentary (rev. ed.).

6. Hess's commentary, one of the best in the Tyndale series, is particularly strong on historical and archaeological background. Howard brings the strengths he exhibited in his *Introduction to the Old Testament Historical Books* (Moody, 1993) to his commentary. Throughout, he is keen to bring out the theology in the text. The strength of the commentary is the in-depth philological investigations that accompany every word or phrase of significance in the text. For comparisons with conquest accounts you would need to consult the monograph of Younger. For reference to cognate literature on border descriptions, land grants, and place-name lists, the commentary of Hess is needed.

L/Cr   2. Hamlin, E. ITC (Eerdmans, 1983).

E   **3. Hawk, Daniel. *Berit Olam* (Liturgical, 2000).**

C/M   4. Merling, David. *The Book of Joshua* (Andrews University Press, 1997). Especially archaeology.

L/Cr   5. Polzin, Robert. *Moses and the Deuteronomist* (Indiana University Press, 1993). Deuteronomy through Judges.

E   **6. Younger, Lawson. *Ancient Conquest Accounts* (Sheffield Academic Press, 1990).**

Judges[*]
Technical, Semitechnical

E   **1. Block, Daniel. NAC (Broadman & Holman, 1999).** Literary/theological analysis. With Ruth.[7]

L/Cr   **2. Boling, Robert. AB (Doubleday, 1975).** Significant redaction based on pre-monarchical traditions, though reflecting many actual events.

C/M   3. Lindars, Barnabas. *Judges 1–5* (T & T Clark, 1995). Examination of versions, targums, ancient-medieval sources.

L/Cr   4. Soggin, J. Alberto. OTL (Westminster John Knox, 1981). Survey of Continental scholarship.

Exposition

L/Cr   1. Auld, Graeme. DSB (Westminster John Knox, 1984). With Joshua and Ruth.

E   2. Brensinger, Terry. BCBC (Herald, 1999). Especially Judges 19–21.

E   3. Cundall, Arthur. TOTC (IVP, 1968). With Ruth.

---

* Forthcoming: Jack Sasson, AB (Doubleday); Trent Butler, WBC (Thomas Nelson, 2007); Alan Groves, Two Horizons (Eerdmans); Klaus Spronk, HCOT (Peeters); Gordon Hugenberger, Apollos (IVP); Barry Webb, NICOT (Eerdmans); Richard Nelson, ECC (Eerdmans); Mark Boda, EBC (Zondervan); and A. D. H. Mayes, ICC (T & T Clark). Use Webb with Block.

7. Block's commentary is almost as good as his two-volume work on Ezekiel, which, both in my mind and in the mind of many others, is the best Old Testament commentary extant.

C/M   4. Gunn, David. BBC (Blackwell, 2004). History of interpretation.

E/Cr   5. Matthews, Victor. *Judges and Ruth*. NCamBC (Cambridge University Press, 2004). Socio-literary study.

L/Cr   6. Olson, Dennis. NIB, vol. 2 (Abingdon, 1998).

E   7. Wilcock, Michael. BST (IVP, 1992).

E   8. Wood, Leon. *The Distressing Days of the Judges* (Zondervan, 1975; Wipf & Stock, 2000).

E   **9. Younger, Lawson. NIVAC (Zondervan, 2002).** With Ruth.[8]

Special Studies

E   **1. Bluedorn, Wolfgang. *Yahweh versus Baalism* (Sheffield Academic Press, 2001).** Gideon-Abimelech.

L/Cr   **2. Klein, Lillian. *The Triumph of Irony in the Book of Judges* (Almond, 1988).**

C/M   **3. O'Connell, Robert. *The Rhetoric of the Book of Judges* (Brill, 1996).**

L/Cr   **4. Schneider, Tammi. *Berit Olam* (Liturgical, 2000).**

E/Cr   **5. Webb, Barry. *The Book of Judges* (Sheffield Academic Press, 1987).** Structural coherence; replay of key motifs.

E   **6. Wong, Gregory. *Compositional Strategy in the Book of Judges* (Brill, 2006).**

L/Cr   7. Yee, Gale. *Judges and Method* (Fortress, 1995; Wipf & Stock, 1999). Numerous methods applied to select passages.

---

8. Younger's commentary uses most of his thirty-page introduction to address the book's literary features. In the commentary proper he focuses almost exclusively on its original context rather than its application. That Younger heavily references all of the major exegetical commentaries and monographs on Judges and Ruth and defers from mentioning expositional commentaries ought to tell you just what sort of "popular" commentary this is. It, too, is a hallmark of erudition if not a faithful representative of the series to which it belongs.

Ruth

Technical, Semitechnical

E 1. Block, Daniel. NAC (Broadman & Holman, 1998). With Judges.

E/Cr 2. **Bush, Frederic. WBC (Word, 1996).** With Esther, especially ANE background.

L/Cr 3. **Campbell, Edward. AB (Doubleday, 1975).** Especially theology and archaeology.

E 4. **Hubbard, Robert. NICOT (Eerdmans, 1988).** Especially literary criticism.

L/Cr 5. **Sasson, Jack. *Ruth*, 2d ed. (Sheffield Academic Press, 1989).** Supports MT; especially ANE background.

Exposition*

E 1. **Atkinson, David. BST (IVP, 1983).** Especially kinsman-redeemer issue.

E/Cr 2. Harris, J. Gordon, Cheryl Brown, and Michael Moore. NIBCOT (Hendrickson, 2000).

L/Cr 3. LaCocque, Andre. Continental (Fortress, 2004). Sturdy, yet post-exilic conclusions. Posits female author.

E 4. Morris, Leon. TOTC (IVP, 1968).

E 5. Roop, Eugene. BCBC (Herald, 2002). With Jonah and Esther.

L/Cr 6. Sakenfeld, Katharine. IBC (Westminster John Knox, 1999).

E 7. Younger, Lawson. NIVAC (Zondervan, 2002). With Judges.

Special Studies

L/Cr 1. Fewell, Danna, and David Gunn. *Compromising Redemption* (Westminster John Knox, 1990).

E/Cr 2. **Gow, Murray. *The Book of Ruth* (Apollos, 1992).** Contribution of rhetoric to structure.

---

* Forthcoming: Marjo Korpel, HCOT (Peeters).

L/Cr 3. Korpel, Marjo. *The Structure of the Book of Ruth* (Van Gorcum, 2001).
C/M 4. **Larkin, Katrina. Ruth and Esther, OTG (Sheffield Academic Press, 1996).**
L/Cr 5. Nielsen, Kirsten. OTL (Westminster, 1997). Narrative-critical commentary, especially intertextualism.
L/Cr 6. Trible, Phyllis. *God and the Rhetoric of Sexuality* (Fortress, 1978). Feminist.
L/Cr 7. Van Wolde, E. J. *Ruth and Naomi* (SCM, 1998). Narrative-critical commentary.

Samuel*
Technical, Semitechnical

C/M 1. **Anderson, Arnold. WBC (Word, 1989).** 2 Samuel only.
L/Cr 2. Hertzberg, H. OTL (Westminster, 1964).
C/M 3. **Klein, Ralph. WBC (Word, 1983).** 1 Samuel only; survey of previous work and canonical approach.
L/Cr 4. **McCarter, P. Kyle. AB, 2 vols. (Doubleday, 1980, 1984).** Especially textual criticism, relationship to Greek and DSS.
E 5. **Tsumura, David. NICOT, 2 vols. (Eerdmans, 2007–).**

Exposition

E/Cr 1. **Arnold, Bill. NIVAC (Zondervan, 2003).**
E/Cr 2. Baldwin, Joyce. TOTC (IVP, 1988).
E 3. **Bergen, Robert. NAC (Broadman & Holman, 1996).** Semitechnical; especially discourse analysis, linguistics.
L/Cr 4. Brueggemann, Walter. IBC (John Knox, 1990). Theological insights, Samuel as literature.

---

* Forthcoming: David Firth, Apollos (IVP); Graeme Auld, OTL (Westminster John Knox); Åke Viberg, 1 Samuel, HCOT (Peeters); Daniel Block, BCBC (Herald); and Jichan Kim, 2 Samuel, HCOT (Peeters). The wealth of background knowledge Tsumura, Block, and Arnold bring perfectly countenances the discourse analysis of Bergen. Keep Klein on 1 Samuel (under revision) and McCarter on 2 Samuel.

L/Cr 5. Cartledge, Tony. SHBC (Smyth & Helwys, 2001).
C/M   6. Evans, Mary. NIBCOT (Hendrickson, 2000). Detailed endnotes.
E   7. **Gordon, Robert.** *1 and 2 Samuel* **(Zondervan, 1988).**
E   8. Youngblood, Ronald. EBC, vol. 3 (Zondervan, 1992).

Special Studies

L/Cr 1. Brueggemann, Walter. *David's Truth,* 2d ed. (Fortress, 2002).
L/Cr 2. Eslinger, Lyle. *Kingdom of God in Crisis* (Almond, 1985). 1 Samuel 1–2.
L/Cr 3. Fokkelman, J. P. *Narrative Art and Poetry in the Books of Samuel,* 4 vols. (Van Gorcum, 1981–93). Ca. 2,000 pages.
L/Cr 4. Halpern, Baruch. *David's Secret Demons* (Eerdmans, 2001).
E/Cr 5. **Klement, Herbert.** *2 Samuel 21–24* **(Lang, 2000).**
L/Cr 6. Polzin, Robert. *Samuel and the Deuteronomist* (Indiana University Press, 1993). 1 Samuel.
———. *David and the Deuteronomist* (Indiana University Press, 1993). 2 Samuel.
L/Cr 7. Schniedewind, William. *Society and the Promise to David* (Oxford University Press, 1999). 2 Samuel 7:7–17.

Kings*
Technical, Semitechnical

C/M   1. **Cogan, Mordechai. AB (Doubleday, 2001).** 1 Kings.
C/M   2. **Cogan, Mordechai, and Hayim Tadmor. AB (Doubleday, 1988).** 2 Kings; especially helpful on philological, historical issues; Assyrian context of later monarchy, particularly Hezekiah.

---

* Forthcoming: Jurie le Roux, 1 Kings 12–22, HCOT (Peeters); Kevin Cathcart, 2 Kings, HCOT (Peeters); Richard Hess, NICOT (Eerdmans); Marvin Sweeney, OTL (Westminster John Knox); Robert Wilson, Hermeneia (Fortress); Marvin Sweeney, OTL (Westminster John Knox); and Richard Patterson (EBC). Wait for Hess and Patterson and use with Provan. Keep Cogan on 1 Kings and Hobbs on 2 Kings.

E/Cr 3. DeVries, Simon. WBC, rev. ed. (Thomas Nelson, 2004). 1 Kings; especially for compositional history of the text and textual criticism.

E/Cr **4. Hobbs, T. R. WBC (Word, 1985).** 2 Kings; especially literary, historical, and theological issues. Sees book as "tragic drama" of covenant failure.

L/Cr 5. Montgomery, James, and J. S. Gehman. ICC (T & T Clark, 1951).

C/M 6. Mulder, M. HCOT (Peeters, 1998). 1 Kings 1–11.

Exposition

L/Cr 1. Auld, Graeme. DSB (Westminster John Knox, 1986).

L/Cr 2. Brueggemann, Walter. *1 and 2 Kings* (Smyth and Helwys, 2000). Contains CD that duplicates content.

E 3. Davis, Dale. *The Wisdom and the Folly* (Christian Focus, 2002). 1 Kings.

L/Cr 4. Fritz, Volkmar. *1 and 2 Kings*. Continental (Fortress, 2003). Especially 1 Kings 1:1–2:46.

E **5. House, Paul. NAC (Broadman & Holman, 1995).** Theological and literary synthesis.

L/Cr 6. Jones, Gwilym. NCBC, 2 vols. (Eerdmans, 1984). Historical-critical issues and textual criticism.

E **7. Konkel, Gus. NIVAC (Zondervan, 2006).**

L/Cr 8. Nelson, Richard. IBC (Westminster John Knox, 1987). Rich in its theological insight.

E **9. Provan, Iain. NIBCOT (Hendrickson, 1995).** Like House's commentary, with excurses on canonical connections. Does not address MT, LXX issue adequately.

———. OTG (Sheffield Academic Press, 1997). Conservative apologetic emphasizing literary features.

C/M **10. Seow, Choon-Leong. NIB, vol. 3 (Abingdon, 1999).**

E **11. Wiseman, Donald. TOTC (IVP, 1993).** Especially archaeological studies.

Special Studies

L/Cr 1. Fretheim, Terence. WBComp (Westminster John Knox, 1999). Study guide emphasizing rhetoric and purpose.

E 2. **Gallagher, William.** *Sennacherib's Campaign to Judah* **(Brill, 1999).** 2 Kings 18–19.

L/Cr 3. Grabbe, Lester, ed. *"Like a Bird in a Cage": The Invasion of Sennacherib in 701 BCE* (Sheffield Academic Press, 2003).

E/Cr 4. **Hauser, Alan, and Russell Gregory.** *From Carmel to Horeb* **(Almond, 1990).** 1 Kings 12–2 Kings 2.

L/Cr 5. **Knoppers, Gary.** *Two Nations Under God,* **2 vols. (Scholars, 1993–94).** Historical-critical.

C/M 6. Laato, Antti. *Josiah and David Redivivus* (Almqvist and Wiksell, 1992). Messianic expectations in 2 Kings 14–25.

L/Cr 7. Long, Burke. FOTL, 2 vols. (Eerdmans, 1984, 1991). Genre and form analysis.

E 8. Moore, Rick. *God Saves* (Sheffield Academic Press, 1990). 2 Kings 5–6.

L/Cr 9. Sweeney, Marvin. *King Josiah of Judah* (Oxford University Press, 2000). 2 Kings 22–23; 2 Chronicles 34–35.

Chronicles*
Technical, Semitechnical

E/Cr 1. **Braun, Roddy. WBC (Word, 1986).** 1 Chronicles only.

E/Cr 2. **Dillard, Raymond. WBC (Word, 1987).** 2 Chronicles only, with greatest debt to Rudolf (1955) and Williamson (1976–82).

---

* Forthcoming: Rodney Duke, Apollos (IVP); Gus Konkel, BCBC (Herald); William Schniedewind, NCamBC (Cambridge University Press); Keith Bodner, NICOT (Eerdmans); Mark Boda, CBC (Tyndale); Tyler Williams, EBC (Zondervan); and Isaac Kalimi, 2 Chronicles, HCOT (Peeters). Use Hill with Japhet, Klein, and Knoppers. Otherwise, Selman and Dirksen are excellent. Japhet's commentary, which supports her contention that 1–2 Chronicles was essentially written by a single author with a peculiar literary style, is a model of erudition.

C/M   3. **Dirksen, Peter. 1 Chronicles. HCOT (Peeters, 2005).**
      Like, Japhet, entirely attributable to Chronicler.
C/M   4. **Japhet, Sara. OTL (Westminster John Knox, 1993).**
      Theological and sensitive to Chronicles as history.
C/M   5. Johnstone, William. *1 and 2 Chronicles,* 2 vols. (Sheffield
      Academic Press, 1997). Especially literary and rhetorical
      features.
C/M   6. **Klein, Ralph W. *1 Chronicles,* Hermeneia (Fortress,
      2006).**
C/M   7. **Knoppers, Gary. AB, 2 vols. (Doubleday, 2003, 2004).**
      1 Chronicles only. Especially text-critical analysis.
      Connection with Ezra. Consideration of considerable
      redaction.

Exposition

E/Cr 1. **Allen, Leslie. NIB, vol. 3 (Abingdon, 1999).** Almost
      literal recasting of TPC.
      ———. **TPC (Word, 1987).**
E   2. Boda, Mark. CBC (Tyndale, 2007).
E/Cr 3. **Hill, Andrew. NIVAC (Zondervan, 2003).**
L/Cr 4. Hooker, Paul. WBComp (Westminster John Knox,
      2001).
C/M   5. McConville, Gordon. DSB (Westminster, 1984).
C/M   6. McKenzie, Steven. AOTC (Abingdon, 2004).
E   7. Payne, Barton. EBC, vol. 4 (Zondervan, 1988).
E   8. Sailhamer, John. EvBC (Moody, 1983).
E   9. **Selman, Martin. TOTC, 2 vols. (IVP, 1994).** Espe-
      cially theology.
E   10. Stewart, Andrew. *A House of Prayer* (Evangelical Press,
      2002). 2 Chronicles.
E   11. Thompson, John. NAC (Broadman & Holman, 1994).
      Especially genealogies.
C/M   12. Tuell, Steven. IBC (John Knox, 2001). Especially
      theology, fourth century B.C. composition, link with
      Ezra/Nehemiah.

E   13. Wilcock, Michael. BST (IVP, 1987).

C/M   14. **Williamson, Hugh. NCBC (Eerdmans, 1982).** Essentially historical with creative theological development.

Special Studies

E   1. Crockett, William. *A Harmony of Samuel, Kings, and Chronicles* (Baker, 1956).

L/Cr   2. DeVries, Simon. FOTL (Eerdmans, 1989).

L/Cr   3. **Endres, John, William Millar, and John Burns, eds.** *Chronicles and Its Synoptic Parallels in Samuel, Kings, and Related Biblical Texts* **(Liturgical, 1998).**

All   4. Graham, Patrick, Kenneth Hoglund, and Steven McKenzie, eds. *The Chronicler as Historian* (Sheffield Academic Press, 1997).

All   5. **Graham, Patrick, Steven McKenzie, and Gary Knoppers, eds.** *The Chronicler as Theologian* **(T & T Clark, 2004).** Ralph Klein tribute.

C/M   6. Japhet, Sara. *The Ideology of the Book of Chronicles and Its Place in Biblical Thought,* 2d ed. (Lang, 1997). Theological supplement to her commentary above.

C/M   7. **Kalimi, Isaac.** *The Reshaping of Ancient Israelite History in Chronicles* **(Eisenbrauns, 2005).**

E/Cr   8. Kelly, Brian. *Retribution and Eschatology in Chronicles* (Sheffield Academic Press, 1996). Postexilic.

E   9. Newsome, John. *A Synoptic Harmony of Samuel, Kings, and Chronicles* (Baker, 1986).

L/Cr   10. Schniedewind, William. *The Word of God in Transition* (Sheffield Academic Press, 1995). Redaction-critical.

C/M   11. Thiele, Edwin. *The Mysterious Numbers of the Hebrew Kings* (Kregel, 1994).

Ezra/Nehemiah*

Technical, Semitechnical

L/Cr 1. Blenkinsopp, Joseph. OTL (Westminster, 1988). Especially Persian background.

L/Cr 2. Clines, David. NCBC (Eerdmans, 1984). Especially introductions. With Esther.

E 3. Fensham, F. Charles. NICOT (Eerdmans, 1982). Especially historical and archaeological background.

C/M 4. Williamson, Hugh. WBC (Word, 1985). Ezra and Nehemiah independent of Chronicles; takes archaeology into account.

Exposition

E/Cr 1. Allen, Leslie. NIBCOT (Hendrickson, 2003). With Esther.

E 2. Breneman, Mervin. NAC (Broadman & Holman, 1993). With Esther.

E 3. Brown, Raymond. BST (IVP, 1998). Nehemiah only.

E 4. Kidner, Derek. TOTC (IVP, 1979). Especially for relating exposition to theology.

L/Cr 5. Klein, Ralph. NIB, vol. 3 (Abingdon, 1999). Posits traditional date, emphasizes message.[9]

---

* Forthcoming: Lizbeth Fried, ECC (Eerdmans); Bob Becking, Ezra, HCOT (Peeters); and Edward Noort, Nehemiah, HCOT (Peeters); T. C. Eskanazi, AB (Doubleday); Shemaryahu Talmon, Hermeneia (Fortress); Hannah Harrington, NICOT (Eerdmans); Mark Boda, TOTC (IVP); Edwin Yamauchi, EBC (Zondervan); and Douglas Green, NIVAC (Zondervan). Williamson is a superior exegetical commentary. Use with Harrington and Klein.

9. The clear-cut expositional leader is Ralph Klein's entry in the NIB, vol. 3 (Abingdon, 1999). This is the best volume in the series and can supply your expositional needs with excellent commentaries on 1–2 Kings and 1–2 Chronicles by Choon-Leong Seow and Leslie Allen, respectively. Seow is noted for his Hebrew grammar and exegesis of Ecclesiastes. Allen is noted for commentaries on Psalms 101–150, Ezekiel, and Joel, Obadiah, Jonah, and Micah. He is also author (with Timothy Laniak on Esther) of a commentary on Ezra/Nehemiah, NIBCOT (Hendrickson). His NIB entry is essentially a barely disguised rehash of his earlier TPC entry with an updated bibliography and a smattering of post-1987 footnotes, but it is still superior. Purchasing this volume is a bargain at seventy dollars for these three commentaries, with the additional bonus of a commentary on Esther.

E/Cr   6. McConville, Gordon. DSB (Westminster, 1985). With Esther.

L/Cr   7. Throntveit, Mark. IBC (John Knox, 1992). Especially theology, proposes multiple chiasmuses.

E   8. Yamauchi, Edwin. EBC, vol. 4 (Zondervan, 1988).

Special Studies

L/Cr   1. Davies, Gordon. Berit Olam series (Liturgical, 1999). Rhetorical analysis.

L/Cr   2. Eskanazi, Tamara. *In an Age of Prose* (Scholars, 1988).

L/Cr   3. Grabbe, Lester. *Ezra and Nehemiah* (Routledge, 1998).

L/Cr   4. Hoglund, Kenneth. *Achaemenid Imperial Administration in Syria-Palestine and the Missions of Ezra and Nehemiah* (Scholars, 1992). Reconstructing society from archaeology.

L/Cr   5. Holmgren, Fredrick. ITC (Eerdmans, 1987).

E   6. Ingram, Chip. *Holy Ambition* (Moody, 2002). Illuminating application of Nehemiah.

L/Cr   7. Van Wijk-Bos, Johanna. WBComp (Westminster John Knox, 1998). With Esther.

L/Cr   8. Weinberg, Joel. *The Citizen-Temple Community* (Sheffield Academic Press, 1992). Political and economic background.

Esther*
Technical, Semitechnical

L/Cr   1. Berlin, Adele. JPSTC (JPS, 2001). Draws from Greek literature of Persian period for context.

E/Cr   2. Bush, Frederic. WBC (Word, 1995). Especially ANE background, literary analysis that divides books into acts, scenes, and episodes. With Ruth.

---

* Forthcoming: Michael O'Connor, Hermeneia (Fortress); Robert Hubbard, NICOT (Eerdmans); and Marjo Korpel, HCOT (Peeters). Wait for Hubbard and use with Jobes. Fox is heavy wading, but it is by far the best commentary on Esther available.

L/Cr 3. Clines, David. NCBC (Eerdmans, 1984). With Ezra/ Nehemiah.

L/Cr **4.** **Fox, Michael.** *Character and Ideology in the Book of Esther,* **2d ed. (Eerdmans, 2001).** Commentary. Especially text-critical, literary features, including characters and motifs.

L/Cr 5. Levenson, Jon. OTL (Westminster John Knox, 1997). Especially biblical theology. Assesses LXX, MT divergence, and also comments on additions.

L/Cr 6. Moore, Carey. AB (Doubleday, 1971).

Exposition

E/Cr **1.** **Baldwin, Joyce. TOTC (IVP, 1984).**

L/Cr 2. Bechtel, Carol. IBC (Westminster John Knox, 2002).

C/M 3. Day, Linda. AOTC (Abingdon, 2005). *See* monograph below.

E 4. Duguid, Iain. *Esther and Ruth.* REC (Presbyterian & Reformed, 2005).

E **5.** **Jobes, Karen. NIVAC (Zondervan, 1999).** Strong introduction, theology.[10]

E/Cr 6. Laniak, Timothy. NIBCOT (Hendrickson, 2003). With Ezra, Nehemiah.

E/Cr 7. McConville, Gordon. DSB (Westminster, 1985). With Ezra, Nehemiah.

E 8. Roop, Eugene. *Ruth, Jonah, Esther.* BCBC (Herald, 2002).

L/Cr 9. White Crawford, Sidnie. NIB, vol. 3 (Abingdon, 1999). As fiction with historical elements; includes five additions.

Special Studies

All 1. Crawford White, Sidnie, and Leonard Greenspoon, eds.

---

10. I think you would be delighted with how well Karen Jobes treats the literary and theological nuances of Esther. It is a model for the goals of the NIVAC series, which is to provide an overview of its exegesis and suggest possible applications.

The Book of Esther in Modern Research (T & T Clark, 2003).

C/M   2. Day, Linda. *Three Faces of a Queen* (Sheffield Academic Press, 1995). Comparison of Esther with two Greek versions.

E   3. Laniak, Timothy. *Shame and Honor in the Book of Esther* (Scholars, 1998).

L/Cr   4. Larkin, Katrina. *Ruth and Esther*, OTG (Sheffield Academic Press, 1996).

Job*
Technical, Semitechnical

L/Cr   **1. Clines, David. WBC, 3 vols. (Word, 1989; Thomas Nelson, 2005, 2006, 2007).** Literary study.

L/Cr   2. Dhorme, Edouard. *A Commentary on the Book of Job* (Thomas Nelson, 1984).

L/Cr   3. Gordis, Robert. *The Book of Job* (KTAV, 1978). Interpretation of difficult words and phrases.

C/M   4. Habel, Norman. OTL (Westminster, 1985). Literary background.

E/Cr   **5. Hartley, John. NICOT (Eerdmans, 1988).** Especially ANE background.

L/Cr   6. Newsom, Carol. NIB, vol. 4 (Abingdon, 1995). Persian date with earlier sources.

L/Cr   7. Pope, Marvin. AB, 2d ed. (Doubleday, 1965). ANE parallels.

L/Cr   8. Rowley, H. H. NCBC (Eerdmans, 1970).

E   9. Smick, Elmer. EBC, vol. 4 (Zondervan, 1988). Technical for series.

---

* Forthcoming: Tremper Longman, BCOTWP (Baker); Michael Coogan, Hermeneia (Fortress); Dennis Magary, NIVAC (Zondervan); Choon-Leong Seow, ECC (Eerdmans); Richard Hess, HCOT (Peeters); Michael Fox, OTL (Westminster John Knox); and Gerald Wilson, NIBCOT (Hendrickson). Clines, Seow, and Hess would be the primary exegetical choices, with Longman to consider. Look for Magary or Wilson as an exposition.

Exposition

E   1.   Alden, Robert. NAC (Broadman & Holman, 1994).

E/Cr   2.   **Andersen, Francis. TOTC (IVP, 1976).** Linguistic study. Especially ANE background, history of interpretation.

E   3.   Atkinson, David. BST (IVP, 1991).

C/M   4.   **Balentine, Samuel. SHBC (Smyth & Helwys, 2006).**

L/Cr   5.   Gibson, John. DSB (Westminster, 1985).

L/Cr   6.   Janzen, Gerald. IBC (John Knox, 1989). Existential and theological.

E   7.   **Konkel, August, and Tremper Longman.** *Job, Ecclesiastes, and Songs.* **CBC (Tyndale, 2006).** Konkel on Job.

Special Studies

E/Cr   1.   **Fyall, Robert.** *Now My Eyes Have Seen You: Images of Creation and Evil in the Book of Job* **(IVP, 2002).** Behemoth-Leviathan typology.

C/M   2.   Lo, Alison. *Job 28 as Rhetoric* (Brill, 2003).

L/Cr   3.   Newsom, Carol. *The Book of Job* (Oxford University Press, 2003). Penetrating literary analysis, though speculative.

L/Cr   4.   Perdue, Leo, and Clark Gilpin, eds. *The Voices from the Whirlwind* (Abingdon, 1992).

L/Cr   5.   Van der Lugt, P. *Rhetorical Criticism and the Poetry of the Book of Job* (Brill, 1995).

L/Cr   6.   Van Wolde, Ellen. *Mr. and Mrs. Job* (SCM, 1997).

Psalms[*]
Technical, Semitechnical

E/Cr   1.   **Allen, Leslie.** *Psalms 101–150,* **rev. ed., WBC (Thomas Nelson, 2002).**

---

[*]   Forthcoming: Phil Botha and Gert Prinsloo, HCOT (Peeters); William Bellinger, SHBC (Smyth & Helwys); Jamie Grant, *Psalms*, vol. 2, NIVAC (Zondervan); Rolf Jacobsen (Pss. 1–41), Nancy deClaisse-Walford (Pss. 42–63; 107–150), and Beth LaNeel Tanner (Pss. 64–106) NICOT (Eerdmans); A. M. Cooper, AB

C/M   2. Anderson, Alan. NCBC, 2 vols. (Eerdmans, 1972). Valuable survey of scholarship now dated on literary and shaping issues.

E/Cr 3. Craigie, Peter. *Psalms 1–50,* rev. ed. **with supplement by Marvin Tate, WBC (Thomas Nelson, 2004).** Ugaritic background and theology, shaping, structure, and style analysis.[11]

E/Cr 4. **Goldingay, John. BCOTWP, 3 vols. (Baker, 2006–).**

L/Cr 5. Hossfeld, Frank-Lothar, and Erich Zenger. Hermeneia, 3 vols. (Fortress, 2005–).[12]

L/Cr 6. Kraus, Hans-Joachim. Continental, 2 vols. (Augsburg, 1988–89). Form-critical, surveys continental scholarship.

E/Cr 7. **Tate, Marvin. *Psalms 51–100,* WBC (Word, 1990).**

L/Cr 8. Terrien, Samuel. ECC (Eerdmans, 2002). Especially theology, exhaustive.

L/Cr 9. Weiser, Artur. OTL (Westminster, 1962). Usage of Psalms in Covenant Renewal Festival.

Exposition

E/Cr 1. **Broyles, Craig. NIBCOT (Hendrickson, 1999).** Especially strong on theology and relationship to rest of canon.

C/M   2. Clifford, Richard. AOTC, 2 vols. (Abingdon, 2002–03).

(Doubleday); Benjamin Sommer (JPS); William Brown, OTL (Westminster John Knox); and Gordon Wenham, Apollos (IVP). Craigie, Tate, and Allen are still the technical commentaries of choice, which has improved with the Craigie revision and Allen's revision of volume 3. Add to these Wenham and Goldingay. For exposition, choose Allen Ross, VanGemeren (rev. ed.), Wilson, and Grant.

11. In the same fashion as other recent WBC "revisions" (i.e., John and I Kings), this revision is actually the addition of a supplement covering recent scholarship, but in this case with a much more satisfying result as Tate chronicles the influence of Kugel, Fokkelman, Watson, and many others. Also, the updated bibliography by Dennis Tucker is excellent.

12. This commentary deviates from the usual Hermeneia style in that technical details are in footnotes rather than parallel to the main exposition. Much can be gleaned from Hossfeld and Zenger despite their heavy reliance on redaction history.

E   3. Kidner, Derek. TOTC, 2 vols. (IVP, 1973, 1975). Espe-
            cially theology and attention to musical features; dated
            in regard to form criticism.

C/M   4. **Mays, James. IBC (John Knox, 1994).** Theologically
            profound; covers history of interpretation.

L/Cr   5. **McCann, Clinton. NIB, vol. 4 (Abingdon, 1995).**
            Especially sensitive to form, theology, and key words.

E   6. **VanGemeren, Willem. EBC, vol. 5 (Zondervan,
            1991).**

E   7. Wilcock, Michael. BST, 2 vols. (IVP, 2001). Meaning of
            Psalms discerned through pattern and order (i.e., Psalms
            1–2 summons to obedience; 146–50 the consequent
            expression of praise and confidence in God).

E   8. Williams, Donald. TPC, 2 vols. (Word, 1986–89).

E   9. **Wilson, Gerald. *Psalms*, vol. 1. NIVAC (Zondervan,
            2002).**

Shaping of the Psalms[13]

L/Cr   1. Anderson, Bernhard. *Out of the Depths,* 3d ed. (West-
            minster John Knox, 2000).

L/Cr   2. Avishur, Yitzhak. *Studies in Hebrew and Ugaritic
            Psalms* (Magnes, 1994).

C/M   3. Bellinger, William. *A Hermeneutics of Curiosity and
            Readings of Psalm 61* (Mercer, 1995).

E   4. Creach, Jerome. *Yahweh as Refuge and the Editing of
            the Hebrew Psalter* (Sheffield Academic Press, 1996).

L/Cr   5. Crow, Loren. *The Song of Ascents (Psalms 120–134)*
            (Scholars, 1996).

L/Cr   6. deClaissé-Walford, Nancy. *Reading from the Beginning*
            (Mercer University Press, 1997).

C/M   7. Eaton, J. *Psalms of the Way and the Kingdom* (Sheffield
            Academic Press, 1995). Surveys key commentators of
            Psalms 1; 19; 119 (Torah) and 93; 97; 99 (Kingship).
            ———. *Psalms* (T & T Clark, 2003).

---

13. Because Special Studies on Psalms fell into the two following categories, I have
    taken the liberty to delineate accordingly.

All 8. **Flint, Peter, and Patrick Miller, eds.** *The Book of Psalms: Composition and Reception* **(Brill, 2005).**

C/M 9. Freedman, David. *Psalm 119* (Eisenbrauns, 1999). Acrostics.

L/Cr 10. Gerstenberger, Erhard. FOTL, 2 vols. (Eerdmans, 1988, 2001). Includes Lamentations.[14]

E 11. Howard, David. *The Structure of Psalms 93–100* (Eisenbrauns, 1997).

L/Cr 12. McCann, Clinton, ed. *The Shape and Shaping of the Psalter* (Sheffield Academic Press, 1993).

C/M 13. **Schaeffer, Konrad. Berit Olam (Liturgical, 2001).** Especially "A School of Prayer" in introduction.

L/Cr 14. **Westermann, Claus.** *The Living Psalms* **(Eerdmans, 1989).**

E 15. **Wilson, Gerald.** *The Editing of the Hebrew Psalter* **(Scholars, 1985).** Groundbreaking study.

Theology of the Psalms

E/Cr 1. Broyles, Craig. *The Conflict of Faith and Experience in the Psalms* (Sheffield Academic Press, 1989).

C/M 2. Davidson, Robert. *The Vitality and Richness of Worship* (Eerdmans, 1998). Commentary.

E 3. Day, John. *Crying for Justice* (Kregel, 2005).

C/M 4. Fløysvik, Ingvar. *When God Becomes My Enemy* (Concordia Academic Press, 1997). Covers complaint Psalms: 6; 44; 74; 88; 90.

E 5. Futato, Mark. *Transformed by Praise* (Presbyterian & Reformed, 2002).

E 6. **Grogan, Geoffrey.** *Prayer, Praise, and Prophecy* **(Christian Focus, 2001).**

L/Cr 7. Kraus, Hans-Joachim. *Theology of the Psalms,* Continental (Fortress, 1986).

---

14. Gerstenberger's second volume on Psalms with Lamentations focuses on the songs and prayers in Psalms in light of their sociohistorical setting and is meant for advanced students.

L/Cr   8. Lohfink, Norbert, and Erich Zenger. *The God of Israel and the Nations* (Liturgical, 2000). Isaiah, Psalms 25; 33; 87; 90–106.

L/Cr   9. Mays, James. *The Lord Reigns* (Westminster John Knox, 1994).

C/M   10. Mitchell, David. *The Message of the Psalter* (Sheffield Academic Press, 1997).

E   11. Travers, Michael. *Encountering God in the Psalms* (Kregel, 2003).

L/Cr   12. Zenger, Erich. *A God of Vengeance?* (Westminster John Knox, 1996). Advocacy of enmity psalms for worship.

        13. *See* Old Testament Introduction, Survey, and Theology: Introduction to the Psalms.

Proverbs*
Technical, Semitechnical

L/Cr   1. Clifford, Richard. OTL (Westminster John Knox, 1999). Especially structure and context.

L/Cr   2. Fox, Michael. AB, 2 vols. (Doubleday, 2000, 2003). Frequent LXX citings, numerous excursuses; however, lack of reference to Clifford and Murphy in volume 1.

E   3. Longman, Tremper. BCOTWP (Baker, 2006).

L/Cr   4. McKane, William. OTL (Westminster, 1970). Evolution of secular wisdom to Biblical proverbs.

L/Cr   5. Murphy, Roland. WBC (Thomas Nelson, 1998). Especially literary context and theological application.

E   6. Waltke, Bruce. NICOT, 2 vols. (Eerdmans, 2004, 2005).

L/Cr   7. Whybray, Norman. NCBC (Eerdmans, 1994). Especially textual criticism and literary context.

Exposition

E   1. Alden, Robert. *Proverbs* (Baker, 1983).

---

* Forthcoming: Paul Overland, Apollos (IVP); James Loader, HCOT (Peeters); Allen Ross (EBC); and Richard Schulz, CBC (Tyndale). Longman, Waltke, and Koptak will probably be your best choices, with a nod to Kitchen.

E   2. Atkinson, David. BST (IVP, 1996). Topical.
E   3. Garrett, Duane. NAC (Broadman & Holman, 1993).
        With Ecclesiastes and Song of Songs. Summary of in-
        terpretative options. Suggests theological application.
E/Cr   4. **Hubbard, David. TPC (Word, 1989).**
E   5. Kidner, Derek. TOTC (IVP, 1964). Especially introduc-
        tion to themes.
E   6. **Kitchen, John. Mentor (Christian Focus, 2006).**
E   7. **Koptak, Paul. NIVAC (Zondervan, 2003).**
E   8. Miller, John. BCBC (Herald, 2004).
L/Cr   9. Perdue, Leo. IBC (Westminster John Knox, 2000).
        Attributes Proverbs to immediate postexilic period.
        Wise versus fools reflect political tensions between pro-
        Persians and malcontents.
E   10. Steinmann, Andrew. Concordia Commentary (Concor-
        dia, 2006).
E/Cr   11. **Van Leeuwen, Raymond. NIB, vol. 5 (Abingdon, 1997).**
        Especially role of context in determining meaning.

Special Studies

L/Cr   1. Camp, Claudia. *Wisdom and the Feminine in the Book
        of Proverbs* (Almond, 1985).
E/Cr   2. Dell, Katherine. *The Book of Proverbs in Social and
        Theological Context* (Cambridge University Press,
        2006).
E   3. Estes, Daniel. *Hear, My Son* (IVP, 2001). Proverbs
        1–9.
E   4. **Heim, Martin. *Like Grapes of Gold Set in Silver* (de
        Gruyter, 2001). Proverbs 10–22.**
E   5. **Longman, Tremper. *How to Read Proverbs* (IVP,
        2002).**
E   6. McCreesh, Thomas. *Biblical Sound and Sense* (Sheffield
        Academic Press, 1992). Poetics of 10–29.
        ———. Berit Olam (Liturgical, 2001).
L/Cr   7. Perry, T. A. *Wisdom Literature and the Structure of
        Proverbs* (Penn State University Press, 1993).

E/Cr   8. Van Leeuwen, Raymond. *Context and Meaning in Proverbs 25–27* (Scholars, 1988).

L/Cr   9. Washington, Harold. *Wealth and Poverty in the Instruction of Amenemope and the Hebrew Proverbs* (Scholars, 1994).

L/Cr   10. Westermann, Claus. *Roots of Wisdom* (Westminster John Knox, 1995).

L/Cr   11. Whybray, Norman. *The Composition of the Book of Proverbs* (Sheffield Academic Press, 1994).

———. *The Book of Proverbs: A Survey of Modern Study* (Brill, 1995).

Ecclesiastes*
Technical, Semitechnical

L/Cr   1. Crenshaw, James. OTL (Westminster, 1987). Literary features.

L/Cr   2. Fox, Michael. *A Time to Tear Down and a Time to Build Up* (Eerdmans, 1999).

———. JPS (JPS, 2004).

L/Cr   3. Gordis, Robert. *Koheleth, the Man and His World,* 3d ed. (Schocken, 1968). Especially philology.

C/M   **4. Krüger, Thomas. Hermeneia (Fortress, 2004).** Especially rhetorical features and textual criticism. Engages largely with German critical scholarship which may account for being unable to discern Qohelet's meaning.

L/Cr   5. Loader, J. *Ecclesiastes.* Text and Interpretation (Eerdmans, 1986).

E/Cr   **6. Longman, Tremper. NICOT (Eerdmans, 1997).** Linguistic, literary, and typology study.

L/Cr   **7. Murphy, Roland. WBC (Word, 1992).** Lengthy introduction; theologically profound; sees Ecclesiastes as challenge to conventional wisdom.

---

* Forthcoming: Craig Bartholomew (BCOTWP); Daniel Fredericks, Apollos (IVP); and Anton Schoors, HCOT (Peeters). Pick Seow, Fredericks, and Provan (with Song of Solomon as a bonus), until Bartholomew comes along. Qohelet features many excellent liberal contributions.

L/Cr **8. Seow, Choon-Leong. AB (Doubleday, 1997).** Proposes non-Solomonic author during Persian period; summary of scholarship.

Exposition

L/Cr 1. Brown, William. IBC (John Knox, 2000). Late third to fourth centuries.

L/Cr 2. Davidson, Robert. DSB (Westminster, 1986). With Song of Solomon.

E 3. Eaton, Michael. TOTC (IVP, 1983). Argues for Qohelet as apologetic for faithlessness.

E/Cr 4. Hubbard, David. TPC (Word, 1992). With Song of Solomon.

E 5. Kaiser, Walter. EvBC (Moody, 1979).

E 6. Kidner, Derek. BST (IVP, 1976).

E 7. Provan, Iain. NIVAC (Zondervan, 2001). With Song of Solomon. Concentrates on bringing out message.

L/Cr 8. Towner, Sibley. NIB, vol. 5 (Abingdon, 1997). Brief but helpful.

L/Cr 9. Whybray, Norman. NCBC (Eerdmans, 1989). Proposes Hellenistic author.

Special Studies

E 1. Barth, Craig. *Reading Ecclesiastes* (Pontifical Biblical Institute, 1998).

L/Cr 2. Farmer, Kathleen. ITC (Eerdmans, 1991).

E 3. Fredericks, Daniel. *Qohelet's Language* (Mellon, 1986). Possibly preexilic.
——. *Coping with Transcience* **(Sheffield Academic Press, 1993).**

L/Cr 4. Ogden, Graham. *Qoheleth* (Sheffield Academic Press, 1987). Commentary on structure, argument, and word meaning.

L/Cr 5. Schoors, A., ed. *Qohelet in the Context of Wisdom* (Peeters, 1998).

L/Cr	6.	Whitley, Charles. *Koheleth* (de Gruyter, 1979). Post-Maccabean composition. Highlights literary features.

Song of Songs*
Technical, Semitechnical

L/Cr	1.	Exum, Cheryl. OTL (Westminster John Knox, 2005).
E	**2.**	**Garrett, Duane, and Paul House. WBC (Thomas Nelson, 2004).** With Lamentations.
L/Cr	3.	Gordis, Robert. *The Song of Songs and Lamentations,* rev. ed. (KTAV, 1974).
E	**4.**	**Hess, Richard. BCOTWP (Baker, 2005).** Literary-theological emphasis.
L/Cr	5.	Keel, Othmar. Continental (Fortress, 1994). Interpretation of images.
E	**6.**	**Longman, Tremper. NICOT (Eerdmans, 2001).** Linguistic, literary, typology study.
L/Cr	**7.**	**Murphy, Roland. Hermeneia (Fortress, 1990).** Egypt-Mesopotamia link.
L/Cr	8.	Pope, Marvin. AB (Doubleday, 1977). Especially comparative customs, history of interpretation.
L/Cr	9.	Snaith, John. NCBC (Eerdmans, 1993). Explores link to Egyptian songs.

Exposition

E	1.	Carr, Lloyd. TOTC (IVP, 1984).
E	**2.**	**Gledhill, Tom. BST (IVP, 1994).**
E/Cr	3.	Hubbard, David. TPC (Word, 1992). With Ecclesiastes.
C/M	4.	Jenson, Robert. IBC (Westminster John Knox, 2005).

---

* Forthcoming: Frederick Dobbs-Alsopp, ECC (Eerdmans); Daniel Estes, Apollos (IVP); Michael Fishbane (JPS); and Wilfred Watson, HCOT (Peeters). Hess and Garrett, WBC (Word) stand ahead of the conservative pack with thorough-going analysis of the Hebrew text, social and literary background, as well as demonstrating familiarity with cognate literature; particularly the Egyptian love songs. Hess will prove especially helpful to the pastor untrained in Hebrew as it is transliterated throughout. Use with Longman, NICOT (Hendrickson), Estes, Carr, or Gledhill.

E   5.   Kinlaw, Dennis. EBC, vol. 5 (Zondervan, 1991).

E   6   Mitchell, Christopher. *The Song of Songs* (Concordia, 2003). Massive theological commentary.

E   **7. Provan, Iain. NIVAC (Zondervan, 2001).** With Ecclesiastes.

Special Studies

L/Cr   1.   Bergant, Dianne. Berit Olam (Liturgical, 2001).

L/Cr   2.   Brenner, Athalya, ed. *A Feminist Companion to the Song of Songs* (Sheffield Academic Press, 1993).

L/Cr   3.   Falk, Marcia. *The Song of Songs* (HarperSanFrancisco, 1990).

L/Cr   **4. Fox, Michael. *The Song of Songs and the Ancient Egyptian Love Songs* (University of Wisconsin, 1985).** Detailed comparison.

L/Cr   5.   LaCocque, Andre. *Romance, She Wrote* (Trinity Press International, 1998). Proposes female author.

E   6.   Norris, Richard, ed. *The Song of Songs: Interpreted by the Early Church and Medieval Commentators*. The Church's Bible (Eerdmans, 2003). Interpretation in first one thousand years.

Isaiah*
Technical, Semitechnical

L/Cr   1.   Baltzer, Klaus. *Deutero-Isaiah,* Hermeneia (Fortress, 2001). Covers chapters 40–55. Sees as postexilic liturgical drama (fifth century).

L/Cr   **2. Beuken, W. *Isaiah Part II,* vol. 2, HCOT (Peeters, 2000).** Covers chapters 28–39. Multiredactions for

---

* Forthcoming: Hendrik Leene, Isaiah 1–12, HCOT (Peeters); and Willem Beuken, 13–27, HCOT (Peeters); Geoffrey Grogan, EBC (Zondervan); Andrew Bartelt and Paul Raabe, *First Isaiah,* ECC (Eerdmans); Shalom Paul, *Second Isaiah,* ECC (Eerdmans); H. G. Williamson, Isaiah 6–27, ICC (T & T Clark); and Richard Schultz, Apollos (IVP). Meanwhile, stick with Oswalt's semitechnical two-volume commentary and Motyer's *Prophecy of Isaiah.* In view of the excellence of his monograph (see Special Studies), definitely obtain Schultz when it comes out. Also, keep in mind John Goldingay's coverage of Isaiah 40–55.

Isaiah. Some parts recast in light of Babylonian conquest of Jerusalem.

L/Cr   3. Blenkinsopp, Joseph. AB, 3 vols. (Doubleday, 2000, 2002–3). Serial interpretation.

L/Cr   4. Childs, Brevard. OTL (Westminster John Knox, 2000). Replacement for Kaiser and Westermann. Canonical approach. Especially literary features, theology, history of interpretation.

C/M   5. Clements, R. E. NCBC (Eerdmans, 1980). Covers chapters 1–39.

E/Cr   6. Goldingay, John. *The Message of Isaiah 40–55* (T & T Clark, 2005). Theological analysis.

E/Cr   7. Goldingay, John, and David Payne. ICC, 2 vols. (T & T Clark, 2006). Covers chapters 40–55.

L/Cr   8. Kaiser, Otto. OTL, 2 vols. (Westminster, 1983, 1974). Covers chapters 1–39, late date.

C/M   9. Koole, J. HCOT, 3 vols. (Peeters, 1997–99). Covers chapters 40–66.

E   10. Oswalt, John. NICOT, 2 vols. (Eerdmans, 1986, 1998).[15]

C/M   11. Watts, John. WBC, rev. ed., 2 vols. (Thomas Nelson, 2006).

L/Cr   12. Westermann, Claus. OTL (Westminster, 1969). Covers chapters 40–66.

L/Cr   13. Whybray, R. N. NCBC (Eerdmans, 1981). Covers chapters 40–66.

---

15. Moderate and liberal scholars alike often criticize Oswalt on two points: being cavalier in response to alternatives and not adequately addressing matters of form and structure concerning Isaiah. Ironically, Brevard Childs (whose introduction is unsurprisingly short in view of his contention that the final reading of Isaiah is that which is to be regarded as authoritative), does a far better job of consistently engaging these scholars over the course of his exposition. Nevertheless, a need for a technical, semitechnical, and conservative commentary on Isaiah that interacts with Beuken, Koole, Childs, and Blenkinsopp, etc., still exists. Shalom Paul on Isaiah 40–66 promises to be conservative in light of his earlier work on Amos.

C/M 14. **Wildberger, Hans. Continental, 3 vols. (Fortress, 1991, 1996, 2002).** Covers chapters 1–39, form-critical.
C/M 15. **Williamson, Hugh.** *Isaiah 1–5.* **ICC (T & T Clark, 2006).** Two volumes on Isaiah 6–27 to follow.
E 16. Young, Edward. *The Book of Isaiah,* 3 vols. (Eerdmans, 1965–72). Amillennial.

Exposition

E/Cr 1. **Goldingay, John.** *The Message of Isaiah 40–55* **(T & T Clark, 2006).**
————. **NIBCOT (Hendrickson, 2001).** Especially literary structure.
E 2. Grogan, Geoffrey. EBC, vol. 6 (Zondervan, 1986).
L/Cr 3. Hanson, Paul. IBC (John Knox, 1995). 40–66, overall unity.
E 4. McKenna, David. TPC, 2 vols. (Word, 1993–94).
E 5. **Motyer, Alec.** *The Prophecy of Isaiah* **(IVP, 1993).** Premillennial. Connection of text to structure.
————. **TOTC (IVP, 1999).**
E/Cr 6. **Oswalt, John. NIVAC (Zondervan, 2003).**
E 7. Ridderbos, Herman. BSC (Zondervan, 1985).
L/Cr 8. **Seitz, Christopher. NIB, vol. 6 (Abingdon, 2001).** Argues for single author (40–66) from immediate post-exile; connects servant to Jesus. Especially literary features.
————. **IBC (John Knox, 1993).** 1–39, somewhat semitechnical.
E 9. Walker, Larry, and Elmer Martens. *Isaiah, Jeremiah, and Lamentations.* CBC (Tyndale, 2006). Walker on Isaiah.
E 10. Webb, Barry. BST (IVP, 1996). All-around but brief.
E 11. Wolf, Herbert. *Interpreting Isaiah* (Zondervan, 1985).

Special Studies

E/Cr 1. Broyles, Craig, and Craig A. Evans, eds. *Writing and Reading the Scroll of Isaiah,* 2 vols. (Brill, 1997).

L/Cr   2.   **Childs, Brevard.** *The Struggle to Understand Isaiah as Christian Scripture* **(Eerdmans, 2004).**

L/Cr   3.   de Waard, Jan. *A Handbook on Isaiah* (Eisenbrauns, 1997).

All   4.   Janowski, Bernd, and Peter Stuhlmacher, eds. *The Suffering Servant* (Eerdmans, 2004). Isaiah 53.

E   5.   **Lessing, R. Reed.** *Interpreting Discontinuity: Isaiah's Tyre Oracle* **(Eisenbrauns, 2004).** Isaiah 23.

E   6.   Ma, Wonsuk. *Until the Spirit Comes* (Sheffield Academic Press, 1999). Spirit passages.

L/Cr   7.   Miller, P. *Rhetoric and Redaction in Trito-Isaiah* (Brill, 1995).

C/M   8.   **O'Connell, Robert.** *Concentricity and Continuity* **(Sheffield Academic Press, 1994).**

L/Cr   9.   Polaski, Donald. *Authorizing an End* (Brill, 2001). Isaiah 24–27.

E   10.   **Schultz, Richard.** *The Search for Quotation* **(Sheffield Academic Press, 1999).** Analysis of prophetic parallels with five Isaianic passages.

C/M   11.   **Sweeney, Marvin.** *Isaiah 1–39.* **FOTL (Eerdmans, 1996).** Redaction-critical.

L/Cr   12.   Van Ruiten, J., ed. *Studies in the Book of Isaiah* (Peeters, 1997).

E   13.   **Wegner, Paul.** *An Examination of Kingship and Messianic Expectation* **(Mellon, 1992).**

L/Cr   14.   **Williamson, Hugh.** *The Book Called Isaiah: Deutero-Isaiah's Role in Composition and Redaction* **(Oxford University Press, 1994).**

         ———. *Variations on a Theme* **(Paternoster, 1998).**

Jeremiah[*]
Technical, Semitechnical

C/M   1.   Bright, John. AB (Doubleday, 1965). Especially introduction.

---

[*] Forthcoming: Ben Oosterhoff and Erik Peels, HCOT (Peeters); Tremper Longman, NIBCOT (Hendrickson), with Lamentations; Pamela Scalise, NICOT

L/Cr 2. Brueggemann, Walter. ITC (Eerdmans, 1997). Especially theology.

L/Cr 3. Carroll, Robert. OTL (Westminster, 1986). Text as ideological creation. Comments on literary reconstruction.

E/Cr 4. Craigie, Peter, Page Kelley, and Joel Drinkard. WBC (Word, 1991), 1–25.

C/M 5. Holladay, William. Hermeneia, 2 vols. (Fortress, 1986, 1989). Datable to time of Jeremiah. Wealth of textual, exegetical notes.

L/Cr 6. Jones, Douglas. NCBC (Eerdmans, 1992).

E 7. Keown, Gerald, Pamela Scalise, and Thomas Smothers. WBC (Word, 1995). Covers chapters 26–52.

L/Cr 8. Lundbom, Jack. AB, 3 vols. (Doubleday, 1999, 2004).[16]

L/Cr 9. McKane, William. ICC, 2 vols. (T & T Clark, 1986, 1996). Especially textual criticism, Baruch core with Deuteronomic redaction.

E/Cr 10. Thompson, J. A. NICOT (Eerdmans, 1980).

Exposition

L/Cr 1. Clements, Ronald. IBC (John Knox, 1988). Form critical.

C/M 2. Davidson, Robert. DSB, vol. 1 (Westminster, 1985). Covers chapters 1–20.

E 3. Dearman, Andrew. NIVAC (Zondervan, 2002). With Lamentations.

C/M 4. Fretheim, Terence. SHBC (Smyth & Helwys, 2002).

(Eerdmans). Scalise drew particular praise for her responsibilities in the WBC commentary on Jeremiah 26–52, which bodes well. Use with Dearman and Lundbom (see below). I also recommend sticking with Thompson, which, though dated, is still worth having.

16. Lundbom's first volume on Jeremiah 1–20 is particularly valuable because he believes these particular chapters are written by Jeremiah. He holds that the ministry of Jeremiah was stimulated by the discovery of the Torah in 622 B.C. The first edition of Lundbom's earlier work on Jeremiac rhetoric has drawn substantial notice and is considered a standard in the field. Others have pointed to Jeremiah's prayers, sermons, and biographical accounts as devices that set Jeremiah apart from all the other prophets.

E	5.	Guest, John. TPC (Word, 1988). With Lamentations.
E	6.	Harrison, R. K. TOTC (IVP, 1973). With Lamentations.
E	**7.**	**Huey, F. NAC (Broadman & Holman, 1993).** With Lamentations.
E	8.	Kidner, Derek. BST (IVP, 1987).
E	9.	Martens, Elmer. CBC (Tyndale, 2006).
L/Cr	10.	McKeating, Henry. Epworth (Epworth, 1999).
L/Cr	11.	Miller, Patrick. NIB, vol. 6 (Abingdon, 2001).
E	12.	Ryken, Philip. *Jeremiah and Lamentations* (Crossway, 2001).
C/M	**13.**	**Stulman, Louis. AOTC (Abingdon, 2005).**

Special Studies

E	1.	Adeyẹmi, Fẹmi. *The New Covenant Torah in Jeremiah and the Law of Christ in Paul* (Lang, 2006).
E/Cr	2.	Biddle, Mark. *Polyphony and Symphony in Prophetic Literature: Rereading Jeremiah 7–20* (Mercer University Press, 1996).
L/Cr	**3.**	**Curtis, A., and T. Römer. *The Book of Jeremiah and Its Reception* (Leuven University Press, 1997).**
C/M	4.	Diamond, Pete, Kathleen O'Connor, and Louis Stulman, eds. *Troubling Jeremiah* (Sheffield Academic Press, 1999).
E/Cr	**5.**	**Friebel, Kelvin. *Jeremiah's and Ezekiel's Sign Acts* (Sheffield Academic Press, 1999).**
ALL	6.	Goldingay, John, ed. *Uprooting and Planting* (T & T Clark, 2006). Leslie Allen tribute.
E/Cr	7.	Hill, J. *Friend or Foe?* (Brill, 1999). Babylon.
L/Cr	**8.**	**King, Philip. *Jeremiah: An Archaeological Companion* (Westminster John Knox, 1993).**
L/Cr	**9.**	**Lundbom, Jack. *Jeremiah,* 2d ed. (Eisenbrauns, 1997).** Rhetoric.
		———. *The Early Career of the Prophet Jeremiah* (Mellen, 1993).
C/M	**10.**	**McConville, Gordon. *Judgment and Promise* (Eisenbrauns, 1993).** Anti-Deuteronomic redaction.

C/M 11. O'Connor, Kathleen. *The Confessions of Jeremiah* (Scholars, 1988). Fine treatment of laments in 1–25.

C/M 12. Parke-Taylor, G. *The Formation of the Book of Jeremiah* (Society of Biblical Literature, 2000).

C/M 13. Stulman, Louis. *Order Amid Chaos* (Sheffield Academic Press, 1998).

L/Cr 14. Thompson, Henry. *The Book of Jeremiah: An Annotated Bibliography* (Scarecrow, 1997).

Lamentations*
Technical, Semitechnical

L/Cr 1. **Berlin, Adele. OTL (Westminster John Knox, 2002).** Especially background, architecture, and theology.

L/Cr 2. **Hillers, Delbert. AB, rev. ed. (Doubleday, 1992).** Especially philology, poetry, and structure.

E 3. **House, Paul. WBC (Thomas Nelson, 2004).** With Song of Solomon.

E 4. **Provan, Iain. NCBC (Eerdmans, 1991).** Especially literary features.

C/M 5. **Renkema, J. HCOT (Peeters, 1998).** Especially insights on poetic structure.

Exposition

L/Cr 1. Bergant, Dianne, AOTC (Abingdon, 2003).

C/M 2. Davidson, Robert. DSB, vol. 2 (Westminster, 1985). With Jeremiah 21–52.

E 3. Dearman, Andrew. NIVAC (Zondervan, 2002). With Jeremiah.

---

* Forthcoming: Robert Hubbard, NICOT (Eerdmans); and Edward Greenstein (JPS). Use Hubbard and House with Provan (if you can get it), which packs an enormous amount of information into 142 pages (a little more than a page per line). Renkema is superb at 641 pages but might also be difficult to obtain. Adele Berlin builds on the strength of her earlier work, *The Dynamics of Biblical Parallelism* (Indiana University Press, 1985), to dissect the complex acrostic patterns of Lamentations' five poems; focusing on the hope that can be found in the midst of human suffering.

C/M   4. **Dobbs-Allsopp, F. IBC (Westminster John Knox, 2000).**[17]

E   5. Ellison, Henry. EBC, vol. 6 (Zondervan, 1986).

E   6. Harrison, R. K. TOTC (IVP, 1973). With Jeremiah.

E   7. Huey, F. NAC (Broadman & Holman, 1993). With Jeremiah.

E   8. Kaiser, Walter. *A Biblical Approach to Personal Suffering* (Moody, 1982; Wipf & Stock, 2003).

C/M   9. O'Connor, Kathleen. NIB, vol. 6 (Abingdon, 2001).

E   10. Ryken, Philip. *Jeremiah and Lamentations* (Crossway, 2001).

Special Studies

L/Cr   1. **Dobbs-Allsopp, F. *Weep, O Daughter of Zion* (Pontifical Biblical Institute, 1993).**

L/Cr   2. Linafelt, Tod. *Surviving Lamentations* (University of Chicago, 1999).

L/Cr   3. Martin-Achard, Robert, and S. Paul Re'emi. ITC (Eerdmans, 1984). Includes Amos.

L/Cr   4. **Salters, Robin. *Jonah and Lamentations*, OTG (Sheffield Academic Press, 1994).**

L/Cr   5. Westermann, Claus. *Lamentations* (Fortress, 1994). Recent history of interpretation.

Ezekiel[*]
Technical, Semitechnical

E/Cr   1. **Allen, Leslie. WBC, 2 vols. (Word, 1990, 1994).** Especially text criticism, theology, and ANE background. Volume 1 replacement for Brownlee.

---

17. Dobbs-Allsopp, the author of a major monograph and seven journal articles on Lamentations in the last ten years, builds on his earlier work. He goes somewhat against the supposed intentions of the Interpretation series by not providing easily discernable segments devoted to application, yet weaves in such an impressive array of mostly secular literature (especially on the Holocaust) that is just as delightful to read as it is to study.

* Forthcoming: Steven Tuell, NIBCOT (Hendrickson); Herrie van Rooy, Ezekiel 1–24, HCOT (Peeters); and Corrine Patton, Ezekiel 25–48, HCOT (Peeters). Block, Odell, and Duguid provide the most thoroughgoing coverage.

E   2. **Block, Daniel. NICOT, 2 vols. (Eerdmans, 1997, 1998).**[18]
L/Cr 3. Eichrodt, Walther. OTL (Westminster, 1970). Emends text and posits expansions from traditio-historical approach. Also, ANE background, literary analysis.
C/M   4. Greenberg, Moshe. AB, 3 vols. (Doubleday, 1983, 1997–). As holistic final form essentially from prophet.
L/Cr 5. **Zimmerli, Walther. Hermeneia, 2 vols. (Fortress, 1979–1983).** Form/tradition-critical.

Exposition

E   1. Alexander, Ralph. EBC, vol. 6 (Zondervan, 1986). Especially the excursus on the millennial temple.
L/Cr 2. Blenkinsopp, Joseph. IBC (John Knox, 1990).
L/Cr 3. Clements, Ronald. WBComp (Westminster John Knox, 1996).
E   4. Cooper, Lamar. NAC (Broadman & Holman, 1994). Dispensational.
E/Cr 5. **Craigie, Peter. DSB (Westminster, 1983).**
E   6. **Duguid, Iain. NIVAC (Zondervan, 2000).** 568 pages of exposition.
E   7. Feinberg, Charles. *The Prophecy of Ezekiel* (Moody, 1969). Dispensational.
L/Cr 8. Hens-Piazza, Gina. *1 and 2 Kings,* AOTC (Abingdon, 2006).

---

18. Block's two-volume exegesis is the best commentary on any book of the Old Testament, even better than Wenham on Genesis, Milgrom on Leviticus, Japhet on 1–2 Chronicles, and his own work on Judges/Ruth. In a recent review, Gordon Matties (author of the monograph on the following page) said, "Daniel Block's massive commentary will become a standard for Ezekiel studies for years to come. . . . A commentary as massive as this one that advocates profoundly at every turn *for* Ezekiel and his God, and *against* our own biases, complicity with evil, and idolatries, deserves our deepest respect" (*Ashland Theological Journal* 33 [2001]: 111–12). Block leaves no stone unturned whether it be on textual/grammatical and historical issues, ANE comparative literature, overall literary structures, analysis of symbols as a means of speech, and a theology that points to the restoration of Israel in both a temporal and an eternal sense.

E   9. Lind, Millard. BCBC (Herald, 1996).
C/M   10. **Odell, Margaret. SHBC (Smyth & Helwys, 2005).**
           Careful literary analysis wedded to theology.
C/M   11. **Pfisterer Darr, Katheryn. NIB, vol. 6 (Abingdon, 2001).**
E   12. **Stuart, Douglas. TPC (Word, 1989).**
E   13. Wright, Christopher. BST (IVP, 2001). Organized into groups of related chapters with some omissions.

Special Studies

L/Cr   1. Bodi, Daniel. *The Book of Ezekiel and the Poem of Erra* (Vandenhoeck and Ruprecht, 1991).
All   2. Cook, Stephen, and Corrine Patton, eds. *Ezekiel's Hierarchical World* (SBL, 2004).
L/Cr   3. **Davis, Ellen. *Swallowing the Scroll* (Almond, 1989).** Discourse analysis.
E   4. **Duguid, Iain. *Ezekiel and the Leaders of Israel* (Brill, 1994).**
E/Cr   5. **Friebel, Kelvin. *Jeremiah's and Ezekiel's Sign-Acts* (Sheffield Academic Press, 1999).**
L/Cr   6. Galumbush, Julie. *Jerusalem in the Book of Ezekiel* (Scholars, 1992). Especially Ezekiel 16; 23.
L/Cr   7. **Hals, Ronald. FOTL (Eerdmans, 1989).** Excellent genre analysis.
E/Cr   8. Joyce, Paul. *Divine Initiative and Human Response in Ezekiel* (Sheffield Academic Press, 1989).
C/M   9. Lapsey, Jacqueline. *Can These Bones Live?* (de Gruyter, 2000). Especially 3–48.
E   10. Matties, Gordon. *Ezekiel 18 and the Rhetoric of Moral Discourse* (Scholars, 1990).
L/Cr 11. McKeating, Henry. OTG (Sheffield Academic Press, 1993).
C/M   12. Mein, Andrew. *Ezekiel and His Ethics of Exile* (Oxford University Press, 2002).
E-L/Cr 13. Odell, Margaret, and John Strong, eds. *The Book of Ezekiel* (SBL, 2000).

E   14. **Renz, Thomas.** *The Rhetorical Function of the Book of Ezekiel* **(Brill, 1999).**

L/Cr   15. Stevenson, Kalinda. *The Vision of Transformation* (Scholars, 1996). 40–48.

Daniel*
Technical, Semitechnical

L/Cr   1. **Collins, John. Hermeneia (Fortress, 1993).** Late composition.

E/Cr   2. **Goldingay, John. WBC (Word, 1989).** Amillennial; apocalypse-midrash; valuable (including nonbiblical) cross-references; proposes late composition.

L/Cr   3. Hartman, Louis, and Alexander Dilella. AB (Doubleday, 1978). Maccabean edit.

L/Cr   4. Lacocque, Andre. *The Book of Daniel* (John Knox, 1979). Late-date.

E/Cr   5. Lucas, Ernest. Apollos (IVP, 2002). Canonical approach. Compositional issues in epilogue.

L/Cr   6. Montgomery, James. ICC (T & T Clark, 1927). Especially philology, textual data.

L/Cr   7. Porteous, Norman. OTL, 2d ed. (Westminster, 1979). With supplement updating 1965 edition.

E   8. Young, Edward. *The Prophecy of Daniel* (Eerdmans, 1949; Wipf & Stock, 2000). Addresses millennial debates. Amillennial.

---

* Forthcoming: Jan-Wim Wesselius, HCOT (Peeters); Eugene Carpenter, CBC (Tyndale); Andrew Hill, EBC (Zondervan); and R. Glenn Wooden, NICOT (Eerdmans). Goldingay and Collins are both excellent. However, both propose a late date ranging from the end of the Persian to the Hasmonean period (333–167 B.C.). Nevertheless, Goldingay is still evangelical in perspective. Another option is dispensationalist Miller to obtain a balanced theological perspective. Miller also suggests Danielic authorship. Baldwin is still superior, but shows its age. Choose Goldingay, look for Wooden and Hill, and watch for Carpenter's commentary on Daniel bound together with Ezekiel in a new eighteen-volume series from Tyndale (CBC).

Exposition

E/Cr 1. **Baldwin, Joyce. TOTC (IVP, 1978).** Amillennial, all-around exposition.

E 2. Ferguson, Sinclair. TPC (Word, 1988). Amillennial.

L/Cr 3. Gowan, Donald. AOTC (Abingdon, 2001).

E 4. **Lederach, Paul M. BCBC (Herald, 1999).** Amillennial.

E 5. Longman, Tremper. NIVAC (Zondervan, 1999). Amillennial.

E 6. **Miller, Stephen. NAC (Broadman & Holman, 1994).** Dispensational.

L/Cr 7. Redditt, Paul. NCBC (Sheffield Academic Press, 2000). Final form 160 B.C.

C/M 8. Seow, Choon-Leong. WBComp (Westminster John Knox, 2003).

L/Cr 9. Towner, Sibley. IBC (Westminster, 1984). Late composition.

E 10. **Wallace, Ronald. BST (IVP, 1979).** Amillennial.

E 11. Wood, Leon. *A Commentary on Daniel* (Zondervan, 1973; Wipf & Stock, 2000). Dispensational.

Special Studies

L/Cr 1. **Collins, John. *Daniel with an Introduction to Apocalyptic Literature,* FOTL (Eerdmans, 1984).**

L/Cr 2. **Collins, John, and Peter Flint, eds. *Book of Daniel,* vol. 1 (Brill, 2001).**

L/Cr 3. Fewell, Danna. *Circle of Sovereignty* (Abingdon, 1991).

L/Cr 4. Meadowcroft, T. *Aramaic Daniel and Greek Daniel* (Sheffield Academic Press, 1995).

L/Cr 5. Van der Woude, Adam, ed. *The Book of Daniel in the Light of New Findings* (Leuven University Press, 1993).

Minor Prophets
Entire Twelve Books*

L/Cr 1. Achtemeier, Elizabeth. IBC (John Knox, 1986). Micah–Malachi.

———. *Minor Prophets I*, NIBCOT (Hendrickson, 1996). Hosea–Micah, especially Hosea, Joel.

E 2. **Baker, David.** *Joel, Obadiah, Malachi.* **NIVAC (Zondervan, 2006).**

E 3. Boice, J. M. *The Minor Prophets,* 2 vols. (Baker, 2001).

E/Cr 4. Craigie, Peter. *Twelve Prophets,* DSB, 2 vols. (Westminster, 1984–85).

E 5. Gaebelein, Frank., ed. EBC, vol. 7 (Zondervan, 1985). With Daniel.

E 6. Kaiser, Walter. TPC (Word, 1992). Micah–Malachi.

E-L/Cr 7. Keck, Leander, ed. NIB, vol. 7 (Abingdon, 1996). With Daniel.

L/Cr 8. Limburg, James. IBC (John Knox, 1988). Hosea–Jonah.

E/Cr 9. **McComiskey, Thomas, ed.** *The Minor Prophets,* **3 vols. (Baker, 1992–98).**[19]

L/Cr 10. O'Brien, Julie. AOTC (Abingdon, 2004). Nahum–Malachi.

E 11. Prior, David. *Joel, Micah, and Habakkuk,* BST (IVP, 1999).

L/Cr 12. Simundson, Daniel. AOTC (Abingdon, 2005). Hosea–Micah.

---

* Forthcoming: Duane Christensen and Pamela Scalise, *Minor Prophets II,* NIBCOT (Hendrickson) with Nahum–Malachi.

19. I recommend certain commentaries in McComiskey's three-volume set (noted later under individual volumes) because it is uneven in quality. As an example of the varying ranges of coverage, the three chapters each of Jonah, Nahum, and Habakkuk receive treatments of 47, 64, and 65 pages, respectively (176 total) whereas Waltke's 173-page treatment of the seven chapters in Micah is as good as any exposition anywhere. Only Andersen/Freedman's 720-page treatment exceeds its quality exegetically. The Hermeneia-like size of the three-volume series lends itself to study.

E   **13.**   **Smith, Gary.** *Hosea, Amos, Micah,* **NIVAC (Zondervan, 2001).**

E   **14.**   Smith, Ralph. WBC (Word, 1984). Micah–Malachi.

E   **15.**   **Stuart, Douglas. WBC (Word, 1987).** Hosea–Jonah.[20]

Special Studies

L/Cr   1.   Achtemeier, Elizabeth. *Preaching from the Minor Prophets* (Eerdmans, 1998).

E   2.   Chisholm, Robert. *Interpreting the Minor Prophets* (Zondervan, 1990).

E/Cr   3.   Collins, Terence. *The Mantle of Elijah* (Sheffield Academic, 1993).

L/Cr   4.   Floyd, Michael. *Minor Prophets, Part 2.* FOTL (Eerdmans, 1999).

E/Cr   5.   Gordon, Robert, ed. *The Place Is Too Small for Us* (Eisenbrauns, 1995). Recent scholarship.

L/Cr   6.   Griffin, William. *The Gods of the Prophets* (Sheffield Academic Press, 1997). Statistical analysis of Joel with Isaiah 1–3, Hosea 4–8, Nahum, Malachi, and Zechariah 12–14.

E   7.   Matthews, Victor. *Social World of the Hebrew Prophets* (Hendrickson, 2001).

All   8.   Nogalski, James, and Marvin Sweeney, eds. *Reading and Hearing the Book of Twelve* (SBL, 2000).

All   9.   Redditt, Paul, and Aaron Schart, eds., *Thematic Threads in the Book of the Twelve* (de Gruyter, 2003).

E   10.   Smith, Gary. *The Prophets as Preachers* (Broadman & Holman, 1994).

L/Cr   11.   Sweeney, Marvin. *The Twelve Prophets,* Berit Olam, 2 vols. (Liturgical, 2001).

---

20. Under revision by Stewart.

Minor Prophets
(Individual Books)[21]

(Except where indicated, Technical, Semitechnical, and Expositional commentaries, as well as Special Studies, are subsumed under one category.)

Hosea[*]

C/M   1.   **Andersen, Francis, and David Freedman. AB (Doubleday, 1980).** Especially textual problems, unity, poetics. Written by Hosea.

L/Cr   2.   Ben Zvi, Ehud. FOTL (Eerdmans, 2005).

L/Cr   3.   Davies, Graham. NCBC (Eerdmans, 1992). Especially textual criticism, later redactions.

C/M   4.   **Macintosh, A. A. ICC (T & T Clark, 1997).** Judean redactors reflecting 750–720 B.C. Especially Rabbinics, textual criticism, influence of DSS, new archaeology. One hundred-page introduction.[22]

L/Cr   5.   Mays, James. OTL (Westminster, 1969). Form critical. Added material by later authors. Especially theology.

L/Cr   6.   McKeating, Henry. Cambridge Bible Commentary (Cambridge, 1971). Includes Amos, Micah.

---

21. Once relegated to one- or two-volume treatments of the entire Minor Prophets, individual books in recent years (see following) have presented some astonishingly full treatments. Among these are A. A. Macintosh on Hosea (704 pp.), Paul Raabe on Obadiah (336 pp.), Francis Andersen and David Freedman on Micah (720 pp.), Andersen on Habakkuk (456 pp.), and Andrew Hill on Malachi (464 pp.). By contrast, Douglas Stuart and Ralph Smith covered the entire corpus in 793 pages for the WBC series.

*   Forthcoming: M. Daniel Carroll R., Apollos (IVP); and Dwight Daniels, HCOT (Peeters).

22. Macintosh is conservative in the sense that he believes that the book is essentially a unity flowing from the prophet's own hand. He attributes its well-known linguistic difficulties to the novelty of Hosea's Northern Kingdom dialect. In a lengthy excursus, he suggests that Gomer's promiscuity is "after the fact," which is one of the few places where some redaction has taken place. His concession to redaction includes the possibility that Hosea was further emendated to adjust its message to a successive audience.

L/Cr 7. **Wolff, Hans. Hermeneia (Fortress, 1974).** Form critical, later redactions.

Evangelical Commentaries[23]

1. **Garrett, Duane. NAC (Broadman & Holman, 1997).** Includes Joel and excursuses.
2. Guenther, Allen. BCBC (Herald, 1998).

E/Cr 3. **Hubbard, David. TOTC (IVP, 1990).**
4. Kidner, Derek. BST (IVP, 1987).
5. **McComiskey, Thomas. "Hosea." *The Minor Prophets*, vol. 1. Edited by Thomas McComiskey (Baker, 1992).**
6. **Stuart, Douglas. WBC (Word, 1987).** Especially covenantal background.

Joel[*]

L/Cr 1. Achtemeier, Elizabeth. NIBCOT, vol. 7 (Hendrickson, 1996).

E/Cr 2. **Allen, Leslie. NICOT (Eerdmans, 1976).**

L/Cr 3. Barton, John. OTL (Westminster, 2001). With Obadiah.

E 4. Busenitz, Irvin. *Joel and Obadiah*. Mentor (Christian Focus, 2003).

---

23. Some strictly evangelical commentaries on Hosea exist of which one can avail himself, although some of them are bundled together with one or two other books. Duane Garrett, the author of a recent grammar on classical Hebrew (Broadman & Holman), goes one step further here by explicating the literary features of the text along with its philology. Douglas Stuart's shorter treatment of Hosea joins Jonah as his most cohesive exegesis of the first half of the Minor Prophets (now under revision). Andrew Dearman's forthcoming commentary in the NICOT series is anxiously anticipated. David Hubbard's Tyndale entry is a bargain (234 pp., $12.95 paper), as is McComiskey in volume 1 of his *Minor Prophets*. I should also mention Gary Smith's expositional treatment of Hosea, which, although brief (he understandably devotes half of the book to Amos), is a model of thoughtful exposition, especially the theological implications of Hosea's relationship with Gomer. With Garrett, Dearman, and Smith, you would be set on Hosea for a lifetime, and if you already have Stuart and Hubbard, you should at least obtain Garrett.

* Forthcoming: Gert Kwakkel, HCOT (Peeters); and Robert Gordon, ICC (T & T Clark).

L/Cr **5. Crenshaw, James. AB (Doubleday, 1995).** Especially literary structure.

E/Cr 6. Dillard, Raymond. "Joel," *The Minor Prophets,* vol. 1. Edited by Thomas McComiskey (Baker, 1992).

E **7. Garrett, Duane. NAC (Broadman & Holman, 1997).**

E 8. Patterson, Richard. EBC, vol. 7 (Zondervan, 1985).

E **9. Stuart, Douglas. WBC (Word, 1987).**

L/Cr **10. Wolff, Hans** (*see* Joel, Amos below).

Amos*

C/M **1. Andersen, Francis, and David Freedman. AB (Doubleday, 1989).** Primarily authentic. In addition to an 178-page introduction, each of four sections receives literary introduction. Emphasizes poetics and linguistics. Somewhat obtuse.

L/Cr 2. Gowan, Donald. NIB, vol. 7 (Abingdon, 1996).

L/Cr **3. Jeremias, Jörg. OTL (Westminster John Knox, 1998).** Mostly postdates the fall of Judah. Several redactional stages. An attempt to balance form/redaction-critical and canonical approaches. Against most critical interpretations, recognizes the role of structure in the message.

L/Cr 4. Mays, James. OTL (Westminster, 1969). Form critical.

E 5. McComiskey, Thomas. EBC, vol. 7 (Zondervan, 1986).

E 6. Motyer, Alec. BST (IVP, 1974). Appreciation for Amos as literature.

E 7. Niehaus, Jeffrey. "Amos," *The Minor Prophets,* vol. 1. Edited by Thomas McComiskey (Baker, 1992). Covenant lawsuit.

---

* Forthcoming: Meindert Dijkstra, HCOT (Peeters); and M. Daniel Carroll R., NICOT (Eerdmans). Use with Paul and Smith if you can get it. If you can't get Smith's fuller treatment, his entry on Amos in the NIVAC series (which includes Hosea and Micah) occupies more than half the book. Denver Seminary professor M. Daniel Carroll R's forthcoming commentary should be eagerly anticipated.

C/M 8. **Paul, Shalom. Hermeneia (Fortress, 1991).** Especially ANE parallels and literary background. Numerous excursuses, 68-page bibliography.

E 9. Smith, Billy. NAC (Broadman & Holman, 1995). Particularly textual and theological issues.

E 10. **Smith, Gary. Mentor, rev. ed. (Christian Focus, 1998).** Features "Theological Developments" following each block of exposition. Update of 1989 Zondervan edition includes new, sociorhetorical insights.

————. *Hosea/Amos/Micah,* NIVAC (Zondervan, 2001).

L/Cr 11. **Wolff, Hans** (*see* Joel, Amos below).

Special Studies

E 1. Carroll R., M. Daniel. *Amos, the Prophet and His Oracles* (Westminster John Knox, 2002).

E 2. Hasel, Gerhard. *Understanding Amos* (Baker, 1991).

E/Cr 3. **Möller, Karl.** *A Prophet in Debate: The Rhetoric of Persuasion in the Book of Amos* **(Sheffield Academic Press, 2003).**

C/M 4. Steiner, Richard. *Stockmen from Tekoa, Sycomores from Sheba* (Catholic Biblical Assoc. of America, 2003).

All 5. Thompson, Henry. *The Book of Amos: An Annotated Bibliography* (Scarecrow, 1997).

Obadiah

E/Cr 1. Allen, Leslie. NICOT (Eerdmans, 1976).

E 2. Baker, David, Desmond Alexander, and Bruce Waltke. TOTC (IVP, 1988).

L/Cr 3. Barton, John. OTL (Westminster John Knox, 2001).

L/Cr 4. **Ben Zvi, Ehud.** *A Historical-Critical Study of the Book of Obadiah* **(de Gruyter, 1996).**

L/Cr 5. Coggins, Richard, and S. Re'emi. ITC (Eerdmans, 1985). With Nahum, Esther.

E 6. Finley, Thomas. WEC (Moody, 1990; Biblical Studies, 2003).

E/Cr   7.   **Raabe, Paul. AB (Doubleday, 1996).**

C/M   8.   **Renkema, Jan. HCOT (Peeters, 2003).** Thorough literary analysis; employs proto-LXX, Syriac sources. Essentially unified.

C/M   9.   Watts, John. *Obadiah* (Eerdmans, 1969; Alpha Pub., 1981).

L/Cr   10.   Wolff, Hans. Continental (Fortress, 1991). Form-critical.

Jonah*

E/Cr   1.   Allen, Leslie. NICOT (Eerdmans, 1976). Proposes nonliteral Jonah; especially literary features, theology.

E   2.   Baker, David, Desmond Alexander, and Bruce Waltke. TOTC (IVP, 1988).

E   3.   Ellison, H. EBC, vol. 7 (Zondervan, 1985).

L/Cr   4.   Limburg, James. OTL (Westminster John Knox, 1993). Targumic, rabbinic developments; modern motifs in art, literature.

E   **5.   Nixon, Rosemary. *The Message of Jonah*. BST (IVP, 2003).**

E   6.   Page, Frank. NAC (Broadman & Holman, 1995). Sensitivity to genre, literary issues.

L/Cr   **7.   Sasson, Jack. AB (Doubleday, 1990).** Especially text-critical, philological analysis. Studies parallel ANE, Jewish sources. Argues for postexilic, composite unity.

L/Cr   8.   Simon, Uriel. JPSTC (JPS, 2000).

E   **9.   Stuart, Douglas. WBC (Word, 1987).**

L/Cr   10.   Trible, Phyllis. NIB, vol. 7 (Abingdon, 1996). Rhetorical-critical.

L/Cr   11.   Wolff, Hans. Continental (Fortress, 1991).

---

* Forthcoming: Johannes Potgieter, HCOT (Peeters); and James Kugel, Hermeneia (Fortress). Jonah has not been particularly well served by evangelicals, at least in terms of providing a full-length exegetical commentary, as most of the currently available evangelical commentaries run less than a hundred pages. To put it into perspective, the slightly longer 2 Peter (61 verses to 48) has received a 210-page treatment from Richard Bauckham.

Special Studies

L/Cr   1.   Ben Zvi, Ehud. *The Sign of Jonah* (Sheffield Academic Press, 2003).

C/M   2.   Fretheim, Terence. *The Message of Jonah* (Augsburg, 1977). Theological.

L/Cr   3.   Magonet, J. *Forms and Meaning,* 2d ed. (Almond, 1983).

L/Cr   4.   Sherwood, Yvonne. *A Biblical Text and Its Afterlives* (Cambridge University Press, 2000). History of interpretation.

L/Cr   5.   Trible, Phyllis. *Rhetorical Criticism* (Fortress, 1994). Jonah.

Micah*

C/M   1.   **Andersen, Francis, and David Freedman. AB (Doubleday, 2000).** Especially history of interpretation, 67-page bibliography.

L/Cr   2   Ben Zvi, Ehud. FOTL (Eerdmans, 2000). Literary analysis.

L/Cr   3.   Hillers, Delbert. Hermeneia (Fortress, 1983). Sociological concerns, extensive textual notations.

L/Cr   4.   Mays, James. OTL (Westminster, 1976). Redaction/form-critical.

L/Cr   5.   McKane, William. ICC (T & T Clark, 1998). Excellent textual-linguistic analysis, limited background.

L/Cr   6.   Wolff, Hans. Continental (Fortress, 1990). Redaction/form critical, many textual notes.

          ———. *Micah the Prophet* (Augsburg, 1981).

Evangelical Commentaries

E/Cr   1.   **Allen, Leslie. NICOT (Eerdmans, 1976).** Especially theology, some sections later additions.

E   2.   Barker, Kenneth. NAC (Broadman & Holman, 1999). Dispensational; with Nahum–Zephaniah.

---

* Forthcoming: Johannes de Moor, HCOT (Peeters).

E   3.   Jacobs, Mignon. *The Conceptual Coherence of the Book of Micah* (Sheffield Academic Press, 2001).

E   **4.   McComiskey, Thomas. EBC, vol. 7 (Zondervan, 1986).**

E   5.   Smith, Gary. *Hosea, Amos, Micah,* NIVAC (Zondervan, 2001).

E   **6.   Waltke, Bruce. *A Commentary on Micah* (Eerdmans, 2007).**

————. **"Micah." *The Minor Prophets,* vol. 2. Edited by Thomas McComiskey (Baker, 1993).**[24]

Nahum[*]

E   1.   Armerding, Carl. EBC, vol. 7 (Zondervan, 1985).

E   **2.   Bailey, Waylon. NAC (Broadman & Holman, 1999).**

E   3.   Baker, David. TOTC (IVP, 1988).

E/Cr 4.   Longman, Tremper. "Nahum." *The Minor Prophets,* vol. 2. Edited by Thomas McComiskey (Baker, 1993).

E   **5.   Maier, Walter. *The Book of Nahum* (Concordia, 1959).**

L/Cr **6.   Roberts, J. OTL (Westminster, 1991).** Especially textual, grammatical concerns.

E   7.   Smith, Ralph. WBC (Word, 1984).

L/Cr **8.   Spronk, K. HCOT (Peeters, 1999).** Especially philological, literary analysis. Argues for Nahum as pseudonym and well-structured unity based on strophic analysis.

Habakkuk[†]

C/M **1.   Andersen, Francis. AB (Doubleday, 2001).** Exhaustive. Helpful excursuses.

---

24. Though purchasing a full commentary on a single Minor Prophet might be an extravagance, it speaks well that Waltke's coverage of Micah in the Baker three-volume series was the single, best effort.

* Forthcoming: Duane Christensen, AB (Doubleday).

† Forthcoming: David Hartzfeld, Apollos (IVP); and Gert Prinsloo, HCOT (Peeters).

E 2. Armerding, Carl. EBC, vol. 7 (Zondervan, 1985).
E **3. Bailey, Waylon. NAC (Broadman & Holman, 1999).**
E 4. Baker, David. TOTC (IVP, 1988).
E/Cr 5. Bruce, F. F. "Habakkuk." *The Minor Prophets,* vol. 2. Edited by Thomas McComiskey (Baker, 1993).
L/Cr 6. Gowan, Donald. *The Triumph of Faith in Habakkuk* (John Knox, 1976).
E 7. Haak, Robert. *Vetus Testamentum Supplement* (Brill, 1992). Political background.
E **8. Patterson, Richard. WEC (Moody, 1991; Biblical Studies, 2003).**
L/Cr **9. Roberts, J. OTL (Westminster, 1991).**

Zephaniah

E **1. Bailey, Waylon. NAC (Broadman & Holman, 1999).**
E **2. Baker, David. TOTC (IVP, 1988).**
C/M **3. Ball, Ivan. *Zephaniah: A Rhetorical Study* (Bibal Press, 1988).**
L/Cr **4. Ben Zvi, Ehud. *A Historical-Critical Study of the Book of Zephaniah* (de Gruyter, 1993).**
L/Cr 5. Berlin, Adele. AB (Doubleday, 1994). Especially rabbinic sources, literary cohesion, canonical interpretation. Fictive author.
E 6. House, Paul. *Zephaniah: A Prophetic Drama* (Almond Press, 1988).
E 7. Motyer, Alec. "Zephaniah," *The Minor Prophets,* vol. 3. Edited by Thomas McComiskey (Baker, 1998).
L/Cr **8. Roberts, J. OTL (Westminster, 1991).** Especially textual, grammatical concerns.
E **9. Robertson, O. Palmer. NICOT (Eerdmans, 1990).** Especially theology.
E 10. Smith, Ralph. WBC (Word, 1984).
C/M **11. Sweeney, Marvin. Hermeneia (Fortress, 2002).** Early 6th century provenance attributed mostly to Zephaniah.

L/Cr 12. Vlaardingerbroek, J. HCOT (Peeters, 1999).

Haggai*

E/Cr 1. Baldwin, Joyce. TOTC (IVP, 1972). Especially theology.

E   2. Merrill, Eugene. *Haggai, Zechariah, Malachi* (Moody, 1994; Biblical Studies, 2003).

L/Cr 3. **Meyers, Carol, and Eric Meyers. AB, 2 vols. (Doubleday, 1987, 1993).** Especially historical background, parallels.

L/Cr 4. **Petersen, David. OTL, 2 vols. (Westminster, 1984).** Especially historical, literary features.

E   5. **Taylor, Richard. NAC (Broadman & Holman, 2004).** More scholarly than series average. Especially temple theology.

E   6. Verhoef, Pieter. NICOT (Eerdmans, 1986). Especially theology.

L/Cr 7. Wolff, Hans. Continental (Fortress, 1988). Form critical.

Zechariah†

E/Cr 1. **Baldwin, Joyce. TOTC (IVP, 1972).** Especially authorship and literary features in introduction.

E   2. Barker, Kenneth. EBC, vol. 7 (Zondervan, 1985).

E   3. **Boda, Mark. NIVAC (Zondervan, 2004).**

C/M   4. Conrad, Edgar. *Zechariah* (Sheffield Academic Press, 1999).

E   5. **McComiskey, Thomas. "Zechariah," *The Minor Prophets*, vol. 3. Edited by Thomas McComiskey (Baker, 1998).**

E   6. **Merrill, Eugene. *Haggai, Zechariah, Malachi* (Moody, 1994; Biblical Studies, 2003).** Dispensational, eye to the NT.

---

* Forthcoming: William Koopmans, HCOT (Peeters).

† Forthcoming: Mark Boda, NICOT (Eerdmans); and Al Wolters, HCOT (Peeters).

L/Cr   7. **Meyers, Carol, and Eric Meyers. AB, 2 vols. (Double-day, 1987, 1993).** Excellent historical and linguistic analysis.
L/Cr   8. Ollenburger, Ben. NIB, vol. 7 (Abingdon, 1996).
L/Cr   9. **Petersen, David. OTL, 2 vols. (Westminster, 1984, 1995).** Dates 9–14 and Malachi to Persian period. Especially socioreligious, literary background.
E/Cr   10. Webb, Barry. BST (IVP, 2003).

Malachi*

E/Cr   1. Baldwin, Joyce. TOTC (IVP, 1972).
E   2. **Clendenen, Ray. NAC (Broadman & Holman, 2004).** More scholarly than series average. Especially linguistics and theology.
C/M   3. **Glazier-McDonald, Beth. *Malachi* (Scholars, 1987).** Literary-historical perspective.
E   4. **Hill, Andrew. AB (Doubleday, 1998).** Exceptional, well-balanced commentary. Thoughtful interaction with breadth of scholarship.
E   5. Kaiser, Walter. *God's Unchanging Love* (Baker, 1984).
E   6. Merrill, Eugene. *Haggai, Zechariah, Malachi* (Moody, 1994; Biblical Studies, 2003). Dispensational.
L/Cr   7. Redditt, Paul. NCBC (Eerdmans, 1995).
E   8. Smith, Ralph. WBC (Word, 1984). Under revision by Stuart.
E   9. Stuart, Douglas. "Malachi," *The Minor Prophets,* vol. 3. Edited by Thomas McComiskey (Baker, 1998).
E   10. **Verhoef, Pieter. NICOT (Eerdmans, 1986).** Especially structural analysis.

---

* Forthcoming: S. D. Snyman, HCOT (Peeters); and N. T. Wright, BST (IVP). Moderate liberals, commenting on the uniqueness of an evangelical entry in the *Anchor Bible* series, commend the evenhandedness with which Hill comments on the text, aware of all of the pertinent literature while defending a conservative position.

Combination Volumes

Joel, Amos*

L/Cr 1. Coggins, Richard. NCBC (Sheffield Academic Press, 2000). Brought together in second century B.C.

E 2. **Finley, Thomas. WEC (Moody, 1990; Biblical Studies, 2003).** Includes Obadiah.[25]

E/Cr 3. **Hubbard, David. TOTC (IVP, 1989).** Especially literary features.

L/Cr 4. **Wolff, Hans. Hermeneia (Fortress, 1977).** Form critical. Analysis of genre, style, and composition for each pericope. Six-stage redaction from time of Amos to postexilic. Scarce discussion of literary structure.

Obadiah, Jonah, Micah[†]

E/Cr 1. **Allen, Leslie. NICOT (Eerdmans, 1976).** Includes Joel, nonliteral Jonah, later additions to Micah.

E 2. **Alexander, Desmond, David Baker, and Bruce Waltke. TOTC (IVP, 1988).**

E 3. Finley, Thomas. EvBC (Moody, 1996). Without Jonah, includes Joel.

E/Cr 4. Mason, Rex. *Micah, Nahum, Obadiah,* OTG (Sheffield Academic Press, 1991). Introduction.

E 5. Smith, Billy, and Frank Page. NAC (Broadman & Holman, 1995). Includes Amos, excludes Micah.

L/Cr 6. Wolff, Hans. Continental (Augsburg, 1986). Without Micah, form critical.

Nahum, Habakkuk, Zephaniah[‡]

E 1. Baker, David. TOTC (IVP, 1988).

---

* Forthcoming: Peter Naylor, Apollos (IVP).

25. The commentaries of Thomas Finley, Richard Patterson, and Eugene Merrill (Biblical Studies Press) more than adequately cover all but Hosea, Jonah, and Micah.

† Forthcoming: Karl Möller, Apollos (IVP).

‡ Forthcoming: Kevin Cathcart, ICC (T & T Clark); and Thomas Renz, NICOT (Eerdmans), replacement for Robertson. Use together with Barker/Bailey. Doug Stuart will eventually revise Ralph Smith's Micah–Malachi, WBC (Word).

E   2. **Barker, Kenneth, and Waylon Bailey. NAC (Broadman & Holman, 1999).** Includes Micah.

E/Cr   3. Mason, Rex. *Zephaniah, Habakkuk, Joel,* OTG (Sheffield Academic Press, 1994).

E   4. **Patterson, Richard. WEC (Moody, 1991; Biblical Studies, 2003).**

L/Cr   5. **Roberts, J. J. M. OTL (Westminster John Knox, 1991).** Especially textual criticism, philology, historical background.

E   6. Robertson, O. Palmer. NICOT (Eerdmans, 1990). Especially theology.

Haggai, Zechariah, Malachi*

E/Cr   1. Baldwin, Joyce. TOTC (IVP, 1972). Especially Zechariah and theology.

E   2. Boda, Mark. *Haggai–Zechariah Research: A Bibliographic Survey* (DEO, 2003).

E   ———. **NIVAC (Zondervan, 2004).** Without Malachi.

All   3. Boda, Mark, and Michael Floyd, eds. *Bringing Out the Treasure: Inner Biblical Allusion and Zechariah 9–14* (Sheffield Academic Press, 2003). Interaction with Rex Mason dissertation.

L/Cr   4. Coggins, Richard. OTG (Sheffield Academic Press, 1987).

E   5. Ham, Clay Alan. *The Coming King and the Rejected Shepherd* (Sheffield Phoenix, 2006).

E   6. **Kessler, John. *The Book of Haggai* (Brill, 2002).**

L/Cr   7. Larkin, Katrina. *The Eschatology of Second Zechariah* (Kok Pharos, 1994).

---

* Forthcoming: Boyd Luter, Apollos (IVP); Robert Gordon, ICC (T & T Clark), with Joel and Obadiah; William Koopmans (Haggai), Al Wolters (Zechariah), and S. D. Snyman (Malachi) are slated in the HCOT series (Peeters). Also, Paul Hanson, Hermeneia (Fortress); Mignon Jacob's replacement for Verhoef on Haggai and Malachi (NICOT, Eerdmans); and Mark Boda on Zechariah (NICOT, Eerdmans). Jacobs, Merrill, Boda, and Taylor/Clendenen will serve you best.

C/M   8. Love, Mark. *The Evasive Text* (Sheffield Academic Press, 1999). Zechariah 1–8.

E/Cr   9. Mason, Rex. Cambridge Bible Commentary (Cambridge University Press, 1973). Especially Zechariah's use of earlier tradition.

E   10. **Merrill, Eugene.** *Haggai, Zechariah, Malachi* **(Moody, 1994; Biblical Studies, 2003).** Dispensational, especially Zechariah.

L/Cr   11. **Meyers, Carol, and Eric Meyers. AB, 2 vols. (Doubleday, 1987, 1993).** Without Malachi, attention to parallels.

L/Cr   12. **Petersen, David. OTL, 2 vols. (Westminster, 1984, 1995).** Zechariah 9–14 to Malachi 1–4 dated to Persian period. Especially socioreligious, literary background. Expert on prophetic literature.

L/Cr   13. Redditt, Paul. NCBC (Eerdmans, 1995). Redaction-critical.

E   14. **Taylor, Richard, and Ray Clendenen. NAC (Broadman & Holman, 2004).** Without Zechariah. More scholarly than series average. Especially theology.

C/M   15. Tigchelaar, Eibert. *Prophets of Old and the Day of the End* (Brill, 1996). Intertestamental, Zechariah and apocalyptic.

L/Cr   16. Tollington, Janet. *Tradition and Invention in Haggai and Zechariah 1–8* (Sheffield Academic Press, 1993).

All   17. Tuckett, Christopher, ed. *The Book of Zechariah and Its Influence* (Ashgate, 2003).

E   18. Verhoef, Pieter. NICOT (Eerdmans, 1987). Especially Haggai and theology, without Zechariah.

5

OLD TESTAMENT BACKGROUND

Primary References

1. Arnold, Bill, and Hugh Williamson, eds. *Dictionary of the Old Testament: Historical Books* (IVP, 2005).
2. Baker, David, and Desmond Alexander, eds. *Dictionary of the Old Testament: The Pentateuch* (IVP, 2002).
3. Boardman, John, et al., eds. *The Oxford History of the Classical World* (Oxford University Press, 1986).
4. Coogan, Michael, ed. *The Oxford History of the Biblical World* (Oxford University Press, 2001).
5. Edwards, I., ed. *Cambridge Ancient History,* 2d ed., 14 vols. (Cambridge University Press, 1970–2005).
6. Hoerth, Alfred. *Archaeology and the Old Testament* (Baker, 1998).
7. Matthews, Victor. *Manners and Customs in the Bible,* 3d ed. (Hendrickson, 2006).
8. Perdue, Leo. *The Blackwell Companion to the Hebrew Bible* (Blackwell, 2001).
9. Walton, John. *Chronological and Background Charts of the OT,* rev. ed. (Zondervan, 1994).
10. Walton, John, Victor Matthews, and Mark Chavalas. *The IVP Bible Background Commentary: Old Testament* (IVP, 2000).

Ancient Near East Parallels

1. Arnold, Bill, and Bryan Beyer. *Readings from the Ancient*

Near East (**Baker, 2001**). Companion to their *Encountering the Old Testament.*

2. **Block, Daniel.** *The Gods of the Nations,* **2d ed. (Baker, 2000).**

3. **Hallo, William, and Lawson Younger, eds.** *The Context of Scripture,* **3 vols. (Brill, 1997–2002).**

4. Lichtheim, Miriam. *Ancient Egyptian Literature,* 3 vols. (University of California, 1973–1980).

5. Matthews, Victor, and Don Benjamin. *Old Testament Parallels,* 2d ed. (Paulist, 1997).

6. McCarthy, Dennis. *Treaty and Covenant,* 2d ed. (Pontifical Biblical Institute, 1981). Vassal treaty/covenant.

7. Parker, Simon. *Stories in Scripture and Inscriptions* (Oxford University Press, 1997). Northwest Semitic inscriptions as closest parallel.

8. Pritchard, James. *Ancient Near East Texts Relating to the Old Testament,* 3d ed. (Princeton University Press, 1969).

9. **Sparks, Kenton.** *Ancient Texts for the Study of the Hebrew Bible* **(Hendrickson, 2005).**

10. **Walton, John.** *Ancient Israelite Literature in Its Cultural Context* **(Zondervan, 1989).**

History of Israel Textbooks

1. **Ahlström, Gösta.** *The History of Ancient Palestine* **(Fortress, 1993).** Moderate.

2. Albertz, Rainier. *History of Israelite Religion in the Old Testament,* 2 vols. (Westminster John Knox, 1994–95). Critical.

3. **Bright, John.** *A History of Israel,* **4th ed. (Westminster John Knox, 2000).** Moderate.

4. de Vaux, Roland. *Ancient Israel,* 2 vols. (McGraw-Hill, 1961).

5. Hayes, John, and Maxwell Miller, eds. *Israelite and Judean History* (Trinity Press International, 1990).

6. **Hayes, John, and Sara Mandell.** *The Jewish People in Classical Antiquity: From Alexander to Bar Kochba* **(Westminster John Knox, 1998).** Moderate.

7. **Kaiser, Walter.** *A History of Israel* **(Broadman & Holman, 1998).** Includes brief intertestamental history.

———. Liverani, Mario. *Israel's History and the History of Israel* (Equinox, 2006).

8. Merrill, Eugene. *Kingdom of Priests* (Baker, 1987).

9. Miller, Maxwell, and John Hayes. *A History of Ancient Israel and Judah,* 2d ed. (Westminster John Knox, 2006). Moderate critical.

10. **Provan, Iain, V. Philips Long, and Tremper Longman.** *A Biblical History of Israel* **(Westminster John Knox, 2003).**

11. Shanks, Hershel, ed. *Ancient Israel,* rev. ed. and expanded (BAS, 2000). 2000 B.C.–A.D. 70.

12. Soggin, Alberto. *An Introduction to the History of Israel and Judah,* 3d ed. (Trinity Press International, 1999). Critical synthesis of Continental scholarship.

———. *Israel in the Biblical Period* (T & T Clark, 2001). Brief.

Other Historical References and Helps

1. Albertz, Rainier. *Israel in Exile* (Brill, 2003).

2. Amit, Yairah. *History and Ideology* (Sheffield Academic Press, 1999). Historiography.

3. **Anderson, Robert, and Terry Giles.** *The Keepers* **(Hendrickson, 2002).** Samaritan history.

———. *Tradition Kept: The Literature of the Samaritans* (Hendrickson, 2005).

4. **Begg, Christopher.** *Josephus' Story of the Later Monarchy* **(Peeters, 2000).**

5. **Bruce, F. F., and David Payne.** *Israel and the Nations,* **2d ed. (IVP, 1999).**

6. Campbell, Antony, and Mark O'Brien. *Unfolding the Deuteronomistic History* (Fortress, 2000).

7. Coote, Robert. *Early Israel* (Fortress, 1990).

8. Davies, Philip. *In Search of "Ancient Israel"* (JSOT Press, 1992).

9. **Day, John, ed. *In Search of Pre-exilic Israel.* Journal for the Study of the Old Testament Supplement (T & T Clark, 2004).**

10. Dever, William. *What Did the Bible Writers Know and When Did They Know It?* (Eerdmans, 2001).

11. Dever, William, and Seymour Gitin, eds. *Symbiosis, Symbolism, and the Power of the Past* (Eisenbrauns, 2003).

12. **Fritz, Volkmar. *The City in Ancient Israel* (Sheffield Academic Press, 1995).**

13. Fritz, Volkmar, and Philip Davies, eds. *The Origins of the Ancient Israelite States* (Sheffield Academic Press, 1996).

14. Gilbert, Martin. *Israel* (William Morrow, 1999).

15. Grabbe, Lester. *Can a "History of Israel" Be Written?* (Sheffield Academic Press, 1997).
    ———. *A History of the Jews and Judaism in the Second Temple Period*, 4 vols. (T & T Clark, 2004–).
    ———, ed. *Like a Bird in a Cage: The Invasion of Sennacherib in 701 B.C.* (Sheffield Academic Press, 2003).

16. Hester, H. *The Heart of Hebrew History* (Broadman & Holman, 1998).

17. Hinson, D. *Old Testament Introduction,* vol. 1: *History of Israel,* rev. ed. (SPCK, 1990).

18. **Hoffmeier, James. *Israel in Egypt* (Oxford University Press, 1997).** Exodus validation.

19. Howard, David, and Michael Grisanti, eds. *Giving the Sense: Understanding and Using Old Testament Historical Texts* (Kregel, 2003).

20. **Isserlin, B. *The Israelites* (Fortress, 2001).** Thirteenth century–586 B.C.

21. Jagersma, Henk. *A History of Israel in the Old Testament Period* (Fortress, 1983).
    ———. *A History of Israel from Alexander to Bar Kochba* (Fortress, 1986).

22. **Kitchen, Kenneth. *On the Reliability of the Old Testament* (Eerdmans, 2003).** Vigorous defense of OT history.

23. **Knoppers, Gary, and Gordon McConville, eds. *Reconsidering Israel and Judah* (Eisenbrauns, 2000).**

24. Kofoed, Jens Bruun. *Text and History: Historiography and the Study of the Biblical Text* (Eisenbrauns, 2005). Validation of historical veracity of Kings.

25. Lemche, Niels. *Ancient Israel* (Sheffield Academic Press, 1988).

———. *Early Israel* (Brill, 1985). Evaluates three premonarchical establishment of Israel theories.

———. *Prelude to Israel's Past* (Hendrickson, 1998).

———. *The Israelites in History and Tradition* (Westminster John Knox, 1998).

26. Lipschits, Oded, and Joseph Bleckinsopp, eds. *Judah and the Judeans in the Neo-Babylonian Period* (Eisenbrauns, 2003).

27. Long, V. Philips. *The Art of Biblical History* (Zondervan, 1994).

———. *Israel's Past in Present Research* (Eisenbrauns, 1999).

28. Long, V. Philips, David Baker, and Gordon Wenham, eds. *Windows into Old Testament History* (Eerdmans, 2002).

29. McDermott, John. *What Are They Saying About the Formation of Ancient Israel?* (Paulist, 1999).

30. Millard, A. R., James Hoffmeier, and David Baker, eds. *Faith, Tradition, and History* (Eisenbrauns, 1994). Old Testament historiography.

31. Miller, Maxwell. *The History of Israel* (Abingdon, 1999). Expanded NIB entry.

32. Miller, Robert. *Chieftains of the Highland Clans: A History of Israel in the 12th and 11th Centuries B.C.* (Eerdmans, 2005).

33. Noll, K. L. *Canaan and Israel in Antiquity* (Sheffield Academic Press, 2001).

34. Schultz, Samuel. *The Old Testament Speaks,* 5th ed. (Harper-Collins, 2000).

35. Thiele, Edwin. *The Mysterious Numbers of the Hebrew Kings,* 3d ed. (Kregel, 1994). Chronology.

36. Thompson, Thomas. *Early History of the Israelite People* (Brill, 1992).

37. Van Seters, John. *In Search of History* (Eisenbrauns, 1997). Historiography.
38. Wesselius, Jan-Wim. *The Origin of the History of Israel* (Sheffield Academic Press, 2002). Unity of Genesis–2 Kings from 440–420 B.C.E. modeled on Herodotus.
39. Wood, Leon. *A Survey of Israel's History,* rev. ed. (Zondervan, 1986).

Principal Archaeological Resources

1. Aharoni, Yohanan. *The Archaeology of the Land of Israel* (Westminster, 1982).
2. **Ben-Tor, Amnon, ed. *The Archaeology of Ancient Israel* (Yale University Press, 1992).**
3. Lance, H. Darrell. *The Old Testament and the Archaeologist* (Fortress, 1981). Introduction.
4. Mazar, Amihai. *Archaeology of the Land of the Bible 10,000– 586 B.C.E.,* vol. 1, ABRL (Doubleday, 1990).
5. **McRay, John, and Alfred Hoerth. *Bible Archaeology* (Baker, 2005).**
6. **Meyers, Eric, ed. *The Oxford Encyclopedia of Archaeology in the Near East,* 5 vols. (Oxford University Press, 1997).**
7. Millard, Alan. *Treasures from Bible Times* (Lion, 1985).
8. Moorey, P. R. S. *A Century of Biblical Archaeology* (Westminster John Knox, 1991).
   ———, ed. *The Bible and Recent Archaeology* (John Knox, 1987).
9. Rast, Walter. *Through the Ages in Palestinian Archaeology* (Trinity Press International, 1992).
10. **Stern, Ephraim. *Archaeology of the Land of the Bible,* vol. 2, ABRL (Doubleday, 2001). 737–530 B.C.**
    ———, ed. ***The New Encyclopedia of Archaeological Excavations in the Holy Land,* 4 vols. (Simon and Schuster, 1993).**

Other Archaeological Resources

1. Athas, George. *The Tel Dan Inscription* (Sheffield Academic Press, 2003).

2. Bahn, Paul, ed. *The Atlas of World Archaeology* (Checkmark Books, 2000).

3. ***The Biblical World in Pictures Revised Edition CD-ROM*** **(BAS, 2003).** Same categories as above at fraction of cost. More than 1,000 images with NT.
   Biblical Archaeological Review: The Archive 1975–2003 **(BAS, 2003).**
   Bible Review: The Archive 1985–2003 **(BAS, 2003).**

4. **Bolen, Todd.** ***Pictorial Library of Bible Lands*** **(Kregel, 2003).** Ten CDs—Galilee, Samaria, Jerusalem, Judah, Negev, Jordan, Egypt, Turkey, Greece, Rome. Ideal for classroom. Six thousand pictures.

5. Coogan, Michael, Cheryl Exum, and Lawrence Stager, eds. *Scripture and Other Artifacts* (Westminster John Knox, 1995).

6. Currid, John. *Doing Archaeology in the Land of the Bible* (Baker, 1999).

7. Finkelstein, Israel. *The Archaeology of the Israelite Settlement* (IES, 1988).

8. Finkelstein, Israel, and Nadav Na'aman, eds. *From Nomadism to Monarchy* (IES, 1994).

9. Fritz, Volkmar. *An Introduction to Biblical Archaeology* (Sheffield Academic Press, 1993).

10. Greenberg, Raphael. *Early Urbanizations in the Levant* (Sheffield Academic Press, 2002). Principally based on evidence from fourth to second millennium B.C. Tels Dan and Hazor.

11. **Harris, Roberta.** ***The World of the Bible*** **(Thames and Hudson, 1995).**

12. Harrison, Timothy. *Megiddo 3* (Oriental Institute, 2004).

13. Hoffmeier, James, and Alan Millard. *The Future of Biblical Archaeology* (Eerdmans, 2004).
   ———. Kaiser, Walter, and Duane Garrett, eds. *The NIV Archaeological Study Bible* (Zondervan, 2006).

14. **King, Philip.** ***Amos, Hosea, Micah: An Archaeological Commentary*** **(Westminster, 1988).**
   ———. ***Jeremiah*** **(Westminster John Knox, 1993).**

15. Levy, Thomas, ed. *The Archaeology of Society in the Holy Land* (Sheffield/Continuum, 1998).
16. Negev, Abraham, ed. (revised by Shimon Gibson). *The Archaeological Encyclopedia of the Holy Land,* 3d ed. (Continuum, 2001).
17. *NIV Archaeological Study Bible* (Zondervan, 2006).
18. *Ritmeyer Archaeological Slides* (Ritmeyer Archaeological Design, 1999). From Sinai to Sakhra, Alec Garrard's Model of the Second Temple (thirty-six slides each), and The Archaeology of Herod's Temple Mount (sixty slides).
19. Schoville, Keith. *Biblical Archaeology in Focus* (Baker, 1978).
20. Shanks, Hershel, and Dan Cole, eds. *Archaeology and the Bible: The Best of Biblical Archaeological Review* (BAS, 1990).
21. Ussishkin, David. *The Renewed Archaeological Excavations at Lachish,* 5 vols. (Tel Aviv University Press, 2004).
22. *Zondervan Image Archives* (Zondervan). Five thousand photos of the Holy Land, Egypt, and Greece on CD.

Jerusalem

1. Ariel, Israel, and Chaim Richman. *Carta's Illustrated Encyclopedia of the Holy Temple in Jerusalem* (Carta, 2005).
2. Auld, Graeme, and Margreet Steiner. *Cities of the Biblical World: Jerusalem,* vol. 1 (Mercer, 1996).
3. Bahat, Dan. *The Illustrated Atlas of Jerusalem* (Simon & Schuster, 1990).
   ———. Carta's *Historical Atlas of Jerusalem* (Carta, 2004).
4. Ben-Dov, Meir. *Jerusalem* (Modan, 1990).
   ———. *Historical Atlas of Jerusalem* (Continuum, 2002). Also provides a highly readable historical and archaeological overview of the city's history.
5. Eliav, Yaron. *God's Mountain: The Temple Mount in Time, Place, and Memory* (Johns Hopkins University Press, 2005).
6. Hess, Richard, and Gordon Wenham, eds. *Zion, City of God* (Eerdmans, 1999). History, religion, and theology of Jerusalem.

7. Hill, Geva, ed. *Ancient Jerusalem Revealed* (IES, 1994).
8. Kaufman, Asher. *The Temple of Jerusalem*, Part 3 (Year'ah, 2004).
9. Levine, Lee, ed. *Jerusalem* (Continuum, 1999). Covers ancient-modern land forms.

———. *Jerusalem: Portrait of the City in the Second Temple Period (538 B.C.E.–70 C.E.)* (JPS, 2002).

10. Mare, Harold. *The Archaeology of the Jerusalem Area* (Baker, 1987; Wipf & Stock, 2002).
11. Poorthuis, M., and S. Safrai, eds. *The Centrality of Jerusalem* (Kok Pharos, 1996).
12. Ritmeyer, Leen, and Kathleen Ritmeyer. *Jerusalem in 30 A.D.* (Carta, 2004). Atlas.

———. *Jerusalem in the Time of Nehemiah* (Carta, 2005). Atlas.

13. Thompson, Thomas, ed. *Jerusalem in Ancient History and Tradition* (T & T Clark, 2004).
14. Vaughn, Andrew, and Anne Killebrew, eds. *Jerusalem in Bible and Archaeology: The First Temple Period* (SBL, 2003).

General Manners and Customs References

1. Barton, John. *The Biblical World* (Routledge, 2002).
2. **Deist, Ferdinand. *The Material Culture of the Bible* (Sheffield Academic Press, 2000).**
3. Gower, Ralph. *The New Manners and Customs of Bible Times* (Moody, 1987).
4. **King, Philip, and Lawrence Stager. *Life in Biblical Israel* (Westminster John Knox, 2001).** An enormously attractive, glossy, and erudite survey of archaeological history as it relates to the common man in ancient Israel, replete with photographs, illustrations, and maps. Highly recommended.
5. Vos, Howard. *Nelson's New Illustrated Bible Manners and Customs* (Thomas Nelson, 1999). Excellent bibliography.
6. *See* Old Testament Background: Primary References.

Daily Life

1. Borowski, Oded. *Life in Biblical Times* (SBL, 2003).
   ———. *Every Living Thing: Daily Use of Animals in Ancient Israel* (AltaMira, 1998).
2. Braun, Joachim. *Music in Ancient Israel/Palestine* (Eerdmans, 2002).
3. Crenshaw, James. *Education in Ancient Israel*. ABRL (Doubleday, 1998).
4. **Hess, Richard, and Daniel Carroll, eds. *The Family in the Bible* (Baker, 2003).**
5. **Perdue, Leo, et al. *Families in Ancient Israel* (Westminster John Knox, 1997).**
6. Walsh, Carey. *The Fruit of the Vine: Viticulture in Ancient Israel* (Eisenbrauns, 2000).

Social Background

1. **Berquist, Jon. *Judaism in Persia's Shadow* (Fortress, 1995).**
2. **Carroll R., M. Daniel, ed. *Rethinking Contexts, Reading Texts* (Sheffield Academic Press, 2000).**
3. Carter, Charles, and Carol Meyers, eds. *Community, Identity, and Ideology* (Eisenbrauns, 1996).
4. Chalcraft, David, ed. *Social-Scientific Old Testament Criticism* (Sheffield Academic Press, 1997). JSOT compendium.
5. **Clements, Ronald. *The World of Ancient Israel* (Cambridge University Press, 1989).**
6. **Cross, Frank. *From Epic to Canon* (John Hopkins University Press, 1998).**
7. **Esler, Philip, ed. *Ancient Israel: The Old Testament in Its Social Context* (Fortress, 2005).**
8. Gordon, R. P., and J. C. de Moor, eds. *The Old Testament in Its World* (Brill, 2005).
9. Gottwald, Norman. *The Hebrew Bible* (Fortress, 1985).
   ———. *The Politics of Ancient Israel* (Westminster John Knox, 1998).

10. **Hugenberger, Gordon.** *Marriage as Covenant* **(Baker, 1998).** Especially Malachi 2.

11. Matthews, Victor. *Social World of the Hebrew Prophets* (Hendrickson, 2001).

12. **Matthews, Victor, and Don Benjamin.** *Social World of Ancient Israel, 1250–587 B.C.E.* **(Hendrickson, 1993).**

13. McNutt, Paula. *Reconstructing the Society of Ancient Israel* (Westminster John Knox, 1999).

14. **Meyers, Carol.** *Women in Scripture* **(Eerdmans, 2001).**

15. **Overholt, Thomas.** *Cultural Anthropology and the Old Testament* **(Fortress, 1996).** Application to prophets.

16. Pleins, David. *The Social Visions of the Hebrew Bible* (Westminster John Knox, 2000).

17. Roaf, Michael. *Cultural Atlas of Mesopotamia and the Ancient Near East* (Facts on File, 1990).

18. Weinfeld, Moshe. *Social Justice in Ancient Israel and in the Ancient Near East* (Fortress, 1995).

19. Wright, Christopher. *God's People in God's Land* (Eerdmans, 1990).

Religious Background[1]

1. Blenkinsopp, Joseph. *Sage, Priest, Prophet* (Westminster John Knox, 1995).

2. Brueggemann, Walter. *Worship in Ancient Israel* (Abingdon, 2005).

3. Cook, Stephen. *The Social Roots of Biblical Yahwism* (SBL, 2004).

4. Dearman, Andrew. *Religion and Culture in Ancient Israel* (Hendrickson, 1992).

5. de Moor, Jacobus. *The Rise of Yahwism* (Peeters, 1990). Important monotheistic perspective.

6. Edelman, Diana. *The Triumph of Elohim* (Eerdmans, 1995).

---

1. I am indebted to the "Annotated Old Testament Bibliography" of Drs. M. Daniel Carroll R. and Richard Hess (*Denver Journal* 5, no. 0101 [2002]) for several of the suggestions here.

7. Gnuse, Robert. *No Other Gods* (Sheffield Academic Press, 1997).

8. Grabbe, Lester. *Priests, Prophets, Diviners, Sages* (Trinity Press International, 1995).

9. Henshaw, Richard. *Female and Male: The Cultic Personnel* (Pickwick, 1994).

10. Keel, Othmar, and Christoph Uehlinger. *Gods, Goddesses, and Images of God in Ancient Israel* (Fortress, 1998). Archaeological evidence.

11. Mettinger, Tryggve. *No Graven Image?* (Almqvist and Wiksell, 1995). ANE aniconism.

12. Miller, Patrick. *The Religion of Ancient Israel* (Westminster John Knox, 2000).

13. Niditch, Susan. *Ancient Israelite Religion* (Oxford University Press, 1997).

14. Schmidt, Brian. *Israel's Beneficent Dead* (Eisenbrauns, 1996).

15. Smith, Mark. *The Origins of Biblical Monotheism* (Oxford University Press, 2001).
    ————. *The Early History of God,* 2d ed. (Eerdmans, 2002). Convergence of deities.

16. Tigay, Jeffrey. *You Shall Have No Other Gods* (Scholars, 1987). Monotheism present throughout monarchy.

17. Van der Toorn, Karel. *The Image and the Book* (Peeters, 1997).
    ————. *Family Religion in Babylonia, Syria and Israel* (Brill, 1996). Ancestor worship versus monotheism.
    ————, et al., eds. *Dictionary of Deities and Demons in the Bible,* 2d ed. (Brill, 1998).

18. Zevit, Ziony. *The Religions of Ancient Israel* (Continuum, 2001). 1200–586 B.C.

6

ANCIENT NEAR EASTERN HISTORY

General References

1. Averbeck, Richard, Mark Chavalas, and David Weisberg, eds. *Life and Culture in the Ancient Near East* (CDL, 2003).
2. **Bienkowski, Piotr, and Alan Millard, eds. *Dictionary of the Ancient Near East* (University of Pennsylvania, 2000).** Ancient–539 B.C.
3. Bosworth, A. *Conquest and Empire: The Reign of Alexander the Great* (Cambridge University Press, 1988).
4. Finley, Moses. *Economy and Society in Ancient Greece* (Penguin, 1983).
5. Frankfort, Henri. *The Art and Architecture of the Ancient Orient,* 5th ed. (Yale University Press, 1996).
6. Gordon, Cyrus, and Gary Rendsburg. *The Bible and the Ancient Near East,* 4th ed. (Norton, 1997).
7. **Hallo, William, and William Simpson. *The Ancient Near East,* 2d ed. (Harcourt Brace, 1998).**
8. **Hillard, T., et al., eds. *Ancient History in a Modern University,* vol. 1 (Eerdmans, 1997).**
9. **Hoerth, Alfred, Gerald Mattingly, and Edwin Yamauchi, eds. *Peoples of the Old Testament World* (Baker, 1994).**
10. Johnston, Sarah Iles, ed. *Religions of the Ancient World* (Harvard University Press, 2004).
11. **Kuhrt, Amelie. *The Ancient Near East: 3000–300 B.C.,* 2 vols. (Routledge, 1995).**
12. Launderville, Dale. *Piety and Politics in Ancient Greece, Israel, and Mesopotamia* (Eerdmans, 2003).

13. Nissinen, Martti. *Prophets and Prophecy in the Ancient Near East* (SBL, 2003).
14. Roberts, J. M. *Ancient History* (Oxford University Press, 2004).
15. **Sasson, Jack, ed. *Civilizations of the Ancient Near East*, 4 vols. (Hendrickson, 2001).**
16. Slater, Elizabeth, et al., eds. *Writing and Ancient Near East Society* (T & T Clark, 2005). Alan R. Millard tribute.
17. Snell, Daniel. *Life in the Ancient Near East* (Yale University Press, 1997).
18. **Van der Mieroop, Marc. *A History of the Ancient Near East*, 2d ed. (Blackwell, 2006).**
19. **Von Soden, Wolfram. *The Ancient Orient* (Eerdmans, 1994).**
20. **Wiseman, Donald, ed. *People of Old Testament Times* (Oxford University Press, 1973).**

Aramaeans

1. Daviau, Michèle, et al., eds. *The World of the Aramaeans*, 2 vols. (Sheffield Academic Press, 2001).
2. Lipinski, Edward. *The Aramaeans* (Peeters, 2000).
3. Pitard, Wayne. *Ancient Damascus* (Eisenbrauns, 1987).

Babylon, Mesopotamia, and Sumeria

1. Arnold, Bill. *Who Were the Babylonians?* (SBL, 2004).
2. Bertman, Stephen. *Handbook to Life in Ancient Mesopotamia* (Oxford, 2005).
3. Black, Jeremy, and Anthony Green. *Gods, Demons, and Symbols of Ancient Mesopotamia: An Illustrated Dictionary* (British Museum, 1992).
4. **Bottéro, Jean. *Mesopotamia* (The University of Chicago Press, 1992).**
———. *Everyday Life in Ancient Mesopotamia* (Johns Hopkins University Press, 2001).
———. *Religion in Ancient Mesopotamia* (University Press of Chicago, 2001).

5. **Chavalas, Mark, and Lawson Younger, eds.** *Mesopotamia and the Bible* **(Baker, 2002).**

6. Crawford, Harriet. *Sumer and the Sumerians* (Cambridge University Press, 1991).

7. Dalley, Stephanie, ed. *The Legacy of Mesopotamia* (Oxford University Press, 1997). Spread of culture through literature to Palestine, Egypt, and Greece.

8. Hunt, Norman. *Historical Atlas of Ancient Mesopotamia* (Checkmark, 2004).

9. Kramer, Samuel. *The Sumerians* (University of Chicago Press, 1963).

10. Leick, Gwendolyn. *Mesopotamia* (Penguin, 2003). Introduction.

11. Michalowski, P. *Letters from Early Mesopotamia* (Scholars, 1993).

12. **Nemet-Nejat, Karen.** *Daily Life in Ancient Mesopotamia* **(Hendrickson, 2002).**

13. **Oates, Joan.** *Babylon,* **rev. ed. (Thames and Hudson, 1986).**

14. **Oppenheim, Leo.** *Ancient Mesopotamia,* **rev. ed. (The University of Chicago Press, 1977).**

15. Pollock, S. *Ancient Mesopotamia* (Cambridge University Press, 1999). Introductory.

16. Postgate, J. *Early Mesopotamia* (Routledge, 1992).

17. Roux, George. *Ancient Iraq,* 3d ed. (Penguin, 1992).

18. **Saggs, H.** *The Greatness That Was Babylon,* **rev. ed. (St. Martin's, 1988).**
———. *The Might That Was Assyria* **(St. Martin's, 1990).**

19. Van DeMieroop, Marc. *The Ancient Mesopotamian City* (Oxford University Press, 1998).
———. *King Hammurabi of Babylon* (Blackwell, 2005).

20. **Wiseman, Donald.** *Nebuchadnezzar and Babylon* **(Oxford University Press, 1985).**

Egypt

1. **Aldred, Cyril.** *The Egyptians,* **3d ed. (Thames and Hudson, 1998).**
2. **Aling, Charles.** *Egypt and Bible History: From Earliest Times to 1000 B.C.* **(Baker, 1981).**
3. Baines, John, and Jaromir Malek. *Cultural Atlas of Ancient Egypt,* rev. ed. (Checkmark Books, 2000).
4. Bierbrier, Morris. *Historical Dictionary of Ancient Egypt* (Scarecrow, 1999).
5. Bowman, A. *Egypt after the Ptolemies* (University of California, 1986). 332 B.C.–A.D. 642.
6. **Currid, John.** *Ancient Egypt and the Old Testament* **(Baker, 1997).**
7. Davies, Gordon. *Israel in Egypt* (Sheffield Academic Press, 1992).
8. Emery, Walter. *Archaic Egypt* (Penguin, 1987).
9. Fagan, Brian. *The Rape of the Nile* (Moyer Bell, 1992).
10. Grimal, Nicolas. *A History of Ancient Egypt* (Blackwell, 1992).
11. Hoffmeier, James. *Israel in Egypt* (Oxford University Press, 1997).
12. **Kemp, Barry.** *Ancient Egypt,* **2d ed. (Routledge, 1992).**
13. Kitchen, Kenneth. *Pharaoh Triumphant* (Aris and Phillips, 1982). Rameses II.
14. Knoppers, Gary, and Antoine Hirsch, eds. *Egypt, Israel and the Ancient Mediterranean World* (Brill, 2004). Redford tribute.
15. Manley, Bill, ed. *The Penguin Historical Atlas of Ancient Egypt* (Penguin, 1996).
16. Murnane, W. *The Penguin Guide to Ancient Egypt,* 2d ed. (Penguin, 1996).
17. **Rainey, A., ed.** *Egypt, Israel, Sinai* **(Tel Aviv University Press, 1987).**
18. **Redford, Donald.** *Egypt, Canaan, and Israel in Ancient Times* **(Princeton University Press, 1992).**

————, ed. *The Oxford Encyclopedia of Ancient Egypt,* **3 vols. (Oxford University Press, 2000).**

19. Robins, Gay. *Women in Ancient Egypt* (Harvard University Press, 1993).

20. Shafer, Byron, ed. *Religion in Ancient Egypt* (Cornell University Press, 1991).

21. Shaw, Ian, and Paul Nicholson. *British Museum Dictionary of Ancient Egypt* (British Museum, 1995).

Hittites

1. Bryce, Trevor. *Life and Society in the Hittite World* (Oxford University Press, 2002).

2. Gurney, O. *The Hittites,* rev. ed. (Penguin, 1991).

3. MacQueen, J. G. *The Hittites* (Thames and Hudson, 1996).

Persia

1. **Briant, Pierre. *From Cyrus to Alexander,* E. T. (Eisenbrauns, 2002).**

2. Cook, John. *The Persian Empire* (Schocken, 1983).

3. Lindsay, Allen. *The Persian Empire* (University Press of Chicago, 2005).

4. Wieserhofer, A. *Ancient Persia from 550 B.C. to A.D. 650* (St. Martin's, 1998).

5. **Yamauchi, Edwin. *Persia and the Bible* (Baker, 1990).**

Philistines

1. **Bierling, Neal. *Giving Goliath His Due* (Baker, 1992).**

2. **Dothan, Trude, and Moshe Dothan. *People of the Sea* (Macmillan, 1992).**

3. Ehrlich, C. *The Philistines in Tradition* (Brill, 1996).

4. Gitin, Seymour, Amihai Mazar, and Ephraim Stern, eds. *Mediterranean Peoples in Transition* (IES, 1998).

5. Margalith, O. *The Sea Peoples in the Bible* (Harrassowitz, 1994).

6. **Sandars, N. K. *The Sea Peoples* (Thames and Hudson, 1978).**

Ugaritic Studies

1. **Smith, Mark.** *Untold Stories* **(Hendrickson, 2001).** Ugaritic studies.
2. Watson, W., and Nicolas Wyatt. *Handbook of Ugaritic Studies* (Brill, 1999). Study of archaeology, socioreligious background, and texts.
3. Yon, M. *The City of Ugarit at Tell Ras Shamra* (Eisenbrauns, 1999).

7

NEW TESTAMENT INTRODUCTION, SURVEY, AND THEOLOGY

New Testament Introduction

1. Carson, D. A., and Douglas Moo. *An Introduction to the New Testament,* 2d ed. (Zondervan, 2005).

2. DeSilva, David. *An Introduction to the New Testament* (IVP, 2004).

3. **Guthrie, Donald. *New Testament Introduction,* 4th ed. (IVP, 1990).**

4. **McDonald, Lee, and Stanley Porter. *Early Christianity and Its Sacred Literature* (Hendrickson, 2000).**

5. Metzger, Bruce. *The New Testament: Its Background, Growth, and Content,* 3d ed. (Abingdon, 2003).

New Testament Survey*

1. Achtemeier, Paul, Joel Green, and Marianne Meye Thompson. *Introducing the New Testament* (Eerdmans, 2001).

2. Bailey, Mark, and Tom Constable. *Nelson's New Testament Survey* (Thomas Nelson, 2003).

3. **Elwell, Walter, and Robert Yarbrough. *Encountering the New Testament* (Baker, 1998).** Includes multimedia, interactive CD-ROM (for companion reader, *see* p. 204).

4. Gundry, Robert. *A Survey of the New Testament,* 4th ed. (Zondervan, 2003).

---

* Forthcoming: Michael Wilkins and Alan Hultberg, *Invitation to the New Testament* (Kregel).

5. Lea, Thomas, and David Alan Black. *The New Testament,* 2d ed. (Broadman & Holman, 2003).

Sectional Survey

1. **Blomberg, Craig.** *From Pentecost to Patmos* **(B & H Publishing Group, 2006).**

    ———. *Jesus and the Gospels* **(Broadman & Holman, 1997).**

2. **Gorman, Michael.** *Apostle of the Crucified Lord* **(Eerdmans, 2003).** Pauline intro.

3. Marshall, I. Howard, Stephen Travis, and Ian Paul. *Exploring the New Testament,* vol. 2 (IVP, 2002). Paul's epistles through Revelation.

4. **Polhill, John.** *Paul and His Letters* **(Broadman & Holman, 1999).**

5. Wenham, David, and Steve Walton. *Exploring the New Testament,* vol. 1 (IVP, 2001). Gospels and Acts.

Critical Introduction

1. **Brown, Raymond E.** *Introduction to the New Testament,* **ABRL (Doubleday, 1997).** Massive.

2. Brown, Schuyler. *The Origins of Christianity: A Historical Introduction to the New Testament,* rev. ed. (Oxford University Press, 1993).

3. Childs, Brevard. *The New Testament as Canon: An Introduction,* rev. ed. (Trinity Press International, 1994). History of research.

4. Ehrman, Bart. *A Brief Introduction to the New Testament* (Oxford University Press, 2004). College-level.

    ———. *The New Testament: A Historical Introduction to the Early Christian Writings,* **3d ed. (Oxford University Press, 2003).** Advanced college level (for companion reader *see* p. 203).

5. Holladay, Carl. *A Critical Introduction to the New Testament* (Abingdon, 2005).

6. **Johnson, Luke.** *The Writings of the New Testament: An Interpretation,* **rev. ed. (Fortress, 1999).** With CD-ROM.
7. Kee, Howard. *Understanding the New Testament,* 5th ed. (Prentice-Hall, 1993). Especially gospels, socioliterary context.
8. Koester, Helmut. *Introduction to the New Testament,* 2d ed., 2 vols. (de Gruyter, 1995–2000). Especially Hellenistic background.
9. Kümmel, W. *Introduction to the New Testament,* rev. and enl. (Abingdon, 1986).
10. Perkins, Pheme. *Reading the New Testament: An Introduction,* rev. ed. (Paulist, 1988).
11. Powell, Mark. *Fortress Introduction to the Gospels* (Fortress, 1997).
12. Reddish, Mitchell. *An Introduction to the Gospels* (Abingdon, 1997). College level, including noncanonical writings, historical Jesus.
13. Schnelle, Udo. *The History and Theology of New Testament Writings* (Fortress, 1998).

New Testament Theology[*]

1. Adam, A. *Making Sense of New Testament Theology* (Mercer University Press, 1995).
2. Balla, Peter. *Challenges to New Testament Theology* (Mohr, 1997; Hendrickson, 1998).
3. Caird, G. B. *New Testament Theology* (Oxford University Press, 1996).
4. **Goppelt, Leonard.** *Theology of the New Testament,* **2 vols. (Eerdmans, 1981–83).** Salvation history.
5. **Guthrie, Donald.** *New Testament Theology* **(IVP, 1981).**
6. **Ladd, George.** *A Theology of the New Testament,* **2d ed. (Eerdmans, 1993).**
7. **Marshall, I. Howard.** *New Testament Theology* **(IVP, 2004).**
8. Räisänen, Heikki. *Beyond New Testament Theology,* 2d ed. (SCM, 2000).

---

[*] Forthcoming: Gregory Beale is also working on a full-blown theology.

9. Rowland, Christopher, and Christopher Tuckett, eds. *The Nature of New Testament Theology* (Blackwell, 2005).

10. Schlatter, Adolf. *New Testament Theology,* 2 vols. (Baker, 1999).

11. Strecker, Georg. *Theology of the New Testament* (Westminster John Knox, 2001). From German (1994).

12. Thielman, Frank. *Theology of the New Testament* (Zondervan, 2005).

13. Wright, N. T. *Jesus and the Victory of God* (Fortress, 1996).

———. *The New Testament and the People of God* (Fortress, 1992).

———. *The Resurrection of the Son of God* (Fortress, 2003).

14. Yarbrough, Robert. *The Salvation-Historical Fallacy?* (DEO, 2004).

15. *See* OT Introduction, Survey, and Theology: Biblical Theologies of Both Testaments.

Pauline Theology[*]

1. Barrett, C. K. *Paul* (Westminster John Knox, 1994). Introduction.

2. Bassler, Jouette, David Hay, and Elizabeth Johnson, eds. *Pauline Theology,* 3 vols. (Fortress, 1991–95). Critical.

3. Bruce, F. F. *Paul* (Eerdmans, 1977).

4. Burke, Trevor. *Adopted into God's Family* (IVP, 2006).

5. Carter, T. L. *Paul and the Power of Sin* (Cambridge University Press, 2002).

6. Dunn, James. *The Theology of Paul the Apostle* (Eerdmans, 1998).

7. Fitzmyer, Joseph. *According to Paul* (Paulist, 1993).

8. Hubbard, Moyer. *New Creation of Paul's Letters and Thought* (Cambridge University Press, 2002). Especially 2 Corinthians and Galatians.

---

[*] Forthcoming: Victor Furnish is producing a Pauline theology for the NTL series (Westminster John Knox).

9. Lovering, Eugene, and Jerry Sumney, eds. *Theology and Ethics in Paul and His Interpreters* (Abingdon, 1996).

10. Martyn, J. Louis. *Theological Issues in the Letters of Paul* (Abingdon, 1997).

11. Pao, David. *Thanksgiving: An Investigation of a Pauline Theme* (IVP, 2003).

12. Pate, Marvin. *The End of the Age Has Come* (Zondervan, 1995).

13. Reymond, Robert. *Paul* (Christian Focus, 2000).

14. Ridderbos, Herman. *Paul* (Eerdmans, 1997).

15. Schreiner, Thomas. *Paul, Apostle of God's Glory in Christ* (IVP, 2001).

16. Strom, Mark. *Reframing Paul* (IVP, 2000).

17. White, John. *Apostle of God* (Hendrickson, 1999).

18. Wiles, Virginia. *Making Sense of Paul* (Hendrickson, 2000). Introduction.

19. Witherington, Ben. *Paul's Narrative Thought World* (Westminster John Knox, 1994).

Paul and the Law

1. Bell, Richard. *No One Seeks for God* (Mohr, 1998).

2. Boers, Hendrikus. *The Justification of the Gentiles* (Hendrickson, 1994). Galatians and Romans, discourse analysis, semiotics.

3. Carson, D. A., Peter O'Brien, and Mark Seifrid, eds. *Justification and Variegated Nomism*, 2 vols. (Mohr/Baker, 2001–02). Response to Sanders.

4. Cummins, Stephen. *Paul and the Crucified Christ in Antioch* (Cambridge University Press, 2001). Both Judaizers and Paul influenced by ideals of Maccabean martyrdom.

5. Das, Andrew. *Paul, the Law, and the Covenant* (Hendrickson, 2001).
   ———. *Paul and the Jews* (Hendrickson, 2004).

6. Donaldson, Terence. *Paul and the Gentiles* (Fortress, 1997).

7. Dunn, James. *Jesus, Paul, and the Law: Studies in Mark and Galatians* (Westminster John Knox, 1990).

————, ed. *Paul and the Mosaic Law* **(Eerdmans, 2001).**

8. Eastman, Brad. *The Significance of Grace in the Letters of Paul* (Lang, 1999).

9. **Elliot, Mark. *The Survivors of Israel* (Eerdmans, 2000).** Sanders corrective.

10. **Gathercole, Simon. *Where Is Boasting?* (Eerdmans, 2002).** Romans 1–5. Dunn critique by Dunn student.

11. Goulder, Michael. *Paul and the Competing Mission in Corinth* (Hendrickson, 2001). Two-mission theory.

12. **Kim, Seyoon. *Paul and the New Perspective* (Eerdmans, 2001).** Rebuttal of Sanders.

13. Koperski, Veronica. *What Are They Saying About Paul and the Law?* (Paulist, 2001).

14. **Kruse, Colin. *Paul, the Law, and Justification* (Hendrickson, 1997).** Recent debate.

15. Laato, Timo. *Paul and Judaism* (Scholars, 1995).

16. Moore, Richard. *The Doctrine of "Justification" in Paul* (Mellen, 2002).

17. Pate, Marvin. *The Reverse of the Curse* (Mohr, 2000). Wisdom as reverse of Deuteronomic blessings and curses.

18. Rapa, Robert. *The Meaning of "Works of the Law" in Galatians and Romans* (Lang, 2001).

19. **Sanders, E. P. *Paul and Palestinian Judaism* (Fortress, 1977).** Law = covenant keeping.

    ————. ***Paul, the Law, and the Jewish People* (Fortress, 1983).**

20. **Schreiner, Thomas. *The Law and Its Fulfillment* (Baker, 1993).**

21. Seifrid, Mark. *Justification by Faith* (Brill, 1992).

22. Stuhlmacher, Peter. *Revisiting Paul's Doctrine of Justification* (IVP, 2001).

23. **Thielman, Frank. *Paul and the Law* (IVP, 1994).** Rebuttal of Dunn, Sanders.

    ————. ***The Law and the New Testament,* CCNT (Herder and Herder, 1999).** Introduction, includes Gospels and Acts.

24. Tomson, Paul. *Paul and the Jewish Law* (Van Gorcum/Fortress, 1990).

25. Vanlandingham, Chris. *Judgment and Justification in Early Judaism and the Apostle Paul* (Hendrickson, 2005).

26. Van Spanje, T. E. *Inconsistency in Paul?* (Mohr, 1999). Heikki Räisänen critique.

27. Waters, Guy. *Justification and the New Perspectives on Paul* (Presbyterian & Reformed, 2004).

28. Westerholm, Stephen. *Israel's Law and the Church's Faith* (Eerdmans, 1988).

29. Wright, N. T. *What Saint Paul Really Said* (Eerdmans, 1997).

30. Young, Brad. *Paul the Jewish Theologian* (Hendrickson, 1997).

8

JESUS AND THE GOSPELS

Synoptics

1. Barr, Allan. *A Diagram of Synoptic Relationships* (T & T Clark, 1938).

2. **Black, David, and David Beck, eds. *Rethinking the Synoptic Problem* (Baker, 2001).** McKnight, Farmer, Osborne, Blomberg, and Bock.

3. Head, Peter. *Christology and the Synoptic Problem* (Cambridge University Press, 1997).

4. Hengel, Martin. *The Four Gospels and the One Gospel of Jesus* (Trinity Press International, 2000).

5. Knight, George W. *A Simplified Harmony of the Gospels* (Holman Bible Publishers, 2001). Sequential HCSB.

6. Koester, Helmut. *Ancient Christian Gospels* (Trinity Press International, 1990). Including Q.

7. **McKnight, Scot. *Interpreting the Synoptic Gospels* (Baker, 1988).**

8. Nickle, Keith. *The Synoptic Gospels*, 2d ed. (Westminster John Knox, 2001).

9. **Orton, David, ed. *The Synoptic Problem and Q* (Brill, 1999).**

10. Paffenroth, Kim. *The Story of Jesus According to L* (Sheffield Academic Press, 1997).

11. Theissen, Gerd. *The Gospels in Context* (Fortress, 1991).

12. Thomas, Robert, ed. *Three Views on the Origins of the Synoptic Gospels* (Kregel, 2002). Grant Osborne and Matthew

Williams: Markan priority; John Niemelä: Two-Gospel theory; David Farnell defends Independent view.

Synoptic Problem
Two-Source (Two-Document) Hypothesis
(Markan Priority and Q)

1. **Bellinzoni, Arthur, ed.** *The Two-Source Hypothesis* **(Mercer University Press, 1985).**

2. Fleddermann, H. *Mark and Q* (Leuven University Press, 1995).

3. **Neville, David.** *Arguments from Order in Synoptic Source Criticism* **(Mercer University Press, 1994).**
———. *Mark's Gospel Prior or Posterior?* **(Sheffield Academic Press, 2002).**

4. New, David. *Old Testament Quotations in the Synoptic Gospels and the Two-Document Hypothesis* (Scholars, 1993).

5. **Stein, Robert.** *Studying the Synoptic Gospels*, **2d ed. (Baker, 2001).**

6. **Tuckett, Christopher.** *Q and the History of Earliest Christianity* **(Hendrickson, 1996).** Wisdom sayings, Cynic influence.

7. **Williams, Matthew.** *Two Gospels from One* **(Kregel, 2006).** Extensive text-critical analysis.

Farrer-Goulder Hypothesis
(Markan Priority sans Q)

1. Goodacre, Mark. *Goulder and the Gospels* (Sheffield Academic Press, 1996).
———. *The Synoptic Problem* (T & T Clark, 2004).

2. Goodacre, Mark, and Nicholas Perrin, eds. *Questioning Q* (IVP, 2005).

3. Goulder, Michael. *Luke: A New Paradigm*, 2 vols. (Sheffield Academic Press, 1989).

4. Sanders, E. P., and Margaret Davies, eds. *Studying the Synoptic Gospels* (Trinity Press International, 1989).

Matthean Priority

1. **Black, David.** *Why Four Gospels?* **(Kregel, 2001).** Provides alternative to Oxford-Griesbach debate.
2. Dungan, David. *A History of the Synoptic Problem,* ABRL (Doubleday, 1999). Assumes anti-Semitism in Markan priority and NA[27] text.
3. Farmer, William. *The Gospel of Jesus* (Westminster John Knox, 1994).
4. Johnson, Sherman. *The Griesbach Hypothesis and Redaction Criticism* (Scholars, 1991).
5. McNicol, Allan. *Jesus' Direction for the Future* (Mercer University Press, 1996). Examination of Paul/Jesus eschatological tradition.
6. **McNicol, Allan, David Dungan, and David Peabody, eds. *Beyond the Q Impasse* (Trinity Press International, 1996).**
7. Neirynck, Frans. *The Minor Agreements of Matthew and Luke Against Mark with a Cumulative List* (Leuven University Press, 1974).
8. Neirynck, Frans, and J. Verhayden. *The Gospel of Matthew and Sayings Source Q: A Cumulative Bibliography,* 2 vols. (Leuven University Press, 1998).
9. **Orchard, Bernard, and Harold Riley. *The Order of the Synoptics* (Mercer University Press, 1987).** Especially patristic evidence.
10. Peabody, David, ed. *One Gospel from Two: Mark's Use of Matthew and Luke* (Trinity Press International, 2001).
11. **Tuckett, Christopher. *The Revival of the Griesbach Hypothesis* (Cambridge University Press, 1983).** Two-source proponent.

Nondocumentary Hypothesis

1. Burkett, Delbert. *Rethinking the Gospel Sources* (T & T Clark, 2004). Proto-Mark.
2. Farnell, David. *Backgrounds to the New Testament.* (Christian Focus Publications/Mentor, 2005).

3. Gerhardsson, Birger. *Memory and Manuscript* (Eerdmans, 1998). Posits extensive oral tradition behind gospels.

———. *The Reliability of the Gospel Tradition* **(Hendrickson, 2001).**

4. Linnemann, Eta. *Is There a Synoptic Problem?* (Baker, 1992).

5. **Wenham, David.** *Redating Matthew, Mark, and Luke* **(IVP, 1992).** Suggests essential independence with Matthew as earliest gospel based on patristic evidence.

Source Q

1. Allison, Dale. *The Jesus Tradition in Q* (Trinity Press International, 1997).

———. *The Intertextual Jesus* (Trinity Press International, 2000).

2. Borg, Marcus, ed. *The Lost Gospel Q* (Ulysses, 1996).

3. **Catchpole, David.** *The Quest for Q* **(T & T Clark, 1993).**

4. **Goodacre, Mark.** *The Case Against Q* **(Trinity Press International, 2001).** Advocates Markan priority and the lack of necessity for Q.

5. Horsley, Richard, and Jonathan Draper. *Whoever Hears You Hears Me* (Trinity Press International, 1999).

6. Jacobson, A. *The First Gospel* (Polebridge, 1992).

7. Kloppenborg, John. *The Formation of Q* (Fortress, 1987).

———. *Q Parallels.* (Polebridge, 1988).

———. *Excavating Q* (Fortress, 2000).

———, ed. *The Shape of Q* (Fortress, 1994).

———, ed. *Conflict and Invention* (Trinity Press International, 1995).

8. Labahn, Michael, and Andreas Schmidt, eds. *Jesus, Mark, and Q* (Sheffield Academic Press, 2001).

9. Lindemann, Andreas, ed. *The Saying Source Q and the Historical Jesus* (Leuven University Press, 2002).

10. Mack, Burton. *The Lost Gospel: The Book of Q and Christian Origins* (HarperSanFrancisco, 1993). Jesus as Cynic sage.

11. Meadors, Edward. *Jesus the Messianic Herald of Salvation* (Hendrickson, 1997). Q rebuttal.

12. **Piper, R., ed.** *The Gospel Behind the Gospels* **(Brill, 1995).**

13. **Robinson, James, John Kloppenborg, and Paul Hoffman.** *Critical Edition of Q,* **Hermeneia (Fortress, 2000).** Synopsis, including Mark, Luke, and Thomas.

14. Vaage, Leif. *Galilean Upstarts* (Trinity Press International, 1994). Q as Cynic document.

15. Valantasis, Richard. *The New Q* (T & T Clark, 2005). Commentary and translation of Robinson et al. above.

Historical Jesus
Conservative Historical Jesus

1. Barnett, Paul. *Jesus and the Logic of History* (Eerdmans, 1998).

2. Bauckham, Richard. *Jesus and the Eyewitnesses* (Eerdmans, 2006).

3. **Bock, Darrell.** *Jesus According to Scripture* **(Baker, 2002).**

   ———. *Studying The Historical Jesus* **(Baker, 2002).** Introduction.

   ———. *The Missing Gospels* **(Thomas Nelson, 2006).**

4. **Bockmuehl, Markus.** *This Jesus: Martyr, Lord, Messiah* **(IVP, 1996).**

5. Boice, J. M., and Philip Ryken. *Jesus on Trial* (Crossway, 2002).

6. Bryan, Steven. *Jesus and Israel's Tradition of Judgment and Restoration* (Cambridge University Press, 2002).

7. Burridge, Richard. *Four Gospels, One Jesus?* rev. ed. (Eerdmans, 2005).

8. Chilton, David, and Craig Evans. *Jesus in Context* (Brill, 1997).

9. Copan, Paul, ed. *Will the Real Jesus Please Stand Up?* (Baker, 1998). Debate between William Lane Craig and John Dominic Crossan.

10. Copan, Paul, and Ronald Tacelli, eds. *Jesus' Resurrection* (IVP, 2000). William Lane Craig versus Gerd Lüdemann debate.

11. Culver, Robert. *The Earthly Career of Jesus, the Christ* (Mentor, 2003).

12. Dunn, James. *Jesus Remembered* (Eerdmans, 2003).
————. *A New Perspective on Jesus* (Baker, 2005).

13. Evans, Craig. *Jesus and His Contemporaries* (Brill, 1995).
————. *The Historical Christ and the Jesus of Faith* (Clarendon, 1996).
————, ed. *The Historical Jesus*, 4 vols. (Routledge, 2004).
————. *Fabricating Jesus* (IVP, 2006).

14. Evans, Craig, and Stanley Porter, eds. *The Historical Jesus* (Sheffield Academic Press, 1995). Annotated bibliography.

15. Green, Joel, and Max Turner, eds. *Jesus of Nazareth* (Eerdmans, 1994; Wipf & Stock, 2000).

16. Komoszewski, J. Ed, M. James Sawyer, and Daniel B. Wallace. *Reinventing Jesus* (Kregel, 2006).

17. McClymond, Michael. *Familiar Stranger* (Eerdmans, 2004). Summation of quests.

18. McKnight, Scot. *A New Vision for Israel* (Eerdmans, 1999).

19. Reymond, Robert. *Jesus, Divine Messiah* (Mentor, 2003).

20. Seccombe, David. *The King of God's Kingdom* (Paternoster, 2003).

21. Spencer, Scott. *What Did Jesus Do?* (Trinity Press International, 2003).

22. Stein, Robert. *Jesus The Messiah* (IVP, 1996).

23. Stanton, Graham. *Gospel Truth?* (Trinity Press International, 1995). Rebuttal to Carsten Thiede.
————. ***The Gospels and Jesus*, 2d ed. (Oxford University Press, 2001).**

24. Thomas, Robert. *Charts of the Life of Christ* (Zondervan, 2000).

25. Twelftree, Graham. *Jesus the Exorcist* (Hendrickson, 1995).
————. *Jesus the Miracle Worker* (IVP, 1999).

26. Van Voorst, Robert. *Jesus Outside the New Testament* (Eerdmans, 2000).

27. Witherington, Ben. *Jesus the Sage* (Fortress, 1994).

———. *The Many Faces of the Christ*, CCNT (Crossroad, 1998).

———. *Jesus the Seer* (Hendrickson, 1999).

———. *What Have They Done to Jesus?* (HarperSanFrancisco, 2006).

28. Wright, N. T. *Who Was Jesus?* (Eerdmans, 1993).

———. *The Original Jesus* (Eerdmans, 1996).

———. *The Challenge of Jesus* (IVP, 1999).

———. *The Contemporary Quest for Jesus* (Fortress, 2002). Booklet.

———. *Judas and the Gospel of Jesus* (Baker, 2006).

Critical Historical Jesus

1. Allison, Dale. *Jesus of Nazareth* (Fortress, 1998).

———. *Resurrecting Jesus* (T & T Clark, 2005).

2. Becker, Jürgen. *Jesus of Nazareth* (de Gruyter, 1998).

3. Bellinger, William, and William Farmer, eds. *Jesus and the Suffering Servant* (Trinity Press International, 1998). Isaiah 53 influence.

4. **Bockmuehl, Markus, ed. *The Cambridge Companion to Jesus* (Cambridge University Press, 2001).**

5. Charlesworth, James, ed. *The Messiah* (Fortress, 1992).

6. Dawes, Gregory, ed. *The Historical Jesus Question* (Westminster John Knox, 2001).

———, ed. *The Historical Jesus Quest* (Westminster John Knox, 2000).

7. denHeyer, Christian. *Jesus Matters: 150 Years of Research* (Trinity Press International, 1997).

8. Ehrman, Bart. *Jesus, Apocalyptic Prophet of the New Millennium* (Oxford University Press, 1999). Believes that Jesus was convinced that a new kingdom would be created on earth.

9. Frederiksen, Paula. *Jesus of Nazareth, King of the Jews* (Knopf, 1999).

10. **Freyne, Sean. *Galilee, Jesus, and the Gospels* (Fortress, 1998).**

11. **Gnilka, Joachim.** *Jesus of Nazareth* **(Hendrickson, 1997).**
12. Hengel, Martin. *Studies in Early Christology* (T & T Clark, 1995).
13. Horsley, Richard. *Sociology and the Jesus Movement,* rev. ed. (Continuum, 1993).
14. Horsley, Richard, and Neil Silberman. *The Message and the Kingdom* (Grossett/Putnam, 1997). Jesus and Paul.
15. Houlden, J. L. *Jesus: The Complete Guide* (Continuum, 2005).
16. Keck, Leander. *Who Is Jesus?* (University of South Carolina, 2000; Fortress, 2001).
17. **Loader, William.** *Jesus' Attitude Towards the Law* **(Eerdmans, 2002).** Gospel study.
18. **Meier, John.** *A Marginal Jew,* **3 vols. (Doubleday, 1991, 1994, 2001).**
19. **Meyer, Ben.** *The Aims of Jesus* **(SCM, 1979; Pickwick, 2002).**
20. Patterson, Stephen. *The God of Jesus* (Trinity Press International, 1998).
21. Powell, Mark. *Jesus as a Figure in History* (Westminster John Knox, 1998).
22. Powell, Mark, and David Bauer, eds. *Who Do You Say That I Am?* (Westminster John Knox, 1999).
23. Reed, Jonathan. *Archaeology and the Galilean Jesus* (Trinity Press International, 2002).
24. **Sanders, E. P.** *Jesus and Judaism* **(Fortress, 1985).**
25. Schnackenburg, Rudolf. *Jesus in the Gospels* (Westminster John Knox, 1995).
26. Theissen, Gerd, and Annette Merz. *The Historical Jesus* (Fortress, 1998).
27. **Vermes, Geza.** *Jesus the Jew* **(Fortress, 1973).**
    ———. *The Changing Faces of Jesus,* **1st American ed. (Viking Compass, 2001).**
28. **Weaver, Walter.** *The Historical Jesus in the Twentieth Century,* **3 vols. (Trinity Press International, 1999–).**

Jesus Seminar

1. Armstrong, Donald, ed. *The Truth About Jesus* (Eerdmans, 1998).

2. Borg, Marcus. *Jesus in Contemporary Scholarship* (Trinity Press International, 1994).

   ———. *Conflict, Holiness, and Politics in the Teachings of Jesus,* rev. ed. (Trinity Press International, 1998).

3. Borg, Marcus, and N. T. Wright. *The Meaning of Jesus* (HarperSanFrancisco, 1999).

4. Boyd, Gregory. *Cynic Sage or Son of God?* (Baker, 1995). Response to Jesus Seminar.

5. Chilton, David, and Craig Evans, eds. *Studying the Historic Jesus* (Brill, 1994).

6. Crossan, John. *The Historical Jesus* (HarperCollins, 1991).

   ———. *Who Killed Jesus?* (HarperSanFrancisco, 1995). Popular response to Raymond Brown's *Death of the Messiah.*

   ———. *After the Crucifixion* (HarperSanFrancisco, 1996).

   ———. *Excavating Jesus* (HarperSanFrancisco, 2002).

7. Downing, Gerald. *Christ and the Cynics* (Sheffield Academic Press, 1988).

8. Funk, Robert, and Roy Hoover. *The Five Gospels* (Macmillan, 1993).

9. Horsley, Richard, and John Hanson. *Bandits, Prophets, and Messiahs* (Winston, 1987).

10. Jenkins, Philip. *Hidden Gospels* (Oxford University Press, 2001). Extracanonicals written late.

11. Johnson, Luke. *The Real Jesus* (HarperSanFrancisco, 1996). Seminar critique.

12. Mack, Burton. *Who Wrote the New Testament?* (HarperSanFrancisco, 1995).

13. Newman, Carey, ed. *Jesus and the Restoration of Israel* (IVP, 1999). Assessment of Wright (see below).

14. Radner, Ephraim, and George Sumner, eds. *The Rule of Faith* (Morehouse, 1997).

15. Sanders, E. P. *The Historical Figure of Jesus* (Penguin, 1993). Popular alternative view to Jesus Seminar.

16. **Strimple, Robert.** *The Modern Search for the Real Jesus* **(Presbyterian & Reformed, 1995).** Evangelical response to the Jesus Seminar.
17. **Wilkins, Michael, and James Moreland, eds.** *Jesus Under Fire* **(Zondervan, 1995).** Response to Jesus Seminar.
18. **Witherington, Ben.** *The Jesus Quest,* **2d ed. (IVP, 1997).**

9

NEW TESTAMENT COMMENTARIES

Matthew[*]
Technical, Semitechnical

L/Cr 1. Boring, Eugene. NIB, vol. 8 (Abingdon, 1995). Dates between A.D. 80–100.

E 2. **Carson, D. A. EBC, vol. 9, rev. ed. (Zondervan, 2005).**

C/M 3. **Davies, W. D., and Dale Allison. ICC, 3 vols. (T & T Clark, 1988–97).** Jewish, extrabiblical background.

C/M 4. Gundry, Robert. *Matthew,* 2d ed. (Eerdmans, 1994). Redactional, literary background.

E/Cr 5. **Hagner, Donald. WBC, 2 vols. (Word, 1993–95).** Occasional doubt on historicity of miracles.

E 6. Keener, Craig. *A Commentary on the Gospel of Matthew* (Eerdmans, 1999). Sociohistorical context. More than ten thousand references to primary sources and more than two thousand to secondary literature in a volume with 720 pages of commentary, 150 pages of bibliography, and almost 170 pages of indices.

L/Cr 7. Luz, Ulrich. Hermeneia, 3 vols. (Fortress, 1989–2005). Redaction critical, history of interpretation.

---

* Forthcoming: R. T. France, NICNT (Eerdmans); Rick Beaton, BNTC (Hendrickson); John Meier, AB (Doubleday); Craig Evans, NCamBC (Cambridge University Press); Grant Osborne, ZEC (Zondervan); and Jack Kingsbury, ECC (Eerdmans). France and Osborne should prove compelling alternatives to Hagner, Nolland, and Carson (rev. ed.). Blomberg is the best exposition, but Turner, CBC (Tyndale) is very good.

L/Cr 8. **Nolland, John. NIGTC (Eerdmans, 2005).** Massive.[1]

Exposition

E   1. **Blomberg, Craig. NAC (Broadman & Holman, 1992).**

C/M   2. Davies, W. D., and Dale Allison. *Matthew: A Shorter Commentary* (T & T Clark, 2005). Six hundred-page condensation of above.

E/Cr 3. **France, Richard. TNTC (Eerdmans, 1988).**

E   4. Green, Michael. BST (IVP, 2001).

L/Cr 5. Harrington, Daniel. Sacra Pagina (Liturgical, 1991). Jewish background.

E   6. Keener, Craig. IVPNTC (IVP, 1997).

E   7. Morris, Leon. PNTC (Eerdmans, 1992).

E   8. Mounce, Robert. NIBCNT (Hendrickson, 1991).

L/Cr 9. Overman, Andrew. *Church and Community in Crisis*, NTC (Trinity Press International, 1996).

L/Cr 10. Senior, Donald. ANTC (Abingdon, 1998).

E   11. Toussaint, Stanley. *Behold the King* (Kregel, 1980).

E   12. Turner, David. BECNT (Baker, 2007).

E   13. **Turner, David, and Darrell Bock. *Matthew and Mark*. CBC (Tyndale, 2006).**

E   14. Wilkins, Michael. NIVAC (Zondervan, 2004).

E   15. Witherington, Ben. SHBC (Smyth & Helwys, 2006).

Sermon on the Mount

C/M   1. Allison, Dale. *The Jesus Tradition in Q* (Trinity Press International, 1997). Includes critique of Betz.

L/Cr 2. Betz, Hans. *The Sermon on the Mount,* Hermeneia (Fortress, 1995). Especially Hellenistic Jewish, Greco-Roman background.

---

1. Nolland has risen to the challenge in response to criticism that his three-volume Luke (WBC) was essentially a compendium of other scholar's positions. In Matthew, he refers to Davies and Allison and Luz with some recourse, but inexplicably mentions Hagner only once and Carson not at all. Nevertheless, this is a standout commentary.

E 3. Carson, D. A. *Jesus' Sermon on the Mount: And His Confrontation with the World* (Baker, 2004). Two 1978 books bound together.

L/Cr 4. Carter, Warren. *What Are They Saying About Matthew's Sermon on the Mount?* (Paulist, 1994).

E/Cr **5. Guelich, Robert. *The Sermon on the Mount* (Word, 1982).**

E 6. Hughes, R. Kent. *The Sermon on the Mount* (Crossway, 2001).

L/Cr 7. Patte, Daniel. *Discipleship According to the Sermon on the Mount* (Trinity Press International, 1996). Strecker, Kingsbury (historical); Edwards (narrative); Luz, Davies, and Allison (figurative); and Patte (thematic).
———. *The Challenge of Discipleship* (Trinity Press International, 1999).

E 8. Stott, John. *The Message of the Sermon on the Mount,* BST (IVP, 1978).

L/Cr 9. Strecker, Georg. *The Sermon on the Mount* (Abingdon, 1988).

C/M 10. Talbert, Charles. *Reading the Sermon on the Mount* (University Press of S. Carolina, 2004).

L/Cr 11. Worth, Roland. *The Sermon on the Mount* (Paulist, 1997). Law validation.

Matthew as Story

E **1. Bauer, David. *The Structure of Matthew's Gospel* (Almond, 1988).**

E-L/Cr 2. Bauer, David, and Mark Powell, eds. *Treasures New and Old* (Scholars, 1996).

C/M 3. Brown, Jeannine. *The Disciples in New Perspective* (SBL, 2002).

L/Cr 4. Carter, Warren. *Matthew,* rev. ed. (Hendrickson, 2004). Reader-response, narrative-critical counterpart to France.

E/Cr **5. France, Richard. *Matthew: Evangelist and Teacher* (Zondervan, 1990; Wipf & Stock, 2004).**

E   6. Garland, David. *Reading Matthew* (Crossroad, 1993). Literary, theological commentary.

L/Cr   7. Howell, David. *Matthew's Inclusive Story* (Sheffield Academic Press, 1990).

L/Cr   8. Kingsbury, Jack. *Matthew as Story,* 2d ed. (Fortress, 1988).

Special Studies

L/Cr   1. Aune, David, ed. *The Gospel of Matthew in Current Study* (Eerdmans, 2000).

L/Cr   2. Balch, David, ed. *Social History of the Matthean Community* (Fortress, 1991).

E   3. Beaton, Richard. *Isaiah's Christ in Matthew's Gospel* (Cambridge University Press, 2002).

L/Cr   4. Brown, Raymond E. *Birth of the Messiah,* ABRL, rev. ed. (Doubleday, 1993). Nativities.
————. ***Death of the Messiah,* ABRL, 2 vols. (Doubleday, 1994).** Passion narratives.[2]

E/Cr   5. Cousland, J. R. C. *The Crowds in the Gospel of Matthew* (Brill, 2002).

E   6. Gibbs, Jeffery. *Jerusalem and Parousia* (Concordia Academic Press, 2000). Eschatological Discourse.

L/Cr   7. Luz, Ulrich. NTT (Cambridge University Press, 1995).
————. *Matthew in History* (Fortress, 1994).
————. *Studies in Matthew* (Eerdmans, 2005). Addendum to commentaries above.

L/Cr   8. Saldarini, Anthony. *Matthew's Christian-Jewish Community* (The University of Chicago Press, 1994).

L/Cr   9. Senior, Donald. IBT (Abingdon, 1997). Survey of modern scholarship.
————. *What Are They Saying About Matthew?* (Paulist, 1996).

---

2. The now-deceased Catholic scholar Raymond E. Brown is to be distinguished from the conservative Raymond Brown (author of BST entries on Numbers, Deuteronomy, Nehemiah, and Hebrews).

C/M 10. Sim, David. *Apocalyptic Eschatology in the Gospel of Matthew* (Cambridge University Press, 1996).
———. *The Gospel of Matthew and Christian Judaism* (T & T Clark, 1998).

C/M **11. Stanton, Graham. *A Gospel for a New People* (Westminster John Knox, 1993).**
———, ed. *The Interpretation of Matthew,* 2d ed. (T & T Clark, 1995).

E/Cr 12. Westerholm, Stephen. *Understanding Matthew* (Baker, 2006).

E **13. Wilkins, Michael. *Discipleship in the Ancient World and Matthew's Gospel,* 2d ed. (Baker, 1995).**

Mark[*]
Technical, Semitechnical

C/M 1. Cranfield, C. E. B. *The Gospel According to St. Mark* (Cambridge University Press, 1959).

E/Cr **2. Evans, Craig. *Mark 8:27–16:20,* WBC (Thomas Nelson, 2001).** Especially rabbinic, Greco-Roman background.

E/Cr **3. France, R. T. NIGTC (Eerdmans, 2002).[3]**

E/Cr **4. Guelich, Robert. *Mark 1:1–8:26,* WBC (Word, 1989).**

E **5. Gundry, Robert. *Mark* (Eerdmans, 1992).** Supports Mark 16:9–20 as original. Through history of interpretation.

---

[*] Forthcoming: Adele Yarbro Collins, Hermeneia (Fortress); Rikki Watts, NICNT (Eerdmans); Robert Stein, BECNT (Baker); Mark Strauss, ZEC (Zondervan); Dieter Luhrmann, Continental (Fortress); Richard Horsley, NTC (Trinity); Alan Culpepper, SHBC (Smyth & Helwys); and Ron Kernaghan, IVPNTC (IVP). Gundry and France make for an effective tandem, as Gundry frequently mines obscure exegetical details lacking in France, while France helps delineate the forest from the trees. It may be that Evans, 2 vols. (Thomas Nelson) best achieves the middle ground. You might want to wait for Stein instead of Edwards or perhaps even Watts and Strauss.

3. Son of Man's coming evident by change in heaven and made visible in temple destruction and growth of the church. Tackles by sections rather than verse-by-verse. Primarily historical/theological than exegetical.

E/Cr   6. **Lane, William. NICNT (Eerdmans, 1974).**

L/Cr   7. Mann, C. S. AB (Doubleday, 1986). Griesbach Hypothesis.

L/Cr   8. Marcus, Joel. AB (Doubleday, 2000). Liturgical drama.[4]

L/Cr   9. Perkins, Pheme. NIB, vol. 8 (Abingdon, 1995). Dates Mark around A.D. 70.

E   10. Witherington, Ben. *The Gospel of Mark* (Eerdmans, 2001). Sociorhetorical.

Exposition

L/Cr   1. Anderson, Hugh. NCBC (Eerdmans, 1981). Redactional, history of critical interpretation.

E   2. **Bock, Darrell, and David Turner. *Matthew and Mark*. CBC (Tyndale, 2006).** Bock on Mark.

E   3. Brooks, James. NAC (Broadman & Holman, 1991).

E   4. Cole, R. Alan. TNTC (Eerdmans, 1989).

L/Cr   5. Donahue, John, and Daniel Harrington. Sacra Pagina (Liturgical, 2002). Donahue: Mark 1–8; 14; Harrington, Mark 9–13; 15–16.

E/Cr   6. **Edwards, James. PNTC (Eerdmans, 2001).** Posits multiple, sandwiched textual interpolations (e.g., the cursing of the fig tree and the cleansing of the temple).

E   7. **Garland, David. NIVAC (Zondervan, 1996).**

E   8. Geddert, Timothy. BCBC (Herald, 2002).

L/Cr   9. Hare, Douglas. WBComp (Westminster John Knox, 1996). Study guide.

C/M   10. **Hooker, Morna. BNTC (Hendrickson, 1993).** Especially Jewish background.

E/Cr   11. Hurtado, Larry. NIBCNT (Hendrickson, 1989).

---

4. Marcus believes that John Mark *might* have written the gospel, and he tends to be skeptical about the historical Jesus. However, his commentary includes three brief appendices, "The Scribes and the Pharisees," "The Messianic Secret Motif," and "The Son of Man." The latter is particularly valuable, tracing its development back to Daniel.

Mark as Story

L/Cr   1.   Anderson, Janice, and Stephen Moore, eds. *Mark and Method* (Fortress, 1992). Five criticisms exemplified.

C/M   2.   Best, Ernest. *Mark: The Gospel of Story* (T & T Clark, 1983).

L/Cr   3.   Dowd, Sharon. *Reading Mark* (Smyth and Helwys, 2000).

L/Cr   4.   Fowler, Robert. *Let the Reader Understand* (Trinity Press International, 2001).

L/Cr   5.   Juel, Donald. IBT (Abingdon, 1999).

C/M   6.   Moloney, Francis. *The Gospel of Mark* (Hendrickson, 2002).

      ———. *Mark: Storyteller, Interpreter, Evangelist* (Hendrickson, 2004).

L/Cr   **7.**   **Rhoads, David, J. Dewey, and Donald Michie. *Mark as Story,* 2d ed. (Fortress, 1999).**

L/Cr   8.   Robbins, Vernon. *Jesus the Teacher* (Fortress, 1992).

E   **9.**   **Santos, Narry. *Slave of All: The Paradox of Authority and Servanthood in the Gospel of Mark* (Sheffield Academic Press, 2003).** Authority-servanthood contrast.

C/M   **10.**   **Telford, William, ed. *The Interpretation of Mark,* 2d ed. (T & T Clark, 1995).**

L/Cr   11.   Tolbert, Mary Ann. *Sowing the Gospel* (Fortress, 1989).

Special Studies

E   **1.**   **Beasley-Murray, George. *Jesus and the Last Days* (Hendrickson, 1993).** Mark 13: Olivet discourse.

L/Cr   2.   Black, Clifton. *Mark: Images of an Apostolic Interpreter* (Fortress, 2001).

E   **3.**   **Bock, Darrell. *Blasphemy and Exaltation in Judaism* (Baker, 2000).** Mark 14:53–65.

E   4.   Bolt, Peter. *The Cross from a Distance: Atonement in Mark's Gospel* (IVP, 2004).

L/Cr   5.   Garrett, Susan. *The Temptations of Jesus in Mark's Gospel* (Eerdmans, 1998).

All   6. Gaventa, Beverly, and Patrick Miller, eds. *The Endings of Mark and the Ends of God* (Westminster John Knox, 2005). Donald Juel tribute.

E   7. Geddert, Timothy. *Watchwords* (JSOT, 1989). Mark 13.

C/M   8. Hengel, Martin. *Studies in the Gospel of Mark* (SCM/ Fortress, 1985).

L/Cr   9. Marcus, Joel. *The Way of the Lord* (Westminster John Knox, 1992). Old Testament usage.

L/Cr   10. Myers, Ched. *Binding the Strong Man* (Orbis, 1988). Liberation perspective commentary.

C/M   11. Oden, Thomas, and Christopher Hall, eds. ACCS (IVP, 1998). Patristic commentary.

C/M   12. Telford, William. *The Theology of the Gospel of Mark*, NTT (Cambridge University Press, 1999).

L/Cr   13. Thurston, Bonnie. *Preaching Mark* (Fortress, 2002). Very informative.

E   14. Watts, Rikki. *Isaiah's New Exodus in Mark* (Mohr, 1997; Baker, 2000).

E   15. Williams, Joel. *Other Followers of Jesus: Minor Characters as Major Figures in Mark's Gospel* (Sheffield Academic Press, 1994).

Luke[*]
Technical, Semitechnical

E   1. Bock, Darrell. BECNT, 2 vols. (Baker, 1994–96). Reviews debated points.

---

[*] Forthcoming: François Bovon, Hermeneia, 2 vols. (Fortress); David Garland, ZEC (Zondervan); Loveday Alexander, BNTC (Hendrickson); Richard Bauckham, ICC (T & T Clark); and Peter Head, PNTC (Eerdmans). I would keep Bock (2 vols.) and wait for Peter Head, David Garland, and Richard Bauckham, but the revised EBC volume looks very promising. Bock is especially strong on historical-grammatical matters and somewhat sparse in addressing Luke as literature. Of course, this is the principal focus of Green's commentary at the expense of historical background (i.e., the relationship between Luke and the synoptics). D. A. Carson believes that Bovon is as deep exegetically and more

L/Cr **2. Bovon, François.** *Luke 1,* **Hermeneia (Fortress, 2002).** Luke 1:1–9:50 from 1989 German edition. Two volumes to follow through 19:27 (German editions, 1996, 2001).

C/M 3. Danker, Frederick. *Jesus and the New Age,* 2d ed. (Fortress, 1988). Especially Greco-Roman context.

L/Cr 4. Evans, C. F. NTC (Trinity Press International, 1990). Cites obscurities, difficulties.

L/Cr **5. Fitzmyer, Joseph. AB, 2 vols. (Doubleday, 1981, 1985).** Especially Aramaic, tradition critical.

E/Cr **6. Green, Joel. NICNT (Eerdmans, 1997).** Needs to be complemented by a standard commentary.

C/M 7. Johnson, Luke. Sacra Pagina (Liturgical, 1991). Literary background.

E/Cr **8. Marshall, I. Howard. NIGTC (Eerdmans, 1978).** Historicity, issues concerning redaction criticism. Dense.

C/M 9. Nolland, John. WBC, 3 vols. (Word, 1989–1993).

L/Cr 10. Tannehill, Robert. ANTC (Abingdon, 1996). Socioliterary, canonical approach.

Exposition

E **1. Bock, Darrell. NIVAC (Zondervan, 1996).** Essentially an abridgement of the author's BECNT volumes.

———. IVPNTC (IVP, 1994).

C/M 2. Culpepper, R. Alan. NIB, vol. 9 (Abingdon, 1995). Dates in the mid-80s.

E/Cr **3. Evans, Craig. NIBCNT (Hendrickson, 1990).** Old Testament background.

E **4. Liefeld, Walter. EBC, vol. 8 (Zondervan, 1984).**

E 5. Morris, Leon. TNTC (Eerdmans, 1988).

E 6. Pate, C. Marvin. *The Gospel of Luke* (Moody, 1995).

---

seminal theologically than any other commentary on Luke (*New Testament Commentary Survey,* 5th ed. [Baker, 2001], 54). However, Bovon holds that Luke represents a specific form of the Pauline school in the third generation of churches, thus dating it rather late.

E   7. **Stein, Robert. NAC (Broadman & Holman, 1993).**
Composition critical.

L/Cr   8. Tiede, David. Augsburg Commentary on the New Testament (Augsburg, 1988). Especially biblical theology.

E   9. Wilcock, Michael. BST (IVP, 1984).

Theology of Luke–Acts

L/Cr   1. Bovon, François. *Luke the Theologian.* 2d rev. ed. (Baylor University Press, 2006). History of interpretation 1950–present.

E   2. Cunningham, Scott. *Through Many Tribulations* (Sheffield Academic Press, 1997).

E/Cr   3. Doble, P. *The Paradox of Salvation* (Cambridge University Press, 1996).

L/Cr   4. **Fitzmyer, Joseph.** *Luke the Theologian* **(Paulist, 1989).**

L/Cr   5. Gillman, J. *Possessions and the Life of Faith* (Liturgical, 1991).

E/Cr   6. Green, Joel. NTT (Cambridge University Press, 1995). Greco-Roman influence.

E   7. McComiskey, Douglas. *Lukan Theology in Light of the Gospel's Literary Structure* (Paternoster, 2004).

L/Cr   8. Moessner, David, ed. *Jesus and the Heritage of Israel* (Trinity Press International, 1999).

C/M   9. Nave, Guy. *The Role of Repentance in Luke–Acts* (SBL, 2002).

C/M   10. Nielsen, Aalders. *Until It Is Fulfilled* (Mohr, 2000). Rhetorical, eschatological study of Luke 22; Acts 20.

CM   11. Squires, John. *The Plan of God in Luke–Acts* (Cambridge University Press, 1993).

E   12. Strauss, Mark. *The Davidic Messiah in Luke–Acts* (Sheffield Academic Press, 1995).

L/Cr   13. Tyson, Joseph, ed. *Luke–Acts and the Jewish People* (Augsburg, 1988).

The Holy Spirit in Luke–Acts

E/Cr 1. Dunn, James. *Jesus and the Spirit* (Eerdmans, 1997).
———. *The Christ and the Spirit,* vol. 2: *Pneumatology* (Eerdmans, 1998).
———. *Baptism in the Holy Spirit* (Westminster, 1970). Rebuts baptism of the Spirit subsequent to salvation.

E 2. Ervin, Howard. *Conversion-Initiation in the Baptism in the Holy Spirit* (Hendrickson, 1984). Contra Dunn.

E/Cr 3. Penney, John. *The Missionary Emphasis of Lukan Pneumatology* (Sheffield Academic Press, 1997).

E 4. Pettegrew, Larry. *The New Covenant Ministry of the Holy Spirit,* 2d ed. (Kregel, 2001). Cessationist.

E 5. Menzies, Robert. *Empowered for Witness* (Sheffield Academic Press, 1994).
———. *The Development of Early Christian Pneumatology with Special Reference to Luke–Acts* (Sheffield Academic Press, 1991). Gift of Spirit as prophetic endowment for special insight, inspired speech.

E 6. Shelton, James. *Mighty in Word and Deed* (Hendrickson, 1991; Wipf & Stock, 1999). Charismatic.

E/Cr 7. Shepherd, William. *The Narrative Function of the Holy Spirit as a Character in Luke–Acts* (Scholars, 1994).

E 8. Stott, John. *Baptism and Fullness,* rev. ed. (IVP, 1999).

E 9. Stronstad, Roger. *The Charismatic Theology of St. Luke* (Hendrickson, 1984).

E/Cr 10. Turner, Max. *Power from On High* (Sheffield Academic Press, 1996). Charismatic.

E 11. Woods, Edward. *The "Finger of God" and Pneumatology in Luke-Acts* (Sheffield Academic Press, 2001).

12. *See* Systematic Theology: The Holy Spirit and Spiritual Gifts (both Traditional, and Pentecostal and Charismatic).

Special Studies

C/M 1. Alexander, Loveday. *The Preface to Luke's Gospel* (Cambridge University Press, 1993). Also Acts 1:1.

L/Cr   2. Arlandson, James. *Women, Class, and Society in Early Christianity* (Hendrickson, 1997).

C/M   3. Aus, Roger David. *My Name Is "Legion": Palestinian Judaic Traditions in Mark 5:1–20 and Other Gospel Texts* (University Press of America, 2003). Luke 8:26–27, etc.

E/Cr   4. Bartholomew, Craig, Anthony Thiselton, and Joel Green. *Reading Luke: Interpretation, Reflection, Formation* (Zondervan, 2005).

L/Cr   5. Bovon, François. *Studies in Early Christianity* (Baker, 2005). Luke–Acts, Apocrypha.

E/Cr   6. Culy, Martin, and Mikeal Parsons. *Acts: A Handbook on the Greek Text* (Baylor University Press, 2004).

L/Cr   7. Esler, Philip. *Community and Gospel in Luke–Acts* (Cambridge University Press, 1987).

E-L/Cr 8. Evans, Craig, and J. A. Sanders, eds. *Luke and Scripture* (Fortress, 1993).

E   9. Forbes, Greg. *The God of Old* (Sheffield Academic Press, 2000). Role of Lukan Parables.

E   10. Ireland, Dennis. *Stewardship and the Kingdom of God* (Brill, 1992). Luke 16:1–13.

L/Cr 11. Kurz, William. *Reading Luke–Acts* (Westminster John Knox, 1993).

C/M 12. Maddox, Robert. *The Purpose of Luke–Acts* (T & T Clark, 1982).

E/Cr 13. Marshall, I. Howard. *Luke,* 2d ed. (Zondervan, 1989; IVP, 1998).

L/Cr 14. Moessner, David. *Lord of the Banquet* (Trinity Press International, 1998). Travel narrative.

C/M 15. Parsons, Mikeal. *Luke: Storyteller, Interpreter, Evangelist* (Hendrickson, 2005).

L/Cr 16. Powell, Mark. *What Are They Saying About Luke?* (Paulist, 1989). Introduction.

L/Cr 17. Sterling, G. *Historiography and Self Definition* (Brill, 1992).

L/Cr 18. Talbert, Charles. *Reading Luke,* rev. ed. (Smyth & Helwys, 2002). Literary, theological commentary.

L/Cr   19.   **Tannehill, Robert.** *The Narrative Unity of Luke–Acts,* **2 vols. (Fortress, 1986–90).**

E-L/Cr 20.   Thompson, Richard, and Thomas Phillips, eds. *Literary Studies in Luke–Acts* (Mercer University Press, 1998).

L/Cr   21.   Verheyden, Jozef, ed. *The Unity of Luke–Acts* (Peeters, 1999).

        22.   *See* New Testament Background: Social Background.

John[*]
Technical, Semitechnical

C/M   1.   Barrett, C. K. *The Gospel According to St. John* (Westminster, 1978).

E   2.   Beasley-Murray, George. WBC, rev. ed. (Thomas Nelson, 1999).

L/Cr   3.   Brown, Raymond E. AB, 2 vols. (Doubleday, 1966, 1970). Sacramental.

E   **4.   Keener, Craig.** *The Gospel of John,* **2 vols. (Hendrickson, 2003).**

E   **5.   Köstenberger, Andreas. BECNT (Baker, 2004).**

L/Cr   6.   Moloney, Francis. Sacra Pagina (Liturgical, 1998). Chapter 21 later addition.

E   7.   Morris, Leon. NICNT, rev. ed. (Eerdmans, 1994). Updated bibliography, footnotes.

---

[*] Forthcoming: Marianne Meye Thompson, NTL (Westminster John Knox); Harold Attridge, Hermeneia (Fortress); John McHugh, ICC (T & T Clark); John Painter (Eerdmans); Richard Bauckham, NIGTC (Eerdmans); and Ramsey Michaels, NICNT (Eerdmans) as a replacement for Morris. No other book of the Bible has received such a spate of recent coverage as the Gospel of John, with commentaries by Keener, Köstenberger, Kruse, and Lincoln appearing within a little more than a two-year period. This embarrassment of riches actually allows for two tiers of extreme-quality recommendations if you take the forthcoming commentaries of Bauckham and Michaels into account. Ultimately, I would go with Bauckham, Köstenberger, and the exposition by Carson in the first tier; Keener, Attridge, and Burge in the second; and Michaels, Meye Thompson, and Kruse in the third. Only Bauckham and Attridge would not be considered evangelical, though Meye Thompson is moderate. Other commentaries by Beasley-Murray, Blomberg, Borchert, Mounce, Ridderbos, and Lincoln give John an unprecedented array of resources to consult.

L/Cr   8. O'Day, Gail. NIB, vol. 9 (Abingdon, 1995). Dates between A.D. 80–100.

E   **9. Ridderbos, Herman. *The Gospel of John: A Theological Commentary* (Eerdmans, 1997).** Dutch original: 1987, 1992.

L/Cr   10. Schnackenburg, Rudolf. *The Gospel According to St. John,* 3 vols. (Seabury/Crossroad, 1968–82).

Exposition

E   **1. Blomberg, Craig. *The Historical Reliability of John's Gospel* (IVP, 2002).**

E   2. Borchert, Gerald. NAC, 2 vols. (Broadman & Holman, 1996, 2002).

E/Cr   3. Bruce, F. F. *The Gospel of John* (Eerdmans, 1983).

E   **4. Burge, Gary. NIVAC (Zondervan, 2000).**

E   **5. Carson, D. A. PNTC (Eerdmans, 1991).**

E/Cr   6. Edwards, Mark. BBC (Blackwell, 2004). History of interpretation commentary.

E   **7. Kruse, Colin. TNTC (Eerdmans, 2004).**

E/Cr   8. Lincoln, Andrew. BNTC (Hendrickson, 2005).

E   9. Mounce, Robert. EBC, vol. 10, rev. ed. (Zondervan, 2006).

L/Cr   10. Smith, D. Moody. ANTC (Abingdon, 1999). Product of Johannine community in three or four stages. No interaction with Motyer or Bauckham below, and limited interaction with others.

E   11. Whitacre, Rodney. IVPNTC (IVP, 1999). Especially theological message.

John as Story

L/Cr   **1. Ashton, John. *Studying John* (Oxford University Press, 1995).**
         ————. *Understanding the Fourth Gospel* (Oxford University Press, 1991). Introduction.
         ————, ed. *The Interpretation of John,* rev. and expanded (T & T Clark, 1997).

C/M 2. **Culpepper, R. Alan. IBT (Abingdon, 1996).** Gospels and Letters.

————, ed. *Critical Readings of John 6* (Brill, 1997).

E 3. Kellum, Scott. *The Unity of the Farewell Discourse* (T & T Clark, 2005). John 13:31–16:33.

C/M 4. Masanobu, Endo. *Creation and Christology* (Mohr, 2002). Prologue.

L/Cr 5. Moloney, Francis. *Belief in the Word: Reading John 1–4* (Fortress, 1993).

————. *Signs and Wonders: Reading John 5–12* (Fortress, 1996; Wipf & Stock, 2004).

————. *Glory Not Dishonor: Reading John 13–21* (Fortress, 1998; Wipf & Stock, 2004).

E 6. **Pryor, John. *John: Evangelist of the Covenant People* (IVP, 1992).** Linkage of Jesus' new covenant community with OT antecedents.

E 7. **Salier, Willis. The Rhetorical Impact of the Semeia in the Gospel of John (Mohr, 2004).**

C/M 8. **Smalley, Stephen. *John: Evangelist and Interpreter,* 2d ed. (IVP, 1998).**

E 9. Stibbe, Mark. *John as Storyteller* (Cambridge University Press, 1992). John 18–19.

L/Cr 10. Talbert, Charles. *Reading John,* rev. ed. (Smyth & Helwys, 1999). Literary-theological commentary; includes Epistles.

Special Studies

E-C/M 1. **Bauckham, Richard, ed. *The Gospel for All Christians* (Eerdmans, 1997).** Refutation of "Johannine community" concept.

E 2. Beasley-Murray, George. *Gospel of Life* (Hendrickson, 1991).

E 3. **Blomberg, Craig. *The Historic Reliability of John's Gospel* (IVP, 2002).** 223 pages of historical commentary, 50 pages of introduction, and an extremely useful 32-page bibliography.

L/Cr   4. Brown, Raymond. *An Introduction to the Gospel of John* (Doubleday, 2003). Revision of commentary introduction.

E   5. Brunson, Andrew. *Psalm 118 in the Gospel of John* (Mohr, 2003).

E   6. Burge, Gary. *Interpreting the Fourth Gospel* (Baker, 1992).

L/Cr   7. Charlesworth, James. *The Beloved Disciple* (Trinity Press International, 1996). Thomas, "the one whom Jesus loved."

C/M   8. Culpepper, Alan. *John, the Son of Zebedee* (Fortress, 2000).

C/M-   9. Culpepper, Alan, and Clifton Black, eds. *Exploring the Gospel of John* (Westminster, 1995).
L/Cr

C/M-   10. Donahue, John, ed. *Life in Abundance* (Liturgical, 2005). Raymond Brown tribute.
L/Cr

E   11. Ensor, Peter. *Jesus and His Works* (Mohr, 1996).

C/M   12. Hengel, Martin. *The Johannine Question* (Trinity Press International, 1994).

E   13. Hill, Charles. *The Johannine Corpus in the Early Church* (Oxford University Press, 2004).

C/M   14. Koester, Craig. *Symbolism in the Fourth Gospel*, rev. ed. (Fortress, 2003).

E   15. Köstenberger, Andreas. *Encountering the Book of John* (Baker, 1999).

L/Cr   16. Kysar, Robert. *Voyages with John* (Baylor University Press, 2006). History of interpretation, 1955–present.

E/Cr   17. Lincoln, Andrew. *Truth on Trial* (Hendrickson, 2000). Lawsuit motif.

E/Cr   18. Meye Thompson, Marianne. *The God of the Gospel of John* (Eerdmans, 2001).

E   19. Morris, Leon. *Jesus Is the Christ* (Eerdmans, 1989).

E/Cr   20. Motyer, Stephen. *Your Father the Devil?* (Paternoster, 1997). John 8:31–59.

L/Cr   21. Schneiders, Sandra. *Written That You May Believe* (Herder and Herder, 1999). Introduction.

L/Cr 22. Smith, D. Moody. NTT (Cambridge University Press, 1995).

E 23. Thatcher, Tom. *Why John Wrote a Gospel* (Westminster John Knox, 2005).

E 24. Um, Stephen. *The Theme of Temple Christology in John's Gospel* (T & T Clark, 2006). John 4:6–26.

L/Cr 25. Van Tilborg, Sjef. *Reading John in Ephesus* (Brill, 1996). Historical setting.

L/Cr 26. Westermann, Claus. *The Gospel of John in Light of the Old Testament* (Hendrickson, 1998).

Acts*
Technical, Semitechnical

C/M **1. Barrett, C. K. ICC, 2 vols. (T & T Clark, 1994, 1999).** Non-Lukan, introduction in volume 2.

E 2. Bock, Darrell. BECNT (Baker, 2007).

E/Cr **3. Bruce, F. F. NICNT, rev. ed. (Eerdmans, 1988).** Historical background.

————. **3d ed. (Eerdmans, 1990; Wipf & Stock, 2000).** Greek.

L/Cr 4. Conzelmann, Hans. Hermeneia (Fortress, 1987).

L/Cr **5. Fitzmyer, Joseph. AB (Doubleday, 1999).** Especially OT in New, table of passages comparing Paul and Acts.

L/Cr 6. Haenchen, Ernst (Westminster, 1971). Early church, interpretation history.

---

* Forthcoming: Loveday Alexander, Luke–Acts, BNTC (Hendrickson); Steve Walton, WBC, 2 vols. (Thomas Nelson); Joel Green, NICNT (Eerdmans); Stanley Porter, NIGTC (Eerdmans); Carl Holladay, NTL (Westminster John Knox); Craig Keener (Eerdmans); and David Peterson, PNTC (Eerdmans), especially for its theology. With Witherington or Barrett's shorter commentary (2002), one should obtain Bock and wait for Porter. Porter will be particularly valuable for his perspective on the function of the aorist. The two-volume commentary by Barrett is outstanding, but is much too obtuse for practical pastoral use, and his view of non-Lukan authorship sometimes colors his interpretation. The expositional field is well-populated with several outstanding middle-level commentaries, especially Longenecker in the recently revised EBC (Zondervan).

C/M   7.   **Johnson, Luke. Sacra Pagina (Liturgical, 1992).** Extrabiblical parallels, as apologetic history.

Sociorhetorical Studies and Commentaries

C/M   1.   Alexander, Loveday. *Acts in its Ancient Literary Context* (T & T Clark, 2005).

E/Cr   2.   Dunn, James. *Acts of the Apostles* (Trinity Press International, 1996).

L/Cr   3.   Gaventa, Beverly. ANTC (Abingdon, 2003).

L/Cr   4.   Kee, Howard. *To Every Nation Under Heaven,* NTC (Trinity Press International, 1998). Especially social context, excellent historicity appendix.

C/M   5.   Marguerat, Daniel. *The First Christian Historian* (Cambridge University Press, 2002).

C/M   6.   **Penner, Todd. *In Praise of Christian Origins: Stephen and the Hellenists in Lukan Apologetic Historiography* (T & T Clark, 2004).**

L/Cr   7.   Pervo, Richard. *Profit with Delight* (Fortress, 1987).

C/M   8.   **Soards, Marion. *The Speeches in Acts* (Westminster John Knox, 1994).**

E/Cr   9.   **Spencer, Scott. *Acts* (Sheffield Academic Press, 1997).**
                  ———. *Journeying through Acts* **(Hendrickson, 2004).**

L/Cr   10. Talbert, Charles. *Reading Acts,* rev. ed. (Smyth & Helwys, 1997). Literary-theological.

E/Cr   **11. Wall, Robert. NIB, vol. 10 (Abingdon, 2002).**

E   **12. Witherington, Ben. *The Acts of the Apostles* (Eerdmans, 1997).** Acts like Thucyclides, Polybius, Jewish historiography.
                  ———, ed. *History, Literature and Society in the Book of Acts* (Cambridge University Press, 1996).

Exposition

C/M   1.   **Barrett, C. K. *Acts: A Shorter Commentary* (T & T Clark, 2002).** Abridgment of above minus technical notes, foreign-language material, and excursuses.

E   2. Fernando, Ajith. NIVAC (Zondervan, 1998).

E   **3. Larkin, William. IVPNTC (IVP, 1995).**

E   **4. Longenecker, Richard. EBC, vol. 10, rev. ed. (Zondervan, 2006).**

E/Cr   **5. Marshall, I. Howard. TNTC (Eerdmans, 1980).**

E   6. Pelikan, Jaroslav. BTCB (Baker, 2005). Church fathers perspective.

E   **7. Polhill, John. NAC (Broadman & Holman, 1992).**

E   **8. Stott, John. BST (IVP, 1990).**

C/M   9. Williams, David. NIBCNT (Hendrickson, 1990). Especially background.

Special Studies

E   1. Arrington, French. *The Acts of the Apostles* (Hendrickson, 1988). Pentecostal commentary.

L/Cr   2. Ascough, Richard. *What Are They Saying About the Formation of the Pauline Churches?* (Paulist, 1998).

L/Cr   3. Cassidy, Richard. *Society and Politics in the Acts of the Apostles* (Orbis, 1987).

E   **4. Gasque, W. Ward. *A History of the Interpretation of the Acts of the Apostles* (Hendrickson, 1989).**

E   **5. Hemer, Colin. *The Book of Acts in the Setting of Hellenistic History* (Mohr, 1989).**

L/Cr   6. Jervell, Jacob. NTT (Cambridge University Press, 1996).

E   **7. Johnson, Dennis. *The Message of Acts in the History of Redemption* (Presbyterian & Reformed, 1997).**

C/M   8. Keathley, Naymond, ed. *With Steadfast Purpose* (Baylor University Press, 1990).

E   9. Liefeld, Walter. *Interpreting the Book of Acts* (Baker, 1995).

L/Cr   10. Lüdemann, Gerd. *Early Christianity According to the Traditions in Acts* (Fortress, 1989).

E/Cr   **11. Marshall, I. Howard, and David Peterson, eds. *Witness to the Gospel* (Eerdmans, 1998).**

E   **12. Pao, David. *Acts and the Isaianic New Exodus* (Baker, 2002).**

E/Cr 13. **Porter, Stanley.** *Paul of Acts* **(Hendrickson, 2001).**[5]
E   14. Smith, David. *The Canonical Function of Acts* (Liturgical, 2002).
E/Cr 15. Spencer, Scott. *The Portrait of Philip in Acts* (Sheffield Academic Press, 1992).
E/Cr 16. **Walton, Steve.** *Leadership and Lifestyle* **(Cambridge University Press, 2000).**
      17. *See* Luke: Theology of Luke–Acts, The Holy Spirit in Luke–Acts, and Special Studies.

Romans[*]
Technical, Semitechnical

C/M   1. **Cranfield, C. E. B. ICC, 2 vols. (T & T Clark, 1975).**
E/Cr 2. Dunn, James. WBC, 2 vols. (Word, 1988). Influenced by Sanders.
L/Cr 3. Fitzmyer, Joseph. AB (Doubleday, 1993). Introduction plus extensive (entire) church history bibliography constitutes two-thirds of the book. Especially Targumic, apocalyptic, DSS parallels.
C/M   4. **Jewett, Paul. Hermeneia (Fortress, 2006).**
L/Cr 5. Kasemann, Ernst. *Commentary on Romans* (Eerdmans, 1980).
E   6. **Moo, Douglas. NICNT (Eerdmans, 1996).** Especially synthetic flow.

---

5. David Pao, assistant professor of New Testament at Trinity Evangelical Divinity School, has reworked his 1998 Harvard dissertation into a monograph of excellence. His thesis concerns the thematic influence of Isaiah's new exodus (especially chap. 40) on Luke's theology of the restoration of the people of God; similar to Rikki Watts's less-successful study of Mark. Incidentally, J. Ross Wagner, following up on his own 1999 Duke dissertation, follows a similar tack in suggesting the influence of the "preaching of good news" (especially Isa. 52:13–53:6) on Paul's thought (*see* Romans: Special Studies).

* Forthcoming: Richard Longenecker, NIGTC (Eerdmans); Beverly Gaventa, NTL (Westminster John Knox); and Robert Jewett, Hermeneia (Fortress). Wait for Longenecker and use it with Moo. Otherwise choose Schreiner (Reformed) or Osborne (Arminian).

E	7.	**Schreiner, Thomas. BECNT (Baker, 1998).**
E	8.	Witherington, Ben. *Paul's Letter to the Romans* (Eerdmans, 2003). Socio-rhetorical.
L/Cr	9.	Ziesler, John. NTC (Trinity Press International, 1989).

Exposition

C/M	1.	Barrett, C. K. BNTC, rev. ed. (Hendrickson, 1993). Completed in 1988.
E/Cr	2.	Bruce, F. F. TNTC (Eerdmans, 1985).
E/Cr	3.	Edwards, James. NIBCNT (Hendrickson, 1992). Influenced by Sanders.
E	4.	Harrison, E. F., and Donald Hagner. EBC, vol. 11, rev. ed. (Zondervan, 2006)
E	5.	Johnson, Alan. EvBC (Moody, 2000). Ideal popular treatment.
L/Cr	6.	Keck, Leander. ANTC (Abingdon, 2005).
E	7.	**Moo, Douglas. NIVAC (Zondervan, 2000).**
E	8.	Morris, Leon. PNTC (Eerdmans, 1988). Somewhat semitechnical; does not interact with Sanders.
E	9.	Mounce, Robert. NAC (Broadman & Holman, 1995). Especially synthetic flow.
E	10.	**Osborne, Grant. IVPNTC (IVP, 2004).** Arminian.
E	11.	**Stott, John. BST (IVP, 1995).**
C/M	12.	Talbert, Charles. SHBC (Smyth & Helwys, 2002).
E	13.	Toews, John. BCBC (Herald, 2004).
E/Cr	14.	Wright, N. T. NIB, vol. 10 (Abingdon, 2002). Interesting perspective on baptism.

Homosexuality
(Romans 1:21–26)

All	1.	Balch, David, ed. *Homosexuality, Science, and the "Plain Sense" of Scripture* (Eerdmans, 2000).
All	2.	**Bradshaw, Timothy, ed. *The Way Forward?: Christian Voices on Homosexuality and the Church*, 2d ed. (Eerdmans, 2003).**
E	3.	**DeYoung, James. *Homosexuality* (Kregel, 2000).**

C/M   4. **Gagnon, Robert.** *The Bible and Homosexual Practice* **(Abingdon, 2002).** Upholds traditional perspective.

E/Cr 5. **Grenz, Stanley.** *Welcoming but Not Affirming* **(West-minster John Knox, 1998).**

E   6. **Jones, Stanley, and Mark Yarhouse.** *Homosexuality: The Use of Scientific Research in the Church's Moral Debate* **(IVP, 2000).**

L/Cr 7. Nissinen, Martti. *Homoeroticism in the Biblical World* (Fortress, 1998).

C/M   8. Pronk, Pim. *Against Nature?* (Eerdmans, 1993).

L/Cr 9. Sample, Tex, and Amy De Long, eds. *The Loyal Opposition* (Abingdon, 2000).

E   10. Satinover, Jeffrey. *Homosexuality and the Politics of Truth* (Baker, 1996).

E   **11. Schmidt, Thomas.** *Straight and Narrow?* **(IVP, 1995).**

E   12. Sears, Alan, and Craig Osten, *The Homosexual Agenda: Exposing the Principal Threat to Religious Freedom Today* (Broadman & Holman, 2003).

E   13. Whitehead, Neil, and Briar Whitehead. *My Genes Made Me Do It!* (Huntington House, 1999).

L/Cr 14. Wilson, Glenn, and Qazi Rahman. *Born Gay? The Psychobiology of Sex Orientation* (Peter Owen, 2005).

L/Cr 15. Wink, Walter, ed. *Homosexuality and the Christian Faith* (Fortress, 1999).

E   16. Wold, Donald. *Out of Order: Homosexuality in the Bible and the Ancient Near East* (Baker, 1998).

Special Studies

C/M   1. Bell, Richard. *No One Seeks for God* (Mohr, 1998). Romans 1:18–3:20.

E   2. Bray, Gerald, ed. ACCS (IVP, 1998).

C/M   3. Cranfield, C. E. B. *On Romans and Other New Testament Essays* (T & T Clark, 1998).

L/Cr 4. Donfried, Karl, ed. *The Romans Debate,* rev. ed. (Hendrickson, 1991).

L/Cr   5. Esler, Philip. *Conflict and Identity in Romans* (Fortress, 2003). Social Background.

L/Cr   6. Goulder, Michael. *Early Christians in Conflict* (Hendrickson, 2001).

E   7. Greenman, Jeffrey, and Timothy Larsen, eds. *Reading Romans Through the Centuries: From the Early Church to Karl Barth* (Baker, 2005).

C/M   8. Johnson, Luke. *Reading Romans* (Smyth & Helwys, 1999).

E   9. Miller, James. *The Obedience of Faith, the Eschatological People of God, and the Epistle of Romans* (SBL, 2000).

E   10. Moo, Douglas. *Encountering the Book of Romans* (Baker, 2002).

L/Cr 11. Morgan, Robert. NTG (Sheffield Academic Press, 1995).

E   12. Piper, John. *The Justification of God*, 2d ed. (Baker, 1993). Romans 9:1–23.

E   13. Reasoner, Mark. *Romans in Full Circle: A History of Interpretation* (Westminster John Knox, 2005).

E/Cr 14. Soderlund, Sven, and N. T. Wright, eds. *Romans and the People of God* (Eerdmans, 1999).

L/Cr 15. Stowers, Stanley. *A Rereading of Romans* (Yale University Press, 1994).

C/M   16. Thorsteinsson, Runar. *Paul's Interlocutor in Romans 2: Function and Identity in the Context of Ancient Epistolography* (Almqvist & Wiksell, 2004).

C/M   17. Tobin, Thomas. *Paul's Rhetoric in Its Contexts* (Hendrickson, 2004). Insightful socio-literary analysis.

C/M   18. Wagner, J. Ross. *Heralds of Good News* (Brill, 2002).

E/Cr 19. Westerholm, Stephen. *Understanding Paul*, 2d ed. (Eerdmans, 2004).

      20. *See* New Testament Introduction, Survey, and Theology: Pauline Theology, Paul and the Law, and New Testament Background: Pauline Background.

1 Corinthians*
Technical, Semitechnical

L/Cr 1. Collins, Raymond. Sacra Pagina (Liturgical, 1999).
L/Cr 2. Conzelmann, Hans. Hermeneia (Fortress, 1975).
E/Cr 3. Fee, Gordon. NICNT (Eerdmans, 1987). Charismatic.
E 4. Robertson, Archibald, and Alfred Plummer. ICC, 2d ed. (T & T Clark, 1914).
E/Cr 5. Thiselton, Anthony. NIGTC (Eerdmans, 2000).[6]

Exposition

C/M 1. Barrett, C. K. BNTC (Hendrickson, 1987).
E 2. Blomberg, Craig. NIVAC (Zondervan, 1995).
E/Cr 3. Bruce, F. F. NCBC (Eerdmans, 1981). 1–2 Corinthians.
C/M 4. Hays, Richard. IBC (Westminster John Knox, 1997). Especially Paul's use of the Old Testament and ethics.
E 5. Johnson, Alan. IVPNTC (IVP, 2004).
E 6. Kistemaker, Simon. *1 Corinthians* (Baker, 1994).
E 7. Morris, Leon. TNTC (Eerdmans, 1983).
L/Cr 8. Murphy-O'Connor, Jerome. DBC (Doubleday, 1998).
E 9. Prior, David. BST (IVP, 1985).
C/M 10. Soards, Marion. NIBCNT (Hendrickson, 1999).
E 11. Verbrugge, Verlyn. EBC, vol. 11, rev. ed. (Zondervan, 2006).

---

* Forthcoming: Paul Gardner, ZEC (Zondervan), Paul Jackson, NAC (Broadman & Holman), Linda Belleville, WBC (Thomas Nelson), Earle Ellis, ICC (T & T Clark), and Brian Rosner, PNTC (Eerdmans). Use Garland and Fee with Johnson. Ellis promises to be his meticulous self in a meticulous series. Belleville, whose middle-level commentary on 2 Corinthians is outstanding in a crowded field, also promises much. Of course, Barrett is still quite outstanding, but Rosner would meet an expository need as well.

6. Not necessarily for the Greek-trained pastor only. Its distinguishing features are its combination of linguistic and hermeneutic theory, its socio-historical emphasis, and its selective interaction with the Greek in a Greek series.

Sociorhetorical Studies and Commentaries

E/Cr **1. Deming, Will. *Paul on Marriage and Celibacy,* 2d ed. (Eerdmans, 2004).**

C/M- 2. Eriksson, Anders. *Traditions and Rhetorical Proof*
L/Cr   (Almqvist and Wiksell, 1998). 1 Corinthians 8:10–16.

L/Cr 3. Horsley, Richard. ANTC (Abingdon, 1998).

E **4. Litfin, Duane. *St. Paul's Theology of Proclamation* (Cambridge University Press, 1994).** 1 Corinthians 1–4.

E **5. Martin, Dale. *The Corinthian Body* (Yale University Press, 1995).**

C/M 6. May, Alistair. *"The Body for the Lord": Sex and Identity in 1 Corinthians 5–7* (T & T Clark, 2004).

L/Cr 7. Mitchell, Margaret. *Paul and the Rhetoric of Reconciliation* (Westminster John Knox, 1992).

L/Cr 8. Murphy-O'Connor, Jerome. *St. Paul's Corinth,* rev. ed. (Liturgical, 2002).

E/Cr- **9. Pogoloff, S. *Logos and Sophia* (Scholars, 1992).**
L/Cr   1 Corinthians 1–4.

L/Cr 10. Talbert, Charles. *Reading Corinthians,* rev. ed. (Smyth & Helwys, 2003). 1–2 Corinthians.

C/M **11. Welborn, Larry. *Politics and Rhetoric in the Corinthian Epistles* (Mercer University Press, 1997).** Especially 2 Corinthians 1–2:13 and 7:1–40, also 1 Corinthians 1–4.

E **12. Witherington, Ben. *Conflict and Community in Corinth* (Eerdmans, 1995).** Commentary, includes 2 Corinthians.

Special Studies

All **1. Adams, Edward, and David Horrell, eds. *Christianity at Corinth* (Westminster John Knox, 2004).**

E 2. Bray, Gerald, ed. ACCS (IVP, 1999). Includes 2 Corinthians.

E 3. Carson, D. A. *Showing the Spirit* (Baker, 1987). 1 Corinthians 12–14.

E/Cr   4.   Chester, Stephen. *Conversion at Corinth* (T & T Clark, 2003).

E/Cr   **5.**   **Cheung, Alex. *Idol Food in Corinth* (Sheffield Academic Press, 1999).** 1 Corinthians 8–10.

E   **6.**   **Clarke, Andrew. *Secular and Christian Leadership in Corinth* (Brill, 1993).** 1 Corinthians 1–6.

L/Cr   7.   Furnish, Victor. NTT (Cambridge University Press, 1999).

E/Cr   **8.**   **Gardner, Paul. *The Gifts of God and the Authentification of a Christian* (University Press of America, 1994).** 1 Corinthians 8–11:1.

L/Cr   9.   Grant, Robert. *Paul in the Roman World* (Westminster John Knox, 2001).

E   10.   Kovacs, Judith, ed. *1 Corinthians: Interpreted by the Early Church and Medieval Commentators.* The Church's Bible (Eerdmans, 2005). Interpretation in first 1,000 years.

E/Cr   11.   Rosner, Brian. *Paul, Scripture, and Ethics* (Brill, 1994). 1 Corinthians 5–7.

E   12.   Thomas, Robert. *Understanding Spiritual Gifts,* rev. ed. (Kregel, 1999). 1 Corinthians 12–14.

E   **13.**   **Williams, Drake. *The Wisdom of the Wise* (Brill, 2001).** 1 Corinthians 1:18–3:23. OT Citations, allusions, and echoes.

E   **14.**   **Winter, Bruce. *Philo and Paul Among the Sophists* (Cambridge University Press, 1997).**

2 Corinthians[*]
Technical, Semitechnical

E   **1.**   **Barnett, Paul. NICNT (Eerdmans, 1997).** Especially biblical theology, historical, social background.

---

[*] Forthcoming: George Guthrie, BECNT (Baker); Calvin Roetzel, ANTC (Abingdon); Ralph Martin, WBC, rev. ed. (Thomas Nelson); and Mark Seifrid, PNTC (Eerdmans). Harris's meticulous exegesis makes the first choice a no-brainer. As for the exposition category, it doesn't get much deeper. Barrett (outstanding for 365 pp.), Garland (for his theology), Belleville (whom many consider to be the

L/Cr 2. Furnish, Victor. AB (Doubleday, 1984). Greco-Roman background.

E **3. Harris, Murray. NIGTC (Eerdmans, 2004).**

E 4. Hughes, Philip. NICNT (Eerdmans, 1962). Annihilationist.

E/Cr 5. Martin, Ralph. WBC (Word, 1986). Especially history of interpretation.

L/Cr 6. Matera, Frank. NTL (Westminster John Knox, 2003).

C/M **7. Thrall, Margaret. ICC, 2 vols. (T & T Clark, 1994).** Three letters in one.

E 8. Witherington, Ben. *Chaos and Community in Corinth* (Eerdmans, 1995). Sociorhetorical, includes 1 Corinthians.

Exposition

C/M **1. Barrett, C. K. BNTC (Harper, 1973; Hendrickson, 1993).**

E/Cr **2. Belleville, Linda. IVPNTC (IVP, 1995).**

L/Cr 3. Fitzgerald, John. ANTC (Abingdon, 2002).

E **4. Garland, David. NAC (Broadman & Holman, 1999).**

E **5. Hafemann, Scott. NIVAC (Zondervan, 2000).**

E 6. Harris, Murray. EBC, vol. 11, rev. ed. (Zondervan, 2006).

E 7. Kistemaker, Simon. *2 Corinthians* (Baker, 1997).

E 8. Kruse, Colin. TNTC (Eerdmans, 1987).

E/Cr 9. Scott, James. NIBCNT (Hendrickson, 1998). Especially Jewish background.

Special Studies

All **1. Burke, Trevor, and J. K. Elliott, *Paul and the Corinthians: Studies on a Community in Conflict* (Brill, 2003).** Margaret Thrall tribute.

first choice), and Hafemann's volume (for exegesis and application) can scarcely be ignored, nor can Harris's revision in the EBC. If you already have one of these, wait for Guthrie or Seifrid and use with Harris, NIGTC (Eerdmans).

E   2.   **Carson, D. A.** *From Triumphalism to Maturity* **(Baker, 1986).** 2 Corinthians 10–13.

E   3.   **Hafemann, Scott.** *Suffering and Ministry in the Spirit* **(Eerdmans, 1990).** 2 Corinthians 2:14–3:3.

         ———. *Paul, Moses, and the History of Israel* **(Mohr, 1995; Hendrickson, 1996).** 2 Corinthians 3.

E   4.   **Long, Frederick.** *Ancient Rhetoric and Paul's Apology: The Compositional Unity of 2 Corinthians* **(Cambridge University Press, 2004).**

L/Cr   5.   Murphy-O'Connor, Jerome. NTT (Cambridge University Press, 1991).

E   6.   **Peterson, Brian.** *Eloquence and the Proclamation of the Gospel in Corinth* **(Scholars, 1998).** 1 Corinthians 1–4; 2 Corinthians 10–13.

E/Cr   7.   **Savage, Timothy.** *Power Through Weakness* **(Cambridge University Press, 1995).** 2 Corinthians 3–4.

E/Cr   8.   Winter, Bruce. *After Paul Left Corinth* (Eerdmans, 2000). Greco-Roman background.

Galatians[*]
Technical, Semitechnical

L/Cr   1.   Betz, Hans. Hermeneia (Fortress, 1979). Rhetorical analysis, Greco-Roman parallels.

E/Cr   2.   **Bruce, F. F. NIGTC (Eerdmans, 1982).**

C/M   3.   Burton, E. ICC (T & T Clark, 1921). Vocabulary index.

E   4.   Fung, Ronald. NICNT (Eerdmans, 1988).

E   5.   **Longenecker, Richard. WBC (Word, 1990).** Rhetorical analysis; surveys disputed points.

---

[*] Forthcoming: D. A. Carson, PNTC (Eerdmans); Doug Moo, BECNT (Baker); Martinus de Boer, NTL (Westminster John Knox); Graham Stanton, ICC (T & T Clark); N. T. Wright, Two Horizons (Eerdmans); and Gerald Borchert, CBC (Tyndale). I'd keep Longenecker and Bruce, and wait for Carson. This is one of four projected commentaries from Carson. He is also slated to comment on Hebrews, BECNT (Baker), 1–3 John, NIGTC (Eerdmans), and Revelation (also PNTC [Eerdmans]).

L/Cr   6. Martyn, J. Louis. AB (Doubleday, 1997). North Galatian, reproclamation of apocalyptic gospel.[7]

L/Cr   7. Matera, Frank. Sacra Pagina (Liturgical, 1992). New perspective on Paul.

Sociorhetorical Studies and Commentaries

E/Cr   1. Hansen, Walter. *Abraham in Galatians* (Sheffield Academic Press, 1989).

E/Cr   2. Kern, Philip. *Rhetoric and Galatians* (Cambridge University Press, 1998).

L/Cr   3. Perkins, Pheme. *Abraham's Divided Children,* NTC (Trinity Press International, 2001).

L/Cr   4. Williams, Sam. ANTC (Abingdon, 1997).

E   **5. Witherington, Ben. *Grace in Galatia* (Eerdmans, 1998).**

Exposition

L/Cr   1. Cousar, Charles. IBC (John Knox, 1982).

E/Cr   **2. Dunn, James. BNTC (Hendrickson, 1993).** New perspective, parallels from ancient Jewish texts.

---

7. The principal sources on which I base my ratings are, not surprisingly, the reviews that appear in theological journals. Recently, a comment made by Carson came to mind while I was reading Craig Blomberg's review of Louis Martyn's Galatians (*Denver Journal* 1:0207 [1998]). Blomberg seemed to be quite taken in by this commentary, especially by Martyn's positive reading of the Law in relation to living by the Spirit. (To be fair, he does rank it fourth after Longenecker, Bruce, and Betz, of whom Martyn interacts with Betz only). Knowing Martyn was Catholic, this perked my suspicions in search of the caveat. This came in the form of his usage of "rectification" instead of "justification," which is precisely the point of departure for Catholic viewpoints on the Rule of Faith. Then, sticking out like a sore finger, came Carson's assessment (see bibliography) warning of Martyn's "unfounded idiosyncracies" and "serious breaches" that "without being easily snookered . . . requires a fair bit of knowledge to spot" (p. 88). All this causes me to especially anticipate Carson's forthcoming commentary on Galatians, which is sure to rectify as well as justify. Martyn, of course, will still be rewarding to scholars by the wealth of minute detail we've come to expect from Catholic scholars of the first rank.

E   3. **George, Timothy. NAC (Broadman & Holman, 1994).** Theology, history of interpretation, rebuttal of new perspective.

E   4. Guthrie, Donald. NCBC (Eerdmans, 1981).

E/Cr   5. **Hansen, Walter. IVPNTC (IVP, 1994).**

C/M   6. **Hays, Richard. NIB, vol. 11 (Abingdon, 2000).**

E/Cr   7. Jervis, Ann. NIBCNT (Hendrickson, 1999). New perspective.

E/Cr   8. McKnight, Scot. NIVAC (Zondervan, 1995). New perspective.

E   9. Morris, Leon. *Galatians* (IVP, 1996).

E   10. Ryken, Philip. REC (Presbyterian & Reformed, 2005). Lay-friendly exposition.

E   11. Stott, John. BST (IVP, 1986).

L/Cr   12. Ziesler, John. Epworth (Epworth, 1992). Available through Trinity Press International.

Special Studies

E/Cr   1. **Barclay, John. *Obeying the Truth* (T & T Clark, 1988).**

E   2. Bonnington, Mark. *Antioch Episode of Galatians 2:11–14 in Historical and Cultural Context* (Paternoster, 2005).

E   3. Ciampa, Roy. *The Presence and Function of Scripture in Galatians 1 and 2* (Mohr, 1998).

E/Cr   4. Dunn, James. NTT (Cambridge University Press, 1993). New perspective.

C/M   5. **Elliott, Susan. *Cutting Too Close for Comfort: Paul's Letter to the Galatians in Its Anatolian Cultic Context* (Sheffield Academic Press, 2003).**

C/M   6. **Hays, Richard. *The Faith of Jesus Christ,* 2d ed. (Eerdmans, 2002).** Galatians 3:1–4:11.

C/M   7. **Longenecker, Bruce. *The Triumph of Abraham's God* (Abingdon/T & T Clark, 1998).**

L/Cr   8. Martyn, Louis. *Theological Issues in the Letters of Paul* (T & T Clark, 1997). Mostly Galatians. Available through Abingdon.

L/Cr   9. Nanos, Mark. *The Irony of Galatians* (Fortress, 2001). Dubious theory of Jewish-Christian relations. Wealth of background, however.

——, ed. *The Galatians Debate* (Hendrickson, 2002).

E   **10. Silva, Moisés. *Interpreting Galatians*, 2d ed. (Baker, 2001).** New appendix on 3:6–14.

Ephesians[*]
Technical, Semitechnical

L/Cr   1. Abbott, T. ICC (T & T Clark, 1897). With Colossians.

C/M   2. Barth, Markus. AB, 2 vols. (Doubleday, 1974). Pauline, extensive theology.

C/M   **3. Best, Ernest. ICC (T & T Clark, 1998).** Ephesians mutually dependent on Colossians; separate authors.

E/Cr   4. Bruce, F. F. NICNT (Eerdmans, 1984). With Colossians/Philemon.

E   **5. Hoehner, Harold. *Ephesians* (Baker, 2002).**

E/Cr   **6. Lincoln, Andrew. WBC (Word, 1990).** Non-Pauline authorship, influence of rhetoric.

L/Cr   7. MacDonald, Margaret. Sacra Pagina (Liturgical, 2000). With Colossians; occasional forced comparisons of epistles.

C/M   8. Mitton, C. NCBC (Eerdmans, 1982). Non-Pauline.

---

* Forthcoming: Frank Thielman, BECNT (Baker); Paul Wolfe, NAC (Broadman & Holman); Clinton Arnold, ZEC (Zondervan); Stephen Fowl, NTL (Westminster John Knox); and Max Turner, NIGTC (Eerdmans). This is a very difficult field to evaluate, as O'Brien, Hoehner, Best, and Lincoln are more than adequate, but Thielman, Wolfe, Arnold, Fowl, and Turner should be eagerly anticipated. Thielman, who is an expert on the law-versus-grace issue, should well illumine the believer's new position in Christ. Turner, whose expertise lies in the function of the Holy Spirit, could well develop this position even further. Hoehner's encyclopedic nine hundred-page work (of which one hundred pages defends Pauline authorship), published as a stand-alone volume by Baker, covers every imaginable issue. Hoehner, along with Best and Arnold, must be consulted for exegetical papers. For exposition, O'Brien retains preeminence, but Klein, Wolfe, and Snodgrass should be considered.

C/M   9. Muddiman, John. BNTC (Continuum, 2001; Hendrickson, 2004).[8]

E/Cr   10. Neufeld, Tom. BCBC (Herald, 2002). Pseudonymous.

E   11. Robinson, J. Armitage. *St. Paul's Epistle to the Ephesians,* 2d ed. (Kregel, 1979; Wipf & Stock, 2003).

C/M   12. Schnackenburg, Rudolf. *Ephesians* (T & T Clark, 2001). Non-Pauline, logical flow and theology.

Exposition

E   **1. Klein, William. EBC, vol. 12, rev. ed. (Zondervan, 2006).**

E/Cr   2. Kreitzer, Larry. Epworth (Epworth, 1997). Pseudonymous. Available through Trinity Press International.

E   3. Liefeld, Walter. IVPNTC (IVP, 1997).

E   4. Morris, Leon. *Expository Reflections on the Letter to the Ephesians* (Baker, 1994).

E   **5. O'Brien, Peter. PNTC (Eerdmans, 1999).**

L/Cr   6. Perkins, Pheme. ANTC (Abingdon, 1997). Especially church fathers, Essene parallels, pseudonymous.

———. NIB, vol. 11 (Abingdon, 2000).

E/Cr   **7. Snodgrass, Klyne. NIVAC (Zondervan, 1996).**

E   **8. Stott, John. BST (IVP, 1979).**

Special Studies

E   **1. Arnold, Clinton. *Power and Magic* (Baker, 1992; Wipf & Stock, 2001).**

C/M   **2. Best, Ernest. NTG (Sheffield Academic Press, 1993).**

---

8. The Black's New Testament Commentaries series usually runs the divide between semitechnical and expositional. Unlike the others, I've included Muddiman's commentary in the Technical, Semitechnical category because it is more technical than its counterparts. Muddiman, who thoroughly engages the secondary literature, believes that Ephesians is the "lost" Laodicean letter plus interpolations that account for more than half the reconstructed letter authored forty years after the fact. The difficulties with such an approach (i.e., the relative innocuousness of the supposed, original Laodicean letter) should not obscure the value of this commentary for its numerous, pertinent insights.

——. *Essays on Ephesians* **(T & T Clark, 1998).**
Expanded introduction to above.

E   3. Caragounis, Chrys. *The Ephesian Mysterion* (Gleerup, 1977).

L/Cr   4. Dahl, Nils. *Studies in Ephesians* (Mohr, 2000).

E/Cr   5. Dawes, Gregory. *The Body in Question* (Brill, 1998). Ephesians 5:21–33.

E   6. Harris, Hall. *The Descent of Christ* (Brill, 1996; Baker, 1998). Ephesians 4:7–11.

E   7. Klein, William. *The Book of Ephesians: An Annotated Bibliography* (Garland, 1996).

E/Cr   8. Lincoln, Andrew, and Arthur Wedderburn. *The Theology of the Later Pauline Epistles,* NTT (Cambridge University Press, 1993).

E/Cr   9. Moritz, Thorsten. *A Profound Mystery: The Use of the Old Testament in Ephesians* (Brill, 1996).

E/Cr   10. Neufeld, Thomas. *"Put On the Armor of God"* (Sheffield Academic Press, 1997). Divine Warrior motif from Isaiah 59; 1 Thessalonians 5; and Wisdom of Solomon.

C/M   11. Strelan, R. *Paul, Artemis, and the Jews in Ephesus* (de Gruyter, 1996).

C/M   12. Trebilco, Paul. *The Early Christians in Ephesus from Paul to Ignatius* (Mohr, 2004).

Philippians*
Technical, Semitechnical

E   1. Fee, Gordon. NICNT (Eerdmans, 1995).

E/Cr   2. Martin, Ralph, and Hawthorne, Gerald. WBC,

---

* Forthcoming: George Guthrie, ZEC (Zondervan); John Reumann, AB (Doubleday); N. T. Wright, ICC (T & T Clark); Todd Still, SHBC (Smyth & Helwys); and Walter Hansen, PNTC (Eerdmans). Look for Hansen, but Philippians is already well represented by Fee, O'Brien, Martin/Hawthorne, Silva, and Bockmuehl. The production of exposition commentaries on Philippians is a virtual cottage industry with only Bockmuehl, Garland, and Thielman standing ahead of the pack, and Thielman too brief at that.

rev. ed. (Thomas Nelson, 2004). Doubles length of original.

E   3. O'Brien, Peter. NIGTC (Eerdmans, 1991).

E   4. Silva, Moisés. BECNT, 2d ed. (Baker, 2005).

E   5. Witherington, Ben. *Friendship and Finances in Philippi*, NTC (Trinity Press International, 1995). Sociorhetorical.

Exposition

L/Cr   1. Beare, Francis. HNTC, 3d ed. (Harper, 1973).

E   2. **Bockmuehl, Markus. BNTC (Hendrickson, 1998).** Socioliterary, theological background. A masterpiece of concise erudition.

E/Cr   3. Bruce, F. F. NIBCNT, 2d ed. (Hendrickson, 1989).

E   4. Fee, Gordon. IVPNTC (IVP, 1999). Somewhat thin condensation of above.

E   5. **Fowl, Stephen. Two Horizons (Eerdmans, 2005).** Theological commentary.

E   6. **Garland, David. EBC, vol. 12, rev. ed. (Zondervan, 2006).**

C/M   7. Hooker, Morna. NIB, vol. 11 (Abingdon, 2000).

E/Cr   8. Marshall, I. Howard. Epworth (Epworth, 1991).

E/Cr   9. Martin, Ralph. NCBC (Eerdmans, 1980). Influenced by Käsemann's "odyssey of Christ."
———. TNTC (Eerdmans, 1987). 1959 edition preferred for the same reasons as given above.

E   10. Motyer, J. Alec. BST (IVP, 1984).

L/Cr   11. Osiek, Carolyn. ANTC (Abingdon, 2000). With Philemon; sociorhetorical.

E   12. **Thielman, Frank. NIVAC (Zondervan, 1995).**

Special Studies

C/M   1. Bakirtzis, C., and Helmut Koester, eds. *Philippi at the Time of Paul and After His Death* (Trinity Press International, 1999).

E/Cr   2. Bloomquist, Gregory. *The Function of Suffering in Phi-*

lippians (Sheffield Academic Press, 1993). Rhetorical analysis.

E/Cr **3. Martin, Ralph. *A Hymn of Christ* (IVP, 1997).** Philippians 2:5–11, *Carmen Cristi* with updated preface, technical.

E/Cr- 4. Martin, Ralph, and Brian Dodd, eds. *Where Christology*
L/Cr *Began* (Westminster John Knox, 1998). Philippians 2.

E **5. Oakes, Peter. *Philippians* (Cambridge University Press, 2000).** Greco-Roman background.

E/Cr 6. Peterlin, Davorin. *Paul's Letter to the Philippians in Light of Disunity in the Church* (Brill, 1995).

E **7. Peterman, Gerald. *Paul's Gift from Philippi* (Cambridge University Press, 1997).** Philippians 4:10–20.

E/Cr 8. Reed, Jeffrey. *Discourse Analysis of Philippians* (Sheffield Academic Press, 1997). Highly technical.

Colossians/Philemon[*]
Technical, Semitechnical

C/M 1. Barth, Markus, and Helmut Blanke. ECC (Eerdmans, 2000). Philemon only, bibliography to 1994, exhaustive study of slavery, ancient world, less than half is exegesis.[9]

———. AB (Doubleday, 1995). Colossians only, bibliography to 1986.

---

[*] Forthcoming: Gregory Beale, BECNT (Baker); Jerry Sumney, NTL (Westminster John Knox); Clint Arnold (revising O'Brien), WBC (Thomas Nelson), and Gerald Hawthorne, PNTC (Eerdmans). Keep O'Brien (rev. ed.) and Garland, and wait for Beale. Meye Thompson should be regarded for theology.

9. Needless to say, scholars will welcome the 255 pages of exegesis on the twenty-five verses in Barth and Blanke's Philemon. Of these, Blanke wrote the last seventy-five pages from Barth's notes, which include sixty-four pages of commentary on Philemon 16 alone! This is in addition to 240 pages of introduction. Fitzmyer is comparatively thin with ninety-two pages of exegesis matched by thirty-six pages of bibliography. Hopefully, the forthcoming commentaries by Beale and Hawthorne will find the middle ground and bring forth the latest scholarship on the practice of slavery in the Greco-Roman world. O'Brien, Dunn, and Garland provide adequate coverage of fifty to eighty pages on Philemon and fuller treatments on Colossians.

E/Cr   2. Bruce, F. F. NICNT (Eerdmans, 1984). Especially Philemon, with Ephesians and Colossians.

E/Cr   3. Dunn, James. NIGTC (Eerdmans, 1996).[10]

L/Cr   4. Fitzmyer, Joseph. AB (Doubleday, 2000). Philemon only.

C/M   5. Lohse, Eduard. Hermeneia (Fortress, 1971). Non-Pauline authorship. Gnostic and syncretistic opponents.

L/Cr   6. McL. Wilson, Robert. ICC (T & T Clark, 2005).

L/Cr   7. Moule, C. F. D. *The Epistle to Colossians and to Philemon* (Cambridge University Press, 1957).

E   8. O'Brien, Peter. WBC (Word, 1982).

Exposition

E   1. Garland, David. NIVAC (Zondervan, 1998).

L/Cr   2. Hay, David. ANTC (Abingdon, 2000). Colossians only.

E   3. Lucas, Raymond. BST (IVP, 1980).

E   4. Martin, Ernest. BCBC (Herald, 1993).

E/Cr   5. Martin, Ralph. NCBC (Eerdmans, 1981). Written from Ephesus.

L/Cr   6. Osiek, Carolyn. ANTC (Abingdon, 2000). Philemon and Philippians; sociorhetorical.

E   7. Rupprecht, Arthur. EBC, vol. 12, rev. ed. (Zondervan, 2006). Philemon.[11]

E   8. Still, Todd. EBC, vol. 12, rev. ed. (Zondervan, 2006). Colossians.

L/Cr   9. Thurston, Bonnie, and Judith Ryan. *Philippians and*

---

10. In Colossians, Dunn believes that Timothy reworked Pauline material just before or after Paul's death, and that the opponents are from the synagogue rather than representatives of a Christian heresy. This necessarily puts a spin on his interpretation.

11. Rupprecht sweetens the deal in considering the purchase of volume 12 in the revised EBC (Zondervan), not to mention Klein (Ephesians), Garland (Philippians), and Köstenberger (Pastorals). His essay on "Slaves, Slavery" in *DPL* (IVP) is now outdated given that recent scholarship favors a harsher perspective of the conditions slaves endured. Hopefully, that will be reflected here.

Philemon. Sacra Pagina (Liturgical, 2005). Especially Philemon.

E/Cr   10.   Wall, Robert. IVPNTC (IVP, 1993).

E   **11.**   **Wright, N. T. TNTC (Eerdmans, 1987).**

Special Studies

E   **1.**   **Arnold, Clinton.** *The Colossian Syncretism* **(Mohr, 1995; Baker, 1997).** Paul combats Christianity/folk belief syncretism.

C/M   **2.**   **Barclay, John.** *Colossians and Philemon* **(Sheffield Academic Press, 1997).**

E   3.   Bevere, Allan. *Sharing in the Inheritance* (Sheffield Academic Press, 2003). Colossians–Galatians parallels.

L/Cr   4.   Cannon, G. *The Use of Traditional Materials in Colossians* (Mercer University Press, 1983).

L/Cr   5.   DeMaris, Richard. *The Colossian Controversy* (Sheffield Academic Press, 1994). Author versus Jewish, Christian, Middle Platonic elements.

E   6.   Harris, Murray. EGGNT (Eerdmans, 1991). Grammatical guide.

C/M   7.   Heppä, Outi. *The Making of Colossians* (Vandenhoek & Ruprecht, 2003).

E   8.   Martin, Troy. *By Philosophy and Empty Deceit* (Sheffield Academic Press, 1996). Response to philosophical cynics.

E/Cr   9.   Meye Thompson, Marianne. Two Horizons (Eerdmans, 2005). Theological commentary.

C/M   10.   Sappington, Thomas. *Revelation and Redemption at Colossae* (Sheffield Academic Press, 1991). Colossians seen through ascetic, mystical piety of Jewish apocalyptic.

E/Cr   11.   Wilson, Ian. *Heavenly Perspective* (T & T Clark, 2006).

L/Cr   12.   Wilson, Walter. *The Hope of Glory* (Brill, 1997). As philosophic moral exhortation.

1 and 2 Thessalonians*
Technical, Semitechnical

E   1. Bruce, F. F. WBC (Word, 1982). Believers receive resurrection body at death; Antichrist excursus.

E   **2. Green, Gene. PNTC (Eerdmans, 2002).** Emphasis on client-patron relations.

C/M   **3. Malherbe, Abraham. AB (Doubleday, 2000).**[12]

E   4. Morris, Leon. NICNT, rev. ed. (Eerdmans, 1991).

L/Cr 5. Richard, Earl. Sacra Pagina (Liturgical, 1995). 2 Thessalonians non-Pauline, lexical, grammatical, literary background.

E   **6. Wanamaker, Charles. NIGTC (Eerdmans, 1990).** Rhetorical analysis.

Exposition

E   **1. Beale, Gregory. IVPNTC (IVP, 2004).** Amillennial.

C/M   2. Best, Ernest. BNTC (Harper, 1972; Hendrickson, 1987). Semitechnical.

E   3. Elias, Jacob. BCBC (Herald, 1995).

L/Cr **4. Furnish, Victor. ANTC (Abingdon, 2002).**

L/Cr 5. Gaventa, Beverly. IBC (Westminster John Knox, 1998). Maternal imagery, persistence of evil.

---

* Forthcoming: Jeffrey Weima, BECNT (Baker); Seyoon Kim, WBC (Thomas Nelson); Karl Donfried, ICC (T & T Clark); Holland Hendrix, NTC (Trinity); Willi Marxsen, Continental (Fortress); and Helmut Koester, Hermeneia (Fortress). First and Second Thessalonians is already well served by Wanamaker, Green, Malherbe, Beale, Holmes, and Marshall, but I would wait to see how Weima and Kim is received. Newer isn't always better, but it usually is. After all, you're drawing on all of the wealth that came before you, including what used to be new! It just costs more. Meanwhile, choose Malherbe, Wanamaker, Witherington, and Beale.

12. Many people might be surprised to discover that Malherbe supports the Pauline authorship of *both* letters around A.D. 50. In response to criticism of his earlier monograph, he also delves much deeper into unpacking Paul's eschatology. Readers should turn to a more conventional explanation of the parousia before wading into Malherbe's rather technical exegesis. The strengths of this commentary are the frequent allusions to Greco-Roman background literature, particularly that of the Epicureans.

E 6. Hiebert, D. Edmond. *1 and 2 Thessalonians,* rev. ed. (Moody, 1992). Pretribulational, dispensational.

E 7. Holmes, Michael. NIVAC (Zondervan, 1998). Posttribulational.

E/Cr 8. **Marshall, I. Howard. NCBC (Eerdmans, 1983).** Semitechnical.

E 9. Martin, Michael. NAC (Broadman & Holman, 1995). Semitechnical, rhetorical analysis, posttribulational.

L/Cr 10. Richard, Earl. Sacra Pagina (Liturgical, 1995). 2 Thessalonians non-Pauline; lexical, grammatical, literary background.

E 11. Stott, John. BST (IVP, 1992).

E 12. Thomas, Robert. EBC, vol. 11 (Zondervan, 1978). Dispensational.

C/M 13. Williams, David. NIBCNT (Hendrickson, 1992).

E 14. Witherington, Ben. *1 and 2 Thessalonians* (Eerdmans, 2006).

Special Studies

E 1. Burke, Trevor. *Family Matters: A Socio-Historical Study of Kinship Metaphors in 1 Thessalonians* (T & T Clark, 2003).

L/Cr 2. Collins, Raymond, ed. *The Thessalonian Correspondence* (Peeters, 1990).

C/M 3. Donfried, Karl. *Paul, Thessalonica, and Early Christianity* (Eerdmans, 2002).

C/M 4. Donfried, Karl, and Johannes Beutler, eds. *The Thessalonians Debate* (Eerdmans, 2000). 1 Thessalonians 2:1–12.

E/Cr 5. Donfried, Karl, and I. Howard Marshall. *The Theology of the Shorter Pauline Letters,* NTT (Cambridge University Press, 1993).

C/M 6. Malherbe, Abraham. *Paul and the Thessalonians* (Fortress, 1987).

E 7. Nicholl, Colin. *From Hope to Despair in Thessalonica*

(Cambridge University Press, 2004). Gordon-Conwell professor.

E   8. Walton, Steve. *Leadership and Lifestyle: The Portrait of Paul in the Miletus Speech and 1 Thessalonians* (Cambridge University Press, 2000).

E-E/Cr 9. Weima, Jeffrey, and Stanley Porter. *An Annotated Bibliography of 1 and 2 Thessalonians* (Brill, 1998).

1 and 2 Timothy, Titus[*]
Technical, Semitechnical

L/Cr   1. Collins, Raymond, NTL (Westminster John Knox, 2003). Noticeable paucity of footnotes.[13]

C/M   2. **Johnson, Luke. AB (Doubleday, 2001).**[14]

E   3. **Knight, George W. III. NIGTC (Eerdmans, 1992).** Complementarian.

E/Cr   4. **Marshall, I. Howard. ICC (T & T Clark, 2000).** Egalitarian.

E   5. **Mounce, William. WBC (Thomas Nelson, 2000).** Complementarian.

C/M   6. **Quinn, Jerome. AB (Doubleday, 1990).** Only Titus, non-Pauline.

C/M   7. Quinn, Jerome, and William Wacker. ECC (Eerdmans, 1999). Especially philology, 1–2 Timothy post-

---

[*] Forthcoming: Gregory Beale, ZEC (Zondervan); Philip Towner, NICNT (Eerdmans); Stanley Porter, BECNT (Baker); Abraham Malherbe, Hermeneia (Fortress); Terry Wilder, Mentor (Christian Focus); and Robert Yarbrough, PNTC (Eerdmans). Once, conservative pastors had to depend upon liberal commentators if they were to continue in utilizing the Greek and Hebrew skills they acquired in seminary. Now that has changed. Nowhere is that more evident than in the Pastoral Letters, where fourteen commentaries in the past thirteen years (of sixteen mentioned) and eight commentaries in the last five years have taken their place on the bookshelf.

13. Erudite to the exclusion of attribution. Confines subordinate role of women to original context (surprising for a Catholic priest). Weak on history of interpretation.

14. In his lengthy introduction, Johnson covers thoroughly the history of interpretation. He also defends Pauline authorship. Finally, he downplays the hierarchical relationship of men to women, another surprising twist from a Catholic.

Pauline (A.D. 80–85), like AB (Doubleday) series with application.

E/Cr 8. **Towner, Philip.** *Letters to Timothy and Titus,* **NICNT (Eerdmans, 2006).** Egalitarian.

Exposition[15]

E 1. Barcley, William. EPSC (Evangelical Press, 2005).

L/Cr 2. Donelson, Lewis. WBComp (Westminster John Knox, 1996).

E 3. **Fee, Gordon. NIBCNT (Hendrickson, 1988).** Egalitarian.

L/Cr 4. Hanson, A. NCBC (Eerdmans, 1982). Post-Pauline.

C/M 5. **Johnson, Luke.** *Letters to Paul's Delegates,* **NTC (Trinity Press International, 1996).**

C/M 6. Kelly, J. N. D. BNTC (Harper, 1963; Hendrickson, 1993). Especially patristic background.

E 7. **Köstenberger, Andreas. EBC, vol. 12, rev. ed. (Zondervan, 2006).**

E 8. Liefeld, Walter. NIVAC (Zondervan, 1999).

C/M 9. **Oden, Thomas. IBC (Westminster John Knox, 1989).** Defends Pauline authorship.

E 10. Stott, John. BST (IVP, 1973). 2 Timothy only.
———. *Guard the Truth,* BST (IVP, 1997). 1 Timothy and Titus only.

E/Cr 11. **Towner, Philip. IVPNTC (IVP, 1994).** Pauline, egalitarian.

Women in Ministry
(1 Timothy 2:9–15)

E 1. **Beck, James, and Craig Blomberg, eds.** *Two Views on Women in Ministry,* **rev. ed. (Zondervan, 2005).** Complementarian vs. Egalitarian.

E/Cr 2. Belleville, Linda. *Women Leaders and the Church: 3 Crucial Questions* (Baker, 2000). Egalitarian.

---

15. Obtain Towner, Beale, and Mounce for technical coverage, and Köstenberger or Johnson (exposition), but watch for Porter and Yarbrough (when they come out).

E	3.	Doriani, Dan. *Women in Ministry* (Crossway, 2003).
E/Cr	4.	France, R. T. *Women in the Church's Ministry* (Eerdmans, 1995). Egalitarian.
E/Cr	5.	Grenz, Stanley, and Denise Muir Kjesbo. *Women in the Church: A Biblical Theology of Women in Ministry* (IVP, 1995). Egalitarian.
E	6.	Grudem, Wayne, ed. *Biblical Foundations for Manhood and Womanhood* (Crossway, 2002).
E	**7.**	**Köstenberger, Andreas, Thomas Schreiner, and Scott Baldwin, eds. *Women in the Church* (Baker, 1995).**
E	8.	Perriman, Andrew. *Speaking of Women: Interpreting Paul* (Apollos, 1998).
E	**9.**	**Pierce, Ronald, and Rebecca Merrill Groothuis, eds. *Discovering Biblical Equality.* 2d ed. (IVP, 2005).** Egalitarian.
E	**10.**	**Piper, John, and Wayne Grudem, eds. *Recovering Biblical Manhood and Womanhood* (Crossway, 1991).**

Special Studies

L/Cr	1.	Collins, J. N. *DIAKONIA* (Oxford University Press, 1990).
L/Cr	**2.**	**Donelson, Lewis. *Pseudepigraphy and Ethical Argument in the Pastoral Epistles* (Mohr, 1986).**
L/Cr	3.	Harding, Mark. *What Are They Saying About the Pastoral Epistles?* (Paulist, 2001).
E	4.	Kidd, Reggie. *Wealth and Beneficence in the Pastoral Epistles* (Scholars, 1990).
E	**5.**	**Lau, Andrew. *Manifest in Flesh: The Epiphany Christology of the Pastoral Epistles* (Mohr, 1996).**
E/Cr	6.	Miller, James. *The Pastoral Letters as Composite Documents* (Cambridge University Press, 1997).
E	7.	Pietersen, Lloyd. *The Polemics of the Pastorals* (T & T Clark, 2004),
E/Cr	**8.**	**Prior, Michael. *Paul the Letter-Writer and the Second Letter to Timothy* (Sheffield Academic Press, 1989).** Defends Pauline authorship.

E 9. Van Neste, Ray. *Cohesion and Structure in the Pastoral Epistle*, Journal for the Study of New Testament Supplement (T & T Clark, 2005). Response to Miller above.

C/M 10. Young, Frances. NTT (Cambridge University Press, 1994). Egalitarian and non-Pauline; especially Patristic theology.

Hebrews[*]
Technical, Semitechnical

L/Cr 1. **Attridge, Harold. Hermeneia (Fortress, 1989).** Primary sources.

E/Cr 2. Bruce, F. F. NICNT, rev. ed. (Eerdmans, 1990). Little change from 1964 edition.

E 3. **deSilva, David. *Perseverance in Gratitude* (Eerdmans, 2000).** Sociorhetorical.[16]

E 4. **Ellingworth, Paul. NIGTC (Eerdmans, 1993).** Especially grammar, textual criticism.

E/Cr 5. Hughes, Philip. *A Commentary on the Epistle to the Hebrews* (Eerdmans, 1977). Especially history of interpretation.

C/M 6. **Johnson, Luke Timothy. AB (Doubleday, 2006).**

C/M 7. Koester, Craig. AB (Doubleday, 2001). Especially rhetoric (sees as sermon), history of interpretation, concept of suffering.

---

[*] Forthcoming: D. A. Carson, BECNT (Baker); Edgar McKnight, SHBC (Smyth & Helwys); David Allen, NAC (Broadman & Holman); Doug Moo, ZEC (Zondervan); and Peter O'Brien, PNTC (Eerdmans). Once again we are faced with a bibliophilic conundrum. For those who have *both* Bruce and Hughes, these will do. However, you should obtain George Guthrie's NIVAC entry for its sensitivity to the overall structure of Hebrews. The same goes for those that possess Attridge, Lane, or Ellingworth. However, in a perfect world, a combination of Lane, Ellingworth, France, Koester, deSilva, and Guthrie would cover the theology, grammar, rhetorical features, social setting, and overall structure quite nicely. Of these, Lane does the best job in addressing each facet of Hebrews. Enter Carson, Moo, and O'Brien. Use with Lane. An embarrassment of riches.

16. I hesitate to recommend specialized commentaries (the other exceptions being Witherington's sociorhetorical commentary on Acts, and Blomberg's historical commentary on John), but deSilva's commentary builds on his much-noticed dissertation *Despising Shame*.

E/Cr   **8.** **Lane, William. WBC, 2 vols. (Word, 1991).** Especially theological flow.

L/Cr   9. McL. Wilson, Robert. NCBC (Eerdmans, 1987).

Exposition

E   1. Brown, Raymond. BST (IVP, 1988).

L/Cr   2. Craddock, Fred. NIB, vol. 12 (Abingdon, 1998). *See* "Reflections" in the back of the volume for applications.

E   3. Ellingworth, Paul. Epworth (Epworth, 1992).

E/Cr   **4.** **France, R. T. EBC, vol. 13, rev. ed. (Zondervan, 2005).**

E   5. Guthrie, Donald. TNTC (Eerdmans, 1983).

E   **6.** **Guthrie, George. NIVAC (Zondervan, 1998).** Especially discourse analysis.

E   7. Hagner, Donald. NIBCNT (Hendrickson, 1990).

E/Cr   8. Lane, William. *Call to Commitment* (Hendrickson, 1988).

L/Cr   9. Pfitzner, Victor. ANTC (Abingdon, 1997). Theological.

Special Studies

E   1. Bateman, Herbert. *Early Jewish Hermeneutics and Hebrews 1:5–13* (Lang, 1997).

————, ed. *Four Views on the Warning Passages in Hebrews* (Kregel, 2007). Grant Osborne, Buist Fanning, Gareth Cockerill, and Randall Gleason.

C/M   **2.** **Croy, Clayton. *Endurance in Suffering* (Cambridge University Press, 1998).** Hebrews 12:1–3.

E   **3.** **deSilva, David. *Despising Shame* (Scholars, 1995).** Honor-shame rhetoric.

E   4. Gheorghita, Radu. *The Role of the Septuagint in Hebrews* (Mohr, 2003).

E   5. Guthrie, George. *The Structure of Hebrews* (Brill, 1994; Baker, 1998).

E   6. Hagner, Donald. *Encountering the Epistle to the Hebrews* (Baker, 2002).

L/Cr   7. Hurst, L. D. *The Epistle to the Hebrews* (Cambridge University Press, 1990).

E   8. Laansma, Jon. *"I Will Give You Rest"* **(Mohr, 1997).**
            Matthew 11 and Hebrews 3–4.
C/M   9. Lindars, Barnabas. NTT (Cambridge University Press,
            1991).
E   10. Peterson, David. *Hebrews and Perfection* (Cambridge
            University Press, 1982).
E   11. **Rhee, Victor.** *Faith in Hebrews* **(Lang, 2001).** Theo-
            logical study.
E   12. **Trotter, Andrew.** *Interpreting the Epistle to the He-
            brews* **(Baker, 1996).**
E   13. Westfall, Cynthia. *A Discourse Analysis of the Letter to
            the Hebrews* (T & T Clark, 2006).

James[*]
Technical, Semitechnical

E/Cr   1. **Davids, Peter. NIGTC (Eerdmans, 1982).**
L/Cr   2. Dibelius, Martin, and Hans Greeven. Hermeneia (For-
            tress, 1975).
C/M   3. **Johnson, Luke. AB (Doubleday, 1995).** Extensive 162-
            page introduction, history of interpretation.[17]
E/Cr   4. **Martin, Ralph. WBC (Word, 1989).**
E/Cr   5. Mayor, Joseph. *The Epistle of James,* 3d ed. (Macmillan,
            1913; Kregel, 1990).
L/Cr   6. Mitton, C. *The Epistle of James* (Eerdmans, 1966).

---

* Forthcoming: Joel Green, NTL (Westminster John Knox); John Kloppenborg,
  Hermeneia (Fortress); Dale Allison, ICC (T & T Clark); Dan McCartney,
  BECNT (Baker); and Scot McKnight, NICNT (Eerdmans). If you have Johnson,
  Davids, Martin, or Moo, you are already pretty well off. If not, obtain Johnson
  and Moo, PNTC (Eerdmans), and wait for the verdict on McCartney. I am also
  encouraged by the spate of special studies that have appeared in the last six
  years, particularly those that affirm James as the brother of Jesus.

17. Luke Johnson's moderate commentary, in which he holds the book of James to
  be authored by James, the brother of Jesus, is the best commentary available.
  It is particularly noteworthy on matters of introduction. He devotes forty pages
  to the history of its interpretation and an even longer section on the relationship
  of James to the rest of the New Testament (especially Paul). In this regard,
  Johnson believes that James and Paul have a lot more in common than is usually recognized. More than four hundred years later, who would have thought
  that a Catholic would correct Luther in this regard?

Exposition

E   1. Baker, William, and T. D. Ellsworth. *Preaching James* (Chalice, 2004).

E/Cr   2. Brosend, William. *James and Jude*, NCBC (Cambridge University Press, 2004). Brief.

E/Cr   3. Davids, Peter. NIBCNT (Hendrickson, 1989).

E   4. Guthrie, George. EBC, vol. 13, rev. ed. (Zondervan, 2005).

C/M   **5. Hartin, Patrick. Sacra Pagina (Liturgical, 2003).** Sociorhetorical. James as kinsman, not brother, of Jesus.

E   6. Hiebert, D. Edmond. *The Epistle of James,* rev. ed. (Moody, 1992).

C/M   7. Johnson, Luke. NIB, vol. 12 (Abingdon, 1998).

L/Cr   **8. Laws, Sophie. BNTC (Harper, 1980; Hendrickson, 1987).** Roman origin.

E   **9. Moo, Douglas. PNTC (Eerdmans, 2000).**
           ———. TNTC (Eerdmans, 1986).

E   10. Nystrom, David. NIVAC (Zondervan, 1997).

E   11. Stulac, George. IVPNTC (IVP, 1993). Appendix: identity of the rich.

E/Cr   12. Wall, Robert. NTC (Trinity Press International, 1997). Socioliterary context; canonical criticism appendix.

Special Studies

E   1. Adamson, James. *James* (Eerdmans, 1989).

E   2. Baker, William. *Personal Speech-Ethics in the Epistle of James* (Mohr, 1995).

C/M   3. Bauckham, Richard. *James* (Routledge, 1999).

L/Cr   4. Bernheim, Pierre. *James, Brother of Jesus* (SCM, 1997). Includes Gospels of Thomas and Hebrews.

E   5. Bratcher, Robert. UBS Helps for Translators (UBS, 1983).

L/Cr   6. Cargal, T. *Restoring the Diaspora* (Scholars, 1993).

E/Cr   7. Chester, A., and Ralph Martin. *The Theology of the Letters of James, Peter, and Jude,* NTT (Cambridge University Press, 1994).

C/M   8. Cheung, Luke. *The Genre, Composition, and Hermeneutics of James* (Paternoster, 2003).

All   9. Chilton, Bruce, and Craig Evans, eds. *James the Just and Christian Origins* (Brill, 1999).
———, eds. *James the Just and Simon Peter* (Brill, 2002).

L/Cr   10. Chilton, Bruce, and Jacob Neusner, eds. *The Brother of Jesus* (Westminster John Knox, 2001).

E   11. Deppe, Dean. *The Sayings of Jesus in James* (Bookcrafters, 1989).

C/M   12. Edgar, David. *Has God Not Chosen the Poor?* (Sheffield Academic Press, 2001).

L/Cr   13. Eisenman, Robert. *James the Brother of Jesus* (Penguin, 1997).

C/M   14. Hartin, Patrick. *James of Jerusalem* (Liturgical, 2004).

C/M   15. Johnson, Luke. *Brother of Jesus, Friend of God* (Eerdmans, 2004).

L/Cr   16. Maynard-Reid, Pedrito. *Poverty and Wealth in James* (Orbis, 1987). Sociological.

E/Cr-L/Cr   17. Neusner, Jacob, and Bruce Chilton, eds. *The Judaism of James the Brother of Jesus* (Westminster John Knox, 2002).

L/Cr   18. Painter, John. *Just James* (Fortress, 1999).

C/M   19. Penner, Todd. *The Epistle of James and Eschatology* (Sheffield Academic Press, 1996). Continuity with early Christian and Jewish texts on ethics and eschatology.

L/Cr   20. Tamez, Elsa. *The Scandalous Message of James.* 2d ed. (Crossroad, 2002).

E   21. Taylor, Mark. *Text-Linguistic Investigation into the Discourse Structure of James* (T & T Clark, 2006).

1 Peter[*]
Technical, Semitechnical

C/M   **1. Achtemeier, Paul. Hermeneia (Fortress, 1996).** Pseudepigraphic.

L/Cr   2. Beare, Francis. *The First Epistle of Peter,* 3d ed. (Basil Blackwell, 1970). Non-Petrine.

E/Cr   **3. Davids, Peter. NICNT (Eerdmans, 1990).** Silvanus by Petrine commission.

L/Cr   4. Elliott, John. AB (Doubleday, 2001). Pseudepigraphic; especially cultural background.

C/M   5. Goppelt, Leonard. *A Commentary on 1 Peter* (Eerdmans, 1993). Sociological background, extracanonical material, links to DSS and OT.

E   **6. Jobes, Karen. BECNT (Baker, 2005).** 1 Peter.

E/Cr   **7. Michaels, Ramsey. WBC (Word, 1988).** Essentially Petrine, written by approved disciple.

E   **8. Schreiner, Thomas. NAC (Broadman, 2003).** With 2 Peter/Jude.

E/Cr   9. Selwyn, Edward. *The First Epistle of St. Peter,* 2d ed. (Macmillan, 1947). Petrine through Silvanus.

Exposition

L/Cr   1. Boring, Eugene. ANTC (Abingdon, 1999). Pseudepigraphic; "Narrative World of Peter" appendix.

E   2. Charles, Daryl. EBC, vol. 23, rev. ed. (Zondervan, 2005). Includes 2 Peter/Jude.

---

[*] Forthcoming: Troy Martin, NIGTC (Eerdmans); David DeSilva, ECC (Eerdmans); Carey Newman, SHBC (Smyth & Helwys); Michael Wilkins, ZEC (Zondervan); David Horrell, ICC (T & T Clark); Lewis Donelson, NTL (Westminster John Knox); and Scott Hafemann, PNTC (Eerdmans). Troy Martin's forthcoming commentary should be very good on the Greek, and Hafemann should be well worth looking forward to. He's also been assigned 2 Peter/Jude, NIGTC (Eerdmans). For 1 Peter, choose Schreiner and Jobes and wait for Martin or Hafemann (Martin if you desire technical, Hafemann if you prefer in-depth expositional). Who would have imagined that a numbers game would ensue in selecting an entirely evangelical slate on 1–2 Peter/Jude?

E   3. Clowney, Edmund. BST (IVP, 1989).

L/Cr   4. Craddock, Fred. WBComp (Westminster John Knox, 1995). 1–2 Peter/Jude.

E   5. Grudem, Wayne. TNTC (Eerdmans, 1988). Petrine, 1 Peter 3:19–20 appendix.

E   6. Hillyer, Norman. NIBCNT (Hendrickson, 1992). 1–2 Peter/Jude.

C/M   7. Kelly, J. N. D. BNTC (Hendrickson, 1993). 1 Peter by Silvanus, denies authenticity of 2 Peter, also includes Jude.

E/Cr 8. Marshall, I. Howard. IVPNTC (IVP, 1992).

L/Cr   9. Richard, Earl. *Reading 1 Peter, Jude and 2 Peter* (Smyth & Helwys, 2000).

L/Cr   10. Senior, Donald, and Daniel Harrington. Sacra Pagina (Liturgical, 2004). With 2 Peter/Jude.

E   11. Waltner, E., and J. Daryl Charles. BCBC (Herald, 1999). 1–2 Peter/Jude.

Special Studies

E   1. Bechtler, Steven. *Following in His Steps* (Scholars, 1998).

E/Cr   2. Campbell, Barth. *Honor, Shame, and the Rhetoric of 1 Peter* (Scholars, 1998).

L/Cr   3. Dalton, W. *Christ's Proclamation to the Spirits,* 2d ed. (Pontifical Biblical Institute, 1989). 1 Peter 3:18–4:6.

E   4. Dubis, Mark. *Messianic Woes in First Peter* (Lang, 2002). 1 Peter 4:12–19.

L/Cr   5. Elliott, John. *A Home for the Homeless,* 2d ed. (Fortress, 1990). Analysis of "aliens and strangers" in 1 Peter.

L/Cr   6. Perkins, Pheme. *Peter* (Fortress, 2000).

C/M   7. Thurén, Lauri. *Argument and Theology in 1 Peter* (Sheffield Academic Press, 1995).

        8. *See* Chester and Martin under James: Special Studies.

2 Peter/Jude*
Technical, Semitechnical

C/M   **1. Bauckham, Richard. WBC (Word, 1983).** Pseudepi-
       graphic, rich extrabiblical material, Jewish background.

E   **2. Davids, Peter. PNTC (Eerdmans, 2006).**

E/Cr   3. Mayor, Joseph B. *The Epistle of St. Jude and the Second
       Epistle of St. Peter* (Baker, 1979). Non-Petrine.

L/Cr   4. Neyrey, Jerome. AB (Doubleday, 1993). Socioliterary
       background, pseudepigraphic.

E   **5. Schreiner, Thomas. NAC (Broadman & Holman,
       2003).** With 1 Peter.

       6. *See* Kelly under 1 Peter: Exposition.

Exposition

E   **1. Green, Michael. TNTC, rev. ed. (Eerdmans, 1987).**
       Annihilationist, solid author defense.

E   2. Hiebert, D. Edmond. *2 Peter and Jude* (Unusual,
       1989).

L/Cr   3. Kraftchick, Stephen. ANTC (Abingdon, 2002).

E   4. Lucas, Dick, and Christopher Green. BST (IVP, 1995).
       Semitechnical, authorship appendix.

E   **5. Moo, Douglas. NIVAC (Zondervan, 1996).**

L/Cr   6. Watson, Duane. NIB, vol. 12 (Abingdon, 1998).

Special Studies

C/M   **1. Bauckham, Richard. *Jude and the Relatives of Jesus
       in the Early Church* (T & T Clark, 1990).**

E   2. Charles, Daryl. *Literary Strategy in the Epistle of Jude*
       (University of Scranton, 1993).

---

* Forthcoming: Peter Davids, PNTC (Eerdmans); Scott Hafemann, NIGTC (Eerdmans); Robert Webb, NICNT (Eerdmans); Gene Green, BECNT (Baker); Watson Mills, SHBC (Smyth & Helwys), and Robert Harvey, IVPNTC (IVP). Green
recently offered an excellent commentary on 1–2 Thessalonians. Hafemann is
slated for a semitechnical effort on 1 Peter. Davids's NICNT entry on 1 Peter
was most serviceable. Therefore, I would recommend Davids, Hafemann, and
Green on 2 Peter/Jude, though Bauckham, WBC (Word) is under revision.

———. *Virtue Amidst Vice* **(Sheffield Academic Press, 1997).** Posits Christianization of Stoicism in 2 Peter 1 as elsewhere in NT. Centrist-Arminian position.

C/M   3.   Landon, Charles. *A Text-Critical Study of the Epistle of Jude* (Sheffield Academic Press, 1996).

E   4.   Lyle, Kenneth. *Ethical Admonition in the Epistle of Jude* (Lang, 1998).

E/Cr   **5.**   **Starr, James. *Sharers in Divine Nature: 2 Peter 1:4 in Its Hellenistic Context* (Almqvist & Wiksell, 2000).**

C/M   **6.**   **Watson, Duane. *Invention, Arrangement, and Style* (Scholars, 1988).**

1–3 John[*]
Technical, Semitechnical

L/Cr   1.   Brown, Raymond. AB (Doubleday, 1982). Sacramental.

L/Cr   2.   Grayston, Kenneth. NCBC (Eerdmans, 1984).

E   **3.**   **Harris, Hall. *1, 2, 3 John: Comfort and Counsel for a Church in Crisis* (Biblical Studies, 2003).** Available through www.bible.org.

E/Cr   **4.**   **Marshall, I. Howard. NICNT (Eerdmans, 1978).**

C/M   5.   Schnackenburg, Rudolf. *The Johannine Epistles,* 7th ed. (Crossroad, 1992). Theological.

---

[*] Forthcoming: D. A. Carson, NIGTC (Eerdmans); Robert Yarbrough, BECNT (Baker); Judith Lieu, NTL (Westminster John Knox); D. Moody Smith, ICC (T & T Clark), and Elizabeth Schüssler Fiorenza, WBComp (Westminster John Knox). I would keep Marshall because it is an admirable recapitulation of previous scholarship and very useful for the pastor. Brown and Schnackenburg are not only dated but do not subscribe to the common authorship of the Gospel and Epistles by the apostle John. Otherwise, Hall Harris' commentary fills a much-needed semitechnical gap. The recent expositions by Daniel Akin and Colin Kruse lean toward the semitechnical and are both very good, but it's time for another more technical commentary. That void will soon be remedied by D. A. Carson and Robert Yarbrough. Carson has already provided an outstanding, semitechnical commentary on the gospel of John (also Eerdmans). Yarbrough's commentary promises to pay close attention to the relationship of the OT and Jesus' teaching to 1–3 John. Frequent allusions will be made to Jewish, Greco-Roman, and patristic authors. Ultimately, go with Carson, Harris, and Kruse, though Smalley, WBC (Word) is under revision.

C/M   6. **Smalley, Stephen. WBC (Word, 1984).**
L/Cr   7. Strecker, Georg. Hermeneia (Fortress, 1996). Presbyter John author of 2–3 John; 1 John non-Johannine. Contra Brown on order of authorship.

Exposition

E   1. **Akin, Daniel. NAC (Broadman & Holman, 2001).**
L/Cr   2. Black, Clifton. NIB, vol. 12 (Abingdon, 1998).
E   3. Burge, Gary. NIVAC (Zondervan, 1996).
E/Cr   4. Johnson, Thomas. NIBCNT (Hendrickson, 1993).
E   5. **Kruse, Colin. PNTC (Eerdmans, 2000).** Extensive use of the early church fathers to establish setting.
E/Cr   6. Meye Thompson, Marianne. IVPNTC (IVP, 1992).
L/Cr   7. Painter, John. Sacra Pagina (Liturgical, 2002).
L/Cr   8. Rensberger, David. ANTC (Abingdon, 1997).
           ———. WBComp (Westminster John Knox, 2001).
L/Cr   9. Sloyan, Gerard. NTC (Trinity Press International, 1998). Social context commentary.
E   10. **Stott, John. TNTC, rev. ed. (Eerdmans, 1988).**
E   11. **Thatcher, Tom. EBC, vol. 13, rev. ed. (Zondervan, 2005).**[18]
E   12. Thomas, John. *1 John, 2 John, 3 John*. The Pentecostal Commentary (T & T Clark, 2004).

Special Studies

E   1. Burge, Gary. *The Anointed Community* (Eerdmans, 1987).
C/M   2. **Lieu, Judith. *The Second and Third Letters of John* (T & T Clark, 1986).**
           ———. NTT (Cambridge University Press, 1991).
C/M   3. Smalley, Stephen. *John,* 2d ed. (IVP, 1998). Especially literary features.
       4. *See* John: John as Story, Special Studies.

---

18. I proofread James–Jude for Zondervan, and Thatcher's exposition was the best of these letters.

Revelation[*]
Technical, Semitechnical

C/M   1. Aune, David. WBC, 3 vols. (Thomas Nelson, 1997–98). Especially grammatical, text-critical analysis; source/ composition critical; extensive introduction; proposes early/late editions; top heavy in extrabiblical citations of Greco-Roman, Jewish parallels; limited use to pastors.

E   2. **Beale, Gregory. NIGTC (Eerdmans, 1999).** Especially OT, Jewish parallels, historical, idealist, amillennial, later date more probable.

E   3. **Mounce, Robert. NICNT, rev. ed. (Eerdmans, 1997).** Posttribulational.

E   4. **Osborne, Grant. BECNT (Baker, 2002).**

L/Cr   5. Roloff, Jürgen. Continental (Fortress, 1993). Amillennial.

C/M   6. **Smalley, Stephen.** *The Revelation to John: A Commentary on the Greek Text of the Apocalypse* **(IVP, 2005).**

E   7. Thomas, Robert. *Revelation,* 2 vols. (Moody, 1992, 1995). Dispensational.

Exposition[19]

E   1. **Beasley-Murray, George. NCBC, rev. ed. (Eerdmans, 1978).** Premillennial.

---

[*] Forthcoming: Elizabeth Schüssler Fiorenza, Hermeneia (Fortress); Craig Koester, AB (Doubleday); Paige Patterson, NAC, 2 vols. (Broadman & Holman); Brian Blount, NTL (Westminster John Knox); and D. A. Carson, PNTC (Eerdmans). At present, Revelation is already well served. I am tempted to say that one could hardly do better than Beale, Osborne, and Mounce for technical/semitechnical commentaries. Of these, I prefer Osborne and Mounce because Beale can leave one's head spinning. Also, Smalley is not to be ignored and preferable to Mounce on the Greek. D. A. Carson's work would be the best choice on the heavy side of exposition. Elizabeth Schüssler Fiorenza has argued previously that Revelation is a collection of traditions unified by a single author.

19. Alan Johnson's entry in the revised EBC (Zondervan) builds on its prior excellence. Keener's commentary weighs on the semitechnical side, but comes closer to an exposition than Carson's probably will. Dennis Johnson's *Triumph*

L/Cr   2. Boring, Eugene. IBC (John Knox, 1989).
C/M   3. Boxall, Ian. BNTC (Hendrickson, 2006). Amillennial.
C/M   4. Caird, George. BNTC (Hendrickson, 1993).
L/Cr   5. Harrington, Wilfred. Sacra Pagina (Liturgical, 1994).
E   6. Hendriksen, William. *More Than Conquerors* (Baker, 1939).
E   7. Johnson, Alan. EBC, vol. 13, rev. ed. (Zondervan, 2003). Semitechnical, premillennial.
E   8. Johnson, Dennis. *Triumph of the Lamb* (Presbyterian & Reformed, 2001). Amillennial.
E   9. Keener, Craig. NIVAC (Zondervan, 2000). Premillennial.
E   10. Kistemaker, Simon. *Exposition of the Book of Revelation* (Baker, 2001). Idealist, amillennial.
L/Cr   11. Kovacs, Judith, and Christopher Rowland. BBC (Blackwell, 2004).
E   12. Ladd, George. *A Commentary on the Revelation of John* (Eerdmans, 1972). Premillennial.
E/Cr   13. Michaels, J. Ramsey. IVPNTC (IVP, 1997).
E   14. Morris, Leon. TNTC, rev. ed. (Eerdmans, 1987). Amillennial.
E   15. Reddish, Mitchell. SHBC (Smyth & Helwys, 2001).
L/Cr   16. Rowland, Christopher. Epworth (Epworth, 1993).
        ———. NIB, vol. 12 (Abingdon, 1998). Numerous excursuses, extensive history of interpretation, early-date advocate. Especially apocalyptic background.
L/Cr   17. Sweet, Leonard. NTC (Trinity Press International, 1990).
E/Cr   18. Wall, Robert. NIBCNT (Hendrickson, 1991).

---

of the Lamb is more layman friendly than Keener and Alan Johnson. An amillennialist, he is to be especially commended for the irenic manner in which he countenances contrary opinions, notably those of dispensationalists. For dispensationalists, Walvoord's shorter commentary is to be preferred over Robert Thomas' two-volume work, which is far too wooden an interpretation.

E   19. Walvoord, John. *The Revelation of Jesus Christ* (Moody, 1966). Dispensational; use with Walvoord's *Daniel.*

E   20. Wilcock, Michael. BST (IVP, 1984). Premillennial.

E   21. Witherington, Ben. NCamBC (Cambridge University Press, 2003).

Sociorhetorical Studies and Commentaries

L/Cr   1. Collins, Adele. *Crisis and Catharis* (John Knox, 1984).

L/Cr   **2. Murphy, Frederick. *Fallen Is Babylon,* NTC (Trinity Press International, 1998).** Written in the 1990s. Highly dependent on Collins above.

E   **3. Pattemore, Stephen. *The People of God in the Apocalypse: Discourse, Structure and Exegesis* (Cambridge University Press, 2004).** Revelation 4:1–22:21.

L/Cr   4. Schüssler Fiorenza, Elizabeth. *Revelation* (Fortress, 1991).

          ———. *The Book of Revelation,* 2d ed. (Fortress, 1999).

L/Cr   5. Talbert, Charles. *The Apocalypse* (Westminster John Knox, 1994).

L/Cr   6. Thompson, Leonard. ANTC (Abingdon, 1998).

          ———. *The Book of Revelation* (Oxford University Press, 1990).

Special Studies

C/M   1. Barker, Margaret. *The Revelation of Jesus Christ* (T & T Clark, 2000).

C/M   **2. Bauckham, Richard. *The Climax of Prophecy* (T & T Clark, 1994).**

          ———. NTT (Cambridge University Press, 1993).

E   **3. Beale, Gregory. *John's Use of the Old Testament in Revelation* (Sheffield Academic Press, 1998).**

          ———. *The Use of Daniel in Jewish Apocalyptic Literature and the Revelation of St. John* (University Press of America, 1984). Links Daniel 7 to Revelation 1:4–20 and Revelation 4–5.

E   **4.**   **Bock, Darrell, ed.** *Three Views on the Millennium and Beyond* **(Zondervan, 1999).**

E   5.   Davis, R. *The Heaven in Court Judgment of Revelation 4–5* (University Press of America, 1992).

E   6.   Gentry, Kenneth. *Before Jerusalem Fell* (Institute for Christian Economics, 1989). Thorough early-date study.

E   7.   Gregg, Steve, ed. *Revelation: Four Views—A Parallel Commentary* (Thomas Nelson, 1997). Preterist, historicist, futurist, idealist. Numerous excerpts from Chilton, Hendriksen, Ladd, Mounce, Russell, Ryrie, Swete, Walvoord, Wilcock, etc.

E   **8.**   **Hemer, Colin.** *The Letters to the Seven Churches of Asia in Their Local Setting* **(JSOT, 1986; Eerdmans, 2001).** Revelation 2–3.

C/M   **9.**   **Koester, Craig.** *Revelation and the End of All Things* **(Eerdmans, 2001).**

E/Cr   **10.**   **Kraybill, Nelson.** *Imperial Cult and Commerce in John's Apocalypse* **(Sheffield Academic Press, 1996).** Socioeconomic perspective culled from archaeological and epigraphical evidence.

E   11.   Lioy, Dan. *The Book of Revelation in Christian Focus* (Lang, 2003).

L/Cr   12.   Malina, Bruce, and John Pilch. *Social-Scientific Commentary on the Book of Revelation* (Fortress, 2000).

E   13.   Mathewson, Dave. *New Heaven and a New Earth: The Meaning and Function of the Old Testament in Revelation 21:1–22:5* (Sheffield Academic Press, 2003). Idealist.

E/Cr   14.   Michaels, Ramsey. *Interpreting the Book of Revelation* (Baker, 1992).

C/M   15.   Moyise, Steve. *The Old Testament in the Book of Revelation* (Sheffield Academic Press, 1995).

E   16.   Pate, Marvin, ed. *Four Views on the Book of Revelation* (Zondervan, 1998). Preterist, idealist, dispensationalist, progressive dispensational.

C/M   **17.** **Stevenson, Gregory.** *Power and Place* **(de Gruyter, 2001).** The temple in Revelation.

L/Cr   **18.** **Wainwright, Arthur.** *Mysterious Apocalypse* **(Abingdon, 1993; Wipf & Stock, 2001).** History of interpretation.

L/Cr   19. Worth, Roland. *The Seven Cities of the Apocalypse,* vol. 2 (Paulist, 1999). Revelation 2–3.

       20. *See* Systematic Theology: The Last Days.

Scholarly One-Volume Commentaries*

1. **Barton, John, and John Muddiman, eds.** *The Oxford Bible Commentary* **(Oxford University Press, 2001).** Moderate-liberal.

2. **Brown, Raymond E., Joseph Fitzmyer, and Roland Murphy, eds.** *New Jerome Bible Commentary,* **2d ed. (Prentice-Hall, 1999).** Catholic, liberal.

3. Bruce, F. F., ed. *New International Bible Commentary* (Zondervan, 1986).

4. Dockery, David, ed. *Holman Bible Handbook* (Broadman & Holman, 1993).

5. **Dunn, James, and John Rogerson, eds.** *Eerdmans Commentary on the Bible* **(Eerdmans, 2003).**

6. Kroeger, Catherine, and Mary Evans, eds. *The IVP Women's Bible Commentary* (IVP, 2002).

7. **Mays, James, ed.** *HarperCollins Bible Commentary,* **rev. ed. (HarperSanFrancisco, 2000).** Moderate-liberal.

8. Mills, Watson, and Richard Wilson, eds. *Mercer Commentary on the Bible* (Mercer University Press, 1995).

9. **Wenham, Gordon, et al., eds.** *New Bible Commentary: Twenty-First Century Edition* **(IVP, 1994).**

---

* Forthcoming: Robert Hubbard and Gordon Fee, eds., *Eerdman's Bible Handbook.*

10

NEW TESTAMENT BACKGROUND

Primary References

1. **Arnold, Clinton, ed.** *The Zondervan Illustrated Bible Backgrounds Commentary: New Testament,* **4 vols. (Zondervan, 2002).**[1]

2. **Evans, Craig, ed.** *The Bible Knowledge Background Commentary,* **3 vols. (Victor, 2003–05).**

3. House, H. Wayne. *Chronological and Background Charts of the New Testament* (Zondervan, 1981).

4. **Keener, Craig.** *The IVP Bible Background Commentary: New Testament* **(IVP, 1994).**

5. Matthews, Victor. *Manners and Customs in the Bible,* rev. ed. (Hendrickson, 1991).

IVP Dictionaries

1. **Evans, Craig, and Stanley Porter, eds.** *Dictionary of New Testament Background* **(IVP, 2000).** Greco-Roman influences, etc. This is not only the best but also the most technical of the IVP dictionaries.

---

1. Especially Mark Strauss on Luke (vol. 1), Andreas Köstenberger on John, and Clinton Arnold on Acts (vol. 2). Choosing the Evans-authored first volume (Matthew–Luke) together with the Evans-edited second volume (Acts to Philemon) of the *Bible Knowledge Background Commentary* (Victor), along with vol. 2 (John; Acts) and vol. 4 (Hebrews–Revelation) of the *ZIBBC* (Zondervan), would be the best route to go. The only redundancy would be Acts (done by Lee McDonald in *Bible Knowledge*), and the cost for the mix n' match approach is about the same for the four Zondervan volumes.

2. **Green, Joel, Scot McKnight, and I. Howard Marshall, eds.** *Dictionary of Jesus and the Gospels* **(IVP, 1992).**
3. **Hawthorne, Gerald, Ralph Martin, and Daniel Reid, eds.** *Dictionary of Paul and His Letters* **(IVP, 1993).**
4. **Martin, Ralph, and Peter Davids, eds.** *Dictionary of the Later New Testament and Its Developments* **(IVP, 1997).** Up to the second-century church fathers.
5. **Reid, Daniel, ed.** *The IVP Dictionary of the New Testament* **(IVP, 2004).**[2]

Primary Source Anthologies

1. Barrett, C. K. *New Testament Background,* 2d ed. (Harper, 1987).
2. Bettenson, Henry, and Chris Maunder, eds. *Documents of the Christian Church,* 3d ed. (Oxford University Press, 1999).
3. Bock, Darrell, and Greg Herrick, eds. *Jesus in Context* (Baker, 2005).
4. Boring, Eugene, Klaus Berger, and Carsten Colpe, eds. *Hellenistic Commentary to the New Testament* (Abingdon, 1995). History-of-religions approach.
5. Doepp, Siegmar, and Wilhelm Geerlings, eds. *Dictionary of Early Christian Literature* (Herder and Herder, 2000).
6. Dungan, David, and David Cartlidge, eds. *Documents for the Study of the Gospels,* rev. ed. and enl. (Fortress, 1994). With noncanonicals.
7. Ehrman, Bart. *The New Testament and Other Early Christian Writings: A Reader* (Oxford University Press, 1997). NRSV and excerpts from anthologies.
    ———. *After the New Testament* (Oxford University Press, 1998).
8. Elliott, J. K., ed. *The Apocryphal New Testament* (Oxford University Press, 1993).

---

2. A first-class abridgement of the above four volumes which slightly favors excerpts from the *DJG* (IVP) and *DPL* (IVP) (about three to two). It would still repay those with a scholarly interest to obtain *DNTB* (IVP) as well.

204 COMMENTARY AND REFERENCE SURVEY

9. Elwell, Walter, and Robert Yarbrough. *Readings from the First Century World* (Baker, 1998). Companion volume for their *Encountering the New Testament.*

10. **Evans, Craig. *Ancient Texts for New Testament Studies* (Hendrickson, 2005).**

11. Kee, Howard. *The Origins of Christianity,* 2d ed. (Prentice-Hall, 1973).

12. Mason, Steve, and Thomas Robinson. *Early Christian Reader* (Hendrickson, 2002). NRSV, NT, Ignatius, 1 Clement, Didache, and Gospel of Thomas.

13. Schneemelcher, Wilhelm. *New Testament Apocrypha,* 2d ed., 2 vols. (Westminster John Knox, 1990–92).

14. Young, Frances, et al., eds. *The Cambridge History of Early Christian Literature* (Cambridge University Press, 2004).

Principal Early Church References[*]

1. **Barnett, Paul. *Jesus and the Rise of Early Christianity* (IVP, 1999).**

   ————. *The Birth of the Church: The First Twenty Years* (Eerdmans, 2005).

2. **Bowersock, G. W., Peter Brown, and Oleg Grabar, eds. *Late Antiquity* (Harvard University Press, 1999).**

3. **Brown, Peter. *The Rise of Western Christendom,* 2d ed. (Blackwell, 2002).**

4. Bruce, F. F. *New Testament History* (Doubleday, 1971).

5. **Chadwick, Henry. *The Church in Ancient Society* (Oxford University Press, 2002).** First six centuries.[3]

6. **Di Berardino, Angelo, ed. *Encyclopedia of The Early Church,* 2 vols. (Oxford University Press, 1992).**

7. Doepp, Siegmar, and Wilhelm Geerlings, eds. *Dictionary of Early Christian Literature* (Herder and Herder, 1999).

---

* Forthcoming: Loveday Alexander, NTL (Westminster John Knox).

3. As a documentary source for early Christianity, this reference has no rivals, especially in its citation of German and French in addition to English references, but it is virtually colorless in composition.

8. Doran, Robert. *Birth of a Worldview* (Rowman and Littlefield, 1999). Author of commentary on 1–2 Maccabees.

9. **Ferguson, Everett. *Backgrounds of Early Christianity*, 2d ed. (Eerdmans, 1993).** Cultural, political, religious background guide.

    ———, ed. *Encyclopedia of Early Christianity*, 2d ed. (Garland, 1997).

10. **Grant, Robert. *Augustus to Constantine*, rev. ed. (Harper, 1990).**

11. **Guy, Laurie. *Introducing Early Christianity* (IVP, 2004).** Centuries 2–4.

12. Lampe, Peter. *From Paul to Valentinus* (Fortress, 1999).

13. Lieu, Judith. *Neither Jew nor Greek?* (T & T Clark, 2003).

14. Malherbe, Abraham, et al., eds. *The Early Church in Its Context* (Brill, 1998).

15. **McKechnie, Paul. *The First Christian Centuries* (IVP, 2002).** First three centuries.

16. Novak, Ralph. *Christianity and the Roman Empire: Background Texts* (Trinity Press International, 2001). The first four centuries.

17. **Patzia, Arthur. *The Emergence of the Church* (IVP, 2001).**

18. Reicke, Bo. *The New Testament Era* (Fortress, 1968). 500 B.C.–A.D. 100.

19. **Stark, Rodney. *The Rise of Christianity* (Princeton University Press, 1996).**

20. **Trocmé, Etienne. *The Childhood of Christianity* (SCM, 1997).** Brief, engaging, moderate history.

21. Winter, Bruce, ed. *The Book of Acts in Its First-Century Setting,* 6 vols. (Eerdmans, 1993–).

22. **Witherington, Ben. *New Testament History* (Baker, 2001).**

Other Early Church References

1. Attridge, Harold, and Gregory Hata. *Eusebius, Christianity, and Judaism* (Wayne State University Press, 1992).

2. **Aune, David. *Prophecy in Early Christianity and the Ancient**

Mediterranean World (**Eerdmans, 1983; Wipf & Stock, 2003**).

————, ed. *The Westminster Dictionary of New Testament and Early Christian Literature and Rhetoric* (**Westminster John Knox, 2003**).

3. Avalos, Hector. *Health Care and the Rise of Christianity* (Hendrickson, 1999).

4. Bauckham, Richard. *Gospel Women* (Eerdmans, 2002).

5. Bockmuehl, Markus. *Jewish Law in Gentile Churches* (T & T Clark, 2000). Influence of halakah.

6. Brox, Norbert. *A History of the Early Church* (SCM, 1994). Available through Trinity Press International, introductory.

7. Capuani, Massimo, et al. *Christian Egypt* (Liturgical, 2002).

8. Charlesworth, James. *The Old Testament Pseudepigrapha and the New Testament* (Trinity Press International, 1998).

9. deSilva, David. *Honor, Patronage, Kinship and Purity* (IVP, 2000).

10. Donfried, Karl, and Peter Richardson, eds. *Judaism and Christianity in First-Century Rome* (Eerdmans, 1998).

11. Evans, Craig. *Noncanonical Writings and Their Use in New Testament Interpretation* (Hendrickson, 1992).

12. Evans, Craig, and Stanley Porter, eds. *New Testament Backgrounds* (Sheffield Academic Press, 1997). JSNT compendium.

13. Hoehner, Harold. *Herod Antipas* (Cambridge University Press, 1972).

14. Horbury, William. *Jewish Messianism and the Cult of Christ* (SCM, 1998).

15. Jensen, Morten. *Herod Antipas in Galilee* (Mohr, 2006).

16. Jeremias, Joachim. *Jerusalem in the Time of Jesus* (Fortress, 1969). Dated.

17. Johnson, Luke. *Religious Experience in New Testament Studies* (Fortress, 1998). Baptism, glossalalia, meals, etc.

18. Kee, Howard. *The Beginnings of Christianity* (T & T Clark, 2005).

19. Kelly, J. N. D. *Early Christian Doctrines,* 5th ed. (Continuum, 2001).

20. Klijn, A. *Jewish-Christian Gospel Tradition* (Brill, 1992). On noncanonical gospels.

21. **Millard, Alan. *Reading and Writing in the Time of Jesus* (Sheffield Academic Press, 2000).**

22. Nobbs, A., et al., eds. *Ancient History in a Modern University,* vol. 2: *Early Christianity and Late Antiquity* (Eerdmans, 1997).

23. **Oakes, Peter, ed. *Rome in the Bible and the Early Church* (Baker, 2002).**

24. Pearson, Brook, ed. *The Future of Early Christianity* (Fortress, 1991).

25. Rousseau, Philip. *The Early Christian Centuries* (Longman, 2002).

26. Schmithals, Walter. *The Theology of the First Christians* (Westminster John Knox, 1997).

27. Sullivan, Francis. *From Apostles to Bishops* (Newman, 2002).

28. **Walker, Peter. *Jesus and the Holy City* (Eerdmans, 1997).**

29. **Williams, P. J., et al., eds. *The New Testament in Its First Century Setting* (Eerdmans, 2004).** Bruce Winters tribute.

30. Wilson, Stephen. *Related Strangers* (Fortress, 1995).

31. **Wright, N. T. *The New Testament and the People of God* (Fortress, 1992).**

32. Young, Frances, et al., eds. *The Cambridge History of Early Christian Literature* (Cambridge University Press, 2004).

33. *See* Church History Resources: Early Church.

Pontius Pilate

1. Bond, Helen. *Pontius Pilate in History and Interpretation* (Cambridge University Press, 1998).

2. Carter, Warren. *Pontius Pilate* (Liturgical, 2003).

3. Wroe, Ann. *Pontius Pilate* (Modern Library, 2000).

Pauline Background

1. Ashton, John. *The Religion of Paul the Apostle* (Yale University Press, 2000).
2. Banks, Robert. *Paul's Idea of Community,* rev. ed. (Hendrickson, 1994).
3. Barrett, C. K. *On Paul* (T & T Clark, 2003).
4. Beck, James. *The Psychology of Paul* (Kregel, 2002).
5. Bockmuehl, Markus. *Revelation and Mystery in Ancient Judaism and Pauline Christianity* (Eerdmans, 1997).
6. Dodd, Brian. *The Problem with Paul* (IVP, 1996). Gender roles, sexuality, slavery, and attitude toward Judaism.
7. Donaldson, Terence. *Paul and the Gentiles* (Fortress, 1997).
8. Dunn, James, ed. *The Cambridge Companion to St. Paul* (Cambridge University Press, 2003).
9. Engberg-Pedersen, Troels, ed. *Paul in Its Hellenistic Context* (Fortress, 1994).
   ———. *Paul and the Stoics* (Westminster John Knox, 2000).
   ———, ed. *Paul Beyond the Judaism/Hellenism Divide* (Westminster John Knox, 2001).
10. Gager, John. *Reinventing Paul* (Oxford University Press, 2000).
11. Goodwin, Mark. *Paul, Apostle of the Living God* (Trinity Press International, 2001).
12. **Hafemann, Scott. *Paul, Moses, and the History of Israel* (Hendrickson, 1996).**
13. Harrison, James. *Paul's Language of Grace in Its Graeco-Roman Context* (Mohr, 2003).
14. **Horrell, David. *The Social Ethos of Corinthian Correspondence* (T & T Clark, 1996).** Comparison of Paul, 1 Clement.
15. Horsley, Richard, ed. *Paul and the Roman Imperial Order* (Trinity Press International, 2004).
16. MacDonald, Margaret. *The Pauline Churches* (Cambridge University Press, 1988).
17. Malina, Bruce, and Jerome Neyrey. *Portraits of Paul* (Westminster John Knox, 1996).

18. McRay, John. *Paul: His Life and Teaching* (Baker, 2002).

19. Meggitt, Justin. *Paul, Poverty, and Survival* (T & T Clark, 1998).

20. Picirilli, Robert. *Paul the Apostle* (Moody, 1986).

21. Porter, Stanley. *Paul in Acts* (Hendrickson, 2001).

22. Roetzel, Calvin. *Paul* (University of South Carolina Press, 1998).

———.*The Letters of Paul*, 4th ed. (Westminster John Knox, 1998).

23. Rosner, Brian. *Understanding Paul's Ethics* (Eerdmans, 1995).

24. Sampley, Paul, ed. *Paul in the Greco-Roman World* (Trinity Press International, 2001).

25. Schnelle, Udo. *Apostle Paul: His Life and Theology* (Baker, 2005).

26. Strom, Mark. *Reframing Paul* (IVP, 2000).

27. Tellbe, Mikael. *Paul Between Synagogue and State* (Almqvist & Wiksell, 2001).

28. Van Bruggen, Jakob. *Paul* (Presbyterian & Reformed, 2004).

29. Wallace, R., and W. Williams. *The Three Worlds of Paul of Tarsus* (Routledge, 1998).

30. Wenham, David. *Paul, Follower of Jesus or Founder of Christianity?* (Eerdmans, 1995).

———. *Paul and Jesus* (Eerdmans, 2002).

31. Westerholm, Stephen. *Preface to the Study of Paul* (Eerdmans, 1997).

32. Williams, David. *Paul's Metaphors* (Hendrickson, 1999).

33. Witherington, Ben. *The Paul Quest* (IVP, 1998).

———. *Paul's Narrative Thought World* (Westminster John Knox, 1994).

34. Wright, N. T. *What Saint Paul Really Said* (Eerdmans, 1997).

35. *See* New Testament Introduction, Survey, and Theology: Pauline Theology, Paul and the Law.

Paul: The Early Years

1. Hengel, Martin. *The Pre-Christian Paul* (Trinity Press International, 1991).
2. **Hengel, Martin, and Ann Schwemer. *Paul Between Damascus and Antioch* (Westminster John Knox, 1997).**
3. Longenecker, Richard, ed. *The Road from Damascus* (Eerdmans, 1997).
4. **Murphy-O'Connor, Jerome. *Paul* (Oxford University Press, 1996).** Childhood, postconversion years.
5. Riesner, Rainer. *Paul's Early Period* (Eerdmans, 1997).

Paul's Imprisonment and Trial

1. Cassidy, Richard. *Paul in Chains* (Herder and Herder, 2001). Especially Philippians.
2. Mauck, John. *Paul on Trial* (Thomas Nelson, 2001). Lawyer Mauck posits Acts as a legal defense treatise. Foreword by Donald Hagner.
3. Rapske, Brian. *Paul in Roman Custody* (Eerdmans, 1995). Social status as measure of jail sentence.
4. Tajra, H. *The Martyrdom of Saint Paul* (Mohr, 1994).
   ———. *The Trial of St. Paul* (Mohr, 1989).
5. Wansink, Craig. *Chained in Christ* (Sheffield Academic Press, 1996).

Greco-Roman Background

1. Alston, Richard. *Aspects of Roman History: A.D. 14–117* (Routledge, 1998).
2. **Aune, David, ed. *Greco-Roman Literature and the New Testament* (Scholars, 1988).**
3. Balch, David, Everett Ferguson, and Wayne Meeks, eds. *Greeks, Romans, and Christians* (Fortress, 1990).
4. Brown, John Pairman. *Israel and Hellas* (de Gruyter, 1995).
5. Burridge, Richard. *What Are the Gospels?* (Cambridge University Press, 1992).
6. **Christopherson, Alf, et al., eds. *Paul, Luke, and the Graeco-Roman World* (Sheffield Academic Press, 2002).**

7. Clarke, Andrew, ed. *First-Century Christians in the Greco-Roman World*, 5 vols. (Eerdmans, 1993–96).

8. Constable, Nick. *Historical Atlas of Ancient Rome* (Checkmark, 2003).

9. Cook, John. *The Interpretation of the New Testament in Greco-Roman Paganism* (Mohr Siebeck, 2000).

10. Goodman, Martin. *The Roman World 44 B.C.–A.D. 180* (Routledge, 1997).

11. Grant, Robert, and R. Kitzinger, eds. *Civilization of the Ancient Mediterranean: Greece and Rome*, 3 vols. (Scribners, 1988).

12. Hornblower, Simon, and Anthony Spaworth, eds. *The Oxford Classical Dictionary*, 3d ed. (Oxford University Press, 1996). ———. *The Oxford Companion to Classical Civilization* (Oxford University Press, 1999).

13. **Jeffers, James. *The Greco-Roman World of the New Testament Era* (IVP, 1999).** Introductory but thorough.

14. Konstam, Angus. *Historical Atlas of Ancient Greece* (Checkmark, 2003).

15. Long, A. *Hellenistic Philosophy* (Duckworth, 1986).

16. **Malherbe, Abraham. *Moral Exhortation*, LEC (Westminster, 1989).**

17. **Millar, Fergus. *The Roman Near East, 31 B.C.–A.D. 337* (Harvard University Press, 1993).**

18. Nash, Ronald. *The Gospel and the Greeks*. 2d ed. (Presbyterian & Reformed, 2003). Refutes Platonic, Stoic, Gnostic and mystery influence on NT.

19. Roberts, John, ed. *The Oxford Dictionary of the Classical World* (Oxford University Press, 2005).

20. Sartre, Maurice. *The Middle East under Rome* (Harvard University Press, 2005).

21. **Starr, C. *A History of the Ancient World*, 4th ed. (Oxford University Press, 1991).** Includes Classical Greek and late Roman period.

22. **Talbert, R., ed. *Barrington Atlas of the Greek and Roman World: Book and CD-ROM* (Princeton University Press, 2000).**

23. Van der Horst, P. *Hellenism-Judaism-Christianity* (Kok Pharos, 1994).

24. Walbank, F. *The Hellenistic World*, rev. ed. (Harvard University Press, 1993).

————, et al., eds. *The Hellenistic World*, CAH, 2d ed., vol. 7.1 (Cambridge University Press, 1984).

————, et al., eds. *The Rise of Rome to 220 B.C.*, CAH, 2d ed., vol. 7.2 (Cambridge University Press, 1990).

25. Wilken, Robert. *The Christians as the Romans Saw Them* (Yale University Press, 2003).

26. Worth, Roland. *The Seven Cities of the Apocalypse and Roman Culture,* 2 vols. (Paulist, 1999). Volume 2: Revelation 2–3.

Greco-Roman Religion

1. Burkert, Walter. *Greek Religion* (Harvard University Press, 1985).

2. Cohn-Sherbok, Daniel, and John Court, eds. *Religious Diversity in the Greco-Roman World* (Sheffield Academic Press, 2001).

3. Finegan, Jack. *Myth and Mystery* (Baker, 1989). Pagan religions.

4. Finn, Thomas. *From Death to Rebirth: Ritual and Conversion in Antiquity* (Paulist, 1997).

5. Fox, Robin Lane. *Pagans and Christians* (Harper, 1987).

6. Frankfurter, David. *Religion in Roman Egypt* (Princeton University Press, 2001). Confrontation between indigenous religion and early Christianity.

7. Grant, Robert. Gods and the One God, LEC (Westminster John Knox, 1986).

8. Klauck, Hans-Josef. *The Religious Context of Early Christianity* (T & T Clark, 2000).

————. *Magic and Paganism in Early Christianity* (Fortress, 2003).

9. MacMullen, Ramsey. *Paganism in the Roman Empire* (Yale University Press, 1981).

10. Tripolitis, Antonia. *Religions of the Hellenistic-Roman Age* (Eerdmans, 2001).

New Testament Archaeology

1. **Akurgal, Ekrem.** *Ancient Civilizations and Ruins of Turkey,* **3d ed. (Istanbul, 1973).**

2. Arav, Rami, and Richard Freund, eds. *Bethsaida*, vol. 2 (Truman State University Press, 1999).

3. *Biblical Archaeological Society Slide Sets* (BAS, 1981–). Approximately 140 slides @ $1.20 per slide (Jerusalem, New Testament Archaeology, Galilee Archaeology, and Archaeology and Religion).
   The Biblical World on CD-ROM **(BAS, 2002).** Same categories as above at fraction of cost with supplemental NT Archaeology and Dead Sea Scrolls. More than one thousand images, including OT.

4. Connolly, Peter. *A History of the Jewish People in the Time of Jesus* (Peter Bedrick, 1987).

5. Finegan, Jack. *The Archaeology of the New Testament,* rev. ed. (Princeton University Press, 1992).

6. **Frend, W.** *The Archaeology of Early Christianity* **(Fortress, 1996).**

7. Koester, Helmut. *Ephesos, Metropolis of Asia* (Trinity Press International, 1995). Includes culture analysis.
   ———, ed. *Pergamon* (Trinity Press International, 1999).

8. Koester, Helmut, and Holland Hendrix, eds. *Archaeological Resources for New Testament Studies,* 2 vols. (Trinity Press International, 1995). Three hundred slides each with indexed text (Ephesus, Philippi, Corinth, Athens, Olympia, and Isthmia).

9. Magness, Jodi. *The Archaeology of Qumran and the Dead Sea Scrolls* (Eerdmans, 2002).

10. **McRay, John.** *Archaeology and the New Testament* **(Baker, 1991).**

11. Meyers, Eric, and James Strange. *Archaeology, the Rabbis and Early Christianity* (Abingdon, 1981).

12. Millard, Alan. *Discoveries from the Time of Jesus* (Lion, 1990).

13. **Murphy-O'Connor, Jerome.** *St. Paul's Corinth,* **rev. ed. (Liturgical, 2002).**

14. Reed, Jonathan. *Archaeology and the Galilean Jesus* (Trinity Press International, 2000).

15. *Ritmeyer Archeological Slides* (Ritmeyer Archeological Design, 1999). Jerusalem in A.D. 30 (thirty-six slides) and The Archaeology of Herod's Temple Mount (sixty slides).

16. Rousseau, John, and Rami Arav. *Jesus and His World* (Fortress, 1995).

17. Stillwell, Richard, ed. *The Princeton Encyclopedia of Classical Sites* (Princeton University Press, 1976).

18. White, Michael. *The Social Origins of Christian Architecture,* vol. 2 (Trinity Press International, 1996).

19. Yamauchi, Edwin. *New Testament Cities in Western Asia Minor* (Baker, 1980).

20. *See* Old Testament Background: Archaeological Resources.

Social Background

1. Arnal, William. *Jesus and the Village Scribes* (Fortress, 2001).

2. Blasi, Anthony, et al., eds. *Handbook of Early Christianity* (AltaMira, 2002).

3. Blount, Brian. *Cultural Interpretation: Reorienting New Testament Criticism* (Fortress, 1995).

4. deSilva, David. *The Hope of Glory* (Liturgical, 1999).

5. Esler, Philip. *The First Christians in Their Social Worlds* (Routledge, 1994).

   ———. *New Testament Theology* (Fortress, 2005).

   ———, ed. *Modeling Early Christianity* (Routledge, 1995).

6. Gehring, Roger. *House Church and Mission* (Hendrickson, 2004).

7. Hanson, K., and Douglas Oakman. *Palestine in the Time of Jesus* (Fortress, 2002). With multiple-link CD.

8. Horsley, Richard. *Galilee: History, Politics, People* (Trinity Press International, 1995).

9. Kee, Howard. *Knowing the Truth* (Fortress, 1989).

   ———. *Who Are the People of God?* (Yale University Press, 1993).

10. Malherbe, Abraham. *Social Aspects of Early Christianity,* 2d ed. (Fortress, 1983; Wipf & Stock, 2003).
11. Meeks, Wayne. *The Moral World of the First Christians,* LEC (Westminster, 1986).
    ———. *The First Urban Christians* (Yale University Press, 1983).
    ———. *The Origins of Christian Morality* (Yale University Press, 1993).
12. Moxnes, Halvor. *The Economy of the Kingdom* (Fortress, 1988; Wipf & Stock, 2003).
    ———. *Putting Jesus in His Place* (Westminster John Knox, 2003).
13. Neyrey, Jerome, ed. *The Social World of Luke–Acts* (Hendrickson, 1991).
    ———. *Honor and Shame in the Gospel of Matthew* (Westminster John Knox, 1998).
14. Roetzel, Calvin. *The World that Shaped the New Testament,* rev. ed. (Westminster John Knox, 2002).
15. Rogerson, John. *Anthropology and the Old Testament* (Sheffield Academic Press, 1984).
16. Smith, Dennis. *From Symposium to Eucharist: The Banquet in the Early Christian World* (Fortress, 2003).
17. Stegemann, Wolfgang. *The Jesus Movement* (Fortress, 1999).
18. Stegemann, Wolfgang, Bruce Malina, and Gerd Theissen, eds. *The Social Setting of Jesus and the Gospels* (Fortress, 2001).
19. Theissen, Gerd. *Social Reality and the Early Christians* (Fortress, 1992).
20. Tidball, Derek. *The Social Context of the New Testament* (Zondervan, 1984).
21. White, Michael, and Larry Yarbrough, eds. *The Social World of the First Christians* (Fortress, 1995).
22. *See* Old Testament Background: General Manners and Customs References, Social Background, Religious Background, and New Testament Background: Primary References.

Social-Scientific

1. **Holmberg, Bengt.** *Sociology and the New Testament* **(Fortress, 1990).** Historical overview.
2. Horrell, David, ed. *Social-Scientific Approaches to New Testament Interpretation* (T & T Clark, 1999).
3. Malina, Bruce. *The Social Gospel of Jesus* (Fortress, 2001).
   ———. *The New Testament World: Insights from Cultural Anthropology.* 3d ed. (Westminster John Knox, 2001).
4. Malina, Bruce, and John Pilch. *Social-Scientific Commentary on the Book of Revelation* (Fortress, 2000).
5. Malina, Bruce, and Richard Rohrbaugh. *Social Science Commentary on the Synoptic Gospels,* 2d ed. (Fortress, 2002).
   ———. *Social Science Commentary on the Gospel of John* (Trinity Press International, 1998).
6. May, David. *Social Scientific Criticism of the New Testament: A Bibliography* (Mercer University Press, 1991).
7. Osiek, Carolyn. *What Are They Saying About the Social Setting of the New Testament?* (Paulist, 1992).
8. Pilch, John, ed. *Social Scientific Models for Interpreting the Bible* (Brill, 2000).
9. Pilch, John, and Bruce Malina. *Handbook of Biblical Social Values,* updated (Hendrickson, 2000).
10. Rohrbaugh, Richard, ed. *The Social Sciences and New Testament Interpretation* (Hendrickson, 1996).
11. **Stambaugh, John, and David Balch.** *The New Testament in Its Social Environment,* **LEC (Westminster John Knox, 1986).** Introduction.

Families

1. **Balch, David, and Carolyn Osiek, eds.** *Early Christian Families in Context* **(Eerdmans, 2003).**
2. Balla, Peter. *The Child-Parent Relationship in the New Testament and Its Environment* (Mohr, 2003).
3. **Burke, Trevor.** *Family Matters* **(T & T Clark, 2004).**
4. **Campbell, Kenneth, ed.** *Marriage and Family in the Biblical World* **(IVP, 2003).**

5. Moxnes, Halvor. *Constructing Early Christian Families* (Routledge, 1997).
6. Osiek, Carolyn, and David Balch. *Families in the New Testament World* (Westminster John Knox, 1997).
7. Osiek, Carolyn, and Margaret MacDonald. *A Women's Place: House Churches in Earliest Christianity* (Fortress, 2005).
8. *See* Old Testament Background: Daily Life.

The Institution of Slavery

1. Bartchy, Scott. *First-Century Slavery and the Interpretation of 1 Corinthians 7:21* (Wipf & Stock, 2002).
2. Bradley, K. R. *Slaves and Masters in the Roman Empire* (Oxford University Press, 1987).
   ———. *Slavery and Society at Rome* (Cambridge University Press, 1994).
3. Braxton, B. R. *The Tyranny of Resolution: 1 Corinthians 7:17–24* (SBL, 2000).
4. Byron, John. *Slavery Metaphors in Early Judaism and Pauline Christianity* (Mohr, 2003).
5. Callahan, Allen, Richard Horsley, and A. Smith, eds. *Slavery in Text and Interpretation* (Scholars Press, 1998).
6. Combes, I. A. H. *The Metaphor of Slavery in the Writings of the Early Church from the New Testament to the Beginning of the Fifth Century* (Sheffield Academic Press, 1998).
7. Garnsey, Peter. *Ideas of Slavery from Aristotle to Augustine* (Cambridge University Press, 1996).
8. Glancy, Jennifer. *Slavery in Early Christianity* (Oxford, 2002).
9. Harrill, J. Albert. *The Manumission of Slaves in Early Christianity* (Mohr, 1995).
   ———. *Slaves in the New Testament* (Fortress, 2005).
10. Martin, Dale. *Slavery as Salvation* (Yale University Press, 1990).
11. *See* Balch and Osiek above.

Early Church Fathers

1. **Bercot, David, ed.** *A Dictionary of Early Christian Beliefs* **(Hendrickson, 1998).**
2. Bradshaw, Paul, Maxwell Johnson, and Edward Phillips. *The Apostolic Tradition* (Fortress, 2002). Attributed to Hippolytus as author (A.D. 170–235).
3. Di Berardino, Angelo, and Basil Studer, eds. *History of Theology: The Patristic Period* (Liturgical, 1997).
4. Diprose, Ronald. *Israel in the Development of Christian Thought* (Italian Biblical Institute, 2000). Claims church fathers instigated replacement theory.
5. **Drobner, Hubertus.** *The Fathers of the Church* **(Hendrickson, 2005).**
6. Evans, G. R. *The First Christian Theologians* (Blackwell, 2005).
7. Hall, Christopher. *Reading Scripture with the Church Fathers* (IVP, 1998).
   ———. *Learning Theology with the Church Fathers* (IVP, 2002).
8. Holmes, Michael, ed. *The Apostolic Fathers,* 2d ed. (Baker, 1998).
9. Jefford, Clayton. *Reading the Apostolic Fathers* (Hendrickson, 1996).
10. Kannengiesser, Charles. *Handbook of Patristic Exegesis,* 2 vols. (Brill, 2004).
11. McGuckin, John. *The Westminster Handbook to Patristic Theology* (Westminster John Knox, 2004).
12. Moreschini, Claudio, and Enrico Norelli. *Early Christian Greek and Latin Literature: A Literary History,* 2 vols. (Hendrickson, 2005).
13. Oden, Thomas, gen. ed. ACCS, 27 vols. (IVP, 1998–).
14. O'Keefe, John, and R. R. Reno. *Sanctified Vision: An Introduction to Early Christian Interpretation of the Bible* (Johns Hopkins University Press, 2005).
15. Osiek, Carolyn. *The Shepherd of Hermas,* Hermeneia (Fortress, 1998).

16. Roberts, Alexander, and James Donaldson, eds. *Ante-Nicene Fathers,* 10 vols. (Eerdmans, 1996). Tagged, cross-referenced, and indexed with introductions.
17. Simonetti, Manlio. *Biblical Interpretation in the Early Church* (T & T Clark, 1994).
18. Tugwell, Simon. *The Apostolic Fathers* (Continuum, 2002).
19. Von Campenhausen, Hans. *The Fathers of the Church* (Hendrickson, 1999).
20. Young, Frances. *Biblical Exegesis and the Formation of Christian Culture* (Cambridge University Press, 1997; Hendrickson, 2002).

The Didache

1. Balabanski, Vicky. *Eschatology in the Making: Mark, Matthew and the Didache* (Cambridge University Press, 1997).
2. Draper, Jonathan, ed. *The Didache in Modern Research* (Brill, 1996).
3. Jefford, Clayton. *The Didache in Context* (Brill, 1994).
4. Milovec, Aaron. *The Didache* (Liturgical/Newman, 2003).
5. Niederwimmer, Kurt. *The Didache.* Hermeneia (Fortress, 1998).
6. Van de Sandt, Huub, ed. *Matthew and the Didache: Two Documents from the Same Jewish-Christian Milieu?* (Van Gorcum, 2005).
7. Van de Sandt, Huub, and David Flusser. *The Didache* (Fortress, 2002). Historical analysis.

Gnosticism

1. Evans, Craig, R. Webb, and R. Wiebe. *Nag Hammadi Texts and the Bible: A Synopsis and Index* (Brill, 1993).
2. Filoramo, G. *A History of Gnosticism* (Blackwell, 1990).
3. Franzmann, Majella. *Jesus in the Nag Hammadi Writings* (T & T Clark, 1996). Simultaneous development.
4. Hanegraaff, Wouter, ed. *Dictionary of Gnosis and Western Esotericism* (Brill, 2005).

5. Hedrick, Charles, and R. Hodgson. *Nag Hammadi, Gnosticism and Early Christianity* (Hendrickson, 1986).
6. Hoeller, Stephan. *Gnosticism* (Quest, 2002).
7. Jonas, Hans. *The Gnostic Religion*, 3d ed. (Beacon, 2001).
8. King, Karen, ed. *Images of the Feminine in Gnosticism* (Trinity Press International, 2000).
9. Klauck, Hans-Josef. *Apocryphal Gospels* (T & T Clark, 2004). Introductory.
10. Layton, Bernard. *The Gnostic Scriptures,* ABRL, 2d ed. (Doubleday, 1995). Translation with introduction and notes.
11. Logan, A. H. B., and A. J. M. Wedderburn, eds. *The New Testament and Gnosis* (T & T Clark, 1983).
12. Logan, Alistair. *Gnostic Truth and Christian Heresy* (Hendrickson/T & T Clark, 1996). Especially the *Apocryphal Gospel of John.*
13. Markschies, Christoph. *Gnosis* (T & T Clark, 2003).
14. Mastrocinque, Attilio. *From Jewish Magic to Gnosticism* (Mohr, 2005).
15. Meyer, Marvin. *The Gnostic Discoveries: The Impact of the Nag Hammadi Library* (HarperSanFrancisco, 2005).
16. Pagels, Elaine. *Beyond Belief* (Random House, 2003). Gospel of Thomas.
17. Patterson, Stephen, and James Robinson. *The Fifth Gospel* (Trinity Press International, 1998). *Gospel of Thomas* analysis.
18. Pearson, Brook. *Gnosticism, Judaism, and Egyptian Christianity* (Fortress, 1990).
———. *Gnosticism and Christianity in Roman and Coptic Egypt* (T & T Clark, 2004).
19. Perkins, Pheme. *Gnosticism and the New Testament* (Fortress, 1993). Simultaneous development.
20. Robinson, James. *The Nag Hammadi Library,* 4th ed. (Brill, 1996).
21. Roukema, R. *Gnosis and Faith in Early Christianity* (Trinity Press International, 1999).

22. Scholer, David, ed. *Gnosticism in the Early Church* (Garland, 1993).
23. Smith, Carl. *No Longer Jews* (Hendrickson, 2004).
24. Tuckett, Christopher. *Nag Hammadi and the Gospel Tradition* (T & T Clark, 1986).
25. Turner, J., and A. McGuire, eds. *The Nag Hammadi Library After Fifty Years* (Brill, 1997).
26. Uro, Risto, ed. *Thomas at the Crossroads* (T & T Clark, 1999).
27. Valantasis, Richard. *The Gospel of Thomas* (Routledge, 1997).
28. Van den Broek, R. *Studies in Gnosticism and Alexandrian Christianity* (Brill, 1996).
29. Williams, M. *Rethinking "Gnosticism"* (Princeton University Press, 1996).
30. Yamauchi, Edwin. *Pre-Christian Gnosticism* (Eerdmans, 1973; Wipf & Stock, 2003).

11

JEWISH BACKGROUND

Original Sources

1. Charlesworth, James. *The Old Testament Pseudepigrapha,* 2 vols. (Doubleday, 1983–85).
2. Coogan, Michael, ed. *The New Oxford Annotated Bible,* 3d ed. (Oxford University Press, 2001).
3. Dupont-Sommer, Andre. *The Essene Writings from Qumran* (Peter Smith, 1973).
4. García Martinez, Florentino. *The Dead Sea Scrolls Translated,* 2d ed. (Eerdmans, 1996).
5. Neusner, Jacob. *The Mishnah* (Yale University, 1988).
6. Reddish, Mitchell, ed. *Apocalyptic Literature: A Reader* (Abingdon, 1990; Hendrickson, 1995).
7. Schenck, Kenneth. *A Brief Guide to Philo* (Westminster John Knox, 2005).
8. Sparks, H., ed. *The Apocryphal Old Testament* (Oxford University Press, 1984). Twenty-five pseudepigraphical translations.
9. Sterling, Gregory. *The Jewish Plato* (Hendrickson, 2005). Philo.
10. Vermes, Geza. *The Complete Dead Sea Scrolls in English,* 4th ed. (Penguin, 1997). Three introductory chapters.
11. Yonge, C. *The Works of Philo* (Hendrickson, 1993).

Josephus

1. Beall, Todd. *Josephus' Description of the Essenes Illustrated by the Dead Sea Scrolls* (Cambridge University Press, 1988).
2. Cohen, Shaye. *Josephus in Galilee and Rome* (Brill, 2003).

3. Feldman, Louis. *Josephus' Interpretation of the Bible* (University of California, 1998).
4. Feldman, Louis, and Gohei Hata, eds. *Josephus, the Bible, and History* (Wayne State University Press, 1989).
5. Mason, Steve. *Flavius Josephus on the Pharisees* (Brill, 1997).
   ———. *Josephus and the New Testament*, 2d ed. (Hendrickson, 2002).
   ———, ed. *Understanding Josephus* (Sheffield Academic Press, 1998).
6. Maier, Paul. *The New Complete Works of Josephus: Translated by William Whiston* (Kregel, 1999). Loeb notes, commentary by Maier.
7. Rajak, Tessa. *Josephus* (Fortress, 1983).

Concordances and Indexes

1. Abegg, Martin, et al. *The Dead Sea Scrolls Concordance* (Brill, 2003–).
2. Borgen, Peder, Kâre Fuglseth, and Roald Skarsten. *The Philo Index* (Eerdmans, 2000).
3. Delamarter, Steve. *A Scripture Index to Charlesworth's The Old Testament Pseudepigrapha* (Sheffield Academic Press, 2002).
4. Schalit, A., ed. *A Complete Concordance to Flavius Josephus,* 4 vols. (Brill, 1998).

Primary Jewish Background References

1. Davies, W. D., et al., eds. *Cambridge History of Judaism,* 3 vols. (1984, 1989, 1999).
2. Kraft, R., and George Nickelsburg, eds. *Early Judaism and its Modern Interpreters* (Scholars, 1986).
3. Neusner, Jacob, and William Green, eds. *Dictionary of Judaism in the Biblical Period* (Hendrickson, 1999).
4. **Nickelsburg, George. *Ancient Judaism and Christian Origins* (Fortress, 2003).**

5. Safrai, S., and M. Stern, eds. *The Jewish People in the First Century,* 2 vols. (Van Gorcum/Fortress, 1974–76).
6. Sanders, E. P. *Judaism: Practice and Belief, 63 B.C.E.–66 C.E.* (Trinity Press International, 1992).
7. Schürer, Emil, ed. *History of the Jewish People in the Age of Jesus Christ,* rev. ed., 3 vols. (T & T Clark, 1973–87).
8. Skarsaune, Oskar. *In the Shadow of the Temple* (IVP, 2002). 200 B.C.–A.D. 300.
9. VanderKam, James. *An Introduction to Early Judaism* (Eerdmans, 2000).
10. Werblowsky, R. J. Zwi, and Geoffrey Wigoder, eds. *The Oxford Dictionary of the Jewish Religion* (Oxford University Press, 1997).

Other Jewish Background References

1. Argall, Randal, Beverly Bow, and Rodney Werline, eds. *For a Later Generation* (Trinity Press International, 2000).
2. Barclay, John, and J. Sweet, eds. *Early Christian Thought in Its Jewish Context* (Cambridge University Press, 1996).
3. Berlin, Andrea, and Andrew Overman, eds. *First Jewish Revolt* (Routledge, 2002).
4. Bocaccini, Gabrielle. *Middle Jewish Thought, 200 B.C.E.– 200 C.E.* (Fortress, 1991).
5. Bockmuehl, Markus. *Jewish Law in Gentile Churches* (Baker, 2003).
6. Dunn, James. *The Parting of the Ways Between Christianity and Judaism* (Trinity Press International, 1991).
7. Fitzmyer, Joseph. *The Semitic Background of the New Testament* (Eerdmans, 1997).
8. Flusser, David. *Judaism and the Origins of Christianity* (Magnes, 1988).
9. Hengel, Martin. The Zealots (T & T Clark, 1989).
10. Ilan, Tal. *Lexicon of Jewish Names in Late Antiquity, Part 1: Palestine 330 B.C.E.–200 C.E.* (Mohr, 2002).
11. Lesses, Rebecca. *Ritual Practices to Gain Power* (Trinity Press International, 1998). Jewish mysticism.

12. Levine, Lee. *The Ancient Synagogue: The First Thousand Years* (Yale University Press, 2000).
13. McCane, Byron. *Roll Back the Stone: Death and Burial in the World of Jesus* (Trinity Press International, 2003).
14. Mendels, Doron. *The Rise and Fall of Jewish Nationalism* (Doubleday, 1992; Eerdmans, 1997).
15. Moore, Carey. *Tobit,* AB (Doubleday, 1996).
16. Murphy, Frederick. *The Religious World of Jesus* (Abingdon, 1991).
17. **Saldarini, Anthony. *Pharisees, Scribes, and Sadducees in Palestinian Society* (Michael Glazier, 1988).**
18. Scott, James. *Geography in Early Judaism and Christianity* (Cambridge University Press, 2002). Especially Jubilees 8–9.
19. **Skarsaune, Oskar, and Reidar Hvalvik, eds. *Jewish Believers in Jesus: The Early Centuries* (Hendrickson, 2007).**
20. Stemberger, Günter. *Jewish Contemporaries of Jesus* (Fortress, 1995).
21. Tomasino, Anthony. *Judaism before Jesus* (IVP, 2003).
22. Wegner, Judith. *Chattel or Person? The Status of Women in the Mishnah* (Oxford University Press, 1988).

Second Temple

1. **Barker, Margaret. *The Great High Priest: The Temple Roots of Christian Liturgy* (T & T Clark, 2003).**
2. **Binder, Donald. *Into the Temple Courts: The Place of the Synagogues in the Second Temple Period* (SBL, 1999).**
3. Bond, Helen. Caiaphas (Westminster John Knox, 2003).
4. **Grabbe, Lester. *History of the Jews and Judaism in the Second Temple Period,* 4 vols. (T & T Clark, 2004–).**
5. **Helyer, Larry. *Exploring Jewish Literature of the Second Temple Period* (IVP, 2002).**
6. Ilan, Tal. *Integrating Women into Second Temple History* (Hendrickson, 2001).
7. **Sacchi, Paolo. *The History of the Second Temple Period* (Sheffield Academic Press, 2000).**

8. Stone, Michael, ed. *Jewish Writings of the Second Temple Period* (Fortress, 1984).

9. **VanderKam, James. *From Joshua to Caiaphas* (Fortress, 2004).** Priesthood.

Intertestamental

1. **Barclay, John. *Jews in the Mediterranean Diaspora from Alexander to Trajan* (T & T Clark, 1996).** Especially Egypt.

2. Bartlett, John. *1 Maccabees* (Sheffield Academic Press, 1998). Introduction.

3. Baumgarten, Albert. *The Flourishing of Jewish Sects in the Maccabean Era* (Brill, 1997).

4. **Cohen, Shaye. *From the Maccabees to the Mishnah,* LEC (Westminster, 1987).**

5. **deSilva, David. *Introducing the Apocrypha* (Baker, 2002).**

6. Doran, Robert. *1–2 Maccabees,* NIB, vol. 4 (Abingdon, 1996). Especially valuable with its allusions to Daniel and references to Josephus and DSS.

7. **Feldman, Louis. *Jew and Gentile in the Ancient World* (Princeton University Press, 1993).**

8. Fine, Steven. *This Holy Place* (University of Notre Dame, 1997).

9. Flannery-Dailey, Frances. *Dreamers, Scribes, and Priests: Jewish Dreams in the Hellenistic and Roman Eras* (Brill, 2004). Analysis of texts from Apocrypha, Pseudepigrapha, and Qumran.

10. **Grabbe, Lester. *Judaism from Cyrus to Hadrian,* 2 vols. (Fortress, 1992).**
    ———. *Yehud: A History of the Persian Province of Judah* (T & T Clark, 2004).

11. Gruen, Robert. *Diaspora: Jews Amidst Greeks and Romans* (Harvard University Press, 2002).

12. **Harrington, Daniel. *Invitation to the Apocrypha* (Eerdmans, 1999).**

13. **Hengel, Martin. *Jews, Greeks, and Barbarians* (Fortress, 1980).**

————. *Judaism and Hellenism,* 2 vols. **(Fortress, 1974; Wipf & Stock, 2003).**

14. Leaney, A. *The Jewish and Christian World: 200 B.C.–A.D. 200* (Cambridge University Press, 1984).

15. **Modrzejewski, Joseph. *The Jews of Egypt: From Rameses II to Emperor Hadrian* (T & T Clark, 1995).**

16. **Murphy, Frederick. *Early Judaism* (Hendrickson, 2002).** Exile-Jewish revolt.

17. Newsome, James. *Greeks, Romans, Jews* (Trinity Press International, 1992).

18. Nickelsburg, George. *Jewish Literature Between the Bible and the Mishnah,* 2d ed. (Fortress, 2005).

19. **Richardson, Peter. *Herod* (Fortress, 1999).**

20. **Scott, J. Julius. *Customs and Controversies* (Baker, 1995).**

21. Van Seters, John. *A Law Book for the Diaspora: Revision in the Study of the Covenant Code* (Oxford University Press, 2002).

Hellenistic Judaism

1. Bartlett, John. *Jews in the Hellenistic and Roman Cities* (Routledge, 2002).

2. Borgen, Peder. *Early Christianity and Hellenistic Judaism* (T & T Clark, 1996).

3. Borgen, Peder, and Søren Giversen, eds. *The New Testament and Hellenistic Judaism* (Hendrickson, 1997).

4. Brown, John Pairman. *Ancient Israel and Ancient Greece* (Fortress, 2003).

5. Collins, John. *Between Athens and Jerusalem,* 2d ed. (Eerdmans, 1999).

6. Collins, John, and Gregory Sterling, eds. *Hellenism in the Land of Israel* (University Press of Notre Dame, 2001).

7. **Freyne, Sean. *Galilee from Alexander the Great to Hadrian 323 B.C.E. to 135 C.E.* (T & T Clark, 1998).**

8. **Goodman, Martin, ed. *Jews in a Greco-Roman World* (Oxford University Press, 1999).**

9. Grabbe, Lester, *An Introduction to First Century Judaism* (T & T Clark, 1996).

10. Levine, Lee. *Judaism and Hellenism in Antiquity* (University of Washington Press, 1998).

11. Levinskaya, Irina. *The Book of Acts in Its Hellenistic Setting*, vol. 5, *The Book of Acts in Its First-Century Setting* (Eerdmans, 1996).

12. Lieu, Judith. *Christian Identity in the Jewish and Graeco-Roman World* (Oxford University Press, 2004).

13. Talmon, Shemaryahu, ed. *Jewish Civilization in the Hellenistic-Roman Period* (Trinity Press International, 1991).

14. *See* Barclay, Sanders, and Skarsaune above.

Dead Sea Scrolls
(Introductions)

1. Cook, Edward. *Solving the Mystery of the Dead Sea Scrolls* (Zondervan, 1994).

2. Fitzmyer, Joseph. *Responses to 101 Questions on the Dead Sea Scrolls* (Paulist, 1992).

3. García Martinez, Florentino, and Julio Trebolle Barrera. *The People of the Dead Sea Scrolls* (Brill, 1995).

4. Pate, Marvin. *Communities of the Last Days* (IVP, 2000). NT parallels, heavily indebted to N. T. Wright.

5. Scanlin, Edward. *Dead Sea Scrolls and Modern Translations of the Old Testament* (Tyndale, 1994).

6. Shanks, Hershel, ed. *Understanding the Dead Sea Scrolls* (Random House, 1992).

7. VanderKam, James. *The Dead Sea Scrolls Today* (Eerdmans, 1994).

8. VanderKam, James, and Peter Flint. *The Meaning of the Dead Sea Scrolls* (HarperSanFrancisco, 2002).

Dead Sea Scrolls

1. Abegg, Martin, Peter Flint, and Eugene Ulrich, eds. *The Dead Sea Scrolls Bible* (HarperCollins, 1999; T & T Clark, 2000).

2. Betz, Otto, and Rainier Riesner. *Jesus, Qumran, and the Vatican* (Crossroad, 1994).

3. Boccaccini, Gabrielle. *Beyond the Essene Hypothesis* (Eerdmans, 1998).

4. Brooke, George. *The Dead Sea Scrolls and the New Testament* (Fortress, 2005).

5. Cansdale, Lena. *Qumran and the Essenes* (Mohr, 1997).

6. Charlesworth, James. *Graphic Concordance to the Dead Sea Scrolls* (Westminster John Knox, 1991).

———. *The Pesharim and Qumran History* (Eerdmans, 2002).

———, ed. *John and the Dead Sea Scrolls* (Crossroad, 1990).

———, ed. *Jesus and the Dead Sea Scrolls,* ABRL (Doubleday, 1992).

———, ed. *The Dead Sea Scrolls,* 10 vols. (Westminster John Knox, 1993–). Hebrew, Aramaic, Greek-English.

———. ed. *The Bible and the Dead Sea Scrolls*, 3 vols. (Baylor University Press, 2006).

7. Charlesworth, James, and Walter Weaver, eds. *Dead Sea Scrolls and the Christian Faith* (Trinity Press International, 1998).

8. Collins, John. *The Scepter and the Star,* ABRL (Doubleday, 1995). Two messiahs of the DSS.

———. *Apocalypticism in the Dead Sea Scrolls* (Routledge, 1997).

9. Collins, John, and Craig Evans, eds. *Christian Beginnings and the Dead Sea Scrolls* (Baker, 2006).

10. Collins, John, and Robert Kugler, eds. *Religion in the Dead Sea Scrolls* (Eerdmans, 2000).

11. Cross, Frank. *The Ancient Library of Qumran and Modern Biblical Studies,* 3d ed. (Fortress, 1995).

12. Cross, Frank, and Shemaryahu Talmon, eds. *Qumran and the History of the Biblical Text* (Harvard University Press, 1975). DSS-MT divergence.

13. Evans, Craig, and Peter Flint, eds. *Eschatology, Messianism and the Dead Sea Scrolls* (Eerdmans, 1997).

14. Fitzmyer, Joseph. *The Dead Sea Scrolls,* 2d ed. (Scholars, 1990). With bibliography.

———. *The Dead Sea Scrolls and Christian Origins* (Eerdmans, 2000).

15. Flint, Peter, ed. *The Bible at Qumran* (Eerdmans, 2001).
    ———. *The Dead Sea Scrolls and the Book of Psalms* (Brill, 1997).

16. Flint, Peter, and James VanderKam, eds. *The Dead Sea Scrolls After 50 Years,* 2 vols. (Brill, 1998).

17. García Martinez, Florentino, and Eibert Tigchelaar, eds. *The Dead Sea Scrolls Study Edition,* 2 vols. (Eerdmans, 1999). Notes and bibliography.

18. Harrington, Daniel. *Wisdom Texts from Qumran* (Routledge, 1996).

19. Henze, Matthias, ed. *Biblical Interpretation at Qumran* (Eerdmans, 2005).

20. Hirschfeld, Yizhar. *Qumran in Context* (Hendrickson, 2004).

21. Lim, Timothy, et al., eds. *The Dead Sea Scrolls in Their Historical Context* (T & T Clark, 2000).

22. Metso, Sarianna. *The Textual Development of the Qumran Community Rule* (Brill, 1997).

23. Murphy-O'Connor, Jerome, ed. *Paul and the Dead Sea Scrolls* (Crossroad, 1990).

24. Porter, Stanley, and Craig Evans, eds. *The Scrolls and the Scriptures* (Sheffield Academic Press, 1997).

25. Ringgren, Helmer. *The Faith of Qumran* (Crossroad, 1995).

26. Schiffman, Lawrence. *Reclaiming the Dead Sea Scrolls* (Jewish Publication Society, 1994; Doubleday, 1995).

27. Schiffman, Lawrence, and James VanderKam, eds. *Encyclopedia of the Dead Sea Scrolls,* 2 vols. (Oxford University Press, 2000).

28. Stegemann, Hartmut. *The Library of Qumran, on the Essenes, Qumran, John the Baptist, and Jesus* (Eerdmans, 1998).

29. Ulrich, Eugene. *The Dead Sea Scrolls and the Origins of the Bible* (Eerdmans, 1999).

30. Vermes, Geza. *An Introduction to the Complete Dead Sea Scrolls,* 3d ed. (Fortress, 2000).

Rabbinics

1. **Boccaccini, Gabrielle.** *Roots of Rabbinic Judaism* **(Eerdmans, 2001).**
2. Hauptman, Judith. *Rereading the Mishnah* (Mohr, 2005). Tosefta earlier.
3. **Instone-Brewer, David.** *Traditions of the Rabbis from the Era of the New Testament: Prayer and Agriculture* **(Eerdmans, 2004).** First of six volumes.
4. Kalimi, Isaac. *Early Jewish Exegesis and Theological Controversy* (Van Gorcum, 2002).
5. Maccoby, Hyam. *Early Rabbinic Writings* (Cambridge University Press, 1988). Introduction.
6. **Neusner, Jacob.** *Introduction to Rabbinic Literature,* **ABRL (Doubleday, 1994).**

     ———. *Judaism and the Interpretation of Scripture* (Hendrickson, 2004). Midrash.

     ———. *Rabbinic Literature and the New Testament* (Trinity Press International, 1994; Wipf & Stock, 2004).

     ———. *Transformations in Ancient Judaism* (Hendrickson, 2004).

     ———. *Rabbinic Literature: An Essential Guide,* **IBT (Abingdon, 2005).**
7. Samely, Alexander. *Rabbinic Interpretation of Scripture in the Mishnah* (Oxford University Press, 2002).
8. Sanders, E. P. *Jewish Law from Jesus to the Mishnah* (SCM/ Trinity Press International, 1990).
9. Stemberger, Günter. *Introduction to the Talmud and Midrash,* 2d ed. (T & T Clark, 1996).

12

POPULAR REFERENCES

Popular Dictionaries

1. Comfort, Philip, and Walter Elwell. *The Complete Book of Who's Who in the Bible* (Tyndale, 2005).
2. Douglas, J. D., ed. *The Illustrated Bible Dictionary,* 3 vols. (Tyndale, 1980).
3. **Elwell, Walter, ed. *Baker Encyclopedia of the Bible*, 2 vols. (Baker, 1988).**
4. **Elwell, Walter, and Philip Comfort, eds. *Tyndale Bible Dictionary* (Tyndale, 2001).**
5. Gardner, Paul, ed. *New International Encyclopedia of Bible Characters* (Zondervan, 1995). Formerly *The Complete Who's Who in the Bible.*
6. Rusten, Michael, and Sharon Rusten. *The Complete Book of When and Where: In the Bible and Throughout History* (Tyndale, 2005).
7. Youngblood, Ronald, et al., eds. *Nelson's New Illustrated Bible Dictionary* (Thomas Nelson, 1995).

Word Studies

1. Bock, Darrell, ed. *The Bible Knowledge Key Word Study: New Testament*, 3 vols. (Victor, 2002, 2006–).
2. Holloman, Henry. *Kregel Dictionary of the Bible and Theology* (Kregel, 2005). Five hundred key theological words and concepts.
3. Merrill, Eugene, ed. *The Bible Knowledge Key Word Study: Old Testament*, 4 vols. (Victor, 2004, 2005–).

4. Mounce, William, ed. *Mounce's Complete Expository Dictionary of Old and New Testament Words* (Zondervan, 2006).
5. Renn, Stephen, ed. *Expository Dictionary of Bible Words* (Hendrickson, 2004). *Vine's* replacement.

Atlases

1. **Dowley, Tim. *Kregel Bible Atlas* (Kregel, 2002).**
2. **Frank, Harry. *Hammond Atlas of the Bible Lands*, rev. ed. (Hammond, 1990).** Thirty-three maps.
3. *Harpur, James, and Marcus Braybrooke. The Collegeville Atlas of the Bible* (Liturgical, 1999).
4. Rogerson, John. *The Atlas of the Bible* (Facts on File, 1985). Excellent illustrations, photos; distributed by Nelson.
5. Wright, Paul. *Holman Quick Source Guide: Atlas of Bible Lands* (Broadman & Holman, 2002).

Other Resources

1. Bailey, Mark, and Tom Constable. *Nelson's New Testament Survey* (Thomas Nelson, 2003).
2. Dyer, Charles, and Eugene Merrill. *Nelson's Old Testament Survey* (Thomas Nelson, 2003).
3. Easley, Kendall. *The Illustrated Guide to Biblical History* (Broadman & Holman, 2003).
4. *WORDsearch 7 Preaching Library.* Available at wordsearchbible.com.

Popular One- and Two-Volume Commentaries[1]

1. Alexander, David, and Pat Alexander. *Zondervan Handbook to the Bible,* rev. ed. (Zondervan, 2005). Updated *Eerdmans/Lion's Handbook.*
2. **Barker, Kenneth, and John Kohlenberger, eds. *Zondervan NIV Bible Commentary,* 2 vols. (Zondervan, 1994).**

---

1. For exposition, the *Zondervan NIV Bible Commentary* (2 vols.) is packed with information. It is a condensation of the Expositor's Bible Commentary minus the more technical information.

3. **Dockery, David, ed.** ***Holman Concise Bible Commentary*** **(Broadman & Holman, 1998).**
4. Elwell, Walter, ed. *Baker Commentary on the Bible* (Baker, 1989).
5. Radmacher, Earl, Ronald Allen, and H. Wayne House, eds. *Nelson's New Illustrated Bible Commentary* (Thomas Nelson, 1999).
6. Unger, Merrill, and Gary Larson. *The New Unger's Bible Handbook* (Moody, 1998).
7. Walvoord, John, and Roy Zuck, eds. *Bible Knowledge Commentary,* 2 vols. (Victor, 1983–85).

Popular Commentary Series[2]

1. Anders, Max, ed. Holman Old Testament Commentary Series (Broadman & Holman, 2002–).
———. Holman New Testament Commentary (Broadman & Holman, 2000–).
2. Boice, J. M. Boice Commentary Series (Baker).
3. Hendriksen, William, and Simon Kistemaker. New Testament Commentary (Baker, 1954–2001).
4. Hughes, R. Kent. Preaching the Word Series (Crossway, 1989–). NT.
5. MacArthur, John. The MacArthur New Testament Commentary Series (Moody, 1983–). NT.
6. McGrath, Alister, and J. I. Packer, eds. Crossway Classic Commentaries (Crossway, 1993–).
7. Phillips, John. The John Phillips Commentary Series (Kregel, 2001–).
8. Wiersbe, Warren. *The Bible Exposition Commentary,* 6 vols. (Chariot Victor Books, 1972–).

---

2. Of these, Hughes and Hendriksen/Kistemaker garner some mention in the commentary survey proper (i.e., *see* New Testament Commentaries: Revelation: Exposition). Although the series themselves bear mention for their general utility, there are better layman-friendly options suggested per biblical book.

13

GENERAL REFERENCES

Parallel Bibles

1. *Comparative Study Bible,* rev. ed. (Zondervan, 1999). NIV, KJV, NASB, AMPLIFIED.
2. *The Hendrickson Parallel Bible* (Hendrickson, 2005). KJV, NKJV, NIV, NLT.
3. **Kohlenberger, John, ed.** *The Evangelical Parallel New Testament* **(Oxford University Press, 2004).** NKJV, NIV, ESV, HCSB, TNIV, NLT, NCV, MSG.

    ———. *The Essential Evangelical Parallel Bible* **(Oxford University Press, 2004).** NKJV, ESV, NLT, MSG.
4. *Today's Parallel Bible* (Zondervan, 2000). NIV, KJV, NASB, NLT.

Bible Dictionaries, Encyclopedias

1. **Achtemeier, Paul, ed.** *HarperCollins Bible Dictionary,* **rev. ed. (HarperSanFrancisco, 1996).** Twenty-five percent new.
2. **Brand, Chad, and Archie England, eds.** *Holman Illustrated Bible Dictionary,* **rev. ed. (Broadman & Holman, 2003).**
3. **Bromiley, Geoffrey, ed.** The *International Standard Bible Encyclopedia,* **4 vols., rev. ed. (Eerdmans, 1979–1988).**[1]
4. Das, A. Andrew, ed. *New Interpreter's Dictionary of the Bible,* 5 vols. (Abingdon, 2006).

---

1. For Bible college or seminary students planning to go into full-time ministry, obtain Geoffrey Bromiley, ed., *International Standard Bible Encyclopedia,* rev. ed., 4 vols. (Eerdmans, 1979–1988).

5. **Freedman, David, ed.** *Anchor Bible Dictionary,* **6 vols. (Doubleday, 1992).**

6. **Freedman, David, ed.** *The Eerdmans Dictionary of the Bible* **(Eerdmans, 2000).** Includes Apocrypha.[2]

7. **Marshall, I. Howard, et al., eds.** *New Bible Dictionary,* **3d ed. (IVP, 1996).**

8. Metzger, Bruce, and Michael Coogan, eds. *The Oxford Companion to the Bible* (Oxford University Press, 1993).

   ————, eds. *The Oxford Guide to Ideas and Issues of the Bible* (Oxford University Press, 2001).[3]

   ————, eds. *The Oxford Guide to People and Places of the Bible* (Oxford University Press, 2001).

9. **Mills, Watson, ed.** *Mercer Dictionary of the Bible* **(Mercer University Press, 1990, 1991).**

---

2. Students will also need a comprehensive, one-volume dictionary for quick reference. For advanced students, the *Eerdmans Dictionary of the Bible* (Eerdmans, 2000), though moderate in overall tone, is a potential choice, along with the *New Bible Dictionary.* Better yet, purchase both dictionaries as they complement each other well. For instance, J. Albert Harrill gives only snapshot coverage to the topic of slavery in *EDB* (giving no indication of the treatment of slaves expressed in his *DNTB* entry) whereas E. A. Judge provides a more thorough, though slightly outdated, essay in *NBD*[3]. Conversely, *EDB* has five thousand entries as opposed to two thousand for *NBD*[3], so you get a little coverage on many more subjects such as the extrabiblical topics "Akkadian," the "Genesis Apocryphon," "Ostraca," and "Zoroastrianism." Elsewhere, diverse topics such as "Lentil," "Millet," "Pomegranate," and "Tamarisk" gain individual attention whereas in *NBD3* they are subsumed under "Food," "Vegetables," and "Trees." *EDB* is also sensitive to the literary background, providing separate entries on Mishnah, midrash, and targum, for instance. Its chief deficit is its lack of cross-references. For instance, the entry "Afterlife, Afterdeath" fails to direct the reader to the entries "Death," "Sheol," and "Grave." In *NBD*[3], relevant cross-references are asterisked in the body of the text. Therefore, in *EDB,* it is up to the reader to exhaust possibilities on his own.

3. These latter two volumes are based on the *Companion,* and essentially winnow and update the *Companion's* seven hundred entries down to five hundred in about the same amount of space and the same price combined. In addition to the standard fare, *Ideas and Issues* is a bit of a historical dictionary covering such issues as "Freud and the Bible" and such ideas as the "Scofield Reference Bible." *People and Places* includes only the most important people and places of the Bible. Neither claims to be encyclopedic and can be recommended only as a novelty supplement (though a very good one).

10. *The New Interpreter's Dictionary of the Bible,* 5 vols. (Abingdon, 2006).

Atlases

1. Aharoni, Yohanan, and Michael Avi-Yonah. *The Macmillan Bible Atlas,* 3d ed. (Macmillan, 1993). Maps of biblical events.
2. Beitzel, Barry. *The Moody Atlas of Bible Lands* (Moody, 1985). Detailed geographical discussion.
3. Bimson, John, and J. P. Kane. *New Bible Atlas* (IVP, 1985).
4. Brisco, Thomas. *The Holman Bible Atlas* (Broadman & Holman, 1998).
5. Lawrence, Paul. *The IVP Atlas of Bible History* (IVP, 2006).
6. May, Herbert. *Oxford Bible Atlas,* 3d ed. (Oxford University Press, 1984).
7. Pritchard, James. *The Times Atlas of the Bible* (Crescent, 1996).
   ———. *HarperCollins Concise Atlas of the Bible* (HarperSanFrancisco, 1997). Especially major events, battles.
8. Rainey, Anson, and Steven Notley. *The Sacred Bridge* (Carta, 2006).
9. Rasmussen, Carl. *Zondervan NIV Atlas of the Bible* (Zondervan, 1989). Superior graphics, mostly Old Testament.
10. *See under* Popular References: Popular One- and Two-Volume Commentaries, and Popular References: Atlases.

Specialty Atlases

1. *Abingdon Bible Map Transparencies* (Abingdon, 1975). Six sets: 41 transparencies (can be ordered individually); Hammond maps from Frank's *Discovering the Biblical World* (Hammond, 1975).
2. Beitzel, Barry. *The Moody Atlas of Bible Lands* (Moody, 1985). Detailed geographical discussion.
3. Brierley, Peter, and Heather Wraight. *Atlas of World Christianity* (Thomas Nelson, 1998).

4. **Cleave, Richard.** *The Holy Land Satellite Atlas,* **2 vols. (Rohr, 1999).**

5. Farrington, Karen. *Historical Atlas of the Holy Lands* (Checkmark, 2002). Including Egypt, Greece, Italy, Turkey.

6. **Mittmann, Siegfried, and Gotz Schmitt, eds.** *Tübinger Bibelatlas* **(ABS, 2004).** Bilingual.

7. Smart, Ninian, ed. *Atlas of the World's Religions* (Oxford University Press, 1999).

Charts and Reconstructions

1. **House, H. Wayne.** *Chronological and Background Charts of the New Testament* **(Zondervan, 1981).**

2. *The Nelson Complete Book of Bible Maps and Charts,* rev. ed. (Thomas Nelson, 1997).

3. *Rose Book of Bible Charts, Maps, and Time Lines* (Rose Publishing, 2005).

4. Smith, Marsha. *Holman Book of Biblical Charts, Maps, and Reconstructions* (Broadman & Holman, 1993).

5. Thomas, Robert. *Charts of the Gospels and the Life of Christ* (Zondervan, 2000).

6. **Walton, John.** *Chronological and Background Charts of the Old Testament,* **rev. ed. (Zondervan, 1994).**

7. **Wilson, Neil, and Linda Taylor.** *Tyndale Handbook of Bible Charts and Maps* **(Tyndale, 2001).** With CD.[4]

Geography

1. **Aharoni, Yohanan.** *The Land of the Bible,* **rev. ed. (Westminster, 1979).**

2. **Beck, John.** *The Land of Milk, Honey, and Hope* **(Concordia Academic Press, 2002).**

3. Bimson, John, ed. *Baker Encyclopedia of Bible Places* (Baker, 1995).

4. **DeVries, Lamoine.** *Cities of the Biblical World* **(Hendrickson, 1997).**

---

4. Contains 400 charts and 200 maps on perforated pages with topical index. CD duplicates contents with NLT text.

5. **Dorsey, David. *The Roads and Highways of Ancient Israel* (Johns Hopkins University Press, 1991).**

6. Elitzur, Yoel. *Ancient Place Names in the Holy Land* (Eisenbrauns, 2004).

7. Fant, Clyde, and Mitchell Reddish. *A Guide to Biblical Sites in Greece and Turkey* (Oxford University Press, 2003).

8. **Harris, Roberta. *The World of the Bible* (Thames and Hudson, 1995).**

9. Hepper, Nigel. *Baker Encyclopedia of Bible Plants* (Baker, 1992).

10. **Kallai, Zecharia. *Historical Geography of the Bible* (Magnes, 1986).**

11. **Koester, Helmut. *Cities of Paul* (Fortress, 2005).** Nine hundred photographs on CD-ROM; intended for slideshow presentations.

12. **Murphy-O'Connor, Jerome. *The Holy Land,* 4th ed. (Oxford University Press, 1995).**

13. Orni, Ephraim, and Elisha Efrat. *Geography of Israel,* 4th ed. (Israel University Press, 1980).

14. Robertson, O. Palmer. *Understanding the Land of the Bible* (Presbyterian & Reformed, 1996).

15. **Scott, James. *Geography in Early Judaism and Christianity* (Cambridge University Press, 2001).**

BIBLICAL HEBREW RESOURCES

First-Year Grammar

1. deClaissé-Walford, Nancy. *Biblical Hebrew,* rev. ed. (Chalice, 2005).

2. **Fuller, Russell, and Kyoungwon Choi. *Invitation to Biblical Hebrew* (Kregel, 2006).**

   ———. *Invitation to Biblical Hebrew: Workbook* (Kregel, 2006).

3. Futato, Mark. *Beginning Biblical Hebrew* (Eisenbrauns, 2003).

4. Garrett, Duane. *A Modern Grammar for Classical Hebrew* (Broadman & Holman, 2002).

5. Green, Jennifer, et al. *Handbook to A Grammar for Biblical Hebrew,* rev. ed. (Abingdon, 2005).

6. **Pratico, Gary, and Miles Van Pelt. *Basics of Biblical Hebrew* (Zondervan, 2001).**

   ———. *Basics of Biblical Hebrew: Workbook* (Zondervan, 2001).

   ———. *The Vocabulary Guide to Biblical Hebrew* (Zondervan, 2003).

7. **Ross, Allen. *Introducing Biblical Hebrew* (Baker, 2001).**

8. Seow, C. L. *A Grammar for Biblical Hebrew,* rev. ed. (Abingdon, 1995). Updates Lambdin approach, includes excursuses on using helps, etc.

Other Grammars and Syntaxes

1. Arnold, Bill T., and John H. Choi. *A Guide to Biblical Hebrew Syntax* (Cambridge University Press, 2003).
2. Bartelt, Andrew, and Andrew Steinmann. *Fundamental Biblical Hebrew/Fundamental Biblical Aramaic* (Concordia Academic, 2000). Combo. Workbook available.
3. Ben Zvi, Ehud, Maxine Hancock, and Richard Beinert. *Readings in Biblical Hebrew* (Yale University Press, 1993).
4. Hoffer, Victoria, et al. *Biblical Hebrew*, 2d ed. (Yale University Press, 2004).
5. Kelley, Page. *Biblical Hebrew* (Eerdmans, 1993). Updates Weingreen approach.
6. Kelley, Page, Terry Burden, and Timothy Crawford. *A Handbook to Biblical Hebrew* (Eerdmans, 1994).
7. Lambdin, Thomas. *Introduction to Biblical Hebrew* (Scribner's, 1971).
8. Martin, James. *Davidson's Introductory Hebrew Grammar*, 27th ed. (T & T Clark, 1993). *See* Johnstone, Computer Resources: Language Helps for an interactive study complement to Davidson's revised grammar.
9. Rocine, B. M. *Learning Biblical Hebrew* (Smyth & Helwys, 2000). Discourse analysis approach.
10. Vance, Donald. *Introduction to Classical Hebrew* (Brill, 2004).
11. Walker-Jones, Arthur. *Hebrew for Biblical Interpretation* (SBL, 2003).

Reference Grammars

1. Cowley, A., and E. Kautzsch, eds. *Gesenius' Hebrew Grammar*, 2d ed. (Oxford University Press, 1910).
2. Gibson, J. *Davidson's Introductory Hebrew Grammar: Syntax*, 4th ed. (T & T Clark, 1994).
3. Horsnell, Malcolm. *A Review and Reference Grammar for Biblical Hebrew* (McMaster University Press, 1999).

4. Jouon, Paul. *A Grammar of Biblical Hebrew,* 2 vols. (Pontifical Biblical Institute, 1991).

5. Putnam, Frederic. *A Cumulative Index to the Grammar and Syntax of Biblical Hebrew* (Eisenbrauns, 1996). Index to Gibson, Davidson, Gesenius' Hebrew Grammar, Waltke, O'Connor, Williams, Jouon, and Rosenthal, etc.

   ———. *Hebrew Bible Insert* (Stylus, 1997). Laminated syntax guide.

   ———. *Card Guide to Biblical Hebrew* (Stylus, 1998). Laminated.

6. **Van der Merwe, Christo, et al. *Biblical Hebrew Reference Grammar* (Sheffield Academic Press, 1999).** Includes latest insights on linguistics.

7. **Waltke, Bruce, and Michael O'Connor. *An Introduction to Biblical Hebrew Syntax* (Eisenbrauns, 1990).** Linguistic approach.

8. Williams, R. *Hebrew Syntax,* 2d ed. (University of Toronto, 1976).

Lexicons

1. Armstrong, Terry, Douglas Busby, and Cyril Carr. *A Reader's Hebrew-English Lexicon of the Old Testament,* (Zondervan, 1989).

2. Brown, Francis, S. R. Driver, and Charles Briggs. *Brown-Driver-Briggs Hebrew-English Lexicon of the Old Testament* (Hendrickson, 1995). Coded to Strong's; considerably outdated.

3. Clines, David, ed. *The Dictionary of Classical Hebrew,* 8 vols. (Sheffield Academic Press, 1993–). Includes extrabiblical sources, contextual approach.

4. Davidson, Benjamin. *The Analytical Hebrew and Chaldee Lexicon,* 2d ed. (Hendrickson, 1986).

5. **Holladay, William. *A Concise Hebrew and Aramaic Lexicon of the Old Testament* (Eerdmans, 1971).** Condensed Koehler below.

6. Koehler, L., W. Baumgartner, and John Stamm, eds. *The Hebrew and Aramaic Lexicon of the Old Testament: Study Edition*, 2 vols. (Brill, 2001).[1]

Theological Dictionaries[2]

1. Botterweck, G. Johannes, Helmer Ringgren, and Heinz-Josef Fabry, eds. *Theological Dictionary of the Old Testament,* 14 vols. (Eerdmans, 1977–).[3]
2. Carpenter, Eugene. *The Complete Word-Study Dictionary of the Old Testament* (AMG, 2003).
3. Gowan, Donald, ed. *The Westminster Theological Wordbook of the Bible* (Westminster John Knox, 2003).
4. Harris, R. Laird, Gleason Archer, and Bruce Waltke, eds. *A Theological Wordbook of the Old Testament,* 2 vols. (Moody, 1980).
5. Jenni, Ernst, and Claus Westermann, eds. *Theological Lexicon of the Old Testament,* 3 vols. (Hendrickson, 1997).
6. **VanGemeren, Willem, ed. *New International Dictionary of Old Testament Theology and Exegesis*, 5 vols. (Zondervan, 1997).**

Concordances

1. Even-Shoshan, E. *A New Concordance of the Old Testament,* 2d ed. (Baker, 1989).
2. Katz, Eliezer, ed. *Topical Concordance of the Old Testament* (Baker, 1992). Hebrew-English.

---

1. The most important feature of this lexicon is that it is alphabetized according to how each word appears in BHS rather than by root. It is also eminently more current than *BDB* relative to etymology and ANE parallels. If not for its exorbitant cost ($180 retail), it would be vastly preferable to *BDB*. Nevertheless, obtain it.
2. A worthy companion to *NIDOTTE* (covering the three hundred most important Hebrew and Aramaic words) is Jenni and Westermann's *Theological Lexicon of the Old Testament,* 3 vols. (Hendrickson, 1997), especially for its thorough statistical data and synthetic treatment of each word's theological development.
3. Fourteen volumes have appeared with more to come.

3. **Kohlenberger, John, and James Swanson.** *The Hebrew-English Concordance to the Old Testament* **(Zondervan, 1998).**
4. Mandelkern, Solomon. *Veteris Testamenti Concordantiae* (Schocken, 1971; P. Shalom Publications, 1988).
5. Wigram, George. *The New Englishman's Hebrew and Chaldee Concordance of the Old Testament,* 5th ed. (Hendrickson, 1984).

Interlinears and Parallel Old Testament

1. Dotan, Aron, ed. *The Parallel Bible Hebrew-English Old Testament* (Hendrickson, 2002). *BHL,* KJV.
2. *JPS Hebrew-English Tanakh* (JPS, 1999).
3. **Kohlenberger, John.** *The* NIV *Hebrew-English Interlinear Old Testament* **(Zondervan, 1987).**

Study Aids

1. Beall, Todd, William Banks, and Colin Smith. *Old Testament Parsing Guide,* rev. ed. (Broadman & Holman, 2001). Parses only verbs.
2. Carpenter, Eugene, and Philip Comfort. *Holman Treasury of Key Bible Words* (Broadman & Holman, 2000). Two hundred Hebrew, two hundred Greek.
3. **Chisholm, Robert.** *From Exegesis to Exposition* **(Baker, 1998).** Sermon preparation.
   ———. *A Workbook for Intermediate Hebrew: Grammar, Exegesis, and Commentary on Jonah and Ruth* **(Kregel, 2006).**
4. Davis, John. *Hebrew Language* (Stylus, 1999). Laminated verb analysis.
5. Einspahr, Bruce. *Index to the B-D-B Hebrew Lexicon* (Moody, 1976).
6. Kelley, Page, Daniel Mynatt, and Timothy Crawford. *The Masorah of the BHS* (Eerdmans, 1998).
7. Landes, George. *Building Your Biblical Hebrew Vocabulary* (SBL, 2001). All roots that occur ten times or more.

8. Long, Gary. *Grammatical Concepts 101 for Biblical Hebrew* (Hendrickson, 2002). English grammar for Hebrew.
9. Mitchel, Larry. *A Student's Vocabulary for Biblical Hebrew and Aramaic* (Zondervan, 1984).
10. Murphy, Todd. *Pocket Dictionary for the Study of Biblical Hebrew* (IVP, 2003).
11. **Owens, John. *Analytical Key to the Old Testament*, 4 vols. (Baker, 1989–1992).**
12. Pratico, Gary, and Miles Van Pelt. *Biblical Hebrew* (Zondervan, 2005). Laminated chart.
13. Silzer, Peter, and Thomas Finley. *How Biblical Languages Work: A Student's Guide to Learning Hebrew and Greek* (Kregel, 2004).
14. Tucker, Dennis. *Jonah: A Handbook on the Hebrew Text* (Baylor University Press, 2006).
15. **Van Pelt, Miles, and Gary Pratico. *Graded Reader of Biblical Hebrew* (Zondervan, 2006).**
16. **Vance, Donald. *Hebrew Reader for Ruth* (Hendrickson, 2002).**

Palm OS/Audio/Video Helps

1. Fuller, Russell T. *Invitation to Biblical Hebrew—DVDs* (Kregel, 2006).[4]
2. *Hebrew Masoretic Text Old Testament* (Olive Tree).
3. *Hebrew Masoretic Text with Parsing* (Olive Tree). Palm OS/ Pocket PC.
4. Hildebrandt, Ted. *Hebrew Tutor* (Parsons Technology, 1997). Reviews grammar, parsing, translation skills, quizzes. 800-644-6344.
5. Lee, Jin. *Basics of Biblical Hebrew FlashCards for Palm OS* (Zondervan, 2003).
6. *MiniFlash Scholar's Edition 3.1.1* (Southpaw Solutions, 2004). Palm OS flash cards for Greek/Hebrew. 877-865-1639.

---

4. This component complements the grammar by Fuller and Choi. A six-disk set, it includes thirty-eight classroom lectures.

7. Pennington, Jonathan. *Old Testament Hebrew Vocabulary* (Zondervan, 2003). CDs.

Textual Criticism

1. **Brotzman, Ellis. *Old Testament Textual Criticism* (Baker, 1993).**
2. McCarter, Kyle. *Textual Criticism* (Fortress, 1982).
3. Scott, William. *A Simplified Guide to BHS* (Bibal, 1987). Critical apparatus guide.
4. **Tov, Emmanuel. *Textual Criticism of the Hebrew Bible*, 2d ed. (Fortress, 2001).** Technical praxis and witness description.
5. Würthwein, Ernst. *The Text of the Old Testament* (Eerdmans, 1995).

Special Studies

1. Bergen, Robert, ed. *Biblical Hebrew and Discourse Linguistics* (SIL, 1994). Available through Eisenbrauns.
2. Bodine, Walter. *Discourse Analysis of Biblical Literature* (Scholars, 1995).
   ———. *Linguistics and Biblical Hebrew* (Eisenbrauns, 1992).
3. Goldfajn, Tal. *Word Order and Time in Biblical Hebrew Narrative* (Oxford University Press, 1998).
4. Groom, Sue. *Linguistic Analysis of Biblical Hebrew* (Paternoster, 2003).
5. Kaltner, John, and Steven L. McKenzie, eds. *Beyond Babel: A Handbook for Biblical Hebrew and Related Languages* (SBL, 2002).
6. Young, Ian. *Diversity in Pre-Exilic Hebrew* (Mohr, 1993). Biblical Hebrew as continuation of earlier language.
   ———, ed. *Biblical Hebrew: Studies in Chronology and Typology* (T & T Clark, 2003).
7. Zevit, Ziony, ed. *Hebrew Studies* (University Press of Wisconsin, 2000).

15

NEW TESTAMENT GREEK RESOURCES

First-Year Grammars and Helps[*]

1. Adam, A. K. M. *A Grammar for New Testament Greek* (Abingdon, 1999).
2. Croy, Clayton. *A Primer of Biblical Greek* (Eerdmans, 1999).
3. Culy, Martin. *1, 2, 3 John: A Handbook on the Greek Text* (Baylor University Press, 2004).
4. Duff, Jeremy. *The Elements of New Testament Greek,* 3d ed. (Cambridge University Press, 2005).
5. Machen, J. Gresham, and Dan McCartney. *New Testament Greek for Beginners,* 2d ed. (Prentice Hall, 2004).
6. **Mounce, William. *Basics of Biblical Greek,* 2d ed. (Zondervan, 2003).** Includes interactive CD-ROM.
   ———. *Basics of Biblical Greek: Workbook,* **2d ed. (Zondervan, 2003).**
7. Stevens, Gerald. *New Testament Greek,* 2d ed. (University Press of America, 1997). Combined beginners, intermediate.
   ———. *New Testament Greek Workbook,* 2d ed. (University Press of America, 1997).
   ———. *New Testament Greek Primer* (Cascade, 2004).
8. Summers, Ray, and Thomas Sawyer. *Essentials of New Testament Greek,* rev. ed. (Broadman & Holman, 1995).

---

[*] Forthcoming: A grammar with a greater emphasis on vocabulary and syntax is planned by Buist Fanning and Jay Smith (Kregel).

9. Swetnam, James. *An Introduction to the Study of New Testament Greek,* 2d ed., 2 vols. (Pontifical Biblical Institute, 1997). Advanced beginners.
10. Vlachos, Chris, and Marvin Wilson. *A Workbook for New Testament Greek* (Hendrickson, 1998). 1 John.
11. Voelz, James. *Fundamental Greek Grammar,* 2d ed. (Concordia Academic Press, 1998).

Second Year

1. Baugh, Steven. *A First John Reader: Intermediate Greek* (Presbyterian & Reformed, 1999).
2. Black, David. *It's Still Greek to Me* (Baker, 1998).
3. Gorman, Frank. *The Elements of Biblical Exegesis* (Hendrickson, 2001). Brief, guidelines, exegetical models.
4. **Guthrie, George, and Scott Duvall. *Biblical Greek Exegesis* (Zondervan, 1998).**
5. Mounce, William. *A Graded Reader of Biblical Greek* (Zondervan, 1996). Second and third semesters.
6. Trenchard, Warren. *The Complete Vocabulary Guide to the Greek New Testament,* rev. ed. (Zondervan, 1999).
7. **Wallace, Daniel. *The Basics of New Testament Syntax* (Zondervan, 2000).** Third semester; abridgement of *Greek Grammar Beyond the Basics.*

Reference Grammars

1. Blass, A., F. Debrunner, and Robert Funk. *A Greek Grammar of the New Testament* (The University of Chicago Press, 1962). German edition, 1990.
2. Brooks, James, and Carlton Winbery. *Syntax of New Testament Greek* (University Press of America, 1979).
3. McKay, K. *A New Syntax of the Verb in New Testament Greek* (Lang, 1994).
4. Moulton, James, W. Howard, and Nigel Turner. *A Grammar of New Testament Greek,* 4 vols. (T & T Clark, 1906–76). Especially volumes 1–2.

5. Owings, Timothy. *A Cumulative Index to New Testament Greek Grammars* (Baker, 1983). Indexed to Scripture.

6. Perschbacher, Wesley. *New Testament Greek Syntax* (Moody, 1995).

7. Robertson, A. T. *A Grammar of the Greek New Testament,* 4th ed. (Broadman & Holman, 1934).

8. Wallace, Daniel. *Greek Grammar Beyond the Basics* (Zondervan, 1996).

9. Young, Richard. *Intermediate New Testament Greek* (Broadman & Holman, 1994).

10. Zerwick, Maximilian. *Biblical Greek Illustrated by Examples* (Pontifical Biblical Institute, 1963). Especially verb structure.

Lexicons

1. Bauer, Walter, Frederick Danker, William Arndt, and F. Wilbur Gingrich. *A Greek-English Lexicon of the New Testament and Other Early Christian Literature,* 3d ed. (The University of Chicago Press, 2000).[1]

2. Fraser, P., and E. Matthews, eds. *A Lexicon of Greek Personal Names* (Oxford University Press, 1987). Ancient Greek–A.D. 600.

3. Kubo, Sakae. *A Reader's Greek-English Lexicon of the New Testament* (Zondervan, 1975).

4. Lampe, G., ed. *A Patristic Greek Lexicon* (Oxford University Press, 1961).

---

1. The Danker-edited revision of the 1988 German lexicon (6th ed.) is a most significant improvement, especially in two respects. First, an extended definition is given for each word (e.g., the word *plasma* is defined as "that which is formed or molded" followed by the equivalents "image, figure"). Second, this extension of meaning eliminates the need to subcategorize every equivalent with its respective examples. For instance, in the previous edition (BAGD), five equivalents and examples of usage were given for *adelphos*. In the new edition, the use of extended definitions enables Danker to implement only two subcategories. The astonishing amount of work that went into this lexicon will be repaid by the astonishing amount of labor it will save.

5. Liddell, H., and R. Scott. *A Greek-English Lexicon,* 9th ed. with rev. supplement (Oxford University Press, 1996). Pre-300 B.C.

6. **Louw, Johannes, and Eugene Nida.** *Greek-English Lexicon of the New Testament: Based on Semantic Domains,* **2d ed., 2 vols. (UBS, 1989).**

   ————. *Lexical Semantics of the Greek New Testament: A Supplement* (Scholars, 1992).

7. **Moulton, James, and G. Milligan.** *The Vocabulary of the Greek Testament* **(Hendrickson, 1997).** Coded to Strong's; NT index.[2]

Theological Dictionaries

1. Balz, Horst, and Gerhard Schneider. *Exegetical Dictionary of the New Testament,* 3 vols. (Eerdmans, 1990–93).

2. Brown, Colin, ed. *The New International Dictionary of New Testament Theology,* 4 vols. (Zondervan, 1975–78).

3. Kittel, Gerhard, and Gerhard Friedrich, eds. *Theological Dictionary of the New Testament,* 10 vols. (Eerdmans, 1964–76). Dated.

4. **Spicq, Ceslas.** *Theological Lexicon of the New Testament,* **3 vols. (Hendrickson, 1994).** Especially papyri, extrabiblical usage.

5. **Verbrugge, Verlyn, ed.** *The New International Dictionary of New Testament Theology,* **abridged ed. (Zondervan, 2000).**[3] Condensation of Colin Brown's *NIDNTT.* Use with Mounce interlinear (below).

---

2. Currently under revision by G. H. R. Horsely and John Lee.

3. This is an ample abridgement of the *NIDNTT* (35 percent plus 7 percent new entries), excising classical references, topical articles, theological digressions, bibliographies, etc. Also, all entries are now wholly evangelical. Similarly useful as Verbrugge is Mounce, *Interlinear for the Rest of Us* (Zondervan, 2006), a reverse interlinear with cross-references to Vebrugge that doubles as an analytical GNT. A $250 savings can be made by purchasing Verbrugge and Mounce in favor of the full *NIDNTT,* a standard interlinear and an analytical GNT.

Concordances

1. Bachmann, H., and W. A. Slaby, eds. *Computer Concordance to the Novum Testamentum Graece* (de Gruyter, 1985).
2. **Kohlenberger, John, Edward Goodrick, and James Swanson. *The Exhaustive Concordance to the Greek New Testament* (Zondervan, 1995).**
   ————. *The Greek-English Concordance of the New Testament* (Zondervan, 1997).
3. Köstenberger, Andreas, and Raymond Bouchoc. *The Book Study Concordance of the Greek New Testament* (Broadman & Holman, 2003). Greek words in context of NT books.
4. **Marshall, I. Howard, ed. *Moulton and Geden: A Concordance to the Greek New Testament*, 6th ed. (T & T Clark, 2002).**
5. Wigram, George. *The Englishman's Greek Concordance and Lexicon* (Hendrickson, 1997). Coded to Strong's.

Analytical Lexicons

1. **Friberg, Timothy, Barbara Friberg, and Neva Miller. *Analytical Lexicon of the Greek New Testament* (Baker, 2000).** Grammatical tags.
2. Mounce, William. *Analytical Lexicon to the Greek New Testament* (Zondervan, 1992).
3. Perschbacher, Wesley. *The New Analytical Greek Lexicon* (Hendrickson, 1990).

Parallel New Testament

1. Aland, Kurt. *Synopsis of the Four Gospels, Nestle-Aland 27th ed.–RSV,* 10th ed. (UBS, 1994).
   ————. *Synopsis Quattuor Evangeliorum,* **14th ed. (GBS, 1990).**
2. Kohlenberger, John. *The Greek New Testament: UBS⁴ with the NRSV and NIV* (Zondervan, 1994).
   ————, ed. *The Precise Parallel New Testament* (Oxford University Press, 1995). Greek, AMPLIFIED, NASB, NRSV, NIV, etc.

3. *Nestle-Aland Greek-English New Testament*, 9th ed. (GBS, 2001). NA[27] with RSV, 2d ed.

4. **NET Bible and Nestle-Aland (27th edition) Greek-English Diglot New Testament (Biblical Studies, 2004).** Available at www.bible.org.

Interlinears

1. Douglas, J. D. *The New Greek-English Interlinear New Testament* (Tyndale, 1990). NA[26], UBS[4], NRSV.

2. **McReynolds, Paul. *Word Study Greek-English New Testament* (Tyndale, 1998).** With complete concordance.

3. **Mounce, William. *Interlinear for the Rest of Us* (Zondervan, 2006).** Includes complete Greek text at bottom of page and dictionary.

4. **Schwandt, John, and C. John Collins, eds. *The English-Greek Reverse Interlinear New Testament: ESV* (Crossway, 2006).**

Study Aids

1. **Chapman, Benjamin, and Gary Shogren. *Greek New Testament Insert*, rev. ed. (Stylus, 1994).**
   ———. *Card Guide to New Testament Greek*, rev. ed. (Stylus, 1994).

2. **DeMoss, Matthew. *Pocket Dictionary for the Study of New Testament Greek* (IVP, 2001).** Immensely useful guide to most commonly used terms in GNT and commentaries.

3. Diewert, David, and Richard Goodrich. *A Summer Greek Reader* (Zondervan, 2001). Between first and second year Greek.

4. **Friberg, Timothy, and Barbara Friberg, eds. *Analytical Greek New Testament* (Baker, 1981).** Exhaustive morphology.

5. **Han, Nathan. *A Parsing Guide to the Greek New Testament* (Herald, 1971).**

6. Magill, Michael. *New Testament TransLine* (Zondervan, 2002). Literal NT translation in outline form with textual notes in parallel.

7. Metzger, Bruce. *Lexical Aids for Students of New Testament Greek*, 3d ed. (Baker, 1998).

8. Mounce, William. *Greek for the Rest of Us* (Zondervan, 2003). Designed for providing enough familiarization to access language resources.

————. *Biblical Greek* (Zondervan, 2005). Laminated chart.

9. Rogers Jr., Cleon, and Cleon Rogers III. *The New Linguistic and Exegetical Key to the Greek New Testament* (Zondervan, 1998).

10. Scott, Bernard, et al. *Reading New Testament Greek: Complete Word Lists* (Hendrickson, 1993).

11. Silzer, Peter, and Thomas Finley. *How Biblical Languages Work: A Student's Guide to Learning Hebrew and Greek* (Kregel, 2004).

12. Swanson, James. *That's Greek to Me* (Broadman & Holman, 1998). One hundred key words, first semester.

13. Wilson, Mark. *Mastering New Testament Greek Vocabulary Through Semantic Domains* (Kregel, 2002).[4]

14. Zerwick, Max, and Mary Grosvenor. *A Grammatical Analysis of the Greek New Testament*, 5th ed. (Biblical Institute, 1996).

Palm OS/Audio Helps

1. Archer, Gleason. *HeavenWord GreekMaster* (HeavenWord, 1997). Archer recitation of all Greek words, links to NASB[95] and UBS[4] dictionary. 888-726-4715.

2. *GRAMCORD Lite* (Olive Tree). Morphology-tagged NA[27] for Palm OS/Pocket PC.

3. *Greek New Testament-NA[27] on Palm OS* (Olive Tree). Also *Pocket PC.*

4. Hildebrandt, Ted. *Mastering New Testament Greek: An Interactive Guide for Beginners* (Baker, 2003).

5. *LXX (Septuaginta) Greek Old Testament* (Olive tree).

---

4. A means by which 3,900 Greek words (72% of the NT) can be memorized in groups rather than the usual 500 suggested words for first-year Greek students.

6. *LXX (Septuaginta) Parsed* (Olive Tree).
7. *MiniFlash Scholar's Edition 3.1.1* (Southpaw Solutions, 2004). Palm OS flash cards for Greek/Hebrew. 877-865-1639.
8. **NET Bible for Handhelds (Biblical Studies).** Palm OS/ WinCE/Pocket PC/Blackberry version to help get started on sermon prep while on the run. Includes NET notes. Available at www.bible.org.
9. **Pennington, Jonathan. *Vocabulary Words for New Testament Greek* (Cambridge University Press, 2004).** Companion to Duff's revision of Wenham's grammar. Audio CD.

    ———. *Readings in the Greek New Testament* (Zondervan, 2003). Two CD pronunciation guide from selected passages.

    ———. **New Testament Greek Vocabulary (Zondervan, 2001).** Two CDs.

Textual Criticism Guides for Exegesis

1. Aland, Kurt, and Barbara Aland. *The Text of the New Testament,* 2d ed. (Eerdmans, 1989).
2. **Comfort, Philip. *Encountering the Manuscripts: An Introduction to New Testament Paleography and Textual Criticism* (Broadman & Holman, 2005).**
3. DeLobel, Joel. *New Testament Textual Criticism and Exegesis* (Peeters, 2002).
4. **Greenlee, J. Harold. *Introduction to New Testament Textual Criticism* (Hendrickson, 1995).**
5. Kilpatrick, George. *The Principles and Practice of New Testament Textual Criticism* (Peeters, 1990).
6. **Metzger, Bruce. *A Textual Commentary of the GNT,* 2d ed. (UBS, 1994).** Companion to UBS[4].
7. **Metzger, Bruce, and Bart Ehrman. *The Text of the New Testament,* 4th ed. (Oxford, 2005).**
8. Vaganay, Leon. *An Introduction to New Testament Textual Criticism*, 2d ed. (Cambridge University Press, 1992).
9. Wegner, Paul. *A Student's Guide to Textual Criticism of the Bible* (IVP, 2005). OT and NT.

Textual Criticism Studies

1. Black, David. *Rethinking New Testament Textual Criticism* (Baker, 2002).
2. Bruce, F. F. *The New Testament Documents: Are They Reliable?* 5th ed. (IVP, 1960).
3. Clarke, Kent. *Textual Optimism: A Critique of the UBSGNT* (Sheffield Academic Press, 1997).
4. Comfort, Philip. *Early Manuscripts and Late Translations of the New Testament* (Baker, 1996; Wipf & Stock, 2002).
5. Ehrman, Bart. *The Orthodox Corruption of Scripture* (Oxford University Press, 1993).
6. Epp, Eldon, and Gordon Fee. *Studies in the Theory and Method of New Testament Textual Criticism* (Eerdmans, 1993). Contra Aland and Kilpatrick.
7. Holmes, Michael, and Bart Ehrman, eds. *The Text of the New Testament in Contemporary Research* (Eerdmans, 1994).
8. Parker, David. *The Living Text of the Gospels* (Cambridge University Press, 1997). Refutes possibility of "original" text.
9. Read-Heimerdinger, Jenny. *The Bezan Text of Acts* (Sheffield Academic Press, 2002). Asserts Western priority.
10. Rius-Camps, Josep, and Jenny Read-Heimerdinger. *The Message of Acts in Codex Bezae: A Comparison with the Alexandrian Tradition, Volume 1: Acts 1:1–5:42: Jerusalem* (T & T Clark, 2004).
11. Sharpe, John, and Kimberley Van Kampen, eds. *The Bible as Book* (British Library/Oak Knoll, 1997, 2000). Volumes 1 and 3.
12. Taylor, D., ed. *Studies in the Early Text of the Gospels and Acts* (SBL, 2001).

Introductions to the Septuagint

1. **Dines, Jennifer. *The Septuagint* (T & T Clark, 2004).**
2. **Hengel, Martin. *The Septuagint and Christian Scripture* (T & T Clark, 2001).**
3. **Jobes, Karen, and Moisés Silva. *Invitation to the Septuagint* (Baker, 2000).**
4. Marcos, Natalios. *The Septuagint in Context* (Brill, 2001).

Septuagint Tools

1. Brooke, A. E., N. McLean, and H. Thackeray, eds. *The Old Testament in Greek According to the Text of Codex Vaticanus,* 3 vols. (Cambridge University Press, 1906–40).
2. **Hatch, Edwin, and Henry Redpath.** *A Concordance to the Septuagint,* **2d ed. (Baker, 1998).** With Muraoka Hebrew-Aramaic index.
3. **Lust, Johan, Erik Eynikel, and Katrin Hauspie.** *A Greek-English Lexicon of the Septuagint,* **rev. ed. (GBS, 2003).**
4. Muraoka, Takamitsu. *A Greek-English Lexicon of the Septuagint: Twelve Prophets* (Peeters, 1993).

    ———. *The Hebrew-Aramaic Index to the Septuagint: Keyed to the Hatch and Redpath Concordance* (Baker, 1998).
5. **Rahlfs, A.** *Septuaginta* **(GBS, 1935).**
6. Taylor, Bernard. *The Analytical Lexicon to the Septuagint* (Zondervan, 1994).

Septuagint Studies

1. Beck, John. *Translators as Storytellers* (Lang, 2000).
2. Loader, William. *The Septuagint, Sexuality, and the New Testament: Case Studies on the Impact of the LXX in Philo and the New Testament* (Eerdmans, 2004).
3. McLay, Timothy. *The Use of the Septuagint in New Testament Research* (Eerdmans, 2003).
4. **Oloffson, Staffan.** *God Is My Rock* **(Almquist & Wiksell, 1990).** Translation technique.
5. Schenker, Adrian, ed. *The Earliest Text of the Hebrew Bible: The Relationship Between the Masoretic Text and the Hebrew Base of the Septuagint Reconsidered* (SBL, 2003).
6. **Tov, Emmanuel.** *The Text-Critical Use of the Septuagint in Biblical Research,* **2d ed. (Simor, 1997).**

Developments

1. Barr, James. *The Semantics of Biblical Language* (Oxford University Press, 1961/Wipf & Stock, 2004).

2. Black, Stephanie. *Sentence Conjunctions in the Gospel of Matthew* (Sheffield Academic Press, 2002).

3. Caragounis, Chrys. *The Development of Greek and the New Testament* (Mohr, 2004).

4. Decker, Rodney. *Temporal Deixis of the Greek Verb in the Gospel of Mark with Reference to Verbal Aspect* (Lang, 2001).

5. Donaldson, Amy, and Timothy Sailors, eds. *New Testament Greek and Exegesis* (Eerdmans, 2003). Gerald Hawthorne tribute.

6. Fanning, Buist. *Verbal Aspect in New Testament Greek* (Oxford University Press, 1990).

7. Johnston, J. William. *The Use of PAS in the New Testament* (Lang, 2004).

8. Lee, John. *A History of New Testament Lexicography* (Lang, 2003).

9. Moule, C. F. D. *An Idiom Book of New Testament Greek*, 2d ed. (Cambridge University Press, 1963).

10. Porter, Stanley. *Idioms of the Greek New Testament*, 2d ed. (Sheffield Academic Press, 1994).
      ———. *Verbal Aspect in the Greek of the New Testament with Reference to Tense and Mood*, 2d ed. (Lang, 1993).

11. Porter, Stanley, and D. A. Carson, eds. *Biblical Greek Language and Linguistics* (Sheffield Academic Press, 1993).
      ———. *Discourse Analysis and Other Topics in Biblical Greek* (Sheffield Academic Press, 1995).
      ———. *Linguistics and the New Testament* (Sheffield Academic Press, 1999).

12. Taylor, Bernard, et al., eds. *Biblical Greek Language and Lexicography* (Eerdmans, 2004).

16

EXEGESIS, INTERPRETATION, AND HERMENEUTICS

Handbooks for Exegesis*

1. Black, David, and David Dockery, eds. *Interpreting the New Testament,* rev. ed. (Broadman & Holman, 2001). Updated *New Testament Criticism and Interpretation* (Zondervan, 1991).
2. **Bock, Darrell, and Buist Fanning, eds. *Interpreting the New Testament Text* (Crossway, 2006).**
3. **Broyles, Craig, ed. *Interpreting the Old Testament* (Baker, 2001).**
4. Carson, D. A. *Exegetical Fallacies,* 2d ed. (Baker, 1996).
5. Chisholm, Robert B. *Interpreting the Historical Books,* HOTE (Kregel, 2006).[1]
6. **Conzelmann, Hans, and A. Lindemann. *Interpreting the New Testament* (Hendrickson, 1988).**
7. **Erickson, Richard. *A Beginner's Guide to New Testament Exegesis* (IVP, 2005).**
8. **Fee, Gordon. *New Testament Exegesis,* 3d ed. (Westminster John Knox, 2002).**

---

* Forthcoming: John Walton and Andrew Hill, *Orientation to the Old Testament* (Zondervan) by John Walton and Andrew Hill.

1. The Handbooks for Old Testament Exegesis (HOTE) series was announced in 2006 (Kregel). David M. Howard Jr. will serve as the general editor. Forthcoming handbooks will include: Peter T. Vogt, *Interpreting the Pentateuch*; Mark D. Futato, *Interpreting the Psalms*; Richard L. Schultz, *Interpreting the Wisdom Literature*; Michael A. Grisanti, *Interpreting the Prophets*; and Richard A. Taylor, *Interpreting Apocalyptic Literature*.

9. Marshall, I. Howard, ed. *New Testament Interpretation* (Eerdmans, 1977).

10. **Piñero, Antonio, and Jesus Peláez.** ***The Study of the New Testament* (Deo, 2003).**

11. **Porter, Stanley, ed.** ***Handbook to Exegesis of the New Testament* (Brill, 1997).**

12. **Rogerson, John, and Judith Lieu, eds.** ***The Oxford Handbook of Biblical Studies* (Oxford University Press, 2006).**

13. **Silva, Moisés.** ***Interpreting Galatians,* 2d ed. (Baker, 2001).** Galatians 3:6–14 appendix. Uses Galatians as a model for exegesis.

14. Stenger, Werner. *Introduction to New Testament Exegesis* (Eerdmans, 1993).

15. **Stuart, Douglas.** ***Old Testament Exegesis,* 3d ed. (Westminster John Knox, 2001).** Outstanding bibliography.

16. VanGemeren, Willem, ed. *A Guide to Old Testament Theology and Exegesis* (Zondervan, 1999).

References for Interpretation

1. **Barton, John, ed.** ***The Cambridge Companion to Biblical Interpretation* (Cambridge University Press, 1998).**

2. **Coggins, Richard, and Leslie Houlden, eds.** ***Dictionary of Biblical Interpretation* (Trinity Press International, 1990).**

3. **Dockery, David, Kenneth Mathews, and Robert Sloan, eds.** ***Foundations for Biblical Interpretation* (Broadman & Holman, 1994).**

4. **Elwell, Walter, and J. D. Weaver, eds.** ***Bible Interpreters of the Twentieth Century* (Baker, 1999).**

5. **Hayes, John, ed.** ***Dictionary of Biblical Interpretation,* 2 vols. (Abingdon, 1998).**

6. Knight, Douglas. *Methods of Biblical Interpretation* (Abingdon, 2004). Excerpted from Hayes above.

7. Lieu, Judith M., and J. W. Rogerson, eds. *The Oxford Handbook of Biblical Studies* (Oxford University Press, 2006).

8. **McKim, Donald, ed.** ***Historical Handbook of Major Biblical Interpreters* (IVP, 1998).**

9. **Patzia, Arthur, and Anthony Petrotta.** *Pocket Dictionary of Biblical Studies* **(IVP, 2002).**

10. Porter, Stanley, and Brook Pearson, eds. *Dictionary of Biblical Criticism and Interpretation* (Routledge, 2006).

11. **Soulen, Richard, and R. Kendall Soulen.** *Handbook of Biblical Criticism,* **3d ed. (Westminster John Knox, 2001).** Essential glossary.

12. Tate, W. Randolph. *Interpreting the Bible: A Handbook of Terms and Methods* (Hendrickson, 2006).

Old Testament Interpretation

1. **Baker, David, and Bill Arnold, eds.** *The Face of Old Testament Studies* **(Baker, 1999).**

2. Barton, John. *Reading the Old Testament,* rev. ed. (Westminster John Knox, 1997).

3. Fewell, Danna, ed. *Reading Between Texts* (Westminster John Knox, 1996).

4. Goldingay, John. *Approaches to Old Testament Interpretation,* rev. ed. (IVP, 1990).

   ———. *Models for Interpretation of Scripture* (Eerdmans, 1995).

5. Perdue, Leo, ed. *The Blackwell Companion to the Hebrew Bible* (Blackwell, 2001).

6. Sarna, Nahum. *Studies in Biblical Interpretation* (JPS, 2000).

New Testament Interpretation

1. Aune, David, ed. *The Blackwell Companion to the New Testament* (Blackwell, 2006).

2. Evans, Craig, and Stanley Porter, eds. *New Testament Interpretation and Methods* (Sheffield Academic Press, 1997). JSNT compendium.

3. Fitzmyer, Joseph. *To Advance the Gospel* (Eerdmans, 1998). Collected essays.

4. Green, Joel, ed. *Hearing the New Testament* (Eerdmans, 1995; Wipf & Stock, 2004).

5. Green, Joel, and Max Turner, eds. *Between Two Horizons* (Eerdmans, 2000).

6. Longenecker, Richard, ed. *Life in the Face of Death* (Eerdmans, 1998). New Testament resurrection.

7. McKnight, Scot, and Grant Osborne, eds. *The Face of New Testament Studies* (Baker, 2004).

8. Meyer, Paul. *The Word in This World,* NTL (Westminster John Knox, 2004).

9. Porter, Stanley, and Craig Evans, eds. *New Testament Interpretation and Methods* (Sheffield Academic Press, 1997).

10. Porter, Stanley, and D. Tombs, eds. *Approaches to New Testament Study* (Sheffield Academic Press, 1995).

Old Testament in the New[*]

1. Baker, David L. *Two Testaments, One Bible,* 2d ed. (IVP, 1991).

2. **Beale, Gregory, ed. *The Right Doctrine from the Wrong Text?* (Baker, 1994).**

3. **Bock, Darrell. *Proclamation from Prophecy and Pattern* (Sheffield Academic Press, 1987).** OT in Luke.

4. **Carson, D. A., and Hugh Williamson, eds. *It Is Written: Scripture Citing Scripture* (Cambridge University Press, 1988).**

5. **Ellis, E. Earle. *The Old Testament in Early Christianity* (Baker, 1992).**
   ————. *Prophecy and Hermeneutic in Earliest Christianity* (Eerdmans, 1978).

6. **Evans, Craig, ed. *From Prophecy to Testament* (Hendrickson, 2004).**
   ————. *Of Scribes and Sages* (T & T Clark, 2004).

7. **Evans, Craig, and J. A. Sanders, eds. *Paul and the Scriptures of Israel* (Sheffield Academic Press, 1994).** Response to Richard Hays.
   ————. ***Early Christian Interpretation of the Scriptures of Israel* (Sheffield Academic Press, 1997).**

---

[*] Forthcoming: D. A. Carson and Gregory Beale, eds., *Commentary on the Use of the Old Testament in the New* (Baker).

8. Evans, Craig, and Werner Stegner, eds. *The Gospels and the Scripture of Israel* (Sheffield Academic Press, 1994).

9. Feinberg, John. *Continuity and Discontinuity* (Crossway, 1988).

10. France, R. T., and David Wenham, eds. *Studies in Midrash and Historiography* (JSOT, 1983).

11. Hays, Richard. *Echoes of Scripture in the Letters of Paul* (Yale University Press, 1989).

12. Juel, Donald. *Messianic Exegesis* (Fortress, 1988).

13. Kaiser, Walter. *The Uses of the Old Testament in the New* (Moody, 1985).

14. Kimball, Charles. *Jesus' Exposition of the Old Testament in Luke's Gospel* (Sheffield Academic Press, 1994).

15. Lindars, Barnabas. *New Testament Apologetic* (Westminster, 1961).

16. Longenecker, Richard. *Biblical Exegesis in the Apostolic Period,* rev. ed. (Eerdmans, 1999).

17. Marcus, Joel. *The Way of the Lord: Christological Exegesis of the Old Testament in the Gospel of Mark* (Westminster John Knox, 1992).

18. Menken, Maarten. *Matthew's Bible* (Peeters, 2004).
    ———. *Old Testament Quotations in the Fourth Gospel* (Kok Pharos, 1996).

19. Moyise, Steve. *The Old Testament in the New* (T & T Clark, 2004).
    ———, ed. *The Old Testament in the New Testament* (Sheffield Academic Press, 2001).

20. Moyise, Steve, and Maarten Menken, eds. *Isaiah in the New Testament* (T & T Clark, 2005).
    ———. *The Psalms in the New Testament* (T & T Clark, 2004).

21. Porter, Stanley, ed. *Hearing the Old Testament in the New Testament* (Eerdmans, 2006).

22. Stanley, C. *Paul and the Language of Scripture* (Cambridge University Press, 1992). Especially LXX.

23. Swartley, Willard. *Israel's Scripture Tradition and the Synoptic Gospels* (Hendrickson, 1994).
24. Wagner, J. Ross. *The Law and the Prophets Bear Witness.* NTL (Westminster John Knox).
25. Wright, Christopher. *Knowing Jesus Through the Old Testament* (IVP, 1992).

Linguistics and Method

1. Bartholomew, Craig, et al., eds. *Renewing Biblical Interpretation* (Zondervan, 2000).
   ———. *After Pentecost* (Zondervan, 2001). Linguistics.
2. Caird, George. *The Language and Imagery of the Bible,* rev. ed. (Eerdmans, 1997).
3. **Cotterell, Peter, and Max Turner. *Linguistics and Biblical Interpretation* (IVP, 1989).**
4. **Egger, Wilhelm. *How to Read the New Testament* (Hendrickson, 1996).**
5. Porter, Stanley, ed. *DiGlossia and Other Topics in New Testament Linguistics* (Sheffield Academic Press, 2000).
6. Porter, Stanley, and Jeffrey Reed, eds. *Discourse Analysis and the New Testament* (Sheffield Academic Press, 1999).
7. Porter, Stanley, and Dennis Stamps, eds. *Rhetorical Criticism and the Bible* (Sheffield Academic Press, 2002).
8. Reed, Jeffrey. *Discourse Analysis of Philippians* (Sheffield Academic Press, 1997).
9. **Silva, Moisés. *Biblical Words and Their Meaning,* rev. ed. (Zondervan, 1994).**
   ———, ed. *Foundations of Contemporary Interpretation* (Zondervan, 1996). Six volumes in one.

Problem Passages

1. **Archer, Gleason. *New International Encyclopedia of Bible Difficulties* (Zondervan, 1981).**
2. **Kaiser, Walter, et al. *Hard Sayings of the Bible* (IVP, 1996).** Five volumes in one.
3. Laney, Carl. *Answers to Tough Questions* (Kregel, 1997).

4. Stein, Robert. *Interpreting Puzzling Texts in the New Testament* (Baker, 1997).
5. Thomas, Robert, ed. *The Master's Perspective on Difficult Passages* (Kregel, 1998). Articles from *TMSTJ.*

Historical Criticism

1. Byrskog, Samuel. *Story as Story History as Story* (Mohr, 2000). Legitimacy of eyewitnesses.
2. Ellis, E. Earle. *The Making of the New Testament Documents* (Brill, 1999).
3. Gerhardsson, Birger. *The Reliability of the Gospel Tradition* (Hendrickson, 2001).
    ———. *Memory and Manuscript* (Eerdmans, 1998). Posits extensive oral tradition behind gospels.
4. Levenson, Jon. *The Hebrew Bible, the Old Testament, and Historical Criticism* (Westminster John Knox, 1993).
5. Linnemann, Eta. *Biblical Criticism on Trial* (Kregel, 2001).
    ———. *Historical Criticism of the Bible* (Kregel, 2001). Noted critic of Q.
6. McKenzie, Steven, and S. Haynes, eds. *To Each Its Own Meaning,* rev. ed. (Westminster John Knox, 1999). Explains numerous criticisms.

Canon

1. Abraham, William. *Canon and Criterion in Christian Theology* (Oxford University Press, 1998).
2. Barnett, Paul. *Is the New Testament Reliable?* 2d ed. (IVP, 2005).
3. Barr, James. *Holy Scripture* (Westminster, 1983).
4. Barton, John. *Oracles of God* (Longman and Todd, 1986).
    ———. *Holy Writings, Sacred Text* (Westminster John Knox, 1998).
5. Beckwith, Roger. *The Old Testament Canon of the New Testament Church and Its Background in Early Judaism* (Eerdmans, 1985).

6. Blenkinsopp, Joseph. *Prophecy and Canon* (University of Notre Dame, 1977). Old Testament.

7. Brenneman, James. *Canons in Conflict* (Oxford University Press, 1997).

8. Bruce, F. F. *The Canon of Scripture* (IVP, 1988).

9. Chapman, Stephen. *The Law and the Prophets* (Mohr, 2000).

10. Comfort, Philip, ed. *The Origin of the Bible* (Tyndale, 1996).

11. Davies, Philip. *Scribes and Schools* (Westminster John Knox, 1998).

12. Gamble, H. *The New Testament Canon* (Fortress, 1985; Wipf & Stock, 2002).

13. Hahneman, Geoffrey. *The Muratorian Fragment and the Development of the Canon* (Clarendon, 1992).

14. Kaiser, Walter. *The Old Testament Documents* (IVP, 2001).

15. McDonald, Lee. *The Formation of the Christian Biblical Canon,* rev. ed. (Hendrickson, 1995).

16. McDonald, Lee, and James Sanders, eds. *The Canon Debate* (Hendrickson, 2002).

17. Meade, D. *Pseudonymity and Canon* (Eerdmans, 1988).

18. Metzger, Bruce. *Canon of the New Testament* (Clarendon, 1987/1997).

19. Patzia, Arthur. *The Making of the New Testament* (IVP, 1995).

20. Sanders, Jack. *Torah and Canon* (Fortress, 1972; Wipf & Stock 1999).

21. Schniedewind, William. *How the Bible Became a Book: The Textualization of Ancient Israel* (Cambridge University Press, 2004).

22. Steinmann, Andrew. *The Oracles of God* (Concordia Academic Press, 1999). OT.

23. Trebolle Barrera, Julio. *The Jewish Bible and the Christian Bible* (Eerdmans, 1998).

24. VanderKam, James. *From Revelation to Canon* (Brill, 2002). OT.

25. Von Campenhausen, Hans. *The Formation of the Christian Bible* (Fortress, 1972).

History of Interpretation
Hebrew Bible

1. **Harrelson, Walter, and John Hayes.** *Hebrew Bible: History of Interpretation* **(Abingdon, 2004).**
2. **Mays, James, David Petersen, and Kent Richards.** *Old Testament Interpretation* **(Abingdon, 1996).**
3. **Sæbø, Magne.** *Hebrew Bible, Old Testament* **(Vandenhoek & Ruprecht, 1996–).**

Early Church

1. Blowers, Paul. *The Bible in Greek Christian Antiquity* (University of Notre Dame, 1997).
2. Evans, Craig, and James Sanders, eds. *The Function of Scripture in Early Jewish and Christian Tradition* (Sheffield Academic Press, 1999).
3. **Hauser, Alan, and Duane Watson, eds.** *A History of Biblical Interpretation: The Ancient Period* **(Eerdmans, 2002).**
4. Mulder, Martin, and Harry Sysling. *Mikra: Text, Translation, Reading, and Interpretation of the Hebrew Bible in Ancient Judaism and Early Christianity* (Van Gorcum, 1988; Hendrickson, 2004).
5. **Oden, Thomas, gen. ed. ACCS, 27 vols. (IVP, 1998–).**
6. Simonetti, Manlio. *Biblical Interpretation in the Early Church* (T & T Clark, 2001).

New Testament

1. **Baird, William.** *History of New Testament Research***, 2 vols. (Fortress, 1992, 2002).**
2. **Ellis, Earle.** *History and Interpretation in New Testament Perspective* **(Brill, 2001).**
3. **Hayes, John, and Edgar Krentz.** *New Testament: History of Interpretation* **(Abingdon, 2004).**
4. Kealy, Sean. *Matthew's Gospel and the History of Interpretation* (Mellen, 1997).

General

1. **Bray, Gerald. *Biblical Interpretation: Past and Present* (IVP, 1996).**
2. de Lubac, Henri. *Medieval Exegesis*, 2 vols. (Eerdmans, 1998, 2000).
3. de Margerie, Bertrand. *An Introduction to the History of Exegesis*, 3 vols. (St. Bede's Publications, 1993–95).
4. Grant, Robert, and David Tracy. *A Short History of the Interpretation of the Bible*, 2d ed. (Fortress, 1984).
5. Jeffrey, David. *People of the Book* (Eerdmans, 1996).
6. **Kling, David. *The Bible in History* (Oxford University Press, 2004).** Eight pivotal texts.
7. Pelikan, Jaroslav. *Whose Bible Is It?* (Viking, 2005).
8. Wilken, Robert, ed. *The Church's Bible* (Eerdmans, 2003–). First one thousand years.

Modern

1. **Epp, Eldon, and George McRae, eds. *The New Testament and Its Modern Interpreters* (Scholars, 1989).**
2. Harrisville, Roy, and Walter Sundberg. *The Bible in Modern Culture: Baruch Spinoza to Brevard Childs*, 2d ed. (Eerdmans, 2002).
3. Morgan, Robert, and John Barton. *Biblical Interpretation* (Oxford University Press, 1988).
4. Neill, Stephen, and Tom Wright. *The Interpretation of the New Testament, 1861–1986*, 2d ed. (Oxford University Press, 1988).
5. Newport, Kenneth. *Apocalypse and Millennium: Studies in Biblical Eisegesis* (Cambridge University Press, 2000). Book of Revelation; 1600–1800 (Protestant/Catholic) and 1800s (Seventh-Day Adventist).

Translation History

1. **Ackroyd, Peter, and C. F. Evans, eds. *The Cambridge History of the Bible*, 3 vols. (Cambridge University Press, 1963–70).**

2. Comfort, Philip, ed. *The Origin of the Bible* (Tyndale, 1992).
3. **De Hamel, Christopher.** ***The Book: A History of the Bible*** **(Phaidon, 2001).**
4. **Metzger, Bruce.** ***The Bible in Translation*** **(Baker, 2002).**
5. Pelikan, Jaroslav. *Whose Bible Is It?* (Viking, 2005).
6. **Rogerson, John, ed.** ***The Oxford Illustrated History of the Bible*** **(Oxford University Press, 2001).**
7. **Scorgie, Glen, Mark Strauss, and Steven Voth, eds.** ***The Challenge of Bible Translation*** **(Zondervan, 2003).** Youngblood tribute.
8. **Wegner, Paul.** ***The Journey from Texts to Translations*** **(Baker, 1999).** General introduction to whole Bible.

The English Bible

1. Comfort, Philip. *The Essential Guide to Bible Versions* (Tyndale, 2000).
2. **Daniell, David.** ***The Bible in English*** **(Yale University Press, 2003).**
3. **Dewey, David.** ***A User's Guide to Bible Translations*** **(IVP, 2005).**
4. **Gilmore, Alec.** ***A Dictionary of the English Bible and Its Origins*** **(Sheffield Academic Press, 2000).**
5. Katz, David. God's Last Words (Yale University Press, 2004).
6. **Kerr, John.** ***Ancient Texts Alive Today: The Story of the English Bible*** **(ABS, 1999).**
7. Lewis, Jack. *The English Bible from KJV to NIV* (Baker, 1981).
8. **Long, John.** ***The Bible in English: John Wycliffe and William Tyndale*** **(University Press of America, 1998).**
9. **Moynahan, Brian.** ***God's Bestseller: William Tyndale, Thomas More, and the Writing of the English Bible*** **(St. Martin's, 2003).**
10. Ryken, Leland. *The Word of God in English* (Crossway, 2002).

11. Sheeley, Steven, and Robert Nash. *The Bible in English Translation* (Abingdon, 1997).

KJV/NIV

1. Barker, Kenneth. *The Accuracy of the NIV* (Baker, 1996).
     ———. *The Making of the NIV* (Baker, 1997).
     ———. *The Balance of the NIV* (Baker, 1998).
2. Beacham, Roy, and Kevin Bauder, eds. *One Bible Only?* (Kregel, 2001). KJV controversy.
3. Carson, D. A. *The KJV Debate* (Baker, 1979).
4. Martin, Robert. *Accuracy of Translation*, 2d ed. (Banner of Truth, 1997). NIV.
5. **McGrath, Alister. *In the Beginning* (Doubleday, 2001).** Creation of KJV.
6. Nicolson, Adam. *God's Secretaries* (HarperCollins, 2003). KJV.
7. **Norton, David. *A Textual History of the King James Bible* (Cambridge University Press, 2004).**
8. White, James. *The King James Only Controversy* (Bethany House, 1995).

Inclusive-Language Debate

1. **Carson, D. A. *The Inclusive Language Debate* (Baker, 1998).**
2. **Poythress, Vern, and Wayne Grudem. *The Gender Neutral Bible Controversy* (Broadman & Holman, 2000).**
3. Storkey, Elaine. *Origins of Difference* (Baker, 2001). Gender debate.
4. **Strauss, Mark. *Distorting Scripture?* (IVP, 1998).** Gender debate.

Hermeneutics
Textbooks

1. Kaiser, Walter, and Moisés Silva. *An Introduction to Biblical Hermeneutics* (Zondervan, 1994).
2. **Klein, William, Craig Blomberg, and Robert Hubbard.**

Introduction to Biblical Interpretation, rev. ed. (Thomas Nelson, 2004).

3. Osborne, Grant. *The Hermeneutical Spiral,* rev. ed. (IVP, 2006). General hermeneutics, genre, contextualization.

4. Tate, Randolph. *Biblical Interpretation,* rev. ed. (Hendrickson, 1997).

5. Thiselton, Anthony. *New Horizons in Hermeneutics* (Zondervan, 1992).

6. Voelz, James. *What Does This Mean?* 2d ed. (Concordia Academic Press, 1995).

Basic Guides

1. Corley, Bruce, Steve Lemke, and Grant Lovejoy, eds. *Biblical Hermeneutics,* 2d ed. (Broadman & Holman, 2002).

2. Doriani, Daniel. *Getting the Message* (Presbyterian & Reformed, 1996).

3. Duvall, J. Scott, and J. Daniel Hays. *Grasping God's Word,* 2d ed. (Zondervan, 2005).

   ———. *Grasping God's Word Workbook,* 2d ed. (Zondervan, 2005).

4. Fee, Gordon, and Douglas Stuart. *How to Read the Bible for All It's Worth,* 3d ed. (Zondervan, 2003).

5. McCartney, Dan, and Charles Clayton. *Let the Reader Understand,* 2d ed. (Presbyterian & Reformed, 2002).

6. Zuck, Roy. *Basic Biblical Interpretation* (Victor, 1991).

Philosophical and Theological Hermeneutics

1. Croatto, Severino. *Biblical Hermeneutics* (Orbis, 1987).

2. Erickson, Millard. *Evangelical Interpretation* (Baker, 1993).

3. Farmer, Ronald. *Beyond the Impasse* (Mercer University Press, 1997).

4. Fee, Gordon. *To What End Exegesis?* (Eerdmans, 2001).

5. Fitzmyer, Joseph. *The Biblical Commission's Document "The Interpretation of the Bible in the Church"* (Subsidia Biblica, 1995).

6. Fodor, James. *Christian Hermeneutics* (Oxford University Press, 1995). On Paul Ricouer.

7. Gadamer, Hans-Georg. *Truth and Method*, 2d ed. (Continuum, 1989).

8. Hirsch, E. D. *Validity in Interpretation* (Yale University Press, 1967).

    ———. *Aims in Interpretation* (The University of Chicago Press, 1976).

9. Hoy, David. *The Critical Circle* (University of California, 1982).

10. Lundin, Roger, Clarence Walhout, and Anthony Thiselton. *The Promise of Hermeneutics* (Eerdmans, 1999).

11. Madison, G. B. *The Hermeneutics of Postmodernity* (Indiana University Press, 1988).

12. Meyer, Ben. *Reality and Illusion in New Testament Scholarship* (Liturgical, 1995).

13. Mueller-Vollmer, Kurt, et al., eds. *The Hermeneutics Reader* (Continuum, 1989).

14. Noble, Paul. *The Canonical Approach* (Brill, 1995).

15. Patte, Daniel. *Ethics of Biblical Interpretation* (Westminster John Knox, 1995).

16. Ricoeur, Paul. *Interpretation Theory* (Texas Christian University, 1976).

17. Scalise, Charles. *Hermeneutics as Theological Prolegomena: A Canonical Approach* (Mercer University Press, 1994).

    ———. *From Scripture to Theology* (IVP, 1996).

18. Smith, James. *The Fall of Interpretation* (IVP, 2000).

19. Stiver, James. *Theology After Ricouer* (Westminster John Knox, 2001).

20. Thiselton, Anthony. *New Horizons in Hermeneutics* (Zondervan, 1992).

21. Vanhoozer, Kevin. *Is There a Meaning in the Text?* (Zondervan, 1998).

    ———. *First Theology* (IVP, 2002).

    ———. *The Drama of Doctrine* (Westminster John Knox, 2005).

22. Webb, William. *Slaves, Women, and Homosexuals* (IVP, 2001). How to apply cultural background to interpretation.

23. Zimmermann, Jens. *Recovering Theological Hermeneutics* (Baker, 2004).

Postmodernism

1. Adam, A. K. M. *What Is Postmodern Biblical Criticism?* (Fortress, 1995).

  ———, ed. *Handbook of Postmodern Biblical Interpretation* (Chalice, 2000).

2. **Benson, Bruce. *Graven Ideologies* (IVP, 2002).**

3. Braaten, Carl, and Robert Jenson, eds. *The Strange New World of the Gospel* (Eerdmans, 2002).

4. **Carson, D. A. *Telling the Truth: Evangelizing Postmoderns* (Zondervan, 2000).**

  ———. *Becoming Conversant with the Emergent Church* (Zondervan, 2005).

5. **Dockery, David. *The Challenge of Postmodernism,* 2d ed. (Baker, 2001).**

6. Erickson, Millard. *Postmodernizing the Faith* (Baker, 1998). Response to Oden, Grenz, Middleton, Walsh, etc.

  ———. ***Truth or Consequences* (IVP, 2001).**

  ———. ***The Postmodern World* (Crossway, 2002).**

7. **Erickson, Millard, Paul Kjoss Helseth, and Justin Taylor, eds. *Reclaiming the Center* (Crossway, 2004).** Postconservative rebuttal.

8. Franke, John. *The Character of Theology* (Baker, 2005).

9. Gay, Craig. *The Way of the (Modern) World* (Eerdmans, 1999).

10. **Gillingham, Susan. *One Bible, Many Voices* (Eerdmans, 1999).**

11. Grenz, Stanley. *A Primer on Postmodernism* (Eerdmans, 1996).

12. **Groothuis, Douglas. *Truth Decay* (IVP, 2000).**

13. **Horton, Michael, ed. *A Confessing Theology for Postmodern Times* (Crossway, 2000).**

14. Jobling, David, ed. *The Postmodern Bible Reader* (Blackwell, 2001).

15. **Middleton, Richard, and Brian Walsh.** *Truth Is Stranger Than It Used to Be* **(IVP, 1995).**

16. Murphy, Nancey. *Beyond Liberalism and Fundamentalism* (Trinity Press International, 1996).

———. *Anglo-American Postmodernism* (Westview, 1997).

17. Penchansky, David. *The Politics of Biblical Theology* (Mercer University Press, 1995).

18. **Phillips, Timothy, and Dennis Ockholm, eds.** *The Nature of Confession* **(IVP, 1996).**

19. Smith, James. *Who's Afraid of Postmodernism?* (Baker, 2006).

20. **Tanner, Kenneth, and Christopher Hall, eds.** *Ancient and Postmodern Christianity* **(IVP, 2002).**

21. **Thiselton, Anthony.** *Interpreting God and the Postmodern Self* **(T & T Clark, 1995).**

22. Thornhill, John. *Modernity* (Eerdmans, 2000).

23. Ward, Graham, ed. *The Blackwell Companion to Postmodern Theology* (Blackwell, 2001).

24. **Webber, Robert.** *Ancient-Future Faith* **(Baker, 1999).**

———. *The Younger Evangelicals* **(Baker, 2002).**

25. **Wright, N. T.** *The Millennial Myth* **(Westminster John Knox, 1999).**

Literary and Genre Studies

1. Alter, Robert, and Frank Kermode, eds. *The Literary Guide to the Bible* (Belknap-Harvard, 1987). Especially the Old Testament.

2. Cotter, David, ed. *Berit Olam: Studies in Hebrew Narrative and Poetry,* 24 vols. (Liturgical, 1996–).

3. Exum, Cheryl, and David Clines. *The New Literary Criticism and the Hebrew Bible* (Trinity Press International, 1994).

4. **Gabel, John, Charles Wheeler, and Anthony York, eds.** *The Bible as Literature,* **4th ed. (Oxford University Press, 2002).**

5. House, Paul, ed. *Beyond Form Criticism* (Eisenbrauns, 1992). OT.

6. Moore, Stephen. *Literary Criticism and the Gospels* (Yale University Press, 1989).
7. Ryken, Leland, and Tremper Longman, eds. *A Complete Literary Guide to the Bible* (Zondervan, 1993).
8. Ryken, Leland, James Wilhoit, and Tremper Longman, eds. *Dictionary of Biblical Imagery* (IVP, 1998).
9. Strecker, Georg. *History of New Testament Literature* (Trinity Press International, 1997).
10. Wills, Lawrence. *The Quest of the Historical Gospel* (Routledge, 1997). Gospel genre.

Introductions to the Bible as Literature

1. Alter, Robert. *The World of Biblical Literature* (Basic, 1992).
2. Aune, David. *The New Testament in Its Literary Environment,* LEC (Westminster, 1987).
3. Bailey, James, and L. Vander Broek. *Literary Forms in the New Testament* (Westminster John Knox, 1993).
4. Dorsey, David. *The Literary Structure of the Old Testament* (Baker, 1999).
5. Longman, Tremper. *Literary Approaches to Biblical Interpretation* (Zondervan, 1987).
6. Malherbe, Abraham. *Moral Exhortation: A Greco-Roman Sourcebook,* LEC (Westminster, 1986).
7. Petersen, Norman. *Literary Criticism for New Testament Critics* (Fortress, 1978).
8. Ryken, Leland. *Words of Delight* (Baker, 1987).
   ———. *Words of Life* (Baker, 1987). NT.
9. Sandy, Brent, and Ronald Giese, eds. *Cracking Old Testament Codes* (Broadman & Holman, 1995).

Apocalyptic*

1. Barton, John, and Christopher Rowland, eds. *Apocalyptic in History and Tradition* (Sheffield Academic Press, 2002).

---

* Forthcoming: Richard Taylor, *Interpreting Apocalyptic Literature* (Kregel).

2. Collins, Adela Yarbro. *Cosmology and Eschatology in Jewish and Christian Apocalypticism* (Brill, 1996).

3. **Collins, John. *The Apocalyptic Imagination*, 2d ed. (Eerdmans, 1998).**

   ————, ed. *Apocalypse,* **Semeia 14 (Scholars, 1979).**

4. Collins, John, and James Charlesworth. *Mysteries and Revelations* (Sheffield Academic Press, 1991).

5. **Collins, John, Bernard McGinn, and Stephen Stein, eds. *The Encyclopedia of Apocalypticism*, 3 vols. (Continuum, 1998).**

6. Cook, Stephen. *Prophecy and Apocalypticism* (Fortress, 1995).

   ————. *The Apocalyptic Literature.* IBT (Abingdon, 2003).

7. García Martinez, Florentino, ed. *Wisdom and Apocalypticism in the Dead Sea Scrolls and in the Biblical Tradition* (Peeters, 2003).

8. Grabbe, Lester, and Robert Haak. *Knowing the End from the Beginning* (Sheffield Academic Press, 2003).

9. **Hanson, Paul. *The Dawn of Apocalyptic,* rev. ed. (Fortress, 1979).**

10. **Hellholm, David, ed. *Apocalypticism in the Mediterranean World and the Near East* (Mohr, 1983).**

11. **Himmelfarb, Martha. *Ascent to Heaven in Jewish and Christian Apocalypses* (Oxford University Press, 1993).**

12. Nickelsburg, George. *1 Enoch 1,* Hermeneia (Fortress, 2001). 1 Enoch 1–36, 81–108.

13. Nickelsburg, George, and James VanderKam. *1 Enoch 2,* Hermeneia (Fortress, forthcoming). 1 Enoch 37–80.

14. **Rowland, Christopher. *The Open Heaven* (Crossroad, 1982; Wipf & Stock, 2002).**

    ————. *The Book of Revelation,* NIB, vol. 12 (Abingdon, 1998). Extensive bibliography on apocalyptic.

15. **Russell, D. *Prophecy and the Apocalyptic Dream* (Hendrickson, 1994).** Introduction.

16. Sandy, Brent. *Turning Plowshares into Pruning Hooks: Rethinking the Language of Biblical Prophecy and Apocalyptic* (IVP, 2002).

17. VanderKam, James, and William Adler, eds. *The Jewish Apocalyptic Heritage in Early Christianity* (Fortress, 1997).
18. Watson, Duane, ed. *The Interpretation of Apocalyptic Discourse in the New Testament* (Brill/SBL, 2002).

Letter-Writing

1. **Murphy-O'Connor, Jerome.** *Paul the Letter-Writer* **(Liturgical, 1995).**
2. **Richards, E. Randolph.** *The Secretary in the Letters of Paul* **(Mohr, 1991).**
   ———. *Paul and First-Century Letter Writing* **(IVP, 2004).**
3. Stirewalt, M. Luther. *Paul the Letter Writer* (Eerdmans, 2003).
4. **Stowers, Stanley.** *Letter Writing in Greco-Roman Antiquity,* **LEC (Westminster, 1986).**
5. **White, John.** *Light from Ancient Letters* **(Fortress, 1986).**
   ———. *The Form and Function of the Body of the Greek Letter* (Scholars, 1972).
6. **Wilder, Terry.** *Pseudonymity, the New Testament, and Deception* **(University Press of America, 2002).**

Narrative

1. **Alter, Robert.** *The Art of Biblical Narrative* **(Basic, 1981).** Introduction.
2. Amit, Yairah. *Reading Biblical Narratives* (Fortress, 2001).
   ———. *Hidden Polemics in Biblical Narrative* (Brill, 2000).
   ———. *History and Ideology in the Bible* (Sheffield Academic Press, 1997).
3. Bar-Efrat, Shimon. *Narrative Art in the Bible* (Almond, 1989).
4. **Berlin, Adele.** *Poetics and Interpretation of Biblical Narrative* **(Eisenbrauns, 1994).**
5. **Burridge, Richard.** *What Are the Gospels?* **2d ed. (Eerdmans, 2004).**
6. **Fokkelman, J. P.** *Reading Biblical Narrative* **(Westminster John Knox, 2000).** Introduction.

7. Gunn, David, and Danna Fewell. *Narrative in the Hebrew Bible* (Oxford University Press, 1993). Introduction.
8. Husser, Jean-Marie. *Dreams and Dream Narratives in the Biblical World* (Sheffield Academic Press, 2000).
9. Inch, Morris. *Scripture as Story* (University Press of America, 2000).
10. Merenlahti, Petri. *Poetics for the Gospels?* (Sheffield Academic Press, 2002).
11. Miscall, Peter. *The Workings of Old Testament Narrative* (Fortress, 1983). 1 Samuel 16–22.
12. **Powell, Mark. *What Is Narrative Criticism?* (Fortress, 1990).**
13. Resseguie, James. *Narrative Criticism of the New Testament* (Baker, 2005).
14. **Simon, Uriel. *Reading Prophetic Narrative* (Indiana University Press, 1997).**
15. **Sternberg, Meir. *The Poetics of Biblical Narrative* (Indiana University Press, 1985).**
16. Walsh, Jerome. *Style and Structure in Biblical Hebrew Narrative* (Liturgical, 2001).

Parables

1. Bailey, Kenneth. *Jacob and the Prodigal* (IVP, 2003).
2. **Blomberg, Craig. *Interpreting the Parables* (IVP, 1990).** Introduction.
3. Capon, Robert. *Kingdom, Grace, Judgment* (Eerdmans, 2002).
4. Donahue, John. *The Gospel in Parable* (Fortress, 1988).
5. **Forbes, Greg. *The God of Old* (Sheffield Academic Press, 2000).** Luke.
6. Gowler, David. *What Are They Saying About the Parables?* (Paulist, 2000).
7. Hedrick, Charles. *The Parables as Fiction* (Hendrickson, 1994).
———. *Many Things in Parables* (Westminster John Knox, 2004).

8. Herzog, William. *The Parables as Subversive Speech* (Westminster John Knox, 1994).
9. Hultgren, Arland. *The Parables of Jesus* (Eerdmans, 2000). Commentary.
10. Jones, Ivor. *The Matthean Parables* (Brill, 1995).
11. Jones, Peter. *Studying the Parables of Jesus* (Smyth & Helwys, 1999).
12. **Kistemaker, Simon. *The Parables* (Baker, 2002).**
13. **Longenecker, Richard. *The Challenge of Jesus' Parables* (Eerdmans, 1999).**
14. Scott, Bernard. *Hear Then the Parable* (Fortress, 1989).
15. Shillington, George, ed. *Jesus and His Parables* (T & T Clark, 1998).
16. Sider, John. *Interpreting the Parables* (Zondervan, 1995).
17. **Wright, Stephen. *The Voice of Jesus* (Paternoster, 2000).** Study of six parables.
18. Young, Brad. *The Parables* (Hendrickson, 1998).

Poetry

1. **Alter, Robert. *The Art of Biblical Poetry* (Basic, 1985).** Introduction, especially dynamics of parallels.
2. Brensinger, Terry. *Simile and Prophetic Language in the Old Testament* (Mellen, 1996).
3. Cross, Frank, and David Freedman. *Studies in Ancient Yahwistic Poetry* (Eerdmans, 1997).
4. **Fokkelman, J. P. *Major Poems of the Hebrew Bible* (Van Gorcum, 2000).** Eighty-five psalms and Job 4–14.
   ———. *Reading Biblical Poetry* (Westminster John Knox, 2001).
5. Follis, Elaine, ed. *Directions in Biblical Hebrew Poetry* (Sheffield Academic Press, 1997).
6. **Gillingham, Susan. *The Poems and Psalms of the Hebrew Bible* (Oxford University Press, 1994).**
7. Kugel, James. *The Idea of Biblical Poetry* (Johns Hopkins University Press, 1998).

8. Petersen, David, and Kent Richards. *Interpreting Hebrew Poetry* (Fortress, 1992).

9. Watson, Wilfred. *Classical Hebrew Poetry* (T & T Clark, 2005).
    ———. *Traditional Techniques in Classical Hebrew Verse* (Sheffield Academic Press, 1994).

10. *See* Old Testament Introduction, Survey, and Theology: Introduction to the Wisdom Literature.

Prophecy

1. Aune, David. *Prophecy in Early Christianity and the Ancient Mediterranean World* (Eerdmans, 1983; Wipf & Stock, 2003).

2. Ben Zvi, Ehud, and Michael Floyd, eds. *Writing and Speech in Israelite and Ancient Near Eastern Prophecy* (SBL, 2000).

3. Blenkinsopp, Joseph. *A History of Prophecy in Israel* (Westminster John Knox, 1996).

4. Clements, Ronald. *Old Testament Prophecy* (Westminster John Knox, 1996).

5. Davies, Philip, and David Clines, eds. *Among the Prophets* (Sheffield Academic Press, 1993).

6. Forbes, Christopher. *Prophecy and Inspired Speech in Early Christianity and Its Hellenistic Environment* (Hendrickson, 1997).

7. Gitay, Yehoshua, ed. *Prophecy and Prophets* (Scholars, 1997).

8. Glazov, Gregory. *The Bridling of the Tongue and the Opening of the Mouth in Biblical Prophecy* (Sheffield Academic Press, 2001).

9. Kaltner, John, and Louis Stulman, eds. Inspired Speech (T & T Clark, 2004).

10. Nissinen, Martti, with contributions by C. L. Seow and Robert Ritner, *Prophets and Prophecy in the Ancient Near East* (SBL, 2003). Nonbiblical prophecy.

11. Peckham, Brian. *History and Prophecy,* ABRL (Doubleday, 1993).

12. Sandy, Brent. *Ploughshares and Pruning Hooks* (IVP, 2002).

13. Uffenheimer, Benjamin. *Early Prophecy in Israel* (Magnes, 1999).

14. Williams, Michael. *The Prophet and His Message* (Presbyterian & Reformed, 2003). OT.

15. *See* Old Testament Introduction, Survey, and Theology: Introduction to Prophetic Literature.

Rhetoric (OT)

1. De Regt, J., et al., eds. *Literary Structure and Rhetorical Strategies in the Hebrew Bible* (Eisenbrauns, 1996).

2. Eslinger, Lyle. *House of God or House of David* (Sheffield Academic Press, 1994). 2 Samuel 7.

3. Lundbom, Jack. *Jeremiah*, 2d ed. (Eisenbrauns, 1997).

4. Patrick, Dale. *The Rhetoric of Revelation in the Hebrew Bible* (Fortress, 1999).

5. Trible, Phyllis. *Rhetorical Criticism* (Fortress, 1994). Jonah.

6. Watts, James. *Reading Law* (Sheffield Academic Press, 1999).

Rhetoric (NT)

1. Anderson, R. *Ancient Rhetorical Theory and Paul* (Kok Pharos, 1996).

2. Classen, Carl. *Rhetorical Criticism of the New Testament* (Brill, 2002).

3. Gowler, David, Gregory Bloomquist, and Duane Watson, eds. *Fabrics of Discourse* (Trinity Press International, 2003). Robbins tribute.

4. Harvey, John. *Listening to the Text: Oral Patterning in Paul's Letters* (Baker, 1998).

5. Kennedy, G. *New Testament Interpretation Through Rhetorical Criticism* (University of North Carolina, 1984).

6. Kim, Johann. *God, Israel, and the Gentiles* (SBL, 2000). Romans 9–11.

7. Longenecker, Bruce. *Rhetoric at the Boundaries* (Baylor University Press, 2005).

8. Mack, Burton. *Rhetoric and the New Testament* (Fortress, 1990).
9. Porter, Stanley, and Thomas Olbricht, eds. *Rhetoric and the New Testament* (Sheffield Academic Press, 1993).

———. *Rhetoric, Scripture and Theology* (Sheffield Academic Press, 1996).

———. *Rhetorical Analysis of Scripture* (Sheffield Academic Press, 1997).

10. Porter, Stanley, and Dennis Stamps, eds. *Rhetorical Criticism and the Bible* (Sheffield Academic Press, 2002).

———. *Rhetorical Interpretation of Scripture* (Sheffield Academic Press, 1999).

11. Robbins, Vernon. *The Tapestry of Early Christian Discourse* (Routledge, 1996).
12. Shiner, Whitney. *Proclaiming the Gospel: First Century Performance of Mark* (Continuum, 2004).
13. Wilder, Amos. *Early Christian Rhetoric* (Hendrickson, 1999).

Sociorhetorical (General)

1. Eriksson, Anders, et al., eds. *Rhetorical Argumentation in Biblical Texts* (Trinity Press International, 2002).
2. Hens-Piazza, Gina. *Of Methods, Monarchs, and Meanings* (Mercer University Press, 1996).
3. Kingsbury, Jack, ed. *Gospel Interpretation* (Trinity Press International, 1997).
4. Meynet, Roland. *Rhetorical Analysis* (Sheffield Academic Press, 1999).
5. Robbins, Vernon. *Exploring the Texts* (Trinity Press International, 1996).
6. Watson, Duane, and Alan Hauser, eds. *Rhetorical Criticism of the Bible* (Brill, 1994). Nonannotated bibliography.
7. *See* Sociorhetorical Studies and Commentaries under NT Commentaries: Acts, 1 Corinthians, Galatians, and Revelation.
8. *See* New Testament Background: Social-Scientific.

Wisdom

1. Ballard, Wayne, and Dennis Tucker, eds. *Introduction to Wisdom Literature and the Psalms* (Mercer University Press, 2000).
2. Bergant, Dianne. *Israel's Wisdom Literature* (Fortress, 1997).
3. Blenkinsopp, Joseph. *Wisdom and Law in the Old Testament,* 2d ed. (Oxford University Press, 1995).
4. Brenner, Athalya, ed. *A Feminist Companion to Wisdom Literature* (Sheffield Academic Press, 1995).
5. Brown, William. *Character in Crisis* (Eerdmans, 1996).
6. Crenshaw, James. *Urgent Advice and Probing Questions* (Mercer University Press, 1995).
7. Day, John, Robert Gordon, and Hugh Williamson, eds. *Wisdom in Ancient Israel* (Cambridge University Press, 1995).
8. **Gammie, John, and Leo Perdue, eds. *The Sage in Israel and the Ancient Near East* (Eisenbrauns, 1990).**
9. Mack, Burton, and David Clines, eds. *Of Prophet's Visions and the Wisdom of the Sages* (Sheffield Academic Press, 1993).
10. Packer, J. I., and Sven Soderlund, eds. *The Way of Wisdom* (Zondervan, 2000).
11. Perdue, Leo, et al., eds. *In Search of Wisdom* (Westminster John Knox, 1993).
12. Von Rad, Gerhard. *Wisdom in Israel* (Abingdon, 1972).
13. **Weeks, Stuart. *Early Israelite Wisdom* (Clarendon, 1994).** Especially Proverbs.
14. *See* Clements, Perdue (Old Testament Resources: Old Testament Theology).
15. *See* Old Testament Introduction, Survey, and Theology: Introduction to the Wisdom Literature.

17

SYSTEMATIC THEOLOGY
(ALL UNRANKED)

Classic Theologies

1. Bavinck, Herman. *Reformed Dogmatics,* ed. John Bolt (Baker, 2003–).
2. Berkhof, Louis. *Systematic Theology* (Eerdmans, 1996). Combined *Systematic Theology,* 4th ed. (Eerdmans, 1939) and *Introduction to Systematic Theology* (Eerdmans, 1932; Baker, 1979).
3. Berkouwer, G. *Studies in Dogmatics,* 14 vols. (Eerdmans, 1952–76).
4. Buswell, James. *A Systematic Theology of the Christian Religion,* 2 vols. (Zondervan, 1962–63).
5. Chafer, Lewis. *Systematic Theology,* 4 vols. (Kregel, 1993). Unabridged.
6. Hodge, Charles. *Systematic Theology,* 3 vols. (Hendrickson, 1997).
   ———. *Systematic Theology,* abridged 1-vol. ed. (Presbyterian & Reformed, 1997).
7. Shedd, William. *Dogmatic Theology,* 3d ed. (Presbyterian & Reformed, 2003). Also available as a Logos CD (2005).
8. Strong, Augustus. *Systematic Theology* (Judson, 1907).
9. Thiessen, Henry. *Lectures in Systematic Theology,* rev. ed. (Eerdmans, 1977).
10. Warfield, Benjamin. *Works,* 10 vols. (Baker, 1991).

11. Wiley, H. Orton. *Christian Theology,* 3 vols. (Nazarene Publishing, 1940–43). Arminian perspective.

Contemporary Theologies

1. **Bloesch, Donald. *Christian Foundations,* 7 vols. (IVP, 1992–).**
2. Culver, Robert. *Systematic Theology* (Christian Focus, 2005).
3. **Enns, Paul. *Moody Handbook of Theology* (Moody, 1989).**
4. **Erickson, Millard. *Christian Theology,* 2d ed. (Baker, 1998).**

    ———. *Introducing Christian Doctrine,* 2d ed., ed. Arnold Hustad (Baker, 2001). Abridgement of *Christian Theology.*
5. Finger, Thomas. *Christian Theology,* 2 vols. (Herald, 1985, 1989).

    ———. *A Contemporary Anabaptist Theology* (IVP, 2004).
6. Forlines, Leroy. *The Quest for Truth* (Randall House, 2001). Non-Wesleyan Arminian position.
7. Garrett, James. *Systematic Theology,* 2 vols. (Eerdmans, 1990, 1995).
8. Geisler, Norman. *Systematic Theology,* 4 vols. (Bethany House, 2002–). Arminian.
9. Grenz, Stanley. *The Named God and the Question of Being* (Westminster John Knox, 2005).

    ———. *Renewing the Center* (Baker, 2000).

    ———. *The Social God and the Question of Being* (Westminster John Knox, 2001).

    ———. *Theology for the Community of God* (Eerdmans, 2000).
10. Grudem, Wayne. *Systematic Theology* (Zondervan, 1994). Calvinistic charismatic.

    ———. *Bible Doctrine* (Zondervan, 1999). Abridgement of *Systematic Theology.*
11. **Gunton, Colin. *The Christian Faith* (Blackwell, 2001).** Introduction.

12. **Hanson, Paul.** *Introduction to Christian Theology* **(Fortress, 1997).**

13. Henry, Carl. *God, Revelation, and Authority,* 6 vols. (Word, 1976–83; Crossway, 1999).

14. Horton, Stanley, ed. *Systematic Theology,* rev. ed. (Logion, 1995). Pentecostal.

15. Jenson, Robert. *Systematic Theology,* 2 vols. (Oxford University Press, 1997–99).

16. Lewis, Gordon, and Bruce Demarest. *Integrative Theology* (Zondervan, 1987–94). Three volumes in one.

17. Livermore, Paul, Donald Bastien, and Thomas Oden. *The God of Our Salvation* (Light and Life Communications, 1995). Wesleyan.

18. McClendon, James. *Systematic Theology,* 3 vols. (Abingdon, 2002,[1] 1986–2000). Anabaptist.

19. **McGrath, Alister.** *Christian Theology,* **3d ed. (Blackwell, 2001).**

     ———. *Studies in Doctrine* (Zondervan, 1997). Four volumes in one.

     ———, ed. *The Christian Theology Reader,* **2d ed. (Blackwell, 2001).**

20. **McKim, Donald.** *Introducing the Reformed Faith* **(Westminster John Knox, 2001).**

21. Menzies, William, and Stanley Horton. *Bible Doctrines* (Logion, 1993). Pentecostal.

22. Miller, Ed, and Stanley Grenz, eds. *Fortress Introduction to Contemporary Theologies* (Fortress, 1998).

23. Oden, Thomas. *Systematic Theology,* 3 vols. (Harper, 1987–92; Prince, 2000). Methodist.

24. Olson, Roger. *The Mosaic of Christian Belief* (IVP, 2002).

     ———. *Arminian Theology* (IVP, 2006).

25. Pannenberg, Wolfhart. *Systematic Theology,* 3 vols. (Eerdmans, 1991, 1994, 1997).

---

1. At the 2001 annual meeting of the Evangelical Theological Society, thirty papers were delivered on this topic, including many by authors listed here.

26. Peters, Ted. *God: The World's Future,* 2d ed. (Fortress, 2000). Postmodern.

27. Reymond, Robert. *A New Systematic Theology of the Christian Faith* **(Thomas Nelson, 1998).** Reformed introduction.

28. Sawyer, James. *The Survivor's Guide to Theology* (Zondervan, 2002). Introduction.

29. Williams, Rodman. *Renewal Theology* (Zondervan, 1992). Three volumes in one, Pentecostal.

Catholic Theologies

1. Beinert, Wolfgang, and Francis Schüssler Fiorenza, eds. *Handbook of Catholic Theology* (Crossroad, 1995).

2. Brown, Raymond E., Karl Donfried, Joseph Fitzmyer, and John Reumann. *Mary in the New Testament* (Fortress/Paulist, 1978).

3. Chauvet, Louis-Marie. *The Sacraments* (Liturgical, 2001).

4. Collinge, William. *The A to Z of Catholicism* (Scarecrow, 2001).

5. Congar, Yves. *Diversity and Communion* (23rd Community, 1985).

6. de Lubac, Henri. *The Sources of Revelation* (Crossroad, 2000).

7. Dulles, Avery. *The Craft of Theology* (Crossroad, 1992).
   ———. *The Assurance of Things Hoped For* (Oxford University Press, 1994).

8. Fries, Heinrich. *Fundamental Theology* (Catholic University of America, 1996).

9. Kaspar, Walter. *Theology and Church II* (Herder and Herder, 2001).
   ———. *The God of Jesus Christ* (Crossroad, 1984). Idealist Christology.

10. Komanchak, Joseph, Mary Collins, and Dermot Lane, eds. *The New Dictionary of Theology* (Liturgical, 1987).

11. Küng, Hans. *Christianity* (Continuum, 1995).
    ———. *Infallible?* 2d ed. (Continuum, 1994).

12. Latourelle, Rene, and Rino Fisichella, eds. *Dictionary of Fundamental Theology* (Crossroad, 1994).

13. O'Collins, Gerald. *Christology* (Oxford University Press, 1995).

14. Rahner, Karl. *Foundations of Christian Faith* (Seabury, 1978). Idealist Christology.
    —————. *Theological Investigations,* 23 vols. (Helicon/Herder and Herder/Seabury/Crossroad, 1961–92).

15. Ratzinger, John. *In the Beginning* (Eerdmans, 1995).
    —————. *Principles of Catholic Theology* (Ignatius, 1987).

16. Richard, Lucien. *Christ: The Self-Emptying of God* (Paulist, 1997). Kenosis.

17. Schillebeeckx, Edward. *Christ* (Crossroad, 1980).
    —————. *Church* (Crossroad, 1990).

18. Schüssler Fiorenza, Francis, and John Galvin, eds. *Systematic Theology,* 2 vols. (Fortress, 1991).

19. Stuhlmueller, Carroll, ed. *The Collegeville Dictionary of Biblical Theology* (Liturgical, 1996).

20. Tracy, David. *Plurality and Ambiguity* (Harper, 1987).

21. Van Beeck, Frans. *God Encountered,* 6 vols. (Liturgical, 1993–).

22. Von Balthasar, Hans Urs. *Mysterium Paschale* (T & T Clark, 1990).

Theological References and Helps

1. **Alexander, Desmond, et al., eds. *New Dictionary of Biblical Theology* (IVP, 2001).** Three parts: introductory articles, individual book theologies, 215 entries (A–Z).

2. Byrne, Peter, and Leslie Houlden, eds. *Companion Encyclopedia of Theology* (Routledge, 1995).

3. **Elwell, Walter, ed. *Evangelical Dictionary of Theology,* 2d ed. (Baker, 2001).**
   —————, ed. *Baker Theological Dictionary of the Bible* (Baker, 1994). Formerly *Evangelical Dictionary of Biblical Theology.*

4. Ferguson, Sinclair, David Wright, and J. I. Packer, eds. *New Dictionary of Theology* (IVP, 1988).
5. Grenz, Stanley, and Roger Olson. *Twentieth Century Theology* (IVP, 1992). Guidebook.
6. **House, H. Wayne. *Charts of Christian Theology and Doctrine* (Zondervan, 1992).**

    ———. *Charts on Systematic Theology, Volume 1: Prolegomena* (Kregel, 2006).
7. House, H. Wayne, and Randall Price. *Charts of Bible Prophecy* (Zondervan, 2003).
8. House, H. Wayne, with Kyle A. Roberts. *Charts on Systematic Theology* (Kregel, 2006).
9. Lacoste, Jean-Yves, ed. *Encyclopedia of Christian Theology*, 3 vols. (Routledge, 2004).
10. Manser, Martin, et al., eds. *Zondervan Dictionary of Bible Themes* (Zondervan, 1999).
11. McKim, Donald. *The Westminster Handbook to Reformed Theology* (Westminster John Knox, 2001).

    ———, ed. *Encyclopedia of the Reformed Faith* (Westminster John Knox, 1992).
12. Musser, Donald, and Joseph Price, eds. *New and Enlarged Handbook of Christian Theology* (Abingdon, 2003).
13. Olson, Roger. *The Westminster Handbook to Evangelical Theology* (Westminster John Knox, 2004).
14. Richardson, Alan, and John Bowden, eds. *Westminster Dictionary of Theology* (Westminster John Knox, 1983).
15. **Sawyer, James. *Taxonomic Charts of Theology and Biblical Studies* (Zondervan, 1999).**

    ———. *The Survivor's Guide to Theology* (Zondervan, 2006).
16. **Smith, David. *A Handbook of Contemporary Theology* (Baker, 1992).**
17. **Vanhoozer, Kevin, et al., eds. *Dictionary for Theological Interpretation of the Bible* (Baker, 2005).**
18. *See* Church History Resources: History of Theology.

Theological Terms

1. Cairns, Alan. *Dictionary of Theological Terms* (Ambassador Emerald, 1998).
2. **DeMoss, Matthew, and J. Edward Miller. *The Zondervan Dictionary of Bible and Theological Words* (Zondervan, 2002).**
3. González, Justo. *Essential Theological Terms* (Westminster John Knox, 2005).
4. Grenz, Stanley, David Guretski, and Cherith Nordling. *Pocket Dictionary of Theological Terms* (IVP, 2001).
5. McKim, Donald. *Westminster Dictionary of Theological Terms* (Westminster John Knox, 1996).

World Religions, Sects, and Cults

1. Bowker, John, ed. *The Oxford Dictionary of World Religions* (Oxford University Press, 1997).
   ———, ed. *The Cambridge Illustrated History of Religions* (Cambridge University Press, 2002).
2. Caner, Ergun, and Emir Caner. *Unveiling Islam* (Kregel, 2002).
3. Chryssides, George. *Historical Dictionary of New Religious Movements* (Scarecrow, 2001).
   ———. *More Than a Prophet* (Kregel, 2003).
4. **Clarke, Peter, ed. *Encyclopedia of New Religious Movements* (Routledge, 2005).**
5. **Corduan, Winfried. *A Tapestry of Faiths* (IVP, 2002).**
6. Doniger, Wendy, ed. *Merriam-Webster's Encyclopedia of World Religions* (Merriam-Webster, 1999).
7. Douglas, J. D., ed. *The New 20th Century Encyclopedia of Religious Knowledge,* 2d ed. (Baker, 1991).
8. Earhart, Byron, ed. *Religious Traditions of the World* (HarperCollins, 1993).
9. **Enroth, Ronald, ed. *A Guide to New Religious Movements* (IVP, 2005).**
10. **Hexham, Irving, et al., eds. *Encountering New Religious Movements* (Kregel, 2004).**

11. House, H. Wayne. *Charts of Cults, Sects, and Religious Movements* (Zondervan, 2000).
12. Losch, Richard. *The Many Faces of Faith* (Eerdmans, 2001).
13. Marshall, Paul, Roberta Green, and Lela Gilbert. *Islam at the Crossroads* (Baker, 2002).
14. Mather, George, Larry Nichols, and Alvin Schmidt. *Dictionary of Cults, Sects, and World Religion,* rev. ed. (Zondervan, 2005).
15. **Millet, Robert. *A Different Jesus? The Christ of the Latter-day Saints* (Eerdmans, 2005).**
16. Moucarry, Chawkat. *The Prophet and the Messiah* (IVP, 2002). Comparison of Christianity to Islam.
17. Neusner, Jacob, ed. *World Religions in America,* 3d ed. (Westminster John Knox, 2003).
18. Partridge, Christopher, ed. *New Religions: A Guide* (Oxford University Press, 2004).
19. **Partridge, Christopher, and Doug Groothius, eds. *Dictionary of Contemporary Religion in the Western World* (IVP, 2002).**
20. Smith, Jonathan, and William Green, eds. *The HarperCollins Dictionary of Religion* (HarperSanFrancisco, 1995).
21. Stark, Rodney, and Reid Neilson. *The Rise of Mormonism* (Columbia University Press, 2005).
22. Tennent, Timothy. *Christianity at the Religious Roundtable* (Baker, 2002).
23. **Tucker, Ruth. *Another Gospel* (Zondervan, 2004).**

Biblical Authority

1. Bacote, Vincent, Laura Miguélez, and Dennis Okholm, eds. *Evangelicals and Scripture: Tradition, Authority and Hermeneutics* (IVP, 2004).
2. Callahan, James. *The Clarity of Scripture* (IVP, 2002).
3. **Carson, D. A., and John Woodbridge, eds. *Scripture and Truth* (Baker, 1992).**
4. Enns, Peter. *Inspiration and Incarnation* (Baker, 2005).
5. **Goldingay, John. *Models for Scripture* (Eerdmans, 1994).**

6. **Helm, Paul, and Carl Trueman, eds.** *The Trustworthiness of God: Perspectives on the Nature of Scripture* **(Eerdmans, 2002).**
7. Kistler, Don, ed. *Sola Scriptura!* (Soli Deo Gloria, 2001).
8. Mathison, Keith. *The Shape of Sola Scriptura* (Canon, 2001).
9. Saucy, Robert. *Scripture* (Word, 2001).
10. **Warfield, Benjamin.** *The Inspiration and Authority of the Bible,* **2d ed. (Presbyterian & Reformed, 1980).**

Revelation

1. Avis, Paul, ed. *Divine Revelation* (Eerdmans, 1997).
2. Bockmuehl, Markus. *Revelation and Mystery in Ancient Judaism and Pauline Christianity* (Mohr, 1997).
3. **Dulles, Avery.** *Models of Revelation* **(Doubleday, 1985; Orbis, 1991).**
4. Fackre, Gabriel. *The Doctrine of Revelation* (Eerdmans, 1997).
5. Gunton, Colin. *A Brief Theology of Revelation* (T & T Clark, 1995).
6. Jensen, Peter. *The Revelation of God* (IVP, 2002).
7. Tiessen, Terrance. *Revelation, Salvation, and the Religions* (IVP, 2002).

Pluralism

1. Baker, Tim. *Why So Many Gods?* (Thomas Nelson, 2002).
2. **Carson, D. A.** *The Gagging of God* **(Zondervan, 1995).**
3. Clendenin, Daniel. *Many Gods, Many Lords* (Baker, 1995).
4. Edwards, James. *Is Jesus the Only Savior?* (Eerdmans, 2006).
5. Hebblethwaite, Brian. *Ethics and Religion in a Pluralistic Age* (T & T Clark, 1997).
6. Heim, Mark. *The Depth of the Riches* (Eerdmans, 2000).
7. **House, H. Wayne.** *Charts of World Religions* **(Zondervan, 2005).**
8. Monsma, Stephen, and Christopher Soper, eds. *Equal Treatment of Religion in a Pluralistic Society* (Eerdmans, 1998).

————. *The Challenge of Pluralism* (Rowman and Littlefield, 1997).

9. **Netland, Harold. *Encountering Religious Pluralism* (IVP, 2001).**

10. **Okholm, Dennis, and Timothy Phillips, eds. *Four Views on Salvation in a Pluralistic World* (Zondervan, 1996).**

11. Pandiappallil, Joseph. *Jesus the Christ and Religious Pluralism* (Herder and Herder, 2001). Rahnerian Christology.

12. Parry, Robin, and Christopher Partridge, eds. *Universal Salvation?* (Eerdmans, 2004).

13. Quinn, Philip, and Kevin Meeker, eds. *The Philosophical Challenge of Religious Diversity* (Oxford University Press, 1999).

14. Skillen, James, and Rockne McCarthy, eds. *Political Order and the Plural Structure of Society* (Eerdmans, 1991).

15. **Stackhouse, John, ed. *No Other Gods Before Me?* (Baker, 2001).**

————. *Evangelical Landscapes* (Baker, 2002).

16. Tiessen, Terrance. *Who Can Be Saved? Reassessing Salvation in Christ and World Religions* (IVP, 2004).

God and His Qualities

1. Boice, J. M. *Whatever Happened to the Doctrine of Grace?* (Crossway, 2001).

2. Boice, J. M., and Philip Ryken. *The Doctrines of Grace* (Crossway, 2002).

3. **Bray, Gerald. *The Doctrine of God* (IVP, 1993).**

4. **Carson, D. A. *The Difficult Doctrine of the Love of God* (Crossway, 2000).**

5. Coppedge, Allan. *Portraits of God* (IVP, 2001). Holiness.

6. Feinberg, John. *No One Like Him* (Crossway, 2001).

7. **Frame, John. *The Doctrine of God* (Presbyterian & Reformed, 2002).**

8. Geivett, R. Douglas, and Gary Habermas. *In Defense of Miracles* (IVP, 1997).

9. **Grenz, Stanley. *The Named God and the Question of Being* (Westminster John Knox, 2005).**

10. Gunton, Colin. *The Triune Creator* (Eerdmans, 1998).
    ———, ed. *The Doctrine of Creation* (T & T Clark, 1998).
11. **Kennard, Douglas. *The Classical Christian God* (Mellen, 2002).**
12. **Lewis, Peter. *The Message of the Living God*, BST (IVP, 2000).**
13. **McGrath, Alister. *Creation* (Fortress, 2005).**
14. Richards, Jay. *Divine Essence and Accidents* (IVP, 2002).
15. Wilkinson, David. *The Message of Creation*, BST (IVP, 2002).
16. Willis, E. David. *Notes on the Holiness of God* (Eerdmans, 2002).

Trinity

1. Davis, Stephen, et al., eds. *The Trinity* (Oxford University Press, 1999).
2. Edgar, Brian. *The Message of the Trinity.* BST (IVP, 2005).
3. Erickson, Millard. *God in Three Persons* (Baker, 1995).
   ———. ***Making Sense of the Trinity* (Baker, 2000).** Popular.
4. **Giles, Kevin. *Jesus and the Father* (Zondervan, 2006).**
5. **Gunton, Colin. *The Promise of Trinitarian Theology*, rev. ed. (T & T Clark, 1997).**
6. Hunt, Anne. *What Are They Saying About the Trinity?* (Paulist, 1998).
7. Kimel, Alvin, ed. *Speaking the Christian God* (Eerdmans, 1992).
   ———, ed. *This Is My Name Forever* (IVP, 2001).
8. Letham, Robert. *The Holy Trinity* (Presbyterian & Reformed, 2004).
9. Olson, Roger, and Christopher Hall. *The Trinity* (Eerdmans, 2002).
10. Toon, Peter. *Our Triune God* (Victor, 1996).
11. Torrance, J. B. *Worship, Community, and the Triune God of Grace* (IVP, 1997).
12. Torrance, Thomas. *The Christian Doctrine of God* (T & T Clark, 1996).

———. *Trinitarian Perspectives* (T & T Clark, 2000).

13. Vanhoozer, Kevin, ed. *The Trinity in a Pluralistic Age* (Eerdmans, 1997).

14. Ware, Bruce. *Father, Son, and Holy Spirit* (Crossway, 2004).

15. **Witherington, Ben, and Laura Ice. *The Shadow of the Almighty* (Eerdmans, 2001).**

Divine Providence and the Will of God

1. **Beilby, James, and Paul Eddy, eds. *Four Views on Divine Foreknowledge and Divine Freedom* (IVP, 2001).**

2. Boyd, Gregory. *God at War* (IVP, 1997).
   ———. *God of the Possible* (Baker, 2000). Freewill open theistic view.

3. **Carson, D. A. *Divine Sovereignty and Human Responsibility*, 2d ed. (Baker, 1994; Wipf & Stock, 2000).**

4. Cobb, John, and Clark Pinnock, eds. *Searching for an Adequate God* (Eerdmans, 2000).

5. Erickson, Millard. *God the Father Almighty* (Baker, 1998).
   ———. *What Does God Know and When Does He Know It?* (Zondervan, 2003).

6. Feinberg, John. *The One True God* (Crossway, 2002).

7. **Frame, John. *No Other God: A Response to Open Theism* (Presbyterian & Reformed, 2001).**

8. Gannsle, Gregory, ed. *God and Time* (IVP, 2001). Four views.

9. **Geisler, Norman, and H. Wayne House. *The Battle for God* (Kregel, 2001).**

10. Hall, Christopher, and John Sanders. *Does God Have a Future?* (Baker, 2003).

11. **Helm, Paul. *The Providence of God* (IVP, 1994).**

12. House, H. Wayne, and Max Herrera. *Charts on Open Theism and Orthodoxy* (Kregel, 2003).

13. **Huffman, Douglas, and Eric Johnson, eds. *God Under Fire* (Zondervan, 2002).**

14. Pinnock, Clark. *Most Moved Mover* (Baker, 2001). Freewill open theistic view.

15. Pinnock, Clark, et al., eds. *The Openness of God* (IVP, 1995). Freewill open theistic view.

16. Piper, John, Justin Taylor, and Paul Helseth, eds. *Beyond the Bounds* (Crossway, 2003).

17. Sanders, John. *The God Who Risks* (IVP, 1998). Freewill view.

18. Tiessen, Terrance. *Providence and Prayer* (IVP, 2000).

19. Waltke, Bruce. *Finding the Will of God* (Eerdmans, 2002).

20. Ware, Bruce. *God's Lesser Glory* (Crossway, 2000). Rebuttal of Boyd, Sanders, Pinnock, etc.

———. *Their God Is Too Small* (Crossway, 2003).

———. *God's Greater Glory* (Crossway, 2004).

21. Wilson, Douglas, ed. *Bound Only Once* (Canon, 2001).

22. Wright, R. K. *No Place for Sovereignty* (IVP, 1996).

Satan and the Powers of Darkness

1. Arnold, Clinton. *Three Crucial Questions About Spiritual Warfare* (Baker, 1997).

———. *Powers of Darkness* (IVP, 1992). In Paul's Letters.

2. Boyd, Gregory. *Satan and the Problem of Evil* (IVP, 2001).

3. Braaten, Carl, and Robert Jenson, eds. *Sin, Death, and the Devil* (Eerdmans, 1999).

4. Day, Peggy. *An Adversary in Heaven: Satan in the Hebrew Bible* (Scholars, 1988).

5. Ferguson, Everett. *Demonology of the Early Christian World* (Mellen, 1984).

6. Lane, Anthony, ed. *The Unseen World* (Baker, 1997).

7. Mayhue, Richard. *Unmasking Satan* (Kregel, 2001). Popular study.

8. Noll, Stephen. *Angels of Light, Powers of Darkness* (IVP, 1998).

9. Page, Sydney. *Powers of Evil* (Baker, 1995).

10. Pagels, Elaine. *Origin of Satan* (Random House, 1995).

11. Russell, Jeffrey. *Mephistopheles* (Cornell University Press, 1986). Modern.

————. *Satan* **(Cornell University Press, 1981).** NT.

————. *The Devil* **(Cornell University Press, 1977).** Antiquity.

12. **Wink, Walter.** *Naming the Powers* **(Fortress, 1984).**

————. *Unmasking the Powers* **(Fortress, 1986).**

————. *Engaging the Powers* **(Fortress, 1992).**

13. Wright, Archie. *The Origin of Evil Spirits* (Mohr, 2005). Genesis 6:1–4.

Sin and Suffering

1. Beker, Christiaan. *Suffering and Hope* (Eerdmans, 1994).

2. **Blocher, Henri.** *Original Sin* **(IVP, 2001).**

————. *Evil and the Cross: An Analytical Look at the Problem of Pain* (Kregel, 1994/2004).

3. **Carson, D. A.** *Love in Hard Places* **(Crossway, 2002).**

————. *How Long, O Lord?* **rev. ed. (Baker, 2006).**

4. Gestrich, Christof. *The Return of Splendor in the World* (Eerdmans, 1997). Sin and forgiveness.

5. Goldingay, John. *Walk On: Life, Loss, Trust, and Other Realities* (Baker, 2002).

6. Kelly, Joseph. *The Problem of Evil in the Western Tradition* (Liturgical, 2002).

7. Mann, Ivan. *A Double Thirst* (Darton, Longman and Todd, 2001). Suffering.

8. McCartney, Dan. *Why Does It Have to Hurt?* (Presbyterian & Reformed, 1998). Popular study.

9. **Ortlund, Raymond.** *Whoredom* **(Eerdmans, 1996; IVP, 2001).** Spiritual adultery.

10. **Peters, Ted.** *Sin* **(Eerdmans, 1996; Wipf & Stock, 2000).**

11. **Phillips, D. Z.** *The Problem of Evil and the Problem of God* **(Fortress, 2005).**

12. **Plantinga, Cornelius.** *Not the Way It's Supposed to Be: A Breviary of Sin* **(Eerdmans, 1995).**

13. Poe, Harry Lee. *See No Evil* (Kregel, 2005).

14. Reventlow, Henning Graf, and Yair Hoffman, eds. *The Problem of Evil and Its Symbols in Jewish and Christian Tradition* (T & T Clark, 2004).

15. Smith, Barry. *Paul's Seven Explanations of the Sufferings of the Righteous* (Lang, 2002).
16. Tambasco, Anthony, ed. *The Bible on Suffering* (Paulist, 2001).
17. Wenham, John. *The Enigma of Evil* (Eagle, 1994).

Jesus Christ

1. **Bauckham, Richard. *God Crucified* (Paternoster, 1998).**
2. **Brown, Raymond E. *An Introduction to New Testament Christology* (Paulist, 1994).**
3. Dunn, James. *The Christ and the Spirit,* vol. 1: *Christology* (Eerdmans, 1998).
4. Erickson, Millard. *The Word Became Flesh* (Baker, 1991).
5. Haight, Roger. *Jesus, Symbol of God* (Orbis, 2000).
6. Hengel, Martin. *Studies in Early Christology* (T & T Clark, 1995).
7. Horton, Michael. *Lord and Servant* (Westminster John Knox, 2005).
8. **Hurtado, Larry. *Lord Jesus Christ* (Eerdmans, 2003).**
   ———. *One Lord, One God* (Fortress, 1988).
9. Lee, Aquila. *From Messiah to Preexistent Son* (Mohr, 2004). Psalms 110:1 and 2:7.
10. Letham, Robert. *The Work of Christ* (IVP, 2004).
11. Longman, Tremper. *Immanuel in Our Place* (Presbyterian & Reformed, 2001).
12. MacLeod, Donald. *The Person of Christ* (IVP, 1998).
13. Marshall, Bruce, ed. *Christology* (Blackwell, 2005).
14. Marshall, I. Howard. *The Origins of New Testament Christology,* rev. ed. (IVP, 1990).
15. Matera, Frank. *New Testament Christology* (Westminster John Knox, 1999).
16. McIntyre, John. *The Shape of Christology,* 2d ed. (T & T Clark, 1998).
17. Motyer, Alec. *Look to the Rock* (Kregel, 1996, 2004). OT.
18. Powell, Mark, and David Bauer, eds. *Who Do You Say That I Am?* (Westminster John Knox, 1999).

19. Schnackenberg, Rudolf. *Jesus in the Gospels* (Westminster John Knox, 1995).
20. Schwarz, Hans. *Christology* (Eerdmans, 1998).
21. Tuckett, Christopher. *Christology and the New Testament* (Westminster John Knox, 2001).
22. Witherington, Ben. *The Christology of Jesus* (Fortress, 1990).

The Cross

1. **Beasley-Murray, Paul. *The Message of Resurrection*, BST (IVP, 2000).**
2. **Demarest, Bruce. *The Cross and Salvation* (Crossway, 1997).**
3. Gorman, Michael. *Cruciformity* (Eerdmans, 2001). Paul.
4. Green, Joel, and Mark Baker. *Recovering the Scandal of the Cross* (IVP, 2000). New Testament atonement.
5. Hill, Charles, and Frank James, eds. *The Glory of the Atonement* (IVP, 2004).
6. **McGrath, Alister. *The Mystery of the Cross* (Zondervan, 1998).**
7. McKnight, Scot. *Jesus and His Death* (Baylor University Press, 2005). Jesus anticipated His death and atonement.
8. **Morris, Leon. *The Apostolic Preaching of the Cross*, 3d ed. (Eerdmans, 1984).**
   ———. *The Atonement* (IVP, 1983).
   ———. *The Cross in the New Testament* (Eerdmans, 1965).
9. **Tidball, Derek. *The Message of the Cross*, BST (IVP, 2001).**
10. Williams, Rowan. *Resurrection* (Pilgrim, 2002).

Salvation

1. Aune, David, ed. *Rereading Paul Together: Protestant and Catholic Perspectives on Justification* (Baker, 2006).
2. **Bahnsen Greg, ed. *Five Views on Law and Gospel* (Zondervan, 1993).**
3. **Budziszewski, J. *Written on the Heart: The Case for Natural Law* (IVP, 1997).**

4. Geisler, Norman. *Chosen but Free,* 2d ed. (Bethany, 2001). Arminian rebuttal of Calvinism.
5. Husbands, Mark, and Daniel Treier, eds. *Justification* (IVP, 2004).
6. Klein, William. *The New Chosen People: A Corporate View of Election* (Zondervan, 1990; Wipf & Stock, 2000).
7. Levering, Matthew. *Christ's Fulfillment of Torah and Temple: Salvation According to Thomas Aquinas* (University of Notre Dame, 2002).
8. McCormack, Bruce, ed. *Justification in Perspective* (Baker, 2006).
9. Oden, Thomas. *The Justification Reader* (Eerdmans, 2002). Patristic compendium.
10. **Piper, John.** *The Justification of God,* **2d ed. (Baker, 1993).**
11. **Ryken, Philip.** *The Message of Salvation,* **BST (IVP, 2001).**
12. **Seifrid, Mark.** *Justification By Faith* **(Brill, 1992).**
    ———. *Christ Our Righteousness* (IVP, 2000).
13. Smith, Gordon. *Beginning Well* (IVP, 2001). Conversion.
14. Stackhouse, John. *What Does It Mean to Be Saved?* (Baker, 2002).
15. White, James. *The Potter's Freedom* (Calvary, 2001). Calvinist rebuttal of Geisler.

Assurance and Sanctification

1. Dieter, Melvin, et al. *Five Views on Sanctification* (Zondervan, 1987).
2. Eaton, Michael. *No Condemnation* (IVP, 1995).
3. Hafemann, Scott. *The God of Promise and the Life of Faith* (Crossway, 2001). Application of theology to life.
4. Jones, Gregory. *Embodying Forgiveness* (Eerdmans, 1996).
5. **Peterson, David.** *Possessed by God* **(IVP, 2001).** Sanctification as a definitive event rather than process.
6. Pinson, Matt, ed. *Four Views on Eternal Security* (Zondervan, 2002).

7. **Schreiner, Thomas, and Ardel Caneday.** *The Race Set Before Us* **(IVP, 2001).** Perseverance and assurance, lordship salvation.

Church and Its Mission

1. Alston, Wallace. *The Church of the Living God* (Westminster John Knox, 2002).
2. Anthony, Michael, et al., eds. *Evangelical Dictionary of Christian Education* (Baker, 2001).
3. Bock, Darrell. *Purpose-Driven Theology* (IVP, 2002). Revamped ETS address anticipating future direction of church.
4. Clarke, Andrew. *Serve the Community of the Church* (Eerdmans, 2000). First-century paradigm.
5. Clowney, Edmund. *The Church* (IVP, 1995).
6. Dulles, Avery. *Models of the Church,* expanded (Random House, 2002).
7. Ferguson, Everett. *The Church of Christ* (Eerdmans, 1996).
8. Hammett, John. *Biblical Foundations for Baptist Churches: A Contemporary Ecclesiology* (Kregel, 2005).
9. Horrell, J. Scott. *From the Ground Up* (Kregel, 2004).
10. Husbands, Mark, and Daniel Treier. *The Community of the Word* (IVP, 2005).
11. Kärkäinnen, Veli-Matti. *An Introduction to Ecclesiology* (IVP, 2002).
12. Köstenberger, Andreas, and Peter O'Brien. *Salvation to the Ends of the Earth* (IVP, 2001). Missions.
13. Moore, Russell. *The Kingdom of Christ* (Crossway, 2004).
14. Saucy, Robert, *The Church in God's Program* (Moody, 1972).
15. Snyder, Howard. *Decoding the Church: Mapping the DNA of Christ's Body* (Baker, 2002).
16. South, James. *Disciplinary Practices in Pauline Texts* (Mellen, 1992).
17. Stackhouse, John, ed. *Evangelical Ecclesiology* (Baker, 2003).

Sacraments

1. **Armstrong, John, ed.** *Understanding Four Views on Baptism* **(Zondervan, 2007).**

2. Chemnitz, Martin. *The Lord's Supper* (Concordia, 1979). Lutheran perspective.

3. De Arteaga, William. *Forgotten Power: The Significance of the Lord's Supper in Revivals* (Zondervan, 2002).

4. Hahn, Scott. *The Lamb's Supper* (Doubleday, 1999). Catholic perspective.

5. **Hartman, Lars.** *"Into the Name of the Lord Jesus": Baptism in the Early Church* **(T & T Clark, 1997).**

6. Marshall, I. Howard. *Last Supper and Lord's Supper* (Paternoster, 2002).

7. **Mathison, Keith.** *Given for You* **(Presbyterian & Reformed, 2002).** Lord's Supper.

8. Nichols, Aidan. *The Holy Eucharist* (Hyperion, 1992). Catholic perspective.

9. Porter, Stanley, and Anthony Cross, eds. *Baptism, the New Testament, and the Church* (Sheffield Academic Press, 1999).
———. *Dimensions of Baptism* (Sheffield Academic Press, 2003).

10. Schenck, Lewis. *The Presbyterian Doctrine of Children in the Covenant* (Presbyterian & Reformed, 2003). Infant baptism.

11. **Schreiner, Thomas, and Shawn Wright, eds.** *Believer's Baptism.* **NACSBT (B & H Publishing Group, 2007).**

12. **Stander, Hendrick, and Johannes Louw.** *Baptism in the Early Church* **(Evangelical, 2004).** Contra paedobaptism.

13. Strawbridge, Gregg, ed. *The Case for Covenantal Infant Baptism* (Presbyterian & Reformed, 2003).

14. **Vander Zee, Leonard.** *Christ, Baptism and the Lord's Supper: Recovering the Sacraments for Evangelical Worship* **(IVP, 2004).**

Church Government

1. Brand, Chad, and R. Stanton Norman, eds. *Perspectives on Church Government* (Broadman & Holman, 2004).

2. **Cowan, Steven, ed. *Who Runs the Church?: Four Views on Church Government* (Zondervan, 2004).**
3. Cowen, Gerald. *Who Rules the Church? Examining Congregational Leadership and Church Government* (Broadman & Holman, 2003).
4. Getz, Gene. *Elders and Leaders* (Moody, 2003).
5. Merkle, Benjamin. *The Elder and Overseer: One Office in the Early Church* (Lang, 2003).
6. Newton, Phil. *Elders in Congregational Life* (Kregel, 2005).

Worship

1. Bateman, Herbert, ed. *Authentic Worship* (Kregel, 2002). Analyzes styles.
2. Best, Harold. *Unceasing Worship* (IVP, 2003).
3. Carson, D. A., ed. *Worship by the Book* (Zondervan, 2002). Free, Anglican, and Presbyterian.
4. Hart, D. G., and John Muether. *With Reverence and Awe* (Presbyterian & Reformed, 2002).
5. Hill, Andrew. *Enter His Courts With Praise!* (Baker, 1997).
6. Hurtado, Larry. *At the Origins of Christian Worship* (Eerdmans, 1999).
7. Liesch, Barry. *The New Worship*, rev. ed. (Baker, 2001).
8. Peterson, David. *Engaging with God* (IVP, 2002).
9. **Ross, Allen P. *Recalling the Hope of Glory* (Kregel, 2006).**
10. Ryken, Philip, et al., eds. *Give Praise to God* (Presbyterian & Reformed, 2003).
11. **Wainwright, Geoffrey, and Karen Tucker, eds. *The Oxford History of Christian Worship* (Oxford University Press, 2005).**

The Holy Spirit and Spiritual Gifts
Traditional

1. Badcock, Gary. *Light of Truth and Fire of Love* (Eerdmans, 1997).
2. Bloesch, Donald. *Christian Foundations: The Holy Spirit*, vol. 5 (IVP, 2000).

3. Brand, Chad, ed. *Perspectives on Spirit Baptism* (Broadman & Holman, 2004).

4. Budgen, Victor. *The Charismatics and the Word of God* (Evangelical Press, 1985).

5. Dunn, James. *Baptism in the Spirit* (Westminster, 1970).

6. Edgar, Thomas. *Satisfied by the Power of the Spirit* (Kregel, 1996).

7. Ewert, David. *The Holy Spirit in the New Testament* (Herald, 1983).

8. Ferguson, Sinclair. *The Holy Spirit* (IVP, 1997).

9. Gaffin, Richard. *Perspectives on Pentecost* (Presbyterian & Reformed, 1979).

10. Hamilton, James. *God's Indwelling Presence.* NACSBT (B & H Publishing Group, 2006).

11. Kärkäinnen, Veli-Matti. *Pneumatology* (IVP, 2003).

12. McIntyre, John. *The Shape of Pneumatology* (T & T Clark, 1997). History of doctrine.

13. Packer, J. I. *Keep in Step with the Spirit* (Revell, 1984).

14. Schandorff, Esther. *The Doctrine of the Holy Spirit,* 2 vols. (Scarecrow, 1995). Exhaustive bibliography.

15. Thomas, Robert, ed. *The Master's Perspective on Contemporary Issues* (Kregel, 1998). Farnell on Prophecy; Mayhue on Holy Spirit.
    ———. *Understanding Spiritual Gifts,* rev. ed. (Kregel, 1999). 1 Corinthians 12–14.

16. Welker, Michael. *God the Spirit* (Fortress, 1994).

17. *See* New Testament Commentaries: Luke: The Holy Spirit in Luke–Acts.

Pentecostal and Charismatic

1. Albrecht, Daniel. *Rites in the Spirit* (Sheffield Academic Press, 1999). Spirit baptism always postconversion.

2. Arrington, French. *Encountering the Holy Spirit* (Pathway, 2003).

3. Arrington, French, and Roger Stronstad, eds. *Life in the Spirit New Testament Commentary* (Zondervan, 1999).

4. Burgess, Stanley. *The Holy Spirit,* 3 vols. (Hendrickson, 1984–1997).

5. **Fee, Gordon. *God's Empowering Presence* (Hendrickson, 1994).**
    ———. *Gospel and Spirit* (Hendrickson, 1991).
    ———. *Paul, the Spirit, and the People of God* (Hendrickson, 1996).

6. **Green, Michael. *I Believe in the Holy Spirit*, rev. ed. (Eerdmans, 2004).**

7. Grieg, Gary, and Kevin Springer, eds. *The Kingdom and the Power,* rev. ed. (Regal, 1993).

8. **Grudem, Wayne. *The Gift of Prophecy in 1 Corinthians* (University Press of America, 1982; Wipf & Stock, 1999).**
    ———. *The Gift of Prophecy in the New Testament and Today,* rev. ed. (Crossway, 2000).
    ———, ed. *Are Miraculous Gifts for Today? Four Views* (Zondervan, 1996).

9. Hardesty, Nancy. *Faith Cure* (Hendrickson, 2003). Healing.

10. **Hart, Larry. *Truth Aflame* (Zondervan, 2006).** Systematic Theology.

11. Hill, Clifford. *Prophecy, Past and Present,* 1st American ed. (Vine, 1991).

12. Houston, Graham. *Prophecy* (IVP, 1989).

13. Hovenden, Gerald. *Speaking in Tongues* (Sheffield Academic Press, 2002).

14. **Hunter, Harold. *Spirit-Baptism* (University Press of America, 1983).**

15. **Keener, Craig. *Gift and Giver* (Baker, 2001).**

16. Lord, Andrew. *Spirit-Shaped Mission* (Paternoster, 2005).

17. **Macchia, Frank. *Baptized in the Spirit* (Zondervan, 2005).**

18. **McDonnell, Kilian, and George Montague. *Christian Initiation and Baptism in the Holy Spirit* (Liturgical, 1994).**

19. McGee, Gary, ed. *Initial Evidence* (Hendrickson, 1991).

20. **Menzies, William, and Robert Menzies. *Spirit and Power* (Zondervan, 2000).**

21. Palma, Anthony. *The Holy Spirit* (Logion, 2001).
22. Poloma, Margaret M. *Main Street Mystics: The Toronto Blessing and Reviving Pentecostalism* (AltaMira, 2003).
23. **Ruthven, Jon. *On the Cessation of the Charismata* (Sheffield Academic Press, 1993).**
24. **Schatzmann, Siegfried. *A Pauline Theology of Charismata* (Hendrickson, 1987).**
25. Stronstad, Roger. *The Prophethood of All Believers* (Sheffield Academic Press, 1999).
26. Thomas, John Christopher. The Spirit of the New Testament (Deo, 2005).
27. **Turner, Max. *The Holy Spirit and Spiritual Gifts* (Eerdmans, 1998).** OT, intertestamental background.
28. Warrington, Keith. *Discovering the Holy Spirit in the New Testament* (Hendrickson, 2005).
29. Yong, Amos. *Discerning the Spirits* (Sheffield Academic Press, 2001).
    ———. *The Spirit Poured Out on All Flesh* (Baker, 2005).
30. *See* New Testament Commentaries: Luke: The Holy Spirit in Luke–Acts.

The Last Days

1. Baker, David, ed. *Looking Into the Future* (Baker, 2001).
2. Bauckham, Richard, and Trevor Hart. *Hope Against Hope* (Eerdmans, 1999).
3. Benware, Paul. *Understanding Endtime Prophecy* (Moody, 1995). Introduction.
4. **Bock, Darrell, ed. *Three Views on the Millennium and Beyond* (Zondervan, 1999).** Premillennial, amillennial, and postmillennial.
5. Brower, Keith, and Mark Elliott, eds. *Eschatology in the Bible and Theology* (IVP, 1997).
6. Bull, Malcolm, ed. *Apocalypse Theory and the Ends of the World* (Blackwell, 1995).
7. **Clouse, Robert, ed. *The Meaning of the Millennium: Four Views* (IVP, 1977).**

8. Clouse, Robert, Robert Hosack, and Richard Pierard. *The New Millennium Manual* (Baker, 1999).

9. Doyle, Robert. *Eschatology and the Shape of Christian Belief* (Paternoster, 1999).

10. Dumbrell, William. *The Search for Order* (Baker, 1995; Wipf & Stock, 2001).

11. Ellis, E. Earle. *Christ and the Future in New Testament History* (Brill, 2000).

12. Erickson, Millard. *A Basic Guide to Eschatology* (Baker, 1998).

13. Fergusson, John, and Marcel Sarot, eds. *The Future as God's Gift* (T & T Clark, 2000).

14. Grenz, Stanley. *The Millennial Maze* (IVP, 1992).

15. Gundry, Robert. *First the Antichrist* (Baker, 1997). Post-tribulational.

16. Gundry, Stanley, ed. *Three Views on the Rapture* (Zondervan, 1984, 1996).

17. Hill, Charles. *Regnum Caelorum,* 2d ed. (Eerdmans, 2001). Early church views.

18. Holman, Charles. *Till Jesus Comes* (Hendrickson, 1996).

19. Horton, Michael. *Covenant and Eschatology* (Westminster, 2002).

20. Ice, Thomas, and Timothy Demy, eds. *The Return* (Kregel, 1999).

21. Ice, Thomas, and Kenneth Gentry. *The Great Tribulation: Past or Future?* (Kregel, 1999).

22. Kyle, Richard. *The Last Days Are Here Again: A History of the End Times* (Baker, 1998).

23. Lewis, Daniel. *Three Crucial Questions about the Last Days* (Baker, 1998).

24. Mathison, Keith. *Postmillennialism* (Presbyterian & Reformed, 1999).

25. Mealy, Webb. *After the Thousand Years* (Sheffield Academic Press, 1992). Revelation 20.

26. Moltmann, Jürgen. *The Coming of God* (Fortress, 1996).

27. **O'Leary, Stephen.** *Arguing the Apocalypse* **(Oxford University Press, 1994).**
28. Otto, Randall. *Coming in the Clouds* (University Press of America, 1994).
29. Plevnik, Joseph. *Paul and the Parousia* (Hendrickson, 1996).
30. Polkinghorne, John. *The God of Hope and the End of the World* (Yale University Press, 2002).
31. Polkinghorne, John, and Michael Welker, eds. *The End of the World and the End of God* (Trinity Press International, 2000).
32. Robertson, O. Palmer. *The Israel of God* (Presbyterian & Reformed, 2000).
33. Russell, J. Stuart. *The Parousia* (Baker, 1999).
34. Schmidt, Thomas, and Moisés Silva, eds. *To Tell the Mystery* (Sheffield Academic Press, 1994).
35. Stackhouse, Reginald. *The End of the World* (Paulist, 1997).
36. Stone, Jon. *A Guide to the End of the World* (Garland, 1993).
37. Walvoord, John. *Prophecy in the New Millennium* (Kregel, 2001).
38. **Witherington, Ben.** *Jesus, Paul, and the End of the World* **(IVP, 1992).**

The Last Days: Issues in Dispensationalism

1. Bahnsen, Greg, and Kenneth Gentry. *House Divided,* 2d ed. (Institute for Christian Economics, 1997).
2. Bateman, Herbert, ed. *Three Central Issues in Contemporary Dispensationalism* (Kregel, 1999). Hermeneutics, covenant, Israel, and the church.
3. Blaising, Craig, and Darrell Bock. *Progressive Dispensationalism* (Baker, 1993).
———, eds. *Dispensationalism, Israel, and the Church* (Zondervan, 1992).
4. DeWitt, Dale. *Dispensational Theology in America During the Twentieth Century* (Grace Bible College, 2002).

5. Doukhan, Jacques. *Israel and the Church* (Hendrickson, 2002).
6. Fuller, Robert. *Naming the Antichrist* (Oxford University Press, 1995).
7. Holwerda, David. *Jesus and Israel: One Covenant or Two?* (Eerdmans, 1995).
8. House, H. Wayne, ed. *Israel, the Land, and the People* (Kregel, 1998).
9. Mathison, Keith. *Dispensationalism* (Presbyterian & Reformed, 1995).
10. Pate, C. Marvin, ed. *Four Views on the Book of Revelation* (Zondervan, 1998). Preterist, idealist, dispensationalist, progressive dispensationalist.
11. Pate, C. Marvin, and Doug Kennard. *Deliverance Now and Not Yet* (Lang, 2003).
12. Poythress, Vern. *Understanding Dispensationalism,* 2d ed. (Presbyterian & Reformed, 1993).
13. Rossing, Barbara. *The Rapture Exposed: The Message of Hope in the Book of Revelation* (Westview, 2004).
14. Ryrie, Charles. *Dispensationalism,* rev. ed. (Moody, 1995).
15. Saucy, Mark. *The Kingdom of God in the Teaching of Jesus* (Word, 1997).
16. Saucy, Robert. *The Case for Progressive Dispensationalism* (Zondervan, 1993).
17. Walton, John. *Covenant* (Zondervan, 1994). Mediating view with dispensationalism.
18. Willis, Wesley, and John Master, eds. *Issues in Dispensationalism* (Moody, 1994).

Heaven and the Destiny of the Unevangelized

1. Bonda, Jan. *The One Purpose of God* (Eerdmans, 1998). Universalist denial of eternal punishment.
2. **Connelly, Douglas. *After Life? What the Bible Really Says* (IVP, 1995).**
3. Edwards, David. *After Death?* (SCM, 1999).
4. Erickson, Millard. *How Shall They Be Saved?* (Baker, 1996).

5. Fackre, Gabriel, Ronald Nash and John Sanders. *What About Those Who Have Never Heard?* (IVP, 1995).

6. Habermas, Gary, and J. P. Moreland. *Beyond Death* (Crossway, 1998; Wipf & Stock, 2004).
   ———. *Immortality* (Thomas Nelson, 1992).

7. House, Paul, and Greg Thornbury, eds. *Who Will Be Saved?* (Crossway, 2000).

8. Johnston, Philip. *Shades of Sheol* (IVP, 2002).

9. Ludlow, Morwenna. *Universal Salvation* (Oxford University Press, 2001).

10. McGrath, Alister. *A Brief History of Heaven* (Blackwell, 2003).

11. Milne, Bruce. *The Message of Heaven and Hell,* BST (IVP, 2003).

12. Parry, Robin, and Christopher Partridge, eds. *Universal Salvation?* (Eerdmans, 2004).

13. Russell, Jeffrey. *A History of Heaven* (Princeton University Press, 1997). Brilliant evaluation of Christian expectations from Christ to Dante.

14. Sanders, John. *No Other Name* (Eerdmans, 1992; Wipf & Stock, 2001).

15. Stott, John, and David Edwards. *Evangelical Essentials* (Hodder & Stoughton, 1988).

16. Toon, Peter. *Heaven and Hell* (Thomas Nelson, 1986).

17. Twelftree, Graham. *Life after Death* (Monarch, 2002).

18. Walls, Jerry. *Heaven* (Oxford University Press, 2002).

Hell

1. Bernstein, Alan. *The Formation of Hell* (Cornell University Press, 2003).

2. Blanchard, John. *Whatever Happened to Hell?* (Evangelical Press, 2003).

3. Crockett, William, ed. *Four Views on Hell* (Zondervan, 1992). Including doctrine of purgatory.

4. Dixon, Larry. *The Other Side of the Good News* (Mentor, 2003).

5. Fernando, Ajith. *Crucial Questions About Hell* (Crossway, 1994).

6. Fudge, Edward, and Robert Peterson. *Two Views of Hell* (IVP, 2000).

7. Hilborn, David. *The Nature of Hell* (Acute, 2000). Drafted by five British theologians.

8. Kvanvig, Jonathan. *The Problem of Hell* (Oxford University Press, 1993).

9. Llassen, Randy. *What Does the Bible Really Say About Hell?* (Pandora, 2001).

10. Moore, David. *The Battle for Hell* (University Press of America, 1996).

11. Morgan, Christopher, and Robert Peterson, eds. *Hell Under Fire* (Zondervan, 2004).

12. Pawson, David. *The Road to Hell* (Hodder & Stoughton, 1999).

13. Peterson, Robert. *Hell on Trial* (Presbyterian & Reformed, 1995).

14. Powys, David. *Hell* (Paternoster, 1998).

15. Walls, Jerry. *Hell* (University Press of Notre Dame, 1992).

18

CHURCH HISTORY RESOURCES

Textbooks*

1. Atwood, Craig. *Always Reforming* (Mercer University Press, 2000). A.D. 1300–present, use with Hinson.
2. Baker, Robert, and Jon Landers. *A Summary of Christian History,* 3d ed. (Broadman & Holman, 2005).
3. Cairns, Earle. *Christianity Through the Centuries*, 3d ed., rev. ed. (Zondervan, 1996).
4. **Davidson, Ivor. *The Birth of the Church: From Jesus to Constantine, A.D. 30–312* (Baker, 2004).**
   ————. *A Public Faith: From Constantine to the Medieval World, A.D. 312–600* (Baker, 2005).
5. **Dowley, Timothy, ed. *Introduction to the History of Christianity* (Fortress, 1995).**
6. **Ferguson, Everett. *Church History*, 2 vols. (Zondervan, 2005, 2006).**
7. **González, Justo. *The Story of Christianity* (Prince, 2000).**
   ————. *Church History: An Essential Guide* (Abingdon, 1996). Basic introduction.
8. **Hastings, Adrian, ed. *A World History of Christianity* (Eerdmans, 1999).**
9. **Heinze, Rudolph. *Reform and Conflict: From the Medieval World to the Wars of Religion, A.D. 1350–1648* (Baker, 2005).**
10. Hinson, Glenn. *The Church Triumphant* (Mercer University Press, 1995). NT–A.D. 1300, use with Atwood.

*Forthcoming: John Hannah, *Invitation to Church History* (Kregel).

11. McGrath, Alister. *Christianity: An Introduction,* 2d ed. (Blackwell, 2006). Combination history/basic theology.

12. McManners, John, ed. *The Oxford Illustrated History of Christianity* (Oxford University Press, 1993).

13. Moynihan, Brian. *Faith* (Doubleday, 2001).

14. Pearse, Meic. *The Age of Reason: From the Wars of Religion to the French Revolution, 1570–1789* (Baker 2006).

15. Shelley, Bruce. *Church History in Plain Language.* Updated 2d ed. (Thomas Nelson, 1996).

General Church History

1. Armstrong, Karen. *A History of God* (A. A. Knopf, 1993). Covers 2,000 B.C.–present.

    ———. *The Battle for God* (Knopf, 2000). Covers 1492–present. Modernity versus Fundamentalism.

2. Bauman, Michael, and Martin Klauber, eds. *Historians of the Christian Tradition* (Broadman & Holman, 1995).

3. Bingham, D. Jeffrey. *Pocket History of the Church* (IVP, 2002).

4. Clouse, Robert, Richard Pierard, and Edwin Yamauchi. *Two Kingdoms* (Moody, 1994).

5. Edwards, David. *Christianity* (Orbis, 1999).

6. Ellingsen, Mark. *Reclaiming Our Roots,* 2 vols. (Trinity Press International, 1999). Introduction.

7. Irvin, Dale, and Scott Sunquist. *History of the World Christian Movement,* 2 vols. (Orbis, 2002–2003).

8. McGonigle, Thomas, and James Quigley. *A History of the Christian Tradition,* 2 vols. (Paulist, 1988, 1996).

9. Miller, Glenn. *The Modern Church* (Abingdon, 1996). Reformation–present.

10. Noll, Mark. *Turning Points: Decisive Moments in the History of Christianity,* rev. ed. (Baker, 2000).

11. Walker, Williston, et al. *A History of the Christian Church,* 4th ed. (Scribner's, 1985).

12. Wolffe, John. *The Expansion of Evangelicalism: The Age of More, Wilberforce, Chalmers, and Finney* (IVP, 2006).

13. Woodbridge, John. *Great Leaders of the Christian Church* (Moody, 1988).

Church History References and Helps

1. Anderson, Gerald, ed. *Biographical Dictionary of Christian Missions* (Macmillan Reference US, 1998).
2. Barrett, David, et al., eds. *World Christian Encyclopedia,* 2 vols., rev. ed. (Oxford University Press, 2001).
3. **Bassett, Paul M., Ivor J. Davidson, Meic Pearse, and Rudolph Heinz. *The Baker History of the Church,* 5 vols. (Baker, 2004–2006).**
4. Bowden, John. *Encyclopedia of Christianity* (Oxford University Press, 2005).
5. Bradley, James, and Richard Muller. *Church History* (Eerdmans, 1995). Research and bibliographical guide.
6. Cohn-Sherbok, Lavinia. *Who's Who in Christianity* (Routledge, 1998).
7. **Cross, Frank, and E. Livingstone, eds. *Oxford Dictionary of the Christian Church,* 4th ed. (Oxford University Press, 2005).**
8. Douglas, J. D., ed. *Twentieth-Century Dictionary of Christian Biography* (Baker, 1995).
9. Douglas, J. D., and Earle Cairns, eds. *The New International Dictionary of the Christian Church,* rev. ed. (Zondervan, 1978).
10. Douglas, J. D., and Philip Comfort, eds. *Who's Who in Christian History* (Tyndale, 1992).
11. **Dowley, Tim. *The Baker Atlas of Christian History* (Baker, 1997).**
12. **Fahlbusch, Erwin, et al., eds. *The Encyclopedia of Christianity,* 5 vols. (Eerdmans/Brill, 1998–).** All-purpose, including statistics, ethics, church history, theology, world religions, and Scripture.
13. **Hannah, John. *Charts of Ancient and Medieval History* (Zondervan, 2001).** Companion CD replicating contents for audio-visual use and printouts.

———. *Charts of Modern and Postmodern Church History* **(Zondervan, 2004).**

14. **Hillerbrand, Hans.** *Encyclopedia of Protestantism,* **4 vols. (Routledge, 2003).**

15. **Larsen, Timothy, ed.** *Biographical Dictionary of Evangelicals* **(IVP, 2003).**

16. Lewis, Donald, ed. *Dictionary of Evangelical Biographies, 1730–1860,* 2 vols. (Hendrickson, 2004).

17. Littell, Franklin, ed. *Historical Atlas of Christianity* (Continuum, 2001). Especially 1500–present.

18. McKim, Donald, ed. *Historical Handbook of Major Biblical Interpreters* (IVP, 1998).

19. O'Brien, Patrick, gen. ed. *Oxford Atlas of World History* (Oxford University Press, 1999).

20. Parrinder, Geoffrey. *A Concise Encyclopedia of Christianity* (Oneworld, 1998).

21. Sundquist, Scott, ed. *Dictionary of Asian Christianity* (Eerdmans, 2001).

22. Walsh, Michael, ed. *Dictionary of Christian Biography* (Liturgical, 2001).

23. **Walton, Robert.** *Chronological and Background Charts of Church History,* **rev. ed. (Zondervan, 2005).**

History of Theology

1. Anderson, William, ed. *A Journey Through Christian Theology* (Fortress, 2000). Anthology and commentary.

2. Carey, Patrick, Joseph Lienhard, eds. *Biographical Dictionary of Christian Theologians* (Hendrickson, 2004).

3. Cunliffe-Jones, Hubert, ed. *A History of Christian Doctrine* (T & T Clark, 1990).

4. **Di Berardino, Angelo, et al., eds.** *History of Theology,* **4 vols. (Liturgical, 1997–).**

5. Elwell, Walter. *A Handbook of Evangelical Theologians* (Baker, 1993). 20th century.

6. **Ford, David, ed.** *The Modern Theologians,* **2d ed. (Blackwell, 1997).**

7. González, Justo. *A History of Christian Thought,* 3 vols., rev. ed. (Abingdon, 1987).

8. **Hannah, John. *Our Legacy* (NavPress, 2001).**

9. **Hart, Trevor, ed. *Dictionary of Historical Theology* (Eerdmans, 2000).**

10. **Kelly, J. N. D. *Early Christian Doctrines*, 5th ed. (Continuum, 2000).**

11. Kerr, Hugh, ed. *Readings in Christian Thought,* 2d ed. (Abingdon, 1990). Anthology.

12. Lindberg, Carter, ed. *The Pietist Theologians* (Blackwell, 2004).

13. Loshe, Berhard. *A Short History of Christian Doctrine* (Fortress, 1983).

14. Marjanen, Antti, and Petri Luomanen, eds. *A Companion to Second-Century Christian "Heretics"* (Brill, 2005).

15. McGrath, Alister, ed. *The Blackwell Encyclopedia of Modern Christian Thought* (Blackwell, 1993).
————. *Historical Theology* (Blackwell, 1998). Companion to *Christian Theology.*

16. Muller, Richard. *Post-Reformation Reformed Dogmatics,* 4 vols. (Baker, 1987–2002).

17. Oberman, Heiko. *The Harvest of Medieval Theology* (Baker, 2000).

18. **Olson, Roger. *The Story of Christian Theology* (IVP, 1999).**

19. Peterson, Susan. *Timeline Charts of the Western Church* (Zondervan, 1999).

20. Placher, William. *A History of Christian Theology* (Westminster John Knox, 1983).

21. *See* Catholic Church History below.

History of Monasticism

1. **Bredero, Adrian. *Bernard of Clairvaux* (Eerdmans, T & T Clark, 1996).** Eleventh century.

2. **Clenent, Oliver. *The Roots of Christian Mysticism* (New City, 2001).**

3. De Dreuille, Mayeul. *Seeking the Absolute Love* (Herder and Herder, 1999).

————. *From East to West* (Herder and Herder, 1999). Brief introduction.

4. de Waal, Esther. *Seeking God: The Way of St. Benedict*, 2d ed (Liturgical, 2001).

————. *The Way of Simplicity: The Cistercian Tradition* (Orbis, 1999).

5. Evans, G. R. *Bernard of Clairvaux* (Oxford University Press, 2000).

6. Goehring, James. *Ascetics, Society, and the Desert* (Trinity Press International, 1999). Early Egypt.

7. LeClercq, Jean. *The Love of Learning and the Desire for God* (Fordham University Press, 2001).

8. McGinn, Bernard. *The Presence of God*, 4 vols. (Crossroad, 1991–2005).

9. McNary-Zak, Bernadette. *Letters and Asceticism in Fourth-Century Egypt* (University Press of America, 2000).

10. Stewart, Columba. *Prayer and Community: The Benedictine Tradition* (Orbis, 1999).

11. Woods, Richard. *Mysticism and Prophecy: The Dominican Tradition* (Orbis, 1999).

Early Church

1. Carroll, John, et al. *The Return of Jesus Christ in Early Christianity* (Hendrickson, 2000).

2. Carroll, John, and Joel Green, et al. *The Death of Jesus in Early Christianity* (Hendrickson, 1995).

3. Hinson, Glenn. *The Early Church* (Abingdon, 1996).

4. Kelly, J. N. D. *Jerome* (Hendrickson, 1999).

————. *Golden Mouth: The Story of John Chrysostom* (Baker, 1999).

5. Robinson, Thomas, and Brent Shaw. *The Early Church* (Scarecrow, 1993). Abstracts of a thousand books covering the second to sixth centuries.

6. **Stemberger, Günter.** *Jews and Christians in the Holy Land* **(T & T Clark, 1999).** Fourth century.
7. Trigg, Joseph. *Origen* (Routledge, 1999).
8. *See* New Testament Background: Early Church References.

Athanasius, Constantine, and the First Councils

1. Anatolios, Khaled. *Athanasius* (Routledge, 2005).
2. Barnes, Timothy. *Athanasius and Constantius* (Harvard University Press, 1993).
3. Cruse, C. *Eusebius' Ecclesiastical History,* updated ed. (Hendrickson, 1998).
4. **Hanson, R. P. C. *The Search for the Christian Doctrine of God: The Arian Controversy, 318–381* (Baker, 2005).**
5. Lieu, Samuel, and Dominic Montserrat. *Constantine* (Routledge, 1998).
6. Maier, Paul. *Eusebius: The Church History* (Kregel, 1999).
7. Odahl, Charles. *Constantine and the Christian Empire* (Routledge, 2004).
8. Pettersen, Alvyn. *Athanasius* (Morehouse, 1995). Introduction.
9. Seitz, Christopher, ed. *Nicene Christianity* (Baker, 2001). Focus on Creed.
10. Tilley, Maureen. *The Bible in Christian North Africa: The Donatist World* (Fortress, 1997).
11. **Williams, Rowan. *Arius*, rev. ed. (Eerdmans, 2001).**

Eastern Orthodoxy

1. Angold, Michael. *Byzantium* (St. Martin's, 2001).
2. Clendenin, Daniel. *Eastern Orthodox Christianity* (Baker, 2003).
   ———. *Eastern Orthodox Theology* (Baker, 2003).
3. Crowley, Roger. *1453: The Holy War for Constantinople and the Clash of Islam and the West* (Hyperion, 2005).
4. Cunningham, Mary. *Faith in the Byzantine World* (IVP, 2002).

5. Hussey, J. *The Orthodox Church in the Byzantine Empire* (Oxford University Press, 1986).
6. Kazhdan, Alexander, ed. *The Oxford Dictionary of Byzantium,* 3 vols. (Oxford University Press, 1991).
7. Mango, Cyril. *Byzantium* (Weidenfeld and Nicolson, 1980).
8. Nichols, Aidan. *Rome and the Eastern Churches: A Study in Schism* (T & T Clark, 1992).
9. Norwich, John. *A Short History of Byzantium* (Knopf, 1999).
10. Parry, Ken. *The Blackwell Companion to Eastern Christianity* (Blackwell, 2005).
11. Parry, Ken, et al., eds. *The Blackwell Dictionary of Eastern Christianity* (Blackwell, 2001).
12. Prokurat, Michael, Michael Peterson, and Alexander Golitzin. *Historical Dictionary of the Orthodox Church* (Scarecrow, 1996).
13. Rosser, John. *Historical Dictionary of Byzantium* (Scarecrow, 2001).
14. Stamoolis, James, ed. *Three Views on Eastern Orthodoxy and Evangelicalism* (Zondervan, 2004).
15. Treadgold, Warren. *A Concise History of Byzantium* (St. Martin's, 2001).
16. Ware, Timothy. *The Orthodox Church,* rev. ed. (Penguin, 1993).

Catholic Church History

1. **Bokenkotter, Thomas. *A Concise History of the Catholic Church*, rev. ed. (Doubleday, 2004).**
2. Collinge, William. *Historical Dictionary of Catholicism* (Scarecrow, 1997).
3. Hollingsworth, Mary. *The Cardinal's Hat: Money, Ambition, and Everyday Life in the Court of a Borgia Prince* (Overlook, 2005).
4. Johnson, Luke, and William Kurz. *The Future of Catholic Biblical Scholarship* (Eerdmans, 2002).
5. McBrien, Richard, ed. *The HarperCollins Encyclopedia of Catholicism* (HarperCollins, 1994).

6. McNamara, Jo Ann. *Sisters in Arms* (Harvard University Press, 1996). History of nuns.
7. **Morris, Colin. *The Papal Monarchy: The Western Church from 1050 to 1250* (Oxford University Press, 1989).**
8. **O'Collins, Gerald, and Maria Farrugia. *Catholicism* (Oxford University Press, 2003).**
9. *See under* General Church History above and Counter-Reformation below.

Mary

1. Braaten, Carl, and Robert Jenson. *Mary, Mother of God* (Eerdmans, 2004).
2. Pelikan, Jaroslav. *Mary Through the Centuries* (Yale University Press, 1996).
3. Svendsen, Eric. *Who Is My Mother? The Role and Status of the Mother of Jesus in the New Testament and Catholicism* (Calvary, 2001).

The Papacy

1. Chadwick, Owen. *A History of the Popes, 1830–1914* (Oxford, 1998).
2. Coppa, Frank, ed. *Encyclopedia of the Vatican and Papacy* (Greenwood, 1999).
3. Duffy, Eamon. *Saints and Sinners: A History of the Popes* (Yale University Press, 1997).
4. Kelly, J. N. D. *The Oxford Dictionary of Popes* (Oxford University Press, 1986).
5. La Due, William. *The Chair of Saint Peter: A History of the Papacy* (Orbis, 1999).
6. Levillain, Philippe, and John O'Malley, eds. *The Papacy*, 3 vols. (Routledge, 2002).
7. Markus, Robert. *Gregory the Great and His World* (Cambridge University Press, 1998).
8. Maxwell-Stuart, P. *Chronicles of the Popes* (Thames and Hudson, 1997).

9. Steimer, Bruno, ed. *The Dictionary of Popes and the Papacy* (Herder and Herder, 2001).
10. Ullmann, Walter. *A Short History of the Papacy in the Middle Ages* (Routledge, 2002).

Saints

1. Descouvement, Pierre. *Therese and Liseaux* (1962; Eerdmans, 2001).
2. DeVries, Kelly. *Joan of Arc: A Military Leader* (Sutton, 1999).
3. Du Boulay, Shirley. *Teresa of Avila* (Bluebridge, 2004).
4. Farmer, David. *The Oxford Dictionary of Saints*, 4th ed. (Oxford, 1998).
5. Galli, Mark. *Francis Assisi and His World* (IVP, 2002).
6. Gorres, Ida F. *The Hidden Face : A Study of Therese of Lisieux*, 2d ed. (Ignatius, 2003).
7. Le Goff, Jacques. *Saint Francis of Assisi* (Routledge, 2004).
8. Medwick, Cathleen. *Teresa of Avila* (Knopf, 1999). Especially on her relationship with St. John of the Cross and their dealings with both the Spanish and Vatican hierarchies.
9. Nash-Marshall, Siobhan. *Joan of Arc* (Crossroad, 1999).
10. Steimer, Bruno, ed. *Dictionary of Saints and Sainthood* (Herder & Herder, 2005).
11. Ward, Benedicta. *The Venerable Bede* (Cistercian, 1998; Continuum, 2002).
12. Wilson-Smith, Timothy. *Joan of Arc* (Sutton, 2006).

Augustine

1. **Brown, Peter.** *Augustine of Hippo* **(University of California, 1999).**
2. Clark, Mary. *Augustine* (Continuum, 2001).
3. Cooper, Stephen. *Augustine for Armchair Theologians* (Westminster John Knox, 2002).
4. **Fitzgerald, Allan, ed.** *Augustine Through the Ages: An Encyclopedia* **(Eerdmans, 1999).**
5. Harrison, Carol. *Augustine* (Oxford University Press, 2000).

6. **Knowles, Andrew, and Pachomios Penkett.** *Augustine and His World* **(IVP, 2004).**
7. Matthews, Gareth. *Augustine* (Blackwell, 2004).
8. **Stump, Eleanore, and Norman Kretzmann, eds.** *The Cambridge Companion to Augustine* **(Cambridge University Press, 2001).**
9. Wills, Garry. *Saint Augustine* (Viking, 1999).

Aquinas

1. Davies, Brian. *Aquinas* (Continuum, 2000).
2. Healy, Nicholas. *Thomas Aquinas* (Ashgate, 2003).
3. Kretzmann, Norman, and Eleanore Stump, eds. *The Cambridge Companion to Aquinas* (Cambridge University Press, 1993).
4. Nichols, Aidan. *Discovering Aquinas* (Darton, Longman and Todd, 2002).
5. Renick, Timothy. *Aquinas for Armchair Theologians* (Westminster John Knox, 2002).
6. Stump, Eleanore. *Aquinas* (Routledge, 2003).
7. Torrell, Jean-Pierre. *Saint Thomas Aquinas,* vol. 1 (Catholic University of America Press, 1996–).
8. Wawrykow, Joseph. *The Westminster Handbook to Thomas Aquinas* (Westminster John Knox, 2005).

The Crusades

1. **Asbridge, Thomas.** *The First Crusade* **(Oxford University Press, 2004).**
2. France, John. *The Crusades and the Expansion of Catholicism 1000–1714* (Routledge, 2005).
3. Jaspert, Nikolas. *The Crusades* (Routledge, 2006).
4. **Konstam, Angus.** *Historical Atlas of the Crusades* **(Checkmark, 2002).**
5. Lock, Peter. *The Routledge Companion to the Crusades* (Routledge, 2005).
6. **Madden, Thomas.** *The New Concise History of the Crusades* **(Rowman & Littlefield, 2005).**
   ———. *Crusades* **(Duncan Baird, 2004).**

7. Miller, David. *Richard the Lionheart: The Mighty Crusader* (George Weidenfeld & Nicholson, 2004).

8. Phillips, Jonathan. *The Fourth Crusade and the Sack of Constantinople* (Viking, 2004).

9. Phillips, Jonathan, and Martin Hoch, eds. *The Second Crusade* (Manchester University Press, 2002).

10. Richard, Jean. *The Crusades: c.1071–c.1291* (Cambridge University Press, 1999).

11. Riley-Smith, Jonathan. *The Atlas of the Crusades* (Facts on File, 1990).

———. ***The Oxford History of the Crusades* (Oxford University Press, 2002).**

12. Runciman, Steven. *The First Crusade* (Cambridge University Press, 2005).

13. Turner, Ralph, and Richard Turner. *The Reign of Richard Lionheart* (Longman, 2000). Focus on third crusade.

14. Tyerman, Christopher. *Fighting for Christendom* (Oxford University Press, 2005).

———. ***God's War: A New History of the Crusades* (Belknap, 2006).**

The Jesuits

1. LaCouture, Jean. *Jesuits* (Counterpoint, 1997).

2. O'Malley, John. *The First Jesuits* (Harvard University Press, 1993).

———, ed. *The Jesuits* (University Press of Toronto, 2000).

3. Woodrow, Alain. *The Jesuits* (Geoffrey Chapman, 1996).

Medieval

1. Barbero, Alessandro. *Charlemagne: Father of a Continent* (University of California Press, 2004).

2. Bassett, Paul. *The Medieval Church* (Baker, 2006).

3. Berman, Constance. *Medieval Religion* (Routledge, 2005).

4. Brown, Harold. *Heresies* (Hendrickson, 2000).

5. Crowley, Roger. *1453: The Holy War of Constantinople and the Clash of Islam and the West* (Hyperion, 2005).

6. **Evans, Gillian. *The Medieval Theologians* (Blackwell, 2001).**
   ———. *Faith in the Medieval World* (IVP, 2002).
   ———. *John Wyclif* (IVP, 2006).

7. Glick, Leonard. *Abraham's Heirs: Jews and Christians in Medieval Europe* (Syracuse University Press, 1999).

8. Grundmann, Herbert. *Religious Movements in the Middle Ages* (University Press of Notre Dame, 1995).

9. Hamilton, Bernard. *Christian World of the Middle Ages* (Sutton, 2002).

10. Konstam, Angus. *Atlas of Medieval Europe* (Checkmark, 2000).

11. Lambert, Malcolm. *Medieval Heresy: Popular Movement from the Gregorian Reform to the Reformation.* 3d ed. (Blackwell, 1992).

12. Le Goff, Jacques. *The Middle Ages and the Birth of Europe* (Blackwell, 2005).

13. Lowney, Chris. *A Vanished World: Medieval Spain's Golden Age of Enlightenment* (Free, 2005). Jewish/Arab/Christian peaceful coexistence (8th–15th centuries).

14. **MacMullen, Ramsey. *Christianity and Paganism in the Fourth to Eighth Centuries* (Yale University Press, 1999).**

15. McKitterick, Rosamond, ed. *Atlas of the Medieval World* (Oxford University Press, 2005).

16. **Pegg, Mark Gregory. *The Corruption of Angels: The Great Inquisition of 1245–1246* (Princeton University Press, 2005).** France.

17. **Russell, Jeffrey, and Douglas Lumsden. *A History of Medieval Christianity* (Lang, 2005).**

18. Sheppard, J. A. *Christendom at the Crossroads* (Westminster John Knox, 2005).

19. Thomson, John. *The Western Church in the Middle Ages* (Oxford University Press, 1998).

20. Volz, Carl. *The Medieval Church* (Abingdon, 1997).

21. **Wilson, Derek. *Charlemagne* (Doubleday, 2006).**

22. *See* Catholic Church History.

Renaissance

1. Campbell, Gordon, ed. *The Oxford Dictionary of the Renaissance* (Oxford University Press, 2003).
2. D'Onofrio, Giulio, ed. *History of Theology,* vol. 3: *The Renaissance* (Liturgical, 1998).
3. Estep, William. *Renaissance and Reformation* (Eerdmans, 1983).
4. Martin, John. *The Renaissance World* (Routledge, 2006).
5. Nauert, Charles. *Humanism and the Culture of Renaissance Europe* (Cambridge University Press, 1995).
6. Ritchie, Robert. *Historical Atlas of the Renaissance* (Checkmark, 2004).
7. Saari, Peggy, and Aaron Saari. *Renaissance and Reformation* (UXL, 2002).
8. Spitz, Lewis. *The Renaissance and Reformation*, 2 vols. (Concordia Academic, 1980).

Reformation

1. Bagchi, David, and David Steinmetz, eds. *The Cambridge Companion to Reformation Theology* (Cambridge University Press, 2004).
2. Barzun, Jacques. *From Dawn to Decadence: 1500 to the Present* (HarperCollins, 2000).
3. Brady, Thomas, Heiko Oberman, and James Tracy, eds. *Handbook of European History, 1400–1600*, 2 vols. (Eerdmans, 1996).
4. Cameron, Euan. *The European Reformation* (Oxford University Press, 1991).
5. Chadwick, Owen. *The Early Reformation on the Continent* (Oxford University Press, 2002).
6. Collinson, Patrick. *The Reformation* (Modern Library, 2004).
7. d'Aubigne, Jean. *For God and His People* (Bob Jones University Press, 2000). Ulrich Zwingli.
8. Duke, Alastair. *Reformation and Revolt in the Low Countries* (Hambledon, 2003).

9. **George, Timothy.** *Theology of the Reformers,* **rev. ed. (Broadman & Holman, 1999).**

10. Gordon, Bruce. *The Swiss Reformation* (University Press of Manchester, 2002).

11. Gordon, Bruce, and Emidio Campi, eds. *Architect of the Reformation: An Introduction to Heinrich Bullinger, 1504–1575* (Baker, 2005).

12. **Gregory, Brad S.** *Salvation at Stake: Christian Martyrdom in Early Modern Europe* **(Harvard University Press, 1999).**

13. **Hall, Basil.** *Humanists and Reformers, 1500–1900* **(T & T Clark, 1996).** Especially Erasmus.

14. Hannah, John. *Charts of Reformation and Enlightenment Church History* (Zondervan, 2004).

15. Hill, Jonathan. *Faith in the Age of Reason* (IVP, 2004).

16. **Hillerbrand, Hans, ed.** *The Oxford Encyclopedia of the Reformation***, 4 vols. (Oxford University Press, 1996).**
———. *Encyclopedia of Protestantism***, 4 vols. (Routledge, 2003).**

17. Holt, Mack. *The French Wars of Religion, 1562–1629,* 2d ed. (Cambridge University Press, 2005).

18. Hsai, Pet-Chia, ed. *A Companion to the Reformation World* (Blackwell, 2003).

19. Janz, Denis, ed. *A Reformation Reader* (Fortress, 1999). With CD-ROM.

20. **Lindberg, Carter.** *The European Reformations* **(Blackwell, 1995).**

21. Lindsay, Thomas. *A History of the Reformation,* 2 vols. (T & T Clark, 1964; Wipf & Stock, 1999).

22. Lovegrove, Deryck, ed. *The Rise of the Laity in Evangelical Protestantism* (Routledge, 2002).

23. **MacCulloch, Diarmaid.** *The Reformation* **(Viking, 2004).**

24. **McGrath, Alister.** *Reformation Thought,* **3d ed. (Blackwell, 1999).**
———. *The Intellectual Origins of the European Reformation,* 2d ed. (Blackwell, 2003).

25. Monod, Paul. *The Power of Kings: Monarchy and Religion in Europe, 1589–1715* (Yale University Press, 1999).

26. Oberman, Heiko. *The Dawn of the Reformation* (Eerdmans, 1992).

————. *The Reformation* **(Eerdmans, T & T Clark, 1994).**

27. **Ozment, Steven. *Protestants: The Birth of a Revolution* (Doubleday, 1992).**

28. Parker, Geoffrey. *The Thirty Years War,* 2d ed. (Routledge, 1997).

29. **Pearse, Meic. *The Great Restoration* (Paternoster, 1998).**

30. **Pettegree, Andrew. *The Reformation World* (Routledge, 2001).**

31. Steimer, Bruno, ed. *The Dictionary of the Reformation* (Herder & Herder, 2004).

32. **Sunshine, Glenn. *The Reformation for Armchair Theologians* (Westminster John Knox, 2005).**

33. **Thompson, Bard. *Humanists and Reformers* (Eerdmans, 1996).**

34. Tracy, James. *Europe's Reformations, 1450–1650,* rev. ed. (Rowman & Littlefield, 2005).

35. Wandel, Lee. *The Eucharist in the Reformation* (Cambridge University Press, 2005).

36. **Ward, W. R. *Protestant Evangelical Awakening* (Cambridge University Press, 1992).**

37. *See* Renaissance above.

Counter-Reformation

1. Bireley, Robert. *The Refashioning of Catholicism* (Catholic University Press of America, 1999).

2. Hillerbrand, Hans. *Historical Dictionary of the Reformation and Counter-Reformation* (Scarecrow, 2000).

3. M'Crie, Thomas. *The Reformation in Spain* (Hartland, 1998).

4. Mullett, Michael. *The Catholic Reformation* (Routledge, 1999).

5. **O'Malley, John. *Trent and All That* (Harvard University Press, 2000).**
6. Peters, Edward. *Inquisition* (University Press of California, 1989).
7. Rawlings, Helen. *The Spanish Inquisition* (Blackwell, 2005).
8. Williams, George. *The Radical Reformation,* 3d ed. (Truman State University Press, 2000).
9. *See* The Jesuits above.

Martin Luther and Lutheranism

1. Brecht, Martin. *Martin Luther,* 3d ed., 3 vols. (Fortress, 1983).
2. Gassman, Günther, Duane Larson, and Mark Oldenburg. *Historical Dictionary of Lutheranism* (Scarecrow, 2001).
3. **Gritsch, Eric. *A History of Lutheranism* (Fortress, 2002).** Reformation–present.
4. **Kittelson, James. *Luther the Reformer* (Fortress, 2003).**
5. Kolb, Robert. *Martin Luther as Prophet, Teacher, and Hero* (Baker, 1999).
6. **McKim, Donald, ed. *The Cambridge Companion to Martin Luther* (Cambridge University Press, 2003).**
7. Mullett, Martin. *Martin Luther* (Routledge, 2004).
8. Nichols, Stephen. *Martin Luther* (Presbyterian & Reformed, 2002).
9. **Oberman, Heiko. *Luther* (Yale University Press, 1989).**
10. Paulson, Steven. *Luther for Armchair Theologians* (Westminster John Knox, 2004).
11. **Steinmetz, David. *Luther in Context,* 2d ed. (Baker, 1995).**
12. Tomlin, Graham. *Luther and His World* (IVP, 2002).

John Calvin and Reformed Churches

1. **Benedetto, Robert, Darrell Guder, and Donald McKim. *Historical Dictionary of the Reformed Churches* (Scarecrow, 1999).**
2. Benedict, Philip. *Christ's Churches Purely Reformed* (Yale University Press, 2002).

3. Bouwsma, William. *John Calvin* (Oxford University Press, 1987).

4. Cottret, Bernard. *John Calvin* (Eerdmans, 2000).

5. Elwood, Christopher. *Calvin for Armchair Theologians* (Westminster John Knox, 2002).

6. Jones, Serene. *Calvin and the Rhetoric of Piety* (Westminster John Knox, 1995).

7. Lane, Anthony. *John Calvin* (Baker, T & T Clark, 1999).

8. McGrath, Alister. *A Life of John Calvin* (Blackwell, 1990).

9. McKim, Donald, ed. *The Cambridge Companion to John Calvin* (Cambridge University Press, 2002).

10. Muller, Richard. *The Unaccommodated Calvin* (Oxford University Press, 2000).

———. *After Calvin* (Oxford University Press, 2003).

11. Naphy, William. *Calvin and the Consolidation of the Genevan Reformation* (Westminster John Knox, 2003).

12. Parker, T. H. L. *Calvin* (Westminster John Knox, 1975; Continuum, 2002).

13. Pettegree, Andrew, et al., eds. *Calvinism in Europe 1540–1620* (Cambridge University Press, 1994).

14. Steinmetz, David. *Calvin in Context* (Oxford University Press, 1995).

Anabaptist

1. Dyck, Cornelius. *An Introduction to Mennonite History,* 3d ed. (Herald, 1993).

2. Estep, William. *The Anabaptist Story*, 3d ed. (Eerdmans, 1996).

3. Friesen, Abraham. *Erasmus, the Anabaptists, and the Great Commission* (Eerdmans, 1998).

4. Hostetler, John. *Amish Society,* 4th ed. (Johns Hopkins University Press, 1993).

5. Kraybill, Donald. *The Riddle of Amish Culture*, rev. ed. (Johns Hopkins University Press, 2001).

6. Weaver, J. Denny. *Becoming Anabaptist: The Origin and Significance of Sixteenth-Century Anabaptism* (Herald, 1987).

7. Yoder, John Howard. *Anabaptism and Reformation in Swit-zerland* (Herald, 2004).

English Reformation

1. **Bernard, G. W. *The King's Reformation: Henry VIII and the Remaking of the English Church* (Yale University Press, 2005).**
2. Dickens, A. G. *The English Reformation,* 2d ed. (Penn State University Press, 1991).
3. Haigh, Christopher. *English Reformations: Religion, Politics, and Society Under the Tudors* (Oxford University Press, 1993).
4. Hogge, Alice. *God's Secret Agents* (HarperCollins, 2005). Underground RC priests in Elizabethan England.
5. **Jones, Norman. *The English Reformation* (Blackwell, 2002).**
6. Scarisbrick, J. J. *The Reformation and the English People* (Blackwell, 1984).
7. Yarnell, Malcolm. *Royal Priesthood in the English Reformation* (Oxford University Press, 2002).

North American

1. **Ahlstrom, Sydney. *A Religious History of the American People,* 2d ed. (Yale University Press, 2004).**
2. Askew, Thomas, and Richard Pierard. *The American Church Experience* (Baker, 2004).
3. **Bobrick, Benson. *Wide as the Waters: The Story of the English Bible and the Revolution It Inspired* (Simon and Schuster, 2001).**
4. Butler, Jon, Grant Wacker, and Randall Balmer. *Religion in American Life: A Short History* (Oxford University Press, 2003).
5. **Carpenter, Joel. *Revive Us Again* (Oxford University Press, 1997).**
6. **Carwardine, Richard. *Abraham Lincoln: A Life of Purpose and Prayer* (Alfred A. Knopf, 2006).**

7. Delbanco, Andrew. *The Puritan Ordeal* (Harvard University Press, 1989).

8. Gaustad, Edwin, and Leigh Schmidt. *The Religious History of America*, rev. ed. (HarperSanFrancisco, 2002).

9. Gutjahr, Paul. *An American Bible* (Stanford University Press, 1999). Cultural meaning of the Scriptures in American history.

10. Hart, D. J. *Defending the Faith* (Baker, 1995; Presbyterian & Reformed, 2003). Places into historical context J. Gresham Machen's involvement in the Modernist-Fundamentalist debate.

    ————, ed. ***Reckoning with the Past* (Baker, 1996).** Puritan-modern U.S. church history.

11. Hatch, Nathan. *The Democratization of American Christianity* (Yale University Press, 1989).

12. Hein, David, and Gardiner Shattuck. *Christ's Churches Purely Reformed* (Praeger, 2003).

13. Holifield, E. Brooks. *Theology in America* (Yale University Press, 2004). Until Civil War.

14. Hutson, James, ed. *Religion and the New Republic* (Rowman and Littlefield, 1999).

15. Jacobsen, Douglas, and William Trollinger, eds. *Re-Forming the Center* (Eerdmans, 1998). Covers 1900 to the present.

16. Kazin, Michael. *A Godly Hero: The Life of William Jennings Bryan* (Alfred A. Knopf, 2006).

17. Keillor, Steven. *This Rebellious House* (IVP, 1996). Apologetic.

18. Longfield, Bradley. *The Presbyterian Controversy* (Oxford University Press, 1991). Modernism controversy 1922–36.

19. Marsden, George. *Fundamentalism and American Culture* (Oxford University Press, 1980).

    ————. *Reforming Fundamentalism: Fuller Seminary and the New Evangelicalism* (Eerdmans, 1987).

    ————. ***Understanding Fundamentalism and Evangelicalism* (Eerdmans, 1991).**

20. Marty, Martin. *Protestantism in the United States* (Scribners, 1986).

21. **Mullin, Robert. *The Puritan as Yankee* (Eerdmans, 2002).** Critique of popular conception of Horace Bushnell as father of American liberalism.
22. Nichols, Stephen. *J. Gresham Machen* (Presbyterian & Reformed, 2004).
23. **Noll, Mark. *American Evangelical Christianity* (Blackwell, 2001).**
    ———. *America's God: From Jonathan Edwards to Lincoln* (Oxford University Press, 2002).
    ———. *The Civil War as a Theological Crisis* **(University of North Carolina Press, 2006).**
24. Porterfield, Amanda, ed. *American Religious History* (Blackwell, 2002).
25. **Smith, Christian. *American Evangelicalism* (University of Chicago Press, 1998).** Sociology.
26. **Stewart, John, and James Moorhead, eds. *Charles Hodge Revisited* (Eerdmans, 2002).**
27. **Thuessen, Peter. *In Discordance with the Scriptures* (Oxford University Press, 1999).** Battle of translations in American history.
28. Treloar, Geoff. *The Disruption of Evangelicalism: The Age of Mott, Machen, and McPherson* (IVP, 2006).
29. Wacker, Grant. *Religion in Nineteenth Century America* (Oxford University Press, 2000).
30. Wells, Ronald, ed. *The Wars of America: Christian Views* (Mercer University Press, 1991).
31. Williams, D. H., ed. *The Free Church and the Early Church* (Eerdmans, 2002).

North American References and Helps

1. Balmer, Randall. *Encyclopedia of Evangelicalism,* rev. ed. (Westminster John Knox, 2004).
2. Bowden, John. *Dictionary of American Religious Biography,* 2d ed. (Greenwood, 1993).
3. **Gaustad, Edwin, and Philip Barlow. *New Historical Atlas***

of Religion in America, **3d ed. (Oxford University Press, 2001).**

4. Gaustad, Edwin, and Mark Noll, eds. *A Documentary History of Religion in America,* 3d ed. (Eerdmans, 2003).

5. Hart, D. G., and Mark Noll, eds. *Dictionary of Presbyterian and Reformed Tradition in America* (Presbyterian & Reformed, 2005).

6. Lippy, Charles, and Peter Williams, eds. *The Encyclopedia of American Religious Experience,* **3 vols. (Scribners, 1988).**

7. Melton, J. Gordon. *Encyclopedia of American Religions,* **3d ed., 3 vols. (Gale Publishers, 1993).**

8. Murphy Terrence, and Roberto Perin, eds. *A Concise History of Christianity in Canada* (Oxford University Press, 1996).

9. Newman, William, and Peter Halvorson. *Atlas of American Religion* (AltaMira, 2000).

10. Noll, Mark. *The Old Religion in a New World* **(Eerdmans, 2001).** More succinct account of distinctions from European religion than below.

 ———. *A History of Christianity in the United States and Canada* **(Eerdmans, 1992).**

11. Prothero, Stephen, et al., eds. *The Encyclopedia of American Religious History,* 2 vols. (Facts on File, 1996).

12. Reid, Daniel, et al., eds. *Dictionary of Christianity in America* **(IVP, 1991).**

13. Toulouse, Mark, and James Duke, eds. *Makers of Christian Theology in America* (Abingdon, 1997).

 ———, eds. *Sources of Christian Theology in America* (Abingdon, 1999).

14. Weir, David. *Early New England* (Eerdmans, 2005).

American Evangelists

1. Dallimore, Arnold. *George Whitefield* **(Banner of Truth, 1998).**

2. Hambrick-Stowe, Charles. *Charles G. Finney and the Spirit of American Evangelicalism* **(Eerdmans, 1996).**

3. Hardman, Keith. *Charles Grandison Finney, 1792–1875* (Syracuse University Press, 1987; Baker, 1990).
4. Mouw, Richard. *The Smell of Sawdust* (Zondervan, 2000). Brief history of evangelicalism's pietist, revivalist, fundamentalist roots.
5. Noll, Mark. *The Rise of Evangelicalism: The Age of Edwards, Whitefield, and the Wesleys* (IVP, 2004).
6. Stout, Harry. *The Divine Dramatist* (Eerdmans, 1991). George Whitefield.

Jonathan Edwards

1. Hart, D. G., et al., eds. *The Legacy of Jonathan Edwards* (Baker, 2003).
2. Marsden, George. *Jonathan Edwards* (Yale University Press, 2003).
3. McClymond, Michael. *Encounters with God* (Oxford University Press, 1998). Jonathan Edwards' theology.
4. Murray, Iain. *Jonathan Edwards* (Banner of Truth, 1988).
5. Piper, John, and Justin Taylor, eds. *A God-Entranced Vision of All Things: The Legacy of Jonathan Edwards* (Crossway, 2004).

John Wesley

1. Abraham, William. *Wesley for Armchair Theologians* (Westminster John Knox, 2005).
2. Collins, Kenneth. *A Real Christian: The Life of John Wesley* (Abingdon, 1999).
    ———. *John Wesley: A Theological Journey* (Abingdon, 2003).
3. Hattersley, Roy. *The Life of John Wesley* (Random House, 2003).
4. Heitzenrater, Richard. *The Elusive Mr. Wesley,* 2d ed. (Abingdon, 2003).
5. Rack, Henry. *Reasonable Enthusiast,* 2d ed. (Abingdon, 1993).
6. Tomkins, Stephen. *John Wesley* (Eerdmans, 2003).

7. Waller, Ralph. *John Wesley* (Continuum, 2003).
8. *See* Holiness, Methodism, and Wesleyanism below.

D. L. Moody

1. Bailey, Faith. *D. L. Moody* (Moody, 1959). Popular.
2. **Bebbington, David. *The Dominance of Evangelicalism: The Age of Spurgeon and Moody* (IVP, 2005).**
3. **Dorsett, Lyle. *A Passion for Souls: The Life of D. L. Moody* (Moody, 1997).**
4. **Evensen, Bruce. *God's Man for the Gilded Age* (Oxford University Press, 2003).**
5. George, Timothy. *Mr. Moody and the Evangelical Tradition* (T & T Clark, 2004).

Billy Sunday

1. Bruns, Roger. *Billy Sunday and Big Time* (University Press of Illinois, 2000).
2. **Dorsett, Lyle. *Billy Sunday and the Redemption of Urban America* (Mercer University Press, 2004).** Updated from 1991 edition.
3. Martin, Robert. *Hero of the Heartland* (Indiana University Press, 2002).

Religion in the South

1. Blum, Edward, and W. Scott Poole, eds. *Vale of Tears: New Essays on Religion and Reconstruction* (Mercer University Press, 2005). Post-Civil War.
2. Cauthen, Kenneth. *I Don't Care What the Bible Says* (Mercer University Press, 2003).
3. Genovese, Eugene. *A Consuming Fire: The Fall of the Confederacy in the Mind of the White Christian South* (University Press of Georgia, 1998).
4. Hill, Samuel, and Charles Lippy, eds. *Encyclopedia of Religion in the South*, 2d ed., rev. ed. (Mercer University Press, 2005).
5. Mulder, Philip. *A Controversial Spirit: Evangelical Awakenings*

in the South (Oxford University Press, 2002). Church rivalry, 1740–1820.

6. Sparks, Rodney. *On Jordan's Stormy Banks: Evangelicalism in Mississippi, 1773–1876* (University Press of Georgia, 1994).

7. Stowell, Daniel. *Rebuilding Zion: The Religious Reconstruction of the South, 1863–1877* (Oxford University Press, 1998).

African-American

1. Angell, Stephen. *Bishop Henry McNeal Turner and African-American Religion in the South* (University of Tennessee, 1992).

2. Battle, Michael. *The Black Church in America* (Blackwell, 2005).

3. Campbell, James. *Songs of Zion: The African Methodist Episcopal Church in the United States and South Africa* (Oxford University Press, 1995).

4. Daly, John. *When Slavery Was Called Freedom* (University Press of Kentucky, 2002).

5. Fitts, Leroy. *A History of Black Baptists* (Broadman & Holman, 1985).

6. **Frey, Sylvia, and Betty Wood. *Come Shouting to Zion* (University of North Carolina, 1999).** Until 1830.

7. **Fulop, Timothy, and Albert Raboteau, eds. *African-American Religion* (Routledge, 1997).**

8. Glaude, Eddie. *Exodus!* (University Press of Chicago, 2000). Early nineteenth century.

9. **Goodman, Paul. *Of One Blood* (University Press of California, 1998).** Abolitionism.

10. **Haynes, Stephen. *Noah's Curse* (Oxford University Press, 2001).** Studies biblical justification of slavery.

11. Hopkins, Dwight, and George Cummings, eds. *Cut Loose Your Stammering Tongue: Black Theology in the Slave Narratives* (Westminster John Knox, 2005).

12. Jackson, Joseph. *A Story of Christian Activism: History of the National Baptist Convention in the USA, Incorporated* (Townsend, 1980).

13. Johnson, Alonso, and Paul Jersild, eds. *"Ain't Gonna Lay My 'Ligion Down"* (University of South Carolina, 1996).

14. Klein, Martin. *A Historical Dictionary of Slavery and Abolition* (Scarecrow, 2002).

15. Lincoln, C. Eric, and Lawrence Mamiya. *The Black Church in the African American Experience* (Duke University Press, 1990).

16. Mitchell, Henry. *Black Church Beginnings* (Eerdmans, 2004).

17. Montgomery, William. *Under Their Own Vine and Fig Tree: The African-American Church in the South, 1865–1900* (Louisiana State University Press, 1993).

18. Pinn, Anthony. *Varieties of African-American Religious Experiences* (Fortress, 1998).

19. Raboteau, Albert. *African-American Religion* (Oxford University Press, 1999).

———. ***Canaan Land* (Oxford University Press, 2001).**

———. *Slave Religion* (Oxford University Press, 1978).

20. Sanders, Cheryl. *Saints in Exile* (Oxford University Press, 1996). Holiness-Pentecostal background.

21. Sernett, Milton. *Bound for the Promised Land* (Duke University Press, 1997). Great Migration.

22. Sobel, Mechal. *Trabelin' On* (Princeton University Press, 1988).

23. Whelchel, Love. *Hell Without Fire: Conversion in Slave Religion* (Abingdon, 2002).

24. Wimbush, Vincent, ed. *African Americans and the Bible* (Continuum, 2001).

General Baptist History

1. Brackney, William. *A Genetic History of Baptist Thought* (Mercer University Press, 2004).

———. *Baptists in America* (Blackwell, 2006).

———. ***Historical Dictionary of the Baptists* (Scarecrow, 1999).**

———. ***The Baptists* (Greenwood, 1988).**

2. Brackney, William, Paul Fiddes, and John Briggs, eds. *Pilgrim Pathways* (Mercer University Press, 1999).

3. Bush, Russ, and Thomas Nettles. *Baptists and the Bible,* rev. ed. (Broadman & Holman, 1999).

4. Byrd, James. *The Challenges of Roger Williams* (Mercer University Press, 2002).

5. George, Timothy, and David Dockery, eds. *Theologians of the Baptist Tradition,* rev. ed. (Broadman & Holman, 2001).

6. George, Timothy, and Denise George, eds. *Library of Baptist Classics,* 12 vols. (Broadman & Holman, 1997).

7. Glass, William. *Strangers in Zion: Fundamentalists in the South, 1900–1950* (Mercer University Press, 2001). Baptists versus Presbyterians presaging the current conflict.

8. Leonard, Bill, ed. *Dictionary of Baptists in America* (IVP, 1994).

———. *Baptists in America* (Columbia University Press, 2005).

———. *Baptist Ways* (Judson, 2003).

9. McBeth, H. Leon. *The Baptist Heritage* (Broadman, 1987).

10. McGoldrick, James. *Baptist Successionism* (Scarecrow, 1994).

11. Norman, Stan. *Preserving Our Baptist Identity* (Broadman & Holman, 2001).

12. Tull, James. *High-Church Baptists in the South,* ed. Morris Ashcroft, rev. ed. (Mercer University Press, 2001). Landmarkism.

Southern Baptist Convention

1. Fletcher, Jesse. *The Southern Baptist Convention* (Broadman & Holman, 1995).

2. Flynt, Wayne. *Alabama Baptists* (University Press of Alabama, 1998).

3. Gardner, Robert. *A Decade of Debate and Division: Georgia Baptists and the Formation of the Southern Baptist Convention* (Mercer University Press, 1995).

4. Goodwin, Everett. *Baptists in the Balance* (Judson, 1997). Defense of moderate-liberals.

5. Hankins, Barry. *God's Rascal: J. Frank Norris and the Beginnings of Southern Fundamentalism* (University Press of Kentucky, 1996).

6. Harvey, Paul. *Redeeming the South* (University Press of North Carolina, 1996). 1865–1920.

7. Jolley, Marc, and John Pierce, eds. *Distinctively Baptist* (Mercer University Press, 2005). Shurden tribute.

8. Nettles, Tom, and Russell Moore. *Why I Am a Baptist* (Broadman & Holman, 2001).

9. Rogers, James. *Richard Furman* (Mercer University Press, 2001).

10. Simmons, Paul. *The Southern Baptist Tradition* (Park Ridge Center, 2002).

11. Wills, Gregory. *Democratic Religion* (Oxford University Press, 1996). 1785–1900.

Southern Baptist Convention Controversy

1. Ammerman, Nancy. *Baptist Battles* (Rutgers University Press, 1990).

   ———, ed. *Southern Baptists Observed: Multiple Perspectives on a Changing Denomination* (University Press of Tennessee, 1993).

2. Copeland, E. Luther. *The Southern Baptist Convention and the Judgement of History: The Taint of an Original Sin* (University Press of America, 1995).

3. Cothen, Grady. *The New SBC: Fundamentalism's Impact on The Southern Baptist Convention* (Smyth & Helwys, 1995).

   ———. *What Happened to the Southern Baptist Convention: A Memoir of the Controversy* (Smyth & Helwys, 1993).

4. DeWeese, Charles, ed. *Defining Baptist Convictions* (Providence House, 1996).

5. Dilday, Russell. *Columns Glimpses of a Seminary Under Assault* (Smyth & Helwys, 2004).

6. Dockery, David. *Southern Baptists and American Evangelicals* (Broadman & Holman, 1993).

7. Draper, James, and Kenneth Keathley. *Biblical Authority* (Broadman & Holman, 2001).

8. Hefley, James, and Mark Coppenger. *The Truth in Crisis,* 5 vols. (Hannibal Books, 1991).

9. Leonard, William. *God's Last and Only Hope: The Fragmentation of the Southern Baptist Convention* (Eerdmans, 1990).

10. Morgan, David. *The New Crusades, the New Holy Land: Conflict in the Southern Baptist Convention, 1969–1991* (University Press of Alabama, 1996).

11. Nettles, Tom. *Ready for Reformation?* (Broadman & Holman, 2005).

12. Nettles, Tom, and Russell Moore, eds. *Why I Am a Baptist* (Broadman & Holman, 2001).

13. Pool, Jeff. *Against Returning to Egypt* (Mercer University Press, 1998). Moderate.

14. Pressler, Paul. *A Hill on Which to Die* (Broadman & Holman, 1998).

15. Rosenberg, Ellen. *The Southern Baptists: A Subculture in Transition* (University Press of Tennessee, 1989).

16. Shurden, Walter, ed. *The Struggle for the Soul of the SBC* (Mercer University Press, 1993).

17. Staton, Cecil, ed. *Why I Am a Baptist: Reflections on Being Baptist in the 21st Century* (Smyth and Helwys, 1999).

18. Stricklin, David. *A Genealogy of Dissent* (University Press of Kentucky, 1999).

19. Sutton, Jerry. *The Baptist Reformation* (Broadman & Holman, 2000).

Holiness, Methodism, and Wesleyanism

1. **Andrews, Dee. *The Methodists and Revolutionary America, 1760–1800* (Princeton University Press, 2000).**

2. Dieter, Melvin. *The Holiness Movement in the Nineteenth Century,* 2d ed. (Scarecrow, 1996).

3. **Heitzenrater, Richard.** *Wesley and the People Called Methodists* **(Abingdon, 1995).**
4. **Hempton, David.** *Methodism* **(Yale University Press, 2005).**
5. Kent, John. *Wesley and the Wesleyans* (Cambridge University Press, 2002).
6. Kinghorn, Kenneth. *The Heritage of American Methodism* (Abingdon, 1999).
7. Kostevly, William. *Historical Dictionary of the Holiness Movement* (Scarecrow, 2001).
8. Lyerly, Cynthia. *Methodism and the Southern Mind, 1770–1810* (Oxford University Press, 1998).
9. **Wigger, John.** *Taking Heaven by Storm* **(Oxford University Press, 1998).**
10. **Wigger, John, and Nathan Hatch, eds.** *Methodism and the Shaping of American Culture* **(Abingdon, 2001).**
11. **Yrigoyen, Charles, and Susan Warrick, eds.** *Historical Dictionary of Methodism,* **2d ed. (Scarecrow, 2005).**

Pentecostal and Charismatic History

1. Anderson, Allan. *An Introduction to Pentecostalism* (Cambridge University Press, 2004).
2. Anderson, Robert. *Vision of the Disinherited* (Hendrickson, 1993).
3. Blumhofer, Edith. *The Assemblies of God,* 2 vols. (Gospel Publishing House, 1989).
   ———. *Restoring the Faith: The Assemblies of God, Pentecostalism, and American Culture* (University Press of Illinois, 1993).
4. Blumhofer, Edith, Russell P. Spittler, and Grant A. Wacker, eds. *Pentecostal Currents in American Protestantism* (University Press of Illinois, 1999).
5. Burgess, Stanley, ed. *Encyclopedia of Pentecostal and Charismatic Christianity* (Routledge, 2005).
6. **Burgess, Stanley, and Eduard van der Maas, eds.** *The New International Dictionary of Pentecostal and Charismatic Movements,* **rev. ed. (Zondervan, 2002).**

7. Cox, Harvey. *The Rise of Pentecostal Christianity and the Reshaping of Religion in the 21st Century* (DaCapo/Addison-Wesley, 1994).

8. Dayton, Donald. *The Theological Roots of Pentecostalism* (Hendrickson/Scarecrow, 1987).

9. Dayton, Donald, and Robert Johnston, eds. *The Variety of American Evangelicalism* (IVP, 1991; Wipf & Stock, 2001).

10. Faupel, William. *The Everlasting Gospel* (Sheffield Academic Press, 1996).

11. **Gillespie, Thomas. *The First Theologians: A Study in Early Christian Prophecy* (Eerdmans, 1994).**

12. Hollenweger, Walter. *The Pentecostals* (Hendrickson, 1972).
——. *Pentecostalism* (Hendrickson, 1997).

13. Jacobsen, Douglas. *Thinking in the Spirit: Theologies of the Early Pentecostal Movement* (Indiana University Press, 2003).

14. **Jones, Charles. *A Guide to the Study of the Pentecostal Movement*, 2 vols. (Scarecrow, 1983).**
——. *The Charismatic Movement*, **2 vols. (Scarecrow, 1995).** Bibliography with focus on Anglo-American sources.

15. **Kydd, Ronald. *Healing Through the Centuries* (Hendrickson, 1998).**

16. **Land, Steven. *Pentecostal Spirituality* (Sheffield Academic Press, 1993).**

17. Ma, Wonsuk, and Robert Menzies, eds. *Pentecostalism in Context* (Sheffield Academic Press, 1997).

18. **Martin, David. *Pentecostalism* (Blackwell, 2001).**

19. McGee, Gary. *People of the Spirit: The Assemblies of God* (Gospel Publishing House, 2004).

20. Nuñez, David. *Full Gospel, Fractured Minds?* (Zondervan, 2005).

21. **Robeck, Cecil. *The Azusa Street Mission and Revival* (Thomas Nelson, 2006).**

22. Shaull, Richard, and Waldo Cesar. *Pentecostalism and the Future of the Christian Churches* (Eerdmans, 2000).

23. **Synan, Vinson. *The Holiness-Pentecostal Tradition*, 2d ed. (Eerdmans, 1997).**

————. *The Century of the Holy Spirit* (**Thomas Nelson, 2001**).

24. **Wacker, Grant.** *Heaven Below* (**Harvard University Press, 2001**). Early Pentecostalism.

Stone Campbell

1. Baker, William, ed. *Evangelicalism and the Stone-Campbell Movement* (IVP, 2002).
2. Foster, Douglas, et al., eds. *The Encyclopedia of the Stone-Campbell Movement* (Eerdmans, 2004).
3. Hughes, Richard. *Reviving the Ancient Faith: The Story of Churches of Christ in America* (Eerdmans, 1996).
4. Sparks, Elder John. *Raccoon John Smith* (University Press of Kentucky, 2006).

19

EXEGETICAL AND BIBLE STUDY COMPUTER PROGRAMS

When considering the option of going electronic for your personal reference collection, first one must consider the qualifications of the computer you will be using.[1] When I upgraded to a new PC, I deliberately selected a model with a gig of RAM and a Pentium 4 processor (2992 MHz); specifically with biblical software programs in mind. A Pentium 4 or higher narrows the search speed differences between Accordance, BibleWorks, and Scholar's Library: Gold. Get a gig of RAM, because upgrades will inevitably grow more complex.

Recently, while preparing the revision of my reference survey, I reviewed programs that, once purely exegetical, have been expanded to include a full range of references. On the other hand, essentially reference-based programs have improved exegetically. Personally, I have always preferred running one program for exegesis and another for reference,[2] but the budget-minded might prefer a single program that has the advantage of tying in all the references at once to the subject at hand.

A marketing manager for one of the leading Windows-compatible exegetical programs remarked that changes that occur in two years of biblical software development are equivalent to ten years in print

---

1. See http://mysite.verizon.net/vzeojt6o/esucommentaryandreferencrvey/ index.html.
2. For a similar assessment, see Robert Plummer, *Southern Baptist Journal of Theology* (Spring 2005): 98–100.

publishing. Indeed, to use Logos as an example, as recently as ten years ago the equivalent of a scholar's library (*Logos Bible Software 2.0: Level 4*) contained 36 (many superfluous) titles and retailed for $599. Today, the most recent option is Logos Bible Software's *Scholar's Library: Gold* ($1,379.95 retail), which combines a whopping 200 primary references (of which 600 are integral) plus 700 or more additional studies addressing works of theology, Bible history, and apologetics, etc. At a minimum, the base usefulness of Logos has more than quintupled while its cost has only increased by 230 percent.

Having said that, the software program which you should choose depends very much on your initial need while keeping in mind a reference tool that will last you down the road. Nowadays, it is actually possible to find many required texts for Greek/Hebrew in leading software packages, as a core bundle (•) or as add-ons (*).

Comparatively speaking, the essential references for basic exegetical study are contained in the programs above, and if the *BDAG/HALOT* (or *NIDOTTE/NIDNTT* for *Accordance* and Pradis) modules are added for an additional $250, you would have most of what you need for first and second year Greek/Hebrew at about half the cost of the corresponding print volumes. The question remains whether or not you would ultimately choose to build your whole library electronically or choose one of the programs above that offers more than the elementary core program.

For those who plan on going entirely digital, it's difficult to argue against *Scholar's Library: Gold* (hereafter *Gold*) as a primary choice. However, the recommended minimum requirements (128 MB RAM, Pentium 3 processor) is somewhat misleading, as I tried it and it's slow. In *Gold*, at least 256 MB RAM is needed to mount several books at once. For searches, a Pentium 3 (1000 MHz) can do the job but at a slower rate than *BibleWorks* and *Accordance*. Again, you really need Pentium 4. Still further and especially for scholars, Logos could be made more intuitive in carrying out certain complex searches.[3] For

---

3. For a thorough analysis by a professional software programmer, see Van Dyke Parunak's (now dated) review of the *Logos Scholar's Library* (without the *Silver* upgrade) in *JETS* 48 (June 2005): 366–68, and his essay at http://www.cyber-chapel .org/reviews/LibBwkDec2004.pdf. For a more dated analysis, see his "Windows

CORE PROGRAMS ▶	ACCORDANCE $445[4]	BIBLEWORKS $349.99	GRAMCORD $235[6]	LOGOS (LIBRONIX) $415.95[7]	PRADIS (ZONDERVAN) $349.99[8]
NA/BHS	•	•	•	•	•
LXX	*	•	•	•	
Friberg AGNT	•Tagged[5]	•	•Tagged	•Tagged	•Interlinear
Friberg Analytical Lex.	•Tagged	•	•Tagged	•Tagged	•
Greek-Eng. Dict. of the NT	*	•	•	•	G/K Def.
Louw-Nida	•	•	•		
A Greek-Eng. Lexicon of LXX	*	•	•	•LS Lexicon	
TWOT	*	•		•	
BDB Hebrew Lexicon	•	•	•	•	

4. The relative cost of a core bundle consisting of Hebrew *BHS*, *BDB*, and *TWOT* as well as Greek NA[27], LXX, LEH Lexicon, Louw-Nida, and *UBS Dictionary*. In *Accordance*, $445 reflects the cost of their *Scholar's Collection 6.9 Core Bundle* plus additional modules needing purchase (marked by asterisk) to equal the other core modules.
5. Morphological code that identifies each form.
6. The GRAMCORD core bundle lacks *TWOT*.
7. Retail price for *Logos Bible Software Series 3: Original Languages Library*. The retail price for *Silver* is $799.95.
8. Retail price for *Zondervan Bible Study Library: Scholar's Edition* with Pradis operating system. Items listed are those that approximate modules in the other three programs.

instance, to search for constructions that cross chapter boundaries, it is necessary to change the search range to "Special."

Whereas *Accordance* and *BibleWorks* operate from a control panel layout through which all base references pass, *Gold's* desktop approach treats books as free-standing entities yet able to be hyperlinked in a variety of ways. Utilizing a gateway that enables rapid passage, word or exegetical studies, the operator is able to select preferred references from a menu of hyperlinks created by the search in question. For instance, an exegetical study of John 3:16 will bring up a list of links to the desired tools (Louw-Nida, Strong's, *TDNT*, etc.) where it is referenced. Thus, you can choose to look up αγαπη in Strong's, while looking up κοσμο" in *TDNT*. Plus, you can keylink any and all Greek lexicons to NA[27] if you prefer. In addition, *Gold* enables references to be displayed by page number (as does *Accordance*). In fact, it automatically adds citations to paste-ins according to whatever style you choose from its Options menu. *BibleWorks* and Pradis (Zondervan) require a trip to the library to hunt down references utilized for proper page citation in class papers.

Also, like *Accordance* and *BibleWorks*, *Gold* is now capable of advanced searching utilizing a graphical query editor as well as the typical query syntax entry.[9] For comparison, here is a simple Greek syntax search for "angel of the Lord (all forms)" with "appeared (all forms)" within three words in both the LXX/GNT.

Software for Bible Study," *JETS* 46.3 (September 2003): 485–95. For a review of *Logos Silver* more apropos to the pastor, see Matt Blackmon with Hall Harris in *BibSac* 162 (July–September 2005): 366–67. For an overview of some of the chief features offered, see the review of *Logos Silver* by Jan van der Watt on the SBL Web site (http://www.bookreviews.org/pdf/4873_5077.pdf).

9. Rubén Gómez has done a very comparable analysis of the various search qualities of the three programs evaluated here at http://www.bsreview.org/weblog/2005/08/graphical-searches-test-case.html. Tyler Williams likewise compares *Logos* and *Accordance* at http://biblical-studies.ca/blog/2005/08/graphical-searches-logos-and.html. For a critique of the *Logos* GQE see the web log of *Accordance* programmer David Lang at http://www.accordancebible.com/forums/index.php?showtopic=202&st=0&p=796&#entry796.

Logos

To speed up the search in Logos, it is best to open up NA[27] and the LXX first and limit the search to all open resources. In Libronix (the technology platform for *Logos Gold*) it could be entered in an advanced search as αγγελ* **AND** κυρ* **WITHIN 3 Words** *φαιν* or in the Graphical Query Editor:

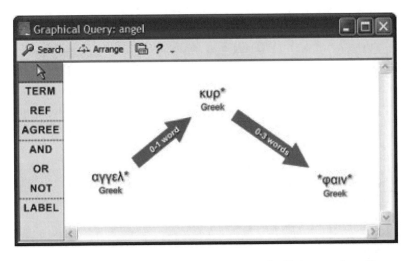

As an added bonus, the search also yields the link to an interlinear (i.e., Matt. 1:20):

αγγελος	Κυριου	κατ	οναρ	εφανη	αυτω	λεγων
an angel	of [the] Lord	in	a dream	appeared	to him,	saying,
ἄγγελος	κύριος	κατά	ὄναρ	φαίνω	αὐτός	λέγω
32	2962	2596	3677	5316	846	3004
NNSM	NGSM	P	ZO	VA2PI3S	RP-DSM	VP-AP-SNM

Accordance

Similarly, *Accordance* runs the query as αγγελ* κυρ* [WITHIN 3 Words] *φαιν*. The Search All function (in the Search button popup menu on the Resource palette) lets users search all their resources or a defined group, very similar to Logos.

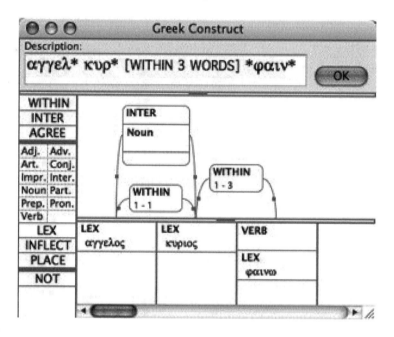

BibleWorks

For *BibleWorks,* the formula would be much the same, although *BibleWorks* has its own codes to denote phrases (') and WITHIN three words (*3). Furthermore, in *BibleWorks* it is necessary to run the query specifically as a morphological search ἀγγελος* κυριος* *3 φαινω = (angel of the Lord) within 3 words (appear) in order to bring up all three results (see below). The search version entered on the command line would be BGM (LXX/GNT morphology) rather than BGT (LXX/GNT text). To find the same results in a BGT search, it is necessary to switch between αγγελ* κυρ* *3 *φαιν or *φαν*.

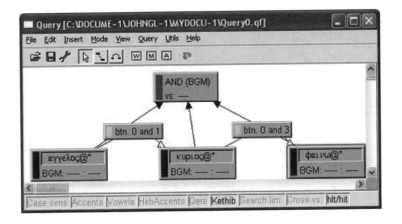

All three programs reveal results in Matthew 1:20; 2:13, 19. No LXX result is found as the translators utilized ο ρ α ω rather than φ α ι ν ω or any other variant in most cases where an "angel of the Lord" is said to have "appeared" in the OT.

Logos' *Scholar's Library: Gold* has the advantage of being able to be expanded with other Libronix-compatible titles like Thomas Nelson's 62-volume Word Biblical Commentary series on 2 CD-ROMS ($1,199 retail). For instance, in the Word Biblical Commentary series, one could match and compare commentary on words and phrases such as "the angel of the Lord" in Greek, Hebrew, English, and seven other languages for that matter (i.e., Gen. 16:7; Exod. 3:2; Num. 22:22; 2 Sam. 24:16; 1 Kings 19:7; 2 Kings 1:3; 1 Chron. 21:30; Ps. 34:7; Isa. 37:36; Matt. 1:20; 28:2; Luke 2:9). There are thousands of other potential Libronix add-ons as well. Broadman & Holman's 31-volume New American Commentary (included in *Gold*), the International Critical Commentary (T & T Clark), the Pillar New Testament Commentary and the New International Greek Testament Commentary (both Eerdmans, NIGTC is packaged with *Gold*) and the WBC and BECNT series are also available as separate modules, and would still function together with *The Essential IVP Reference Collection* ($180 retail) as a single system.[10]

---

10. A search on the obscure phrase "arm of the Lord" in just the IVP, WBC, and NAC series yielded 22 hits in 9 different commentaries and references (excluding Bibles).

For a purely exegetical program, *BibleWorks for Windows 7.0* is extremely user-friendly with context-sensitive popup windows and almost four hours of online instructional videos.[11] One popup window that is particularly helpful is the Lexical and Grammatical Help dialog that keys the relevant passages in the *UBS Dictionary*, Friberg, Wallace's *Greek Grammar, BDAG, HALOT, BDB,* Waltke and O'Connor, *TWOT,* and Tischendorf's *Critical Apparatus,* etc., for quick and easy lookup of biblical terms. *BibleWorks,* however, largely limits itself to original language resources only.

Up to now, *Accordance* (OakTree Software) has been unrivaled in complex searches in the original Hebrew and Greek thanks in large part to the Greek and Hebrew skills of its development team.[12] Like, Logos, *Accordance* has recently added the NIGTC and PNTC (Eerdmans) as well as the WBC series (Thomas Nelson). Another big plus is the availability of the CNTTS Apparatus (Center for New Testament Textual Studies) and the *BHS* and NA[27] Apparatuses available in the *Stuttgart Electronic Study Bible* CD-ROM as add-ons (also available through Logos since 2004).[13] *Accordance 6.9* (OakTree Software) with the *Scholar's Collection 6* can be made Windows-compatible by the employment of the *Basilisk II* Mac Emulator (available as a free download from accordancebible.com). There is a bit of steep learning curve for those unfamiliar with the Mac platform. To start with, installation of the Mac emulator requires close application of the directions

---

11. This edition has 122 reference works and helps (although 90 of these are foreign translations and references in 28 languages, making this collection unique), which includes an advanced search engine for complex constructions, 20 English translations, the *TWOT*, the unabridged *BDB* lexicon, an abridged Liddell-Scott lexicon, Louw-Nida, the Friberg and Miller revised analytical lexicon (2000) and *AGNT*[2] morphological database. See the review by Moisés Silva, *WTJ* 66 (Fall 2004): 449–54. Jan van der Watt has recently reviewed *BibleWorks 6* (http://www.bookreviews.org/pdf/5016_5283.pdf) in January.

12. For instance, see the review of *Accordance 6.4* by Andreas Köstenberger in *JETS* 48 (March 2005): 196–97. For a thorough overview of *Accordance 6.6*, see Frank Ritchel Ames, http://www.sbl-site.org/Article.aspx?ArticleId=433.

13. Generally *Accordance* has been the forerunner in tagged texts like Targums, Qumran Sectarian Documents, the Mishnah, and the Apostolic Fathers. Logos is catching up.

provided. Having said that, *Accordance* is heads and shoulders above all competition for those who use Mac.[14]

Conclusion

- *Accordance* is a Porsche—built for both speed and drivability.
- *BibleWorks* is a Mercedes[15] (sorry BMW).
- *Scholar's Library: Gold* is a Cadillac (for library size and bells and whistles).
- Zondervan's *Scholar's Edition* is a Ford pickup (for utility, especially in the NIV).

---

14. *Accordance* shares some of the advantages of its chief rival in being expandable, and Logos has surpassed all others in being the first to bring syntactically tagged resources to market (a *Logos Scholar's Edition* for Mac will soon be available).

15. See review by Silva, *WTJ* 66:454, who suggested that *BibleWorks'* simple search function is like using a Stealth Fighter to purchase milk at a 7-Eleven.

GREEK/HEBREW LEXICONS	ACCORDANCE	BIBLEWORKS	GRAMCORD	LOGOS	PRADIS
BDAG/HALOT	•	•		•	
NIDOTTE	•				•
NIDNTT	•				•
TDNT				•	
TLNT	•				
TLOT	•				
EDNT		•		•	
Grammars:					
Wallace	•	•		•	•
Joüon/Muraoka				•	
Futato		•		•	
Ross					
Waltke	•	•		•	

COMMENTARIES	ACCORDANCE	BIBLEWORKS	GRAMCORD	LOGOS	PRADIS
Metzger Text. Comm.		•		•	Rogers LK
NIGTC (Eerdmans)	•			•	
WBC (Nelson)	•			•	
ICC (T & T Clark)				•	
NAC (Broadman)				•	
PNTC (Eerdmans)	•			•	
IVPNTC (IVP)				•	
IBC (WJK)				•	
NIVAC (Zondervan)					•
NIBC (Hendrickson)	•				
BECNT (Baker)				•	
Hermeneia (Fortress)				•	

REFERENCE	ACCORDANCE	BIBLEWORKS	GRAMCORD	LOGOS	PRADIS
IVP Essential Collection	•			•	
Eerdmans Dictionary	•			•	ZPBE[16]
Atlas[17]	•	•	•	•	•
Interlinear	•	CNTTS[18]		•	Parallel
NT Intro	•			•	•
OT Intro	•			•	•
SESB[19]	•	CNTTS		•	
Theo. Journal[20]	•			•	

---

16. *Zondervan Pictorial Bible Encyclopedia.*
17. Logos has an atlas, OT Intro, and NT Intro in its *Gold Edition*, as well as an untagged Josephus and tagged Philo. Pradis (Zondervan) comes with an atlas (tied to NIV), an OT Intro, and NT Intro in its *Scholar's Edition.*
18. Center for New Testament Textual Studies.
19. *Stuttgart Electronic Study Bible.* Morphologically tagged LMT/LXX/NA[27] with critical apparatus and variants.
20. *Theological Journal Library CD,* vols. 5–9 (Galaxie Software).

OTHER ORIGINAL-LANGUAGE TEXTS	ACCORDANCE	BIBLEWORKS	GRAMCORD	LOGOS	PRADIS
Josephus	•	•		Untagged	
Philo	•	•		•	
Pseudepigrapha	•			•	
Targums	•	•		•	
Qumran Sectarian	•	•		•	
Mishnah	•			Untagged	
Apostolic Fathers	•	•		•	

Optimal Package

1. *Accordance* (877-339-5855) or *BibleWorks* (888-747-8200) (for language searches).
2. *BDAG* and *HALOT. BibleWorks-, Accordance-,* and Libronix-compatible (Logos).[21]
3. Carson, D. A., ed. The Pillar New Testament Commentary (Eerdmans). Libronix- and *Accordance*-compatible.
4. *The Essential IVP Reference Collection* (IVP, 2001). *Accordance-* and Libronix-compatible (Logos). 630-734-4321.
5. Marshall, I. Howard, and Donald Hagner, eds. The New International Greek Testament Commentary (Eerdmans). Libronix- and *Accordance*-compatible.
6. Metzger, Bruce, ed. Word Biblical Commentary (Thomas Nelson). Libronix- and *Accordance*-compatible. 800-251-4000.
7. *Scholar's Library: Gold* (Logos Research Systems). Includes New American Commentary series (Broadman & Holman) and New International Greek Commentary (Eerdmans). *See under* Computer Resources: References for other add-ons. 800-875-6467.
8. VanGemeren, Willem, ed. *New International Dictionary of Old Testament Theology and Exegesis 6.0* (Zondervan). Pradis-compatible.

---

21. *BibleWorks* corrected many errors in electronic version of *HALOT* provided by publisher.

20

COMPUTER RESOURCES

1. *Accordance Scholar's Collection 6.9* (OakTree Software). Accessible on PC with *Basilisk II* Mac Emulator.[1]

CORE BUNDLE[2]	ADD-ONS

KJV
Greek New Testament NA[27] (tagged)
Louw and Nida Semantic Domain
   Lexicon
BHS with Westminster Hebrew
   Morphology
Brown-Driver-Briggs Abridged
   Hebrew Lexicon
	A Greek-English Lexicon of the NT
	   (BDAG)
	The Hebrew and Aramaic Lexicon of
	   the OT
	New International Dictionary of NT
	   Theology
	Spicq Theological Lexicon of the NT
	Jenni-Westermann Theological
	   Lexicon
	LEH Septuagint Lexicon Second
	   Edition

The modules listed with each package are representative rather than exhaustive.

1. Allen Ross, *Introducing Biblical Hebrew* (requires unlock); Daniel Wallace, *Greek Grammar Beyond the Basics: Exegetical Syntax of the New Testament* (requires unlock); Bruce Waltke and M. O'Connor, *Introduction to Biblical Hebrew Syntax* (requires unlock); L. Koehler, W. Baumgartner, and John Stamm, eds., *The Hebrew and Aramaic Lexicon of the Old Testament*, 4th ed. (requires unlock); *BDAG* (requires unlock).

2. Unlike the other key packages, it is necessary to purchase these add-on modules (price listed) to equate the core bundles of the other programs. A core bundle consists of Hebrew *BHS*, *BDB*, and *TWOT* as well as Greek NA[27], LXX, Liddell-Scott, Louw-Nida, and *UBS Dictionary*.

	New International Dictionary of OT Theology and Exegesis New International Biblical Commentary NIGTC commentary series (Eerdmans) PNTC commentary series (Eerdmans)
UBS Greek Dictionary $25 Theological Wordbook of the Old Testament $70 Rahlfs Septuaginta, revised $80 Liddell and Scott Greek Lexicon (Abridged) $60	Word Biblical Commentary series (2006) Essential IVP Reference Collection Greek Grammar Beyond the Basics Theological Journal Library CD, vols. 5–9 MT/LXX Parallel Database CNTTS Apparatus

2. *BibleWorks for Windows 7.0.*[3]

Friberg's 1999 *AGNT* Friberg's *Analytical Lexicon of the Greek New Testament* (2000 ed.) Whitaker's abridged *BDB* Lexicon Transliterated *BHS* Hebrew OT Aletti/Gieniusz/Bushell/CNTSS Morphologically Analyzed LXX and Lemmas (completed) Groves-Wheeler Westminster Hebrew OT Morphology database vol. 4 The Targumim, parsed, lemmatized, and tied to entries in the Comprehensive Aramaic Lexicon *NET Bible* with full notes and maps *HCSB* Holladay *Complete works of Flavius Josephus* *Works of Philo*	• Diagramming module • Greek and Hebrew paradigms charts, linked to text • Hebrew and Greek vocabulary flashcards (complete sets), supporting print, electronic, and audio flashcards • Popup gloss window (definition and parsing information) displayed over Greek and Hebrew texts when mouse is held over word • Auto-complete morphology codes—popup list opens as you type • Lexical/Grammatical Helps Window—shows all related references for a word/verse as you move over text

---

3. Mark Futato, *Beginning Biblical Hebrew* (full text; requires unlock); Wallace, *Greek Grammar Beyond the Basics* (requires unlock); Waltke and O'Connor, *Introduction to Biblical Hebrew Syntax* (requires unlock); Koehler, Baumgartner, and Stamm, *Hebrew and Aramaic Lexicon of the Old Testament* (requires unlock); *BDAG* (requires unlock); *CNTTS Critical Apparatus.* (requires unlock).

3. *Gramcord for Windows* Ultimate Bundle (Gramcord Institute).

GRAMCORD Hebrew Masoretic Text (*Biblia Hebraica Stuttgartensia* with Revised Westminster Hebrew Morphology) Princeton Edition Expanded *BDB* Hebrew Lexicon GRAMCORD LXX with Rahlf's *Septuaginta* (LXX with Univ. of Pennsylvania/CCAT LXX Morphology) [GRAMCORD LXX includes alternate Theodotian readings!]	LEH Septuagint Lexicon [a GRAMCORD Institute exclusive; a TRUE Septuagint lexicon, not a classical Greek approximation]. *A Handbook of Grammatical Diagramming* (Based on Philippians) Louw-Nida *Semantic Domains*

4. *Scholar's Library: Gold* (Logos Research Systems). $11,700 worth of print titles. 5,000 add-ons available.[4]

Word Study Bible: KJV (Zodhiates) Full *BDB* Lexicon Swanson's *Dictionary of Biblical Languages* (Hebrew OT, Aramaic OT, Greek NT) *Analytical Greek New Testament* *Analytical Lexicon of the Greek NT* *Complete Word Study Dictionary: NT* (Zodhiates) *Theological Dictionary of the New Testament*, Unabridged (*TDNT*) *A Greek-English Lexicon of the Septuagint* (Lust) Syriac Peshitta NT and *Analytical Syriac Lexicon* Complete Works of Josephus. Works of Philo Early Church Fathers (37 vols.)	*Biblical Hebrew Reference Grammar* *Hebrew Syntax*, 3d (Davidson) Greek New Testament Insert (Chapman-Shogren) Hebrew Bible Insert Diagrammatical Analysis *Ancient Egyptian Lit.*, 3 vols. *The DSS and Modern Translations of the OT* Synopses: Analytical Outline of the Books of Samuel, Kings, and Chronicles Synopsis of the Old Testament Synopsis of the Four Gospels (Kurt Aland) Jude–2 Peter

---

4. Futato, *Beginning Biblical Hebrew* (full text; requires unlock); Wallace, *Greek Grammar Beyond the Basics* (requires unlock); Waltke and O'Connor, *Introduction to Biblical Hebrew Syntax* (requires unlock); Koehler, Baumgartner, and Stamm, *Hebrew and Aramaic Lexicon of the Old Testament* (requires unlock); *BDAG* (requires unlock).

New Bible Commentary	*New Manners and Customs of the*
IVP Bible Background Commentary:	*Bible*
New Testament	*Images of the Holy Lands*
New American Commentary (31 vols.)	*Moody Handbook of Theology*
Barclay's Daily Study Series: OT (24	*Oxford Dictionary of the Christian*
vols.)	*Church*
Daily Study Series: NT (17 vols.)	*Hard Sayings of the Bible*
Amarna Letters	*Difficulties in the Bible*
History of the Christian Church	*A Survey of OT Introduction*
Logos Deluxe Map Set	*New Testament Introduction*
	And thousands more . . .

5. *Zondervan Bible Study Library 6.0: Scholar's Edition* (Zondervan, 2003).[5]

NIV Study Bible	*New International Bible Dictionary*
NASB/NIV Parallel Bible	*New Int'l Encyclopedia of Bible Words*
The Greek New Testament UBS⁴ with	*New Int'l Dictionary of the Christian*
NRSV and NIV	*Church*
Kohlenberger Concordances	*Dictionary of Cults, Sects, Religion,*
Hebrew-English Reader's Lexicon of	*and the Occult*
the Old Testament	*New Int'l Dictionary of Biblical*
Greek-English Reader's Lexicon of the	*Archaeology*
New Testament	*Zondervan Pictorial Encyclopedia of*
New Linguistic and Exegetical Key to	*the Bible* (5 vols.)
the Greek New Testament	*Zondervan NIV Bible Commentary*
	(2 vols.)
	Introduction to the New Testament
	An Introduction to the Old Testament
	Is There Meaning in this Text?

---

5. *NIDOTTE* and *NIDNTT* are available as separate modules or combined as one add-on module. The Pradis *Scholar's Edition* includes Wallace's grammar. The NIV Application Commentary series is available in the New Testament, and eventually in the Old Testament as well.

Details of Important Add-On Resources
Commentary Series

1. Barton, John, and John Muddiman, eds. *The Oxford Bible Commentary* (Oxford U., 2001). Unlockable Logos CD with book. 800-334-4249.

2. Carson, D. A., ed. The Pillar New Testament Commentary (Eerdmans). Available from both Logos and *Accordance*. 877-339-5855.

3. Clendenen, Ray, gen. ed. The New American Commentary, 46 vols. (Broadman & Holman). Libronix-compatible, available from Logos Research Systems. Included in *Logos Gold* or as separate component. 800-87LOGOS.

4. Gaebelein, Frank, ed. *The Expositor's Bible Commentary on CD-ROM*, 12 vols. (Zondervan, 1998). Pradis- and *Accordance*-compatible.

5. International Critical Commentary Series. 53 vols. (T & T Clark).

6. Keck, Leander, gen. ed. The New Interpreter's Bible: A Commentary in 12 vols. Electronic edition (Abingdon). 800-251-3320.

7. Machinist, Peter, and Helmut Koesters, eds. Hermeneia (Fortress). Libronix-compatible

8. Marshall, I. H., and Donald Hagner, eds. The New International Greek Testament Commentary (Eerdmans). Available from both Logos and *Accordance*.

9. Metzger, Bruce, gen. ed. Word Biblical Commentary (Thomas Nelson). Includes NA^{26}, *BHS*, *BDB*, Louw-Nida, and 7 translations. Libronix- and *Accordance*-compatible. 800-251-4000.

10. Muck, Terry, gen. ed. *The NIV Application Commentary 6.0: Complete New Testament* (Zondervan, 2004). Pradis-compatible.

References

1. *Bible Review: The Archive, 1985–2003 CD-ROM* (BAS, 2004).

2. *Biblical Archaeology Review: The Archive, 1975–2003 CD-ROM* (BAS, 2004).

3. *Biblical Studies Library 4* (Biblical Studies). NET *Bible* (see above) and 5,000 documents, including many unpublished Bible studies. Logos and Libronix compatible. 800-GALAXIE.

4. *Catalogue of the French Biblical and Archaeological School of Jerusalem* (Brill, 2000). Bibliographical research of École Biblique, French-English, Logos-compatible.

5. *The Essential IVP Reference Collection* (IVP, 2001). Includes the four-volume *DJG, DPL, DLNTD* and *DNTB,* the *New Dictionary of Biblical Theology* (2001), the *NBD³, NBC⁴,* and *Atlas,* the *New Dictionary of Theology,* the *Dictionary of Biblical Imagery, Hard Sayings of the Bible,* and the *IVP Bible Background Commentaries: Old Testament* and *New Testament.* Libronix-compatible. 630-734-4321.

6. Freedman, David, ed. *The Anchor Bible Dictionary on CD-ROM* (Doubleday). Libronix-compatible.

7. Hannah, John. *Charts of Ancient and Medieval History* (Zondervan, 2001). Companion CD replicating contents for audiovisual use and printouts.

8. Hanson, K., and Douglas Oakman. *Palestine in the Time of Jesus* (Fortress, 1996/2002). With multiple-link CD.

9. **Keathley, Hampton, ed. *Theological Journal Library CD,* vols. 5–9 (Galaxie Software).** *ATJ, BibSac, Emmaus, JBMW, JETS, RevExp, SBJT, TJ, TMSTJ, WTJ,* etc.

10. Musser, Donald, and Joseph Price, eds. *The Abingdon Dictionary of Theology: Electronic Edition* (Abingdon, 1997).

11. NET *Bible* (Biblical Studies, 2001). *New English Translation.* Sixty thousand footnotes excellent for identifying key Hebrew, Greek words, and phrases. Logos and Libronix-compatible. 800-GALAXIE.

12. *Thesaurus Linguae Graecae* on CD-ROM (University Press of California).

13. VanGemeren, Willem, and Colin Brown, gen. eds. *Zondervan Theological Dictionaries* (Zondervan, 2002). *NIDOTTE and NIDNTT* bundled together. Pradis-compatible. 800-727-1309.

14. Wilson, Neil, and Linda Taylor. *Tyndale Handbook of Bible Maps and Charts* (Tyndale, 2002). CD replicating book with links to NLT. Also Mac-compatible.

Images

1. *The Biblical World in Pictures Revised Edition CD-ROM* (BAS, 2004). More than 1,300 images.
2. Bolen, Todd. *Pictorial Library of Bible Lands* (Kregel, 2003). Ten CDs—Galilee, Samaria, Jerusalem, Judah, Negev, Jordan, Egypt, Turkey, Greece, Rome. Ideal for classroom. Six thousand pictures.
3. Koester, Helmut. *Cities of Paul: Images and Interpretations from the Harvard New Testament and Archaeology Project* (Fortress, 2005). Nine hundred photos plus maps and detailed site info.

Language Helps

1. Johnstone, William, et al. *A Computerized Introductory Hebrew Grammar* (T & T Clark, 1993). Interactive, cross-referenced complement to Davidson; also Mac.
2. Koehler, L., W. Baumgartner, and J. Stamm, eds. *The Hebrew-Aramaic Lexicon of the Old Testament CD-ROM* (Brill, 2000).
3. *The Lexham Hebrew-English Interlinear Bible* (Logos, 2005).
4. Louw, J., and E. Nida. *A Greek-English Lexicon of the New Testament on CD-ROM* (iExalt).
5. McLean, John. *Handbook of Grammatical Diagramming* (Gramcord Institute). 360-576-3000.
6. *The New Greek-English Interlinear New Testament on CD-ROM* (iExalt). UBS[4], Friberg's *AGNT*, STEP-compatible, vocalizes pronunciation and definition.
7. Swanson, James. *A Dictionary of Biblical Languages with Semantic Domains* (Logos). Available in Hebrew, Greek, and Aramaic.

8. Van der Merwe, H., et al. *A Biblical Hebrew Reference Grammar* (Sheffield). Libronix-compatible.

9. Wallace, Daniel, *Greek Grammar Beyond the Basics* (Galaxie Software). 800-GALAXIE.

Macintosh

1. *Accordance Bible Atlas* (Oaktree Software) in the *Scholar's Collection.*

2. Blum, Ed, ed. *Holman Christian Standard Bible* (Broadman & Holman, 2002). Accordance-compatible. 800-251-3225.

3. Brown, Colin, ed. *The New International Dictionary of New Testament Theology,* 4 vols. (Zondervan, 1975–1978). Accordance-compatible.

4. Clines, David, ed. *The Dictionary of Classical Hebrew,* 8 vols. (Sheffield Academic Press, 1993–).

5. Freedman, David, gen. ed. *The Anchor Bible Dictionary* (Oaktree Software).

6. Gaebelein, Frank, ed. *The Expositor's Bible Commentary for Macintosh* (Zondervan). Accordance-compatible.

7. *The Online Bible* (Yeshua's Ministry). Also Windows-compatible. 888-224-2537.

8. *Scholar's Collection with Accordance 7.0* (Oaktree Software). Best overall exegetical program, see Windows above. 877-339-5855.

9. VanGemeren, Willem, ed. *The New International Dictionary of Old Testament Theology and Exegesis,* 5 vols. (Zondervan, 1997). Accordance-compatible.

10. *Zondervan Scholarly Bible Study Suite for Macintosh* (Zondervan). Accordance-compatible.

21

INTERNET WEB SITES

Publishing Houses and Software

www.bible.org (Biblical Studies Press). 800-575-2425. *NET Bible, NET Bible for Handhelds.*

www.biblestudysoftware.com

www.catholic-resources.org/Bible/Publishers.htm (Comprehensive list of links to print, university, and software publishers).

www.compubible.com

www.discountchristian.com

www.galaxie.com (Galaxie Software) 800-GALAXIE. *The Theological Journal Library CD*, vols. 5–9.

www.heavenword.com (888-726-4715). *GreekMaster, Lightning Study Bible.*

www.OliveTree.com (*Bible Reader, GRAMCORD Lite*).

www.onlinebible.net

www.PalmGear.com

www.rejoicesoftware.com

www.wesleyowen.com/WesleyOwenSite/sunrise/software

www.tlg.uci.edu (Thesaurus Lingua Graecae)

Used Books[1]

www.abebooks.com (Advanced Book Exchange). Search engine, finds location of both new and used books.

www.academicbooks.com (Windows Booksellers). Average 43 percent off secondhand books. 800-779-1701.

---

1. I would first check the Baker and Eerdmans sites, where slightly damaged books can often be found at 40–50 percent off, then I would turn to Windows

www.addall.com (comprehensive used-book search).

www.alibris.com

www.archivesbookshop.com (used books).

www.bakerbookretail.com (616-957-3110, [fax] 616-957-0965). More than 70,000 used and slightly damaged Baker books (including those missing a dust jacket).

www.bookfinder.com (search engine). New and used books.

www.booktown.com (Loome Theo. Booksellers). 250,000 used books.

www.cbebooks.org (Christian Book Exchange).

www.centuryone.com

www.eerdmans.com. Ask for bookstore, where many discontinued, slightly damaged, and overstocked books can be purchased at a significant discount. 800-253-7521.

www.evangelicalbooks.com

www.TheologyBooks.com.

www.UsedTheologyBooks.com.

Academic Sites

www.ats.edu (Association of Theological Schools). Full listing of seminaries and Bible colleges.

www.bible.gospelcom.net/cgi-bin/webcommentary (IVPNTC online).

www.bible-history.com

www.bible.org (Biblical Studies Foundation). Extensive Bible studies, commentaries, pastoral helps, NET translation.

www.bible-researcher.com

www.biblestudytools.com (14 translations, links to commentaries and other references).

www.biblicalstudies.org.uk (Excellent source of online articles and links to print material).

Booksellers, which regularly purchases entire libraries for resale. Another good source is eBay. If a book is particularly difficult to locate, consult abebooks.com. It is conceivable that you could construct a library of completely secondhand titles, and generally these are as good as new. Look out for CBD closeouts also, although it is less likely that you will find frontline references there.

http://bildi.uibk.ac.at/index-theoldi-en.html (THEOLDI).
    Bibliographical search.
www.ccel.org (Christian Classics Ethereal Library); i.e., Charles,
    OT Pseudepigrapha.
www.earth-history.com/
http://faculty.bbc.edu/rdecker/rd–rsrc.htm (Resources for New
    Testament Studies). Rodney Decker list.
www.hypotyposeis.org/weblog (Stephen Carlson on Synoptics,
    links to multiple ancient texts).
www.iclnet.org
www.jnul.huji.ac.il/rambi (RAMBI). Jewish bibliographical search.
www.leaderu.com (Leadership University Press). Articles on
    dozens of topics by pastors, scholars, etc.
http://monergism.com/thethreshold/artciles/topic
http://mysite.verizon.net/vzeojt6o/esucommentaryandreferencrvey/
    index.html (John Glynn site).
www.ntgateway.com (The New Testament Gateway). All New
    Testament studies links, references.
www.ohiolink.edu/search (bibliographical search).
www.otgateway.com (Old Testament Gateway).
www.perseus.tufts.edu (ancient texts, maps, archaeology).
www.theologywebsite.com/internet/Bible/Biblical_Studies
www.tlg.uci.edu (Thesaurus Lingua Graecae).
http://torreys.org/bible (Resource Pages for Biblical Studies).
www.tren.com (Theological Research Exchange Network). 7,800
    unpublished theses, dissertations from 70 institutions plus
    society meeting papers.
www.utoronto.ca/religion/synopsis (A Synopsis of the Gospels).
www.wabashcenter.wabash.edu/Internet

Theological Journals and Christian Magazines

www.acs.ucalgary.ca/~lipton/journals (comprehensive list).
www.arts.ualberta.ca/JHS (*Journal of Hebrew Scriptures*). **Online.**
www.atla.com (ATLA Religion Database). Listing of all journals.
www.bookreviews.org (*Review of Biblical Literature*) Online *JBL*,
    877-725-3334. **Online.**

www.booksandculture.net (numerous book reviews). **Online.**

www.brill.nl (*Novum Testamentum, Vetus Testamentum*).

www.calvin.edu (*Calvin Theological Journal*).

http://cba.cua.edu/CBQ.cfm (*Catholic Biblical Quarterly*).

http://ccmag.gospelcom.net (*Christian Computing magazine*).
    800-456-1868.

www.christianitytoday.com (*Christianity Today, Books and
    Culture, Leadership Journal*). **Online.**

www.churchsociety.org (*Churchman*).

www.cssr.org (*Religious Studies Review*). Numerous brief reviews
    in several categories.

www.denverseminary.edu/dj/index2006 (*Denver Journal*). **Online.**

www.dts.edu/media/publications/bibliothecasacra (*Bibliotheca
    Sacra*).

www.etsjets.org/jets/journal/jets.html (*Journal of the Evangelical
    Theological Society*). **Online.**

www.ingentaconnect.com (*JBI*, JSNT, JSOT, *JTS*, NT, *SJOT, VT*).

www.interpretation.org/reviews (IBC). **Online** (partial).

www.journalofbiblicalstudies.org. **Online.**

http://poj.peeters-leuven.be/content.php (Peeters online journals).

http://rande.org (*Review & Expositor*).

http://rosetta.reltech.org/TC/TC.html (*TC: A Journal of Biblical
    Textual Criticism*). **Online.**

www.rtabst.org (*Religious and Theological Abstracts*). 1959–2001
    editions, Updated annually.

www.sagepub.co.uk/journals.nav (*ExpTim, JPT, JSNT, JSOT*, etc.).

www.sbl-site.org (*Journal of Biblical Literature*). **Online.**

www.tiu.edu (*Trinity Journal*).

www.tms.edu/journal.asp (*The Master's Seminary Theological
    Journal*). (tms.edu/links.asp for thorough listing of online
    journals). **Online.**

www.ubs-translations.org/tictalk (UBS newsletter). **Online.**

www.wts.edu/publications/wtj (Westminster Theological Journal).

22

THE ULTIMATE COMMENTARY COLLECTION

Technical

Genesis
Victor Hamilton (NICOT)
Gordon Wenham (WBC)

Exodus
Brevard Childs (OTL)
Cornelius Houtman (HCOT)

Leviticus
John Hartley (NICOT)
Jacob Milgrom (AB)

Numbers
Timothy Ashley (NICOT)
Jacob Milgrom (JPSTC)

Deuteronomy
Peter Craigie (NICOT)
Gordon McConville (Apollos)

Joshua
Marten Woudstra (NICOT)

Judges
Robert Boling (AB)

Ruth
Fredric Bush (WBC)
Robert Hubbard (NICOT)

1–2 Samuel
Ralph Klein (1 Sam.) (WBC)
K. McCarter (2 Sam.) (AB)
David Tsumura (NICOT)

1–2 Kings
M. Cogan (1 Kings) (AB)
T. Hobbs (2 Kings) (WBC)

1–2 Chronicles
Roddy Braun (1 Chron.) (WBC)
Raymond Dillard (2 Chron.)
    (WBC)
Sara Japhet (OTL)

Ralph Klein (1 Chron.)
   (Hermeneia)
Gary Knoppers (1 Chron.) (AB)

Ezra & Nehemiah
Ralph Klein (Abingdon)
Hugh Williamson (WBC)

Esther
Fredric Bush (WBC)
Michael Fox (Eerdmans)

Job
David Clines (WBC)
John Hartley (NICOT)

Psalms
P. Craigie, M. Tate, and L. Allen
   (WBC)
John Goldingay (BCOTWP)
F. Hossfeld and E. Zenger
   (Hermeneia)

Proverbs
Michael Fox (AB)
Tremper Longman (BCOTWP)
Bruce Waltke (NICOT)

Ecclesiastes
Thomas Krüger (Hermeneia)
Roland Murphy (WBC)
Choon-Leong Seow (AB)

Song of Songs
Duane Garrett (WBC)
Richard Hess (BCOTWP)
Tremper Longman (NICOT)

Isaiah
John Goldingay (Isa. 40–55)
   (ICC)
Alec Motyer (IVP)
John Oswalt (NICOT)
Hugh Williamson (Isa. 1–5)
   (ICC)

Jeremiah
Jack Lundbom (AB)
Louis Stuhlman (Abingdon)
J. A. Thompson (NICOT)

Lamentations
Paul House (WBC)
Iain Provan (Sheffield)

Ezekiel
Leslie Allen (WBC)
Daniel Block (NICOT)
Margaret Odell (SHBC)

Daniel
John Collins (Hermeneia)
John Goldingay (WBC)

Hosea–Amos
A. A. MacIntosh (ICC)
Shalom Paul (Hermeneia)

Obadiah–Micah
Leslie Allen (NICOT)
F. Anderson and D. Freedman
   (AB)
Thomas Finley (Biblical Studies)
Paul Raabe (AB)
Jack Sasson (AB)

Nahum–Zephaniah

Francis Andersen (AB)
Richard Patterson (Biblical
  Studies)
Klaus Spronk (HCOT)
Marvin Sweeney (Hermeneia)

Haggai–Malachi

Andrew Hill (AB)
Eugene Merrill (Biblical
  Studies)[1]
Carol and Eric Meyers (AB)
Pieter Verhoef (NICOT)

Matthew

W. Davies and D. Allison (ICC)
Donald Hagner (WBC)
John Nolland (NIGTC)

Mark

Craig Evans (WBC)
Richard France (NIGTC)
Robert Gundry (Eerdmans)

Luke

Darrell Bock (BECNT)
François Bovon (Hermeneia)

John

Craig Keener (Hendrickson)
Andreas Köstenberger
  (BECNT)

Acts

C. K. Barrett (ICC)
Darrell Bock (BECNT)
Ben Witherington (Eerdmans)

Romans

C. E. B. Cranfield (ICC)
Doug Moo (NICNT)
Thomas Schreiner (BECNT)

1 Corinthians

Gordon Fee (NICNT)
David Garland (BECNT)
Anthony Thiselton (NIGTC)

2 Corinthians

Paul Barnett (NICNT)
Murray Harris (NIGTC)

Galatians

F. F. Bruce (NIGTC)
Richard Longenecker (WBC)

Ephesians

Ernest Best (ICC)
Harold Hoehner (Baker)

Philippians

Markus Bockmuehl
  (Hendrickson)
Gordon Fee (NICNT)
Peter O'Brien (NIGTC)

---

1. Finley, Patterson, and Merrill available through www.bible.org.

Colossians & Philemon
Robert McL. Wilson (ICC)
Peter O'Brien (WBC)

1–2 Thessalonians
Abraham Malherbe (AB)
Charles Wanamaker (NIGTC)

1–2 Timothy & Titus
Luke Johnson (AB)
I. Howard Marshall (ICC)
William Mounce (WBC)
Phillip Towner (NICNT)

Hebrews
Luke Johnson (AB)
William Lane (WBC)

James
Peter Davids (NIGTC)
Patrick Hartin (Liturgical)
Luke Johnson (AB)

1 Peter
Karen Jobes (BECNT)
Ramsey Michaels (WBC)

2 Peter & Jude
Richard Bauckham (WBC)

1–3 John
Hall Harris (Biblical Studies)[2]
I. Howard Marshall (NICNT)

Revelation
Robert Mounce (NICNT)
Grant Osborne (BECNT)
Stephen Smalley (IVP)

Expositional Commentaries

Genesis
Ken Mathews (NAC)
Bruce Waltke, *Genesis*
    (Zondervan)
John Walton (NIVAC)

Exodus
Peter Enns (NIVAC)
Alec Motyer (BST)
Douglas Stuart (NAC)

Leviticus
Roy Gane (NIVAC)
Mark Rooker (NAC)
Allen Ross, *Holiness to the Lord*
    (Baker)

Numbers
Dennis Cole (NAC)
Gordon Wenham (TOTC)

---

2. Available through www.bible.org.

Deuteronomy
Daniel Block (NIVAC)
Eugene Merrill (NAC)

Joshua
Richard Hess (TOTC)
David Howard (NAC)

Judges & Ruth
David Atkinson (BST)
Daniel Block (NAC)
Lawson Younger (NIVAC)

1–2 Samuel
Bill Arnold (NIVAC)
Robert Bergen (NAC)

1–2 Kings
Paul House (NAC)
Gus Konkel (NIVAC)
Donald Wiseman (TOTC)

1–2 Chronicles
Andrew Hill (NIVAC)
Martin Selman (TOTC)

Ezra & Nehemiah
Douglas Green (NIVAC)
Derek Kidner (TOTC)

Esther
Joyce Baldwin (TOTC)
Karen Jobes (NIVAC)

Job
Gus Konkel (CBC)
Dennis Magary (NIVAC)

Psalms
Jamie Grant (NIVAC)
Michael Wilcock (BST)
Gerald Wilson (NIVAC)

Proverbs
David Atkinson (BST)
John Kitchen (Mentor)
Paul Koptak (NIVAC)

Ecclesiastes
Tremper Longman (CBC)
Iain Provan (NIVAC)

Song of Songs
Thomas Gledhill (BST)
Tremper Longman (CBC)

Isaiah
John Oswalt (NIVAC)
Gary Smith (NAC)
Barry Webb (BST)

Jeremiah & Lamentations
Andrew Dearman (NIVAC)
F. B. Huey (NAC)
Elmer Martens (CBC)

Ezekiel
Lamar Cooper (NAC)
Iain Duguid (NIVAC)

Daniel
Joyce Baldwin (TOTC)
Eugene Carpenter (CBC)
Stephen Miller (BST)

Hosea–Amos
Duane Garrett (NAC)
Gary Smith (NIVAC)

Obadiah–Micah
Rosemary Nixon (BST)
B. Smith, F. Page (NAC)

Nahum–Zephaniah
K. Barker, W. Bailey (NAC)
James Bruckner (NIVAC)

Haggai–Malachi
Joyce Baldwin (TOTC)
Mark Boda (NIVAC)
R. Taylor, R. Clendenen (NAC)

Matthew
Craig Blomberg (NAC)
D. A. Carson (EBC)
David Turner (CBC)
Ben Witherington (SHBC)

Mark
Darrell Bock (CBC)
James Brooks (NAC)
David Garland (NIVAC)

Luke
Darrell Bock (NIVAC)
Walter Liefeld and David Pao (EBC)
Robert Stein (NAC)

John
Gary Burge (NIVAC)

Colin Kruse (TNTC)
Robert Mounce (EBC)

Acts
William Larkin (IVPNTC)
Richard Longenecker (EBC)
John Stott (BST)

Romans
Douglas Moo (NIVAC)
Grant Osborne (IVPNTC)
John Stott (BST)

1 Corinthians
George Guthrie (NAC)
Alan Johnson (IVPNTC)
Verlyn Verbrugge (EBC)

2 Corinthians
David Garland (NAC)
Scott Hafemann (NIVAC)
Murray Harris (EBC)

Galatians
Timothy George (NAC)
John Stott (BST)

Ephesians
William Klein (EBC)
Peter O'Brien (PNTC)
Klyne Snodgrass (NIVAC)

Philippians
Stephen Fowl (Two Horizons)
David Garland (EBC)
Frank Thielman (NIVAC)

Colossians & Philemon
David Garland (NIVAC)
N. T. Wright (TNTC)

1–2 Thessalonians
Gregory Beale (IVPNTC)
John Stott (BST)
Ben Witherington (Eerdmans)

1–2 Timothy & Titus
L. Belleville, J. Laansma (CBC)
Andreas Köstenberger (EBC)
Walter Liefeld (NIVAC)

Hebrews
R. T. France (EBC)
George Guthrie (NIVAC)

James
Douglas Moo (PNTC)
David Nystrom (NIVAC)
George Stulac (IVPNTC)

1 Peter
Daryl Charles (EBC)
I. Howard Marshall (IVPNTC)
Tom Schreiner (NAC)

2 Peter & Jude
Peter Davids (PNTC)
Douglas Moo (NIVAC)
Tom Schreiner (NAC)

1–3 John
Daniel Akin (NAC)
Colin Kruse (PNTC)
Tom Thatcher (EBC)

Revelation
Ian Boxall (BNTC)
Alan Johnson (EBC)
Dennis Johnson, *Triumph of the Lamb* (Presbyterian & Reformed)
Craig Keener (NIVAC)

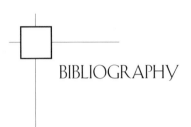

BIBLIOGRAPHY

Barber, Cyril, and Robert Krauss. *An Introduction to Theological Research: A Guide for College and Seminary Students*. University Press of America, 2000.

Barton, John, and John Muddiman, eds. *Oxford Bible Commentary*. Oxford University Press, 2001. Bibliographical guide and extensive individual bibliographies.

Bauer, David. *An Annotated Guide to Biblical Resources for Ministry*. Hendrickson, 2003.

Birch, Bruce, et al. *A Theological Introduction to the Old Testament*. Abingdon, 1999.

Bock, Darrell. *Studying the Historical Jesus*. Baker, 2002.

Brown, Raymond E. *An Introduction to the New Testament*. Doubleday, 1997.

Carroll R., M. Daniel. *Amos: The Prophet and His Oracles*. Westminster John Knox, 2002. Annotated bibliography.

Carson, D. A. *New Testament Commentary Survey*. 6th ed. Baker, 2007.

Childs, Brevard. *The New Testament as Canon*. Trinity Press International, 1994.

Corley, Bruce, Steve Lemke, and Grant Lovejoy. *Biblical Hermeneutics*. 2d ed. Broadman & Holman, 2002.

Danker, Frederick. *Multipurpose Tools for Bible Study*. Rev. ed. Fortress, 1993.

Ehrman, Bart. *The New Testament*. Oxford University Press, 1997. Annotated bibliographies.

Enns, Peter. *Poetry and Wisdom*. IBR. Baker, 1998.

Evans, Craig. *Life of Jesus Research: An Annotated Bibliography*. Rev. ed. Brill, 1996.

Fee, Gordon. *New Testament Exegesis*. 3d ed. Westminster John Knox, 2002.

Fitzmyer, Joseph. *An Introductory Bibliography for the Study of Scripture*. 3d ed. Pontifical Biblical Institute, 1990.

Goldingay, John. *OT Commentary Survey*. Rev. ed. Religious and Theological Studies Fellowship, 1994.

Green, Joel, and Michael McKeever. *Luke–Acts and New Testament Historiography*. IBR. Baker, 1994.

Grudem, Wayne. *Bible Doctrine*. Zondervan, 1999. "Annotated Bibliography of Theologies."

Gundry, Robert. *A Survey of the New Testament*. 4th ed. Zondervan, 2006.

Guthrie, George, and Scott Duvall. *Biblical Greek Exegesis*. Zondervan, 1998. Extensive bibliographical suggestions.

Hagner, Donald. *New Testament Exegesis and Research*. 4th ed. Fuller Seminary, 1999.

Harrington, Daniel. *The New Testament*. Michael Glazier, 1985.

Hill, Andrew, and John Walton. *A Survey to the Old Testament*. 2d ed. Zondervan, 2000. Annotated bibliographies.

Hostetter, Edwin. *Old Testament Introduction*. IBR. Baker, 1995.

Johnston, William M. *Recent Reference Books in Religion*. Rev. ed. Fitzroy-Dearborn, 1998.

Keener, Craig. *The IVP Bible Background Commentary: New Testament*. InterVarsity Press, 1993.

Klein, William, Craig Blomberg, and Robert Hubbard. *Introduction to Biblical Interpretation*. Rev. ed. Thomas Nelson, 2004. Annotated bibliography.

Longman, Tremper. *Old Testament Commentary Survey*. 4th ed. Baker, 2007.

Martens, Elmer. *Old Testament Theology*. IBR. Baker, 1997.

McDonald, Lee, and Stanley Porter. *Early Christianity and Its Sacred Literature*. Hendrickson, 2000.

McKnight, Scot, and Matthew Williams. *The Synoptic Gospels*. IBR. Baker, 2000.

Mills, Watson, ed. *Bibliographies for Biblical Research: The New Testament in 21 Volumes*. Mellen, 1997–.

Moo, Douglas, ed. *An Annotated Bibliography on the Bible and the Church*. 2d ed. Alumni Publications, 1987. Trinity Evangelical Divinity School.

Porter, Stanley, and Lee McDonald. *New Testament Introduction*. IBR. Baker, 1995.

Rosscup, James. *Commentaries for Biblical Expositors*. Rev. ed. Grace Book Shack, 2004.

Sandy, Brent. *Prophecy and Apocalyptic*. IBR. Baker, 2006.

Seifrid, Mark, and Randall Tan. *The Pauline Writings*. IBR. Baker, 2002.

Sparks, Kenton. *The Pentateuch*. IBR. Baker, 2002.

Stewart, David R. *The Literature of Theology: A Guide for Students and Pastors*. Westminster John Knox, 2003.

Stuart, Douglas. *A Guide to Selecting and Using Bible Commentaries*. Word, 1990.

———. *Old Testament Exegesis*. 3d ed. Westminster John Knox, 2001. Excellent suggestions.

Thomas, Derek. *The Essential Commentaries for a Preacher's Library*. Rev. ed. First Presbyterian Press, 2006.

Vos, Howard. *Nelson's New Illustrated Bible Manners and Customs*. Thomas Nelson, 1999. Excellent bibliography.

Walton, John, Victor Matthews, and Mark Chavalas. *The IVP Bible Background Commentary: Old Testament*. IVP, 2000.

Wenham, Gordon, et al., eds. *New Bible Commentary: 21st Century Edition*. IVP, 1994.

Zannoni, Arthur. *The Old Testament: A Bibliography*. Liturgical, 1992.

Annotated Commentary Series

Furnish, Victor, gen. ed. Abingdon New Testament Commentaries (Abingdon).

Keck, Leander, et al., eds. *The New Interpreter's Bible: A Commentary in 12 Volumes* (Abingdon).

Muck, Terry, gen. ed. The NIV Application Commentary Series (Zondervan).

Unpublished, Self-Published, Journal, and Internet Sources

Annotated Bibliographies (various departments) in the *Ashland Theological Journal*. Ashland Theological Seminary, 1996–2001.

Association of Theological Booksellers. *Theological Best Books.* Consortium catalog, 2002.

Blomberg, Craig, and William Klein. "New Testament Exegesis Bibliography." *Denver Journal* 5, no. 20 (2002). Denver Seminary (www.denverseminary.edu/dj).

Building a Basic Ministerial Library. Reformed Theological Seminary, 1993.

Carroll R., M. Daniel, and Richard Hess. "Old Testament Annotated Bibliography." *Denver Journal* 5, no. 20 (2002).

Division of Biblical Studies, *Biblical Resources for Ministry.* Asbury Theological Seminary, 1990.

Evans, John. *A Guide to Biblical Commentaries and Reference Works.* 4th ed. Covenant Theological Seminary, 2005.

Klein, Ralph. *Commentary Recommendations for the Old Testament* (2001). (http://prophetess.lstc.edu/~rklein/).

Lind, Sarah. Bibliographies (http://www.ubs-translations.org/).

McMurray, Heather. *Programmatic Bibliography, Hebrew Bible* (2003).

Metzger, Jim. *Programmatic Bibliography, New Testament* (2003).

Pope, Anthony, and Vernon Ritter. *A Directory of Exegetical Aids for Bible Translators.* 2d ed. (SIL, 1989/1993 supp.). Summer Institute of Linguistics.

Silva, Moisés. *Commentaries on the Greek New Testament.* Rev. ed. 1993.

Stitzinger, James. *Books for Biblical Expositors.* The Master's Seminary (http://tms.edu/850books.asp).

Suggs, Martha, and John Trotti. *Building a Pastor's Library*. Union
    Theological Seminary, VA, 1991.
Swanson, Dennis. *How to Do Library Research*. The Master's
    Seminary (http://tms.edu/research.asp).
VanderHill, Steve. *Top Picks from the Westminster Campus Bookstore*,
    1994, 1996.
Weatherly, Jon. *An Annotated Bibliography of Commentaries and
    Reference Works on the Greek New Testament*. Cincinnati Bible
    College and Seminary, 2003 (www.ccuniversity.edu/seminary/
    annotbib.doc).